THE
BOSTONER

Andrew Buckley

STAGE HARBOR PRESS
Cape Cod, Mass.
Vancouver, British Columbia

Published simultaneously in Canada
Printed in the United States of America

First Edition

Library of Congress Card Number: 99-67795

ISBN 0-9676082-0-1

Design by Andrew Buckley
Cover concept by Katja Lackner
Cover photograph by J. Sanchez
Author photograph by Bonnie Foote

Stage Harbor Press
Box 460
Orleans, MA 02653
www.stageharbor.com

10 9 8 7 6 5 4 3 2

For Meredith,

who saved me

Foreword:

I made a lot of this up.

PROLOGUE

Solstice

I remember Lisa asking me if I was afraid the voices might come back.

It was very tight, neat handwriting, blue ink on narrow lined white paper. Stacks of these notes, graphs and charts lay on the chair, opposite his bed. Shelly had crept into the house, through the French doors rattling in the December chill, and wandered about this strange, empty old house by the sea. She at last found him -- this man she had crossed half the country for -- upstairs, asleep. But she had driven all night and it was still early.

The reports of his short, *voluntary* stay at the county mental hospital in Pocasset years ago were old news by now, so it didn't faze her to be reading about it as she cleared off the chair. Following the bombing in October and the FBI leak, he had granted that interview after Thanksgiving.

But none of that prepared her for what she read now. Damn him, it didn't matter.

She raised her eyes to reassure herself he was still asleep. His thick cocoon of blankets showed only his face and his long brown hair. His beard was as she remembered. Gone was the short scruff she had seen on TV. And longer gone, the goatee he'd worn on Columbus Day. When, he admitted, it truly began. The night he brought another woman to this same house, and thought it was just luck.

It hadn't bothered Shelly about his history. If he could forgive hers, they'd be even. She had come, figuring that by the time she got here, she could stay. It was a risk -- he'd only been with her that one night on the ranch, in the middle of the whole business. But he'd gotten to her. Just wandered right into her soul, through a door she never knew existed. Damn him, whoever he really was.

She had heard him tell Barbara Walters that he had lost his mind at that point. In his drive to understand a psychopath, he had begun to confuse real people with those in history and myth. Weeks before, in Boston, he had given control of the investigation, and his life, to the dark part of him he referred to as *The Rogue*. But once in the Northwest, it was clear he was instead fighting the demons of his own past. Earlier, he had dismissed his ethical side -- THE PRIEST -- when it had led him to destruction, and so only nine days later in Vancouver, he was forced to do the same with *The Rogue*. Then he had been left alone, a boy -- the bard, he had said -- with no guidance, to uncover the truth behind a killer now known to the nation as The Bostoner.

And still none of this mattered to her. She had to know this man. Damn him.

His back to her, John Miles Kendrick -- Miles to her -- hadn't moved a muscle. Good. She settled more comfortably into the chair, pulling the afghan about her shoulders as a slight raw draft puffed through the windows facing the Atlantic. Maybe these folders and notes would hold the answer. If she could understand what he had gone through, maybe she could manage to stay. Damn him.

I remember answering Lisa. It was the first time I answered anyone for the better part of the four weeks I had already been there. I'd be there another two, but this young, goofy intern, out of all the staff, had gotten through. I had checked in to check out, to take a much-needed break from real life. Didn't know for how long, and didn't care.

I told her, 'No, I'm not afraid the voices will come back. I'm afraid they won't.'

Shelly pulled the afghan tighter about her neck.

PART ONE

PRIEST

As the French say, there are three sexes –
men, women, and clergy men.
- Sydney Smith

CHAPTER ONE

Terminus

Sunday, October 15, 1995

"Got a date?" Seth called down the dusty Beacon Hill hallway.

"In a way." In the bathroom mirror, Miles was still fussing with the tie.

"What's his name?"

A flat smile crossed his face, but Miles continued tying the muted green and gold pattern tie. "Arthur. Nice guy -- you'd like him. Prefers academic types -- historians especially."

The maritime history professor leaning against the bathroom doorway returned the flat smile. "So how'd you fool him?" unfolding one arm and pushing up his glasses.

Miles clipped on the brass tie clip in the form of a fly-fishing rod. "Oh, I just remembered what you said works for you -- just lie back and think of *Nautilus*."

The summer house down on the Cape -- the many-chambered *Nautilus*. Seven bedrooms. Five baths. A huge living room. And a front porch laden with wicker rocking chairs. Maps covered his bedroom walls because it made no sense to repair them until after the rewiring. Wax dripped everywhere from the pervasive and necessary candles.

A month ago Paulie had opened his studio off Melcher Street in Boston with his first showing in a few weeks. Maybe he would hit it big and buy *Nautilus*. Or Seth would be granted tenure at Harvard and make an offer to Mrs. Marston's estate (she having just passed on). Whatever the future, the past had been a coup. A free house for the summer in one of the best locations on the East Coast. *My conquest.*

An abbreviated laugh burst forth from the squat frame of his older roommate. Salathiel Mayo Jones, a few months Miles' senior, knew the wordplay with him better than anyone. They had gone to nursery school together. They shared the same shallow gene pool as well as a gallows humor about it. Seth took great pride in claiming his would be the last in the Jones line. And not for any other reason than having realized romantic relationships weren't all that important.

"Oh, so it's politics..." Seth reached into his pocket, pulled a roll of bills out and stuffed them in Miles' jacket. "That's rent," he said, "I got Paulie's share this morning." If Seth never asked how Miles' swung the deal on this huge apartment, or why the rent had to be in cash, he certainly wasn't going to nose into whatever murky tasks called his roommate out into the streets of Boston at any hour.

"I'd almost ask you to come along on this one – there," Miles displayed himself in front of the bathroom mirror: faded gray-green trousers, pale gray shirt, tweed jacket, and brown topsiders. Hair brushed out, parted on the right and pulled back again, by doing this all the sunbleached streaks gathered together to make him appear blond. "Ivy-covered enough?"

In answer, the Professor tapped his bifocals. Miles stared back at him, confused. "You should wear your glasses," said Seth.

"A" Street in South Boston was perfect. Not one brick needed to be changed. Abandoned railways lead up to the forgotten loading docks of waterfront warehouses and factories from the turn of the century. Congress Street, running across stagnant Fort Point Channel from downtown passed over the first story of this area, so that down here you were in a corner of Boston's basement.

But the basement was coming back. These beautiful old four and five-story buildings with their ornate brick work and high ceilings had become a favorite of artists looking for cheap rent and easy access to downtown. This vital, creative community would be dispersed within the next few years when the new Federal Courthouse on nearby Fan Pier was completed. Replaced by higher income tenants -- that most endearing of professions -- lawyers. They'd probably want the streets cleaned.

Cheek-to-jowl with the artists were a more low-key element. Some of these warehouses were still used for their original intent. Not far from the container port, these buildings held God-knows-what. Arms outbound for Northern Ireland. And drugs inbound for the streets of Roxbury, Dorchester and Chelsea. Less thrilling but more pervasive were the more elite smugglers. Like the one resting against his black Audi.

"How'dya like the feel of that?" Arthur asked. He dumped the heavy tin can into Miles' hands, then smoothed one of the glossy white wisps in his tight coif. Strange for such a solidly-built man to have such delicate fingers.

Miles turned it over, then lobbed it back and forth, from one hand to the other. "It's heavier than I thought." He held it up to the bare bulb hanging from the ceiling. The steel casing had hardly a speck of rust. "Smaller, too."

"Most people want cannon balls -- ya know -- the kind about the size of bowling balls. Put 'em on their front porch or in the office."

"Yes, my aunt has a house on Beacon Hill, and beside the fireplace she kept a few. Guess that wouldn't be too smart with this, huh?"

The middle-aged man in a warm-up suit grinned, "Not for long."

It was easy to see that Arthur Lewis liked John M. Kendrick, even though the young man hadn't bought anything on his two previous visits. But here he was -- a young, preppy guy, smelled of old money, and looking for a bargain. John said he heard about the "Collection" of imported antiques through a friend of a friend. And while Arthur used to have a fine store on Charles Street below Beacon Hill, there had been real estate problems a couple years back, and everything, lock, stock and barrel, had been moved to this warehouse near the corner of Melcher and A Streets.

The first time John Kendrick had come "looking for ideas." Arthur was more than happy to let him in and show off. The second time he was "looking on the behalf of friends." This time it was different. "Dad's birthday, ya say?"

"Tomorrow," Miles smiled weakly.

Arthur had handed Miles the old cylinder *after* punching in the combination but *before* sliding the massive door aside. "Cannister," Arthur had said. To Miles, it looked like an old can of beans, but without the label. The contents inside rattled like a child's toy. *It's amazing.*

BE VERY CAREFUL WITH THIS. FOCUS.

"Ya know about these, then?" Arthur asked.

Miles peered over his tortoise shell wire-rim glasses and forced a smile. Inside were dozens of tiny lead balls -- grapeshot -- and a small gunpowder charge. Shot from a cannon at close range, cannister was devastating -- as the tens of thousands of Union soldiers found when storming the Confederate batteries at Fredericksburg in 1862. What Arthur had so carelessly lobbed to Miles was the world's largest shotgun shell.

"As my mother is fond of saying: 'Just enough to make me dangerous.'"

I want it.

In such a low-profile profession as LEWIS IMPORT-EXPORT, you'd think he'd spare for a little oil for the door. The sound of the gears and rollers rumbled out of the alley and filled the entire Fort Point Channel night for all of two seconds. Arthur stepped inside, disappearing into the darkness. "C'mon in."

The flicker, then flash of the fluorescent lights blinded Miles. After a hard blink he beheld the Collection, walled in on every side by whitewashed brick, below pale lights. The pallor of the room was sickly. Stacked to the rafters in the thousand square-foot room were all manner of crates and cardboard boxes, some open and half-emptied, others freshly sealed. They bore few markings, save for some printing of what appeared to be Cyrillic characters. Slavic antiques were Arthur's specialty.

"I know you've already seen the eggs," Arthur pointed to the corner, "but maybe you'd like to see some of what I've just got in." He lumbered over to a sealed box, grabbed the ends of the top and ripped it open. He pulled out a new book that cracked as it opened. Arthur mumbled something flipping pages this way, then that, searching haphazardly for God-knows what. "John -- here -- you can find it -- I can't see a thing." He shoved the book at Miles, turned to the center of the room and threw his arms wide. "God, I'm as blind as a bat in this light!"

Miles bit his lip to keep from snickering at an image of Arthur the bat -- wings opened out and stout body in the middle. My God, he did look like one. Not a sinister vampire bat, but a kindly fruit bat, or maybe one of those that eat mosquitoes.

LOOK AT THE BOOK. "What am I looking for?" Miles asked. The book was full of photos of collectible coins and their values.

"It's in there somewhere." There was a clang of metal against concrete.

I'm in danger.

DON'T LOOK UP. In Miles' peripheral vision he could see Arthur with a crowbar in his hand. "Look up Moldova," Arthur said. The book was broken up by country, so Miles turned to the "M"s. Malawi. Arthur was hauling out with his bare hands a crate about seven feet long by three feet wide. Maybe vampire bat wasn't too far off.

It's a coffin.

DON'T BE PARANOID. Morocco. Monaco. Macao. Working the flat end of the bar under the edge, Arthur looked up. "S'old's ya dad?"

Moldova. "Ah! Here it is!" Miles exclaimed. "Sixty-nine tomorrow."

Arthur pulled off the lid and reached inside. It was a coffin. Arthur looked up and laughed.

Stupid priest. Miles looked back at Arthur, expressionless. Arthur lifted the lid of the coffin. It was full of Styrofoam peanuts. He reached in and fished around. If he pulled up a body -- DON'T BE PARANOID.

Stupid priest.

Miles was curious, but as he leaned forward, holding the book with both hands in case it was needed as shield.

"There!" Arthur pulled out a long string of coins sealed in a strip of perforated plastic. And set against the four Moldovan coins on the page, he caught a massive wave of incongruity. They were gold.

"Why...," he began. Then stopped. FOCUS. "Why do these coins from Moldova have John Kennedy on them?"

Arthur explained that like all former Soviet republics, Moldova was desperate for hard currency and wanted to get in good with the West. First, the regime had dismantled its nuclear arsenal in exchange for a trainload of foreign aid. Now they produced a gold coin, cheap to make because their ore was low-grade, but easy to sell to collectors because of the Kennedy mystique. Save for the Cyrillic lettering, it looked like a JFK half-dollar. Oh, and it was gold. "Nice work." Miles noticed,

"And a collector's item...," Arthur turned the coin over to reveal the seal of Moldova. "I got these 'cause of the flaw." Around the edge of the coin were stars, except that the one at the top was a little different. It had six points. Star of David. Was Arthur Jewish?

"I'll bet their government wasn't too happy to see that!" Miles laughed.

"They ran off several thousand or so before it was caught. Some had already gone to different parts of the country. They had to recall all of them for recasting. All but a few hundred made it back. This is about a quarter of that."

The book displayed the value of the regular version at $250. If Arthur had a hundred of those, it was $25,000. There was no telling how much these flawed ones were worth. Ten -- a hundred -- times that? Miles couldn't help but shoot a glance at the pry bar. *Money. Wealth. Tempting. I could take this all in a swing --*

WHAT IS YOUR DUTY?

Miles was here on assignment. He had an obligation to his client, Attorney Lotta Coolidge, a private litigator for the FDIC, and, ultimately, the taxpayers of the United States. Arthur owed them money. A lot of it -- from a landlord who couldn't pay his mortgages when Arthur failed to pay his rent. This was theirs. Settled. "How much?"

Arthur didn't bat an eye. "Six hundred. Each. Three for fifteen hundred. You know -- and so forth."

I can do this!

STALL. "Mmm... how many do you have?"

Arthur dove into his peanut coffin and came up with two more strands. "'Bout a hundred."

"Mmm... wa-el... let's do this -- I'll take one -- for now -- 'cause he'll appreciate the investment value -- and you throw in the cannister with it -- for fun."

"Deal."

Miles wondered for half a second where this idea of the cannister had come from. "But -- we gotta talk before you sell any more of these or any other rare coins like this."

"Yah... okay." Arthur ripped off one of the coins from the strip and went over to a hutch covered with papers, pens and what-not. He switched on a lamp and searched through drawers and pigeon holes. "Lemme find ya a nice box."

Miles looked down at the coin book. Lotta would love this -- evidence! And the cannister to show Seth and Paulie. He glanced up at the ancient but deadly cannister perched precariously on the corner of the hutch. It could slide off so easily...

"I'll have to check back here." Arthur bounded on past Miles and into another murky area -- blind as a bat? Maybe he had radar -- and started pulling boxes apart.

Miles rechecked his chest pocket -- $700. He had brought it along just in case of such an emergency. It was the combined rent Miles should be forwarding on behalf of Paulie, Seth and himself. But the FDIC, if they wanted the coin, would reimburse him. If not, he could sell it and make a tidy profit. Arthur was known to take merchandise back, no questions asked. No problem. Miles counted out six hundred-dollar bills and handed them to Arthur. "Receipt?"

Arthur glanced convincingly at the hutch -- "Oh, my receipt book is back at my house. Can I send you one?"

Miles smiled innocently as he knew how. "No problem." There would be no receipt.

"I gotta hang back here," Arthur looked over Miles' shoulder, and gripped his hand, "thanks for coming. Tell your Dad happy birthday from me, and I'll see ya soon."

Miles thanked him, took the cannister gingerly off the hutch and placed it in his briefcase. As he stepped out the door, he turned back. "Arthur."

Arthur turned back from his hutch and raised an eyebrow. "Hm?"

"Any idea – they ever find out who put that flaw in the coin?"

Arthur's pleasant face finally lost its facade. "Yeah."

"And...?"

He returned to the shelter of the hutch. "They got caught."

CHAPTER TWO

Venus

Monday, October 16, 1995

"I wish I could dress like that!" Bill Connor looked beaten and defeated in his gray three-piece suit. His pink face was uncomfortable and gray hair tired. At forty, he wanted to be twenty. As an attorney, he wanted to be something else. Miles, standing in the reception area of Connor & Vanzetti, delighted in his own shorts and T-shirt. If he followed Bill's example, he'd look like a lawyer.

As he followed Bill into his office, Miles cocked his head off to the left, and caught sight of Francisco Vanzetti at his desk on the phone. Miles raised his eyebrows in silent greeting, acknowledgment of the other being tied up. Frankie pulled off the receiver for a second with an "Uh-huh" to the party on the other end, covered the mouthpiece and yelled "Johnny!" with a wave, then returned to the phone with another "Uh-huh."

Miles plunked himself down in one of the overstuffed chairs in front of Bill's desk and glanced over at the computer. Most Boston lawyers have them in their offices, complete with the Massachusetts General Laws and West's Case Base on disk. Bill's had a joystick. Forty years old and the man played *Street Fighter III*. Miles fished a sheet of paper out his backpack. "You get my fax of this?"

Bill glanced at it -- a memo with a bill attached. He had asked Miles to track down a few heirs of an estate abutting a local performing arts center. "Yeah,..." Bill slumped in his chair and twisted back and forth. Miles' gaze moved from Bill to his law degrees above, and over to the stereo with its collection of blues and avant-garde rock. "Okay..." Bill reached over for the checkbook. "Is that it?" meaning the amount of $197.97 down at the bottom of the memo.

Miles pulled his eyes back upon Bill, smiling pleasantly. "Yep." He prided himself on low billings. No padding. If in doubt about time, he left it out of that charged. Twenty bucks an hour plus expenses. On a large bill he could have fudged a quarter-hour here, a little more mileage. But that was dishonest. These were his clients. They trusted him. They let him live this existence by continuing their patronage. Not even *The Rogue* was tempted.

It was better than pushing a lawn mower in the cemetery for his father down on the Cape, and, well, fun. Hell, it was pretty much free money. Bill began writing the check. Here it was -- do the work, render the bill, get paid. A client, not an employer. Theoretically, he could refuse any work for any reason at any time. Freedom. The downside was that sometimes there simply wasn't any work.

"Howdja find this last guy?" Bill signed the check, tore it off and handed it across the desk.

Miles paused for half a beat. He smiled and took the check. "Well..." DON'T HAM IT UP TOO MUCH. "... I knew you needed to find this last heir to settle the title to the property. Otherwise your client'd have to pay about ten grand in Land Court costs to clear it -- along with waiting three years before selling it to the Center. So, of course, I felt it my duty to save your client that time and money, and to find the heir."

DUTY. No one else could find him. More experienced, professionals had tried. If Miles could – *then I'm the best. Otherwise, I'm just another hack researcher with his nose in a book and his thumb up his ass.*

DUTY. THIS CAN BE DONE CHEAPLY. IT SHOULD BE DONE SO. NO ONE ELSE WILL DO SO. YOU MUST. YOU SHOULD.

"I remembered talking with your client, Mrs. Malley. She said her aunt had died in 1940 and her aunt's husband, Mulford Langley, had come down from Maine and sold everything before the estate could be administered -- books, furniture, clothes, at a yard sale. Then he disappeared back into Maine, and with good riddance from his in-laws."

Bill wasn't smiling yet. He reached into a file on his desk and found a yellow legal-sized sheet of paper, from which he read, "Yeah, Damariscotta."

Miles leaned forward in his chair, cocked his head to one side and swung it mechanically to the other, "N-no." Then he added, "I checked.

The Damariscotta Town Clerk had no listing for Mulford Langley or anyone else with that last name in the last sixty years."

"Uh-huh." Bill didn't pay for dead ends.

"So, I called Mrs. Malley again to double-check the information. She said she wasn't too sure on the Damariscotta thing, but did remember Mulford as a tall, heavy man *and* that he worked as a conductor on the Boston & Maine Railroad. So I'm left with looking for a big, fat conductor who disappeared into Maine without a trace before World War II at age 33. Hell, he coulda died in France or the Pacific for all I knew."

"Did you check death records?"

"I didn't want to take the trip to Maine." Miles could make road trips like this pay maybe $400, but THE PRIEST wouldn't allow it until cheaper options were exhausted. "Anyway, he was a conductor. He coulda died anywhere. Chicago. Spokane. Anywhere. Maine would've been a shot in the dark. The Washington County Probate Office had no record of a will being entered for him, so Maine seemed pretty erroneous."

"Ya try veteran's records?"

Miles shook his head disapprovingly. "Naw. Railroad personnel weren't drafted and this guy didn't strike me as much of a hero -- from Mrs. Malley's description." He paused and looked up at the law degree. Then he fixed his gaze upon Bill and sat back.

"Conductors, like all railroad personnel, belong to unions. These unions still exist. So I called D.C., and spoke to the Department of Transportation. They gave me the number of the union. I called the union and told 'em I needed the information on where and when Mulford Langley died in order to settle an estate."

Bill was grinning. "Pretty good."

Miles crossed his legs, and examined his cuticles. "'Bout a week later I got a message down on the Cape. My father took it..." He dug a crumpled piece of scrap paper out of his back pocket. "Mulford Langley. Died August 5, 1959. Cambridge, Mass." He looked at the note smugly, and smiled. Then to Bill, who reached for the note. Miles handed it over like an engraved invitation.

"Lemme see this." Bill grinned as he surveyed the report.

Miles feigned an absent-minded turn of the head, "Oh, his social security number's on there, too." In his peripheral vision he caught -- *Someone watching me from the door.*

DON'T LOOK. DON'T EVER APPEAR SURPRISED.

Bill's eyes confirmed the presence of a figure in the doorway. A secretary? Nobody new or he'd've acted surprised, or stopped the telling of the tale.

"So I bopped on over to the Probate Court in Cambridge -- which, I don't have to remind you is just a short walk across the river from here and *not* a long drive to Maine -- and found Langley's estate registered there, complete with a list of his surviving heirs. All living in a Bethel, Maine -- which is on the other side of the state from Damariscotta."

LOOK OVER AT THE WINDOW. Miles could see most of the room reflected in the glass, but the doorway was still dark... save for an image of white -- Frankie. The only person in the office wearing white was Frankie. His starched white dress shirt.

Bill nudged his head upwards in a signal to the door figure. "Whaddya think?"

DON'T LOOK UP. YOU'LL LOOK SURPRISED IF YOU DO.

Frankie's voice rolled into the room like a bowling ball, "I think he doesn't charge enough."

Miles held up his check with both hands, studying it, "*I never do.*"

White marble steps.

Years ago, in a dark, pinstriped three-piece suit, John M. Kendrick had slipped in his black penny loafers and crashed down upon the State House staircase. The bruises stretched from his ankle to his knee. The near-annual sprains had come to a stop then. X-rays revealed bone chips, though worn and rounded -- remnants of countless other missteps -- embedded in the flesh between the heel and Achilles tendon. The doctor at Mass. General told Miles one more injury like this and it'd require surgery. Pins and artificial joints. Pain. Unnecessary pain. And always the possibility of one of those chips, nudged by the surgeon's scalpel, hitching a ride on a vein straight to the heart. To be avoided.

But the life that had bred such injuries had been cashed in -- penny loafers for light hikers, short hair for long, clean shaven for a goatee. He was safer now.

This fresh-faced young man who had tumbled down the slick and hard climb to power, who had worked within the inner sanctums of the Byzantine world of Massachusetts (where people are said to be motivated by only three things: sports, politics, and revenge), who had joked and planned with governors, representatives and senators, now simply lurked its back alleys and waterfronts, cased their houses, checked their deeds and ran their license plates, in the name of the federal government, and, perhaps, an even higher power -- insurance companies.

White marble steps. Twelve, leading up from Connor & Vanzetti on the ninth floor. Entering the office of Lotta Coolidge, P.C., Miles caught sight of the prominent jug waiting to be swung onto the water cooler.

I went to college to fill the water cooler. He said good morning to Jennifer, the red-haired and buxom secretary, as he picked up a memo on the table outside Lotta's office.

```
TO:  JMK
FR:  LBC
DT:  10/16/95
RE:  Of water coolers and coins

Could you use your vast expertise in the physical
world to negotiate one of the large bottles into
position upon the cooler?

As you know, the trial date for Meares is tomorrow.
I expect he will try to settle -- to his advantage
-- just prior to beginning (perhaps just before the
jurors are all seated).

Leave whatever you have on my desk. And could you
drop this file (below) at Jos. Barrell's at One
Post Office Square?
```

He pulled out his report on his evening with Arthur, attached the Moldovan coin, and placed them on Lotta's desk along with his bill. The cooler and the delivery would be gratis. He'd pick up the check tomorrow after the hearing.

One Post Office Square had those highly polished floors that go squitch-squitch when you walked across them in wet rubber soles. Miles went in through the revolving door. Squitch, squitch, squitch. The guard at the desk looked up. Squitch, squitch, squitch. "Can I help you, sir?"

Squeeench! Miles froze in mid-stride. TURN. STAND UP STRAIGHT. SMILE. "Uh,.... yeah." Miles adopted an embarrassed but happy-go-lucky yokel look. He had on a college T-shirt and this guard most likely had never gone beyond high school. Worse, he had to work around suits all day long.

DO NOT CONDESCEND. Miles wandered over to the front desk and searched the directory on the wall above the guard, who was keeping his slightly puffed-up appearance as he stood. Six-three. Maybe 225 pounds. Thick neck. Pale, pink skin. Flat-top. Probably twenty-five years old. The uniform was like something out of a bad sci-fi movie, all gray with red-piping and badges. An Irish storm trooper.

"Lessee...," Miles would drawl out flat A's and soft R's to a lazy equivalent of the Boston accent. This gave the impression of being lazy, himself, and thus no active threat. "Jeez, yah, I guess I do need y'help." His eyes met the guard's -- suspicious. Miles held up the envelope. "Gotta drop this off for Attorney Joseph Barrell." His eyes caught the guard's name tag -- MAGEE -- as the man looked through the list of tenants. First names was probably something like "Buddy."

"Yeah. Barrell," accenting the second syllable (Ba-RRELL). "You can leave it here. I'll call 'em... sir?"

Miles was quite obvious as he watched a red miniskirt leave the lobby through the revolving doors. "Mm-hmmm...," then he started and whipped around with a sheepish grin. The guard raised his eyebrows and craned his neck in the direction of the rapidly fading skirt. Then he shook his head. "Nice traffic ya got here," Miles said, and peaked over the desk. "Ya got it on video, too, huh?"

Buddy flicked on a console of three video monitors and the skirt was shown from above walking around the corner of the building. "Beats the Celtics."

I got him now.

MAKE SURE OF IT. A fluidity worked into Miles' shoulders as he pulled a shade away from the counter, "Oh, sure, the way they're playin' these days."

"Don't I know it."

"Sure -- hey, I'm supposed to give this to the big man personally." Miles pointed up to the directory. "Tha's 25th, right?"

Buddy looked back at his book. "Uh... Barrell... 2501. Yeah. But you hafta go through main reception on the 24th floor."

"Thanks, Buddy." The elevator dinged open and Miles ran inside. Empty. He hit the button marked 25. The doors closed and he looked at himself in the reflection of their mirrored surface. *I am the master.*

At the second floor, the doors opened. A large man of middle age and steel gray hair stepped in. His dress was impeccable but casual -- old brown shoes with a gray Brooks Brothers suit. He had that heavy-lidded look of a patrician, rather bored with the world, living for his responsibilities to lessors and only occasionally amused. The Brahmin smiled close-lipped with a raise of the eyebrows. Miles returned in kind. The doors slid closed. They stood side-by-side. Miles found himself directly under a lamp. YOU ARE BEING WATCHED.

I know.

The Brahmin cleared his throat. DO NOT RESPOND.

I am not a dog. I will not be called like one. Miles continued his survey of the floors as they passed. No one had cleared their throat. Or if they had, what of it?

"Euh..." The Brahmin slur -- one part Downeast Maine and one part British -- was evident already.

I win. Miles looked over at the man with a mix of innocence and earnest helpfulness.

"If you'll wait a minute," the Brahmin said, "my office might have something for you."

Pause. Miles blinked at the man.

"Can you wait?" he added.

Miles regained a look of an American encountering a native-speaker in France. "I beg your pardon?"

The Brahmin's expression instantly changed from simple query to cross-examination. Nothing surprised this man. "You are making a delivery to my office?" the Brahmin indicated the envelope.

Miles looked down at it as if he just realized it was under his arm. "This?" He held it up. "It's for Joseph Barrell," Miles explained. The Brahmin made the slightest nod. "Mr. Barrell," Miles handed over the envelope. WHO IS THE MASTER?

The Brahmin Barrell turned his attention to the envelope, opened it, glanced inside and shut it without further examination. No glimmer of recognition or hint was evident either positive or negative. He turned and continued his lazy ruminations upon the elevator doors. Then he casually hit the button for the 24th floor

The doors opened at 24, the Brahmin hit the "Door Open" button, and he stood aside like a bored maitre d'. "Please sit and wait here while I get together the deliveries."

Miles was about to object when a sandy-haired, blue-eyed, smartly-dressed young woman walked by the elevator. She was 5'7", no more than 125 pounds. The clothes were modest, but the neck and ankles were in perfect tone, speaking to hidden beauty. The bobbed hair and wire-rim glasses finished off Miles' concentration. He gasped.

The Brahmin's voice called out from the elevator, "-- Oh, Meredith. I'm going up to get together those files for Suffolk Superior Court. Could you get this young gentleman something to drink while he's waiting?"

Meredith -- it was hard now to imagine this woman with her legs around Miles' hips. It had been great to find her and bring her back to *Nautilus* Saturday night, but her phone call this morning inviting him to lunch was a little disconcerting. Miles stepped off the elevator before the veiled shock vanished from the woman's face as quickly as it appeared. BE PROFESSIONAL. SHE DESERVES YOUR RESPECT. "Hello."

She looked from the closing elevator doors to him, shielded partly by her glasses. "Hello." Then she turned to the reception area and cast about for its attendant. Under her breath, Miles could hear cursing.

LET HER OFF THE HOOK. "Look, you're busy. I can respect that. I don't need anything to drink. In fact..."

She spun around. "No. You can sit down. This will take a moment. Coffee. Soda?"

Miles sat down on the plush leather sofa. It was apparent she was angry and wanted to be as far away from Miles as she could get. ALLOW HER TO LEAVE. WITH HER PRIDE INTACT. "Really, nothing I--"

"Oh, don't be a pain."

DON'T BE A PAIN. NEVER ALLOW YOURSELF TO BE CONSIDERED NEGATIVELY. Miles dropped all defenses. "Coke, please."

She sighed, followed by a "Finally."

Left alone in the reception room Miles felt horribly exposed. It was apparent that he should leave. *I could pick up a new client and money.*

NO, YOU WOULD COMPROMISE LOTTA'S POSITION.

True. Barrell was Meares' attorney. At the very least it would give Barrell the grounds to postpone the trial until any wrongdoing was thoroughly investigated. Lotta could be taken off the case. Miles would not only lose a current client, but all his others once they heard of this.

I want to see this woman again. She couldn't avoid me if Barrell is my client.
SHE WILL COME TO LOATHE YOU.
At first, but I can wear her down. No one can resist my charm forever.
WHAT IS YOUR DUTY?
Pause.
Shit.

Meredith re-entered with a glass full of Coke complete with ice and straw. She had actually put a little effort into the task, rather than handing him just a can. It almost made him forget his duty. "There you go." There was still that business-like air, but the edge was off it. It was not secretarial, but almost waitress-ish. The cut of her clothes made him realize -- "How long have you been an attorney here?"

The question stopped her pulling away, but she still looked like a deer ready to bolt. "A year. I interned here during law school, so it's more like three." She caught herself, and changed to highly professional again. "So you're a courier."

DO YOUR DUTY. "No." She was unbelieving and frowned. He continued, "And I'd wish you'd tell Mr. Barrell that. I can not take anything anywhere for him -- at least not now." She began to look alarmed.

BE FIRM BUT DON'T THREATEN. Miles stood up. "I perform research and investigations for several attorneys. Lotta Coolidge is a client. I was returning some documents she had requested."

Meredith crossed to the reception desk just as a dowdy, middle-aged woman returned to it. She smiled attentively at Meredith, knowing she had been caught off her watch.

"Could you tell Joseph to hold those documents for Suffolk, that there's been a mistake and I'll be right up?" Meredith turned from the reception desk as an elevator emptied out its lunch crowd of prim paralegals. They all cast curious glances at Miles and his drink. Meredith stepped in the elevator, hit a button and avoided any eye contact with Miles until the doors closed.

Miles sat down. The receptionist smiled sweetly at him. He felt like a small boy brought to the office and left with a drink to keep him quiet and well-behaved. What's worse, with the shorts, he looked it.

No one was going to come back down. Or if they did, he decided it would make Meredith even more uncomfortable. YOU MUST AVOID THIS. There was something in her, familiar but elusive, he had connected with and their imminent lunch date sounded tricky enough.

Get me out of here. Miles looked at his drink. Untouched. He drank down the whole thing. When he was finished, he stood up and approached the receptionist. She was just getting off a call and spied the empty glass. "Would you like me to take that for you?"

Miles adopted a boyish, uncomfortable politeness. "Oh-uh-yes, please." He handed the glass over, "Uh... could you tell Mr. Barrell that I'm sorry about the mix-up?" He checked his watch. "I really must be going."

"Certainly. And your name again was...?"

"John Kendrick. Thank you very much." Miles pulled open the exit door to the stairs, turned and waved. *Thank God I got outta that one!*

Carefully, he picked his way down all 24 flights of stairs. DID YOU?

Space!

"No problem," he said. After lunch, this sub shop wasn't so crowded.

Ah, that word! Space! She wants SPACE!?! I can give her all the space in the world!

NO. YOU HAVE ABSOLUTE OBLIGATIONS. YOU CAN MINIMIZE CONTACT, BUT NOT TO THE DETRIMENT OF YOUR OBLIGATIONS.

It was such a common request. Such a reasonable request. And such a cowardly one. Space.

So today at lunch, Miles looked across the table at Meredith, and realized he had heard an echo. They had met just last Saturday and talked long into the night about the ocean and the land, how it changes peoples and cultures, and how families communicate and get along. The way good conversation flows. Nothing to indicate their professional backgrounds. Nothing to betray that they were on opposing sides of a federal court case.

But when he had first kissed her, she had said "Maybe you shouldn't do that." It had sounded like a warning, but he pressed his luck, and they had spent a most passionate and tender night together at *Nautilus*. Good luck to find her, he had thought. Bad luck, today, to find out whom she was. And maybe that warning of hers had been right.

She had insisted on buying lunch today -- the second bad sign. The first was that she had darkened her hair color back to its original sandy blonde -- a display? "Listen...," she said.

PREPARE YOURSELF.

"... I don't feel the same way you feel about me."

THE PRIEST had to take control. Miles opened his round, sunken eyes a little wider to show thoughtful consideration. THIS IS DATA. GOOD OR BAD, RIGHT OR WRONG, TRUE OR FALSE. IT IS WHAT IT IS. But he couldn't manage to open his mouth. He nodded.

She took this as a cue to continue. "I... I think you are a good person...," she was struggling, he could tell, not wanting to sound cliché, "... but there's just too much in my life right now -- and I don't know if I could ever --"

STOP THIS. Miles raised his hand. The movement froze her mid-sentence, relieved at the stay of execution. "Don't worry about it." Meredith looked at her soup, and poked a stray bit of kale. "I would never want to make you feel uncomfortable," he said. "It would eventually make it impossible to function in everyday life. That wouldn't be good."

She looked up and nodded. "I didn't want to hurt you --"

"IT IS WHAT IT IS."

"-- I'm just not --"

"*Hey* --" *The Rogue* could take no more. He softened, though. "Nobody does anything they don't really want to do."

Her look turned hard. "Do you really believe that?"

All along he had thought she had wanted this lunch to talk about having not used a condom. He brought his gaze slowly back to fix upon her eyes. "I have to."

There were three people in line ahead of him, and an old lady was having trouble getting her bag through the metal detector -- the rubber leaves at the entrance were too heavy for the light bag to push through the conveyor belt. Miles swung his backpack onto the belt and its weight pushed the handbag on through like a snowplow.

Whenever he came to the Suffolk County Courthouse, he entered through the "new building" entrance (built in 1937, but "new" in comparison to the original Second Empire style "old building" from 1888). It also had a less sensitive metal detector. At the old building entrance the guards would never fail to hold onto at least one of his two Swiss Army knives. As Miles headed up the elevator to the 5th floor, he amused himself with the thought that the entrance to the old courthouse, for accessing the inoffensive Registry of Deeds, was more secure than the entrance for the new building, which housed the criminal courts. An expression of Boston priorities?

On the 5th floor trials and hearings were about to start at 1:00 PM. Miles paid little attention to the milling crowds. He had come for a quick fix. Miles straightened up, cracked his shoulder blades and poked his head around an office door.

Beautiful looked up from her terminal. Olive skin. Long black hair, big brown eyes and fluttering lashes. She was wearing a sun dress that showed off her shoulders. Beautiful. Her glance up was quick, and returned just as fast to her typing. A sweet smile appeared. "Hello."

Miles had on his sunny, winning smile. "Hi."

"What can I do for you?"

Be nice to me.... "Wa-el," Miles drawled long enough to see her walk out from behind her desk and up to the counter. The hem of her dress came just above her knee. DON'T LOOK DOWN THERE. "... I need a copy of a docket."

"Is that case 94-8902?"

Miles checked his notebook. As he lifted his head up again, he shook it and smiled. "Good memory!" *She's quick. And beautiful.*

"Well, you always come here for the same docket entry every couple weeks." As she spun around to begin typing out the print request, her dress twirled up just slightly to reveal the back of her thigh.

READ YOUR NOTEBOOK. Meares vs. Lewis. #94-8902. Boston Housing Court. Get copy of docket. Fifth floor.

Beautiful went into the next office to get it. Miles looked out the window to the part of the old courthouse connecting to the new. The top of the former rose up above like a crown beyond the causeway. He could barely see out the grimy windows, but he knew that the Registry of Deeds was in the windows opposite. She came back with the docket sheets, counted them, and handed them slowly to Miles. "That's all of them. Nothing's been added in two weeks. You sure you need them?"

Miles smiled as he took them slowly from her. "Yeah, the attorney I work for asked me to stop here every couple of weeks to pick up a new docket regardless."

"So which side are you on -- plaintiff or defendant?"

"Neither. Well, that's not exactly true." He looked down at the copies and stole a glance at her left hand to re-check for a wedding band -- a horrible habit.

"So who *do* you work for?"

Miles was coy. "The Feds."

She nodded slowly, comprehending. This guy did not look like a government --any government -- type. "Ohh... okay... so that's why you're always by?"

Miles nodded. "Uh-huh." Then he grinned with his eyes and turned away quickly. "Well, uh, thanks."

She slowly walked back to her desk. "You're welcome."

Miles turned quickly and left. She had done it again. How could he not love such a lovely woman with a quick mind and had never, since he had first made it a habit of stopping by for this docket, ever charged him for the copies? It was her power and she used it. Again. That vote of confidence in his charm had done the trick.

FEEL BETTER?

He did. *For now.*

But alone again in the elevator, it came back. Space. The word crashed into his psyche like a baseball through a window. *I'll give her space!*

GOOD.

On my terms!

FINE.

Absolute. Total. All the space in the world!

YOU SMOTHERED HER.

Let her suffocate in her space. Meredith had seen his weaknesses. Miles slammed back against the elevator wall and gripped the bar behind him. He fought against the growling. He flashed on her face looking down at him, stroking his head in afterglow. It was so tender. Then he recalled her pulling away early when he tried to simply hold her the following afternoon.

"AAAAH!" He gripped the bar and jerked his head right, then left as he was thrashed by the impact of the images. The grunts and yells were audible. Then he thought of Meredith with some lowlife J. Crew stonehead lawyer. He shook his head violently to rid himself of the image. A long, pitiful groan whipped out as he did.

The elevator slowed.

CONTROL. Miles stood up. Took a long, deep breath. The doors parted. No one entered from the lobby, thank God. No one had heard. He calmly walked out past the metal detectors.

CHAPTER THREE

~∞~

Queen Charlotte

Tuesday, October 17, 1995

A gray New England day. Blessed rain was in the forecast. These urban dwellers lived for their sun. Snatched bits and pieces during commutes, lunches and cigarette breaks. A man of the earth knew the fantastic rainless summer had been a fantastic drought which would take a full month of rain to recover. As it was, it was simply spitting.

Enough to lose the shorts, though. APPEARANCE IS EVERYTHING. The white sea-island cotton shirt flowed like cream off his shoulders, billowing under the southwest print vest. The pumpkin-taupe jeans and topsiders gave him the look of a rather well-off owner of a head shop or ice cream company. Last weekend this outfit had pushed all of Meredith's buttons when they met at a bar. Perhaps again, it would work. Remind her of what first attracted her to him. If he got the chance to see her today in court, that is.

Miles sauntered into Lotta's office, checking out whatever he could so as to not meet Jennifer's gaze directly. When he did look her way, her eyebrows were raised. A slow smirk emerged. Then a giggle erupted. "Lotta said to wait here in case she needs you before the trial starts at 9:30." She put her head down.

Miles approached the desk slowly, deliberately and hovered over Jennifer. She lifted her head to meet his gaze. Thank God she was wearing a high collar today. "Something funny?" he asked playfully. She shook her head. "My mistake." He turned and abruptly headed around the corner to the meeting room. *See if she runs after me...*

"It's just --", she called out. He stopped dead in his tracks at the corner, and turned to face her. She was playing with her pencil. "-- You're *not* wearing *that* to court."

"Something wrong with this?"

She was apologetic. "No-no, not at all. You look great! Really!" Miles practically blushed. She softened. "But in front of a judge...?"

In a social situation, Miles would have swept down on one knee, taken her hand, and looked deep into her eyes. In the present setting, however, his eyes had to do all the work. In a lowered and softened voice, he said, "I'm not on trial."

The call came ten minutes later. Lotta launched right into it. "Well, you better put on your dark sunglasses -- I just saw Arthur Lewis. He's listed as a witness, but shouldn't have shown up for a few days."

If Arthur saw Miles anywhere near Meares or Lotta,... definitely *not* healthy for Miles. "I thought this wasn't supposed to go to trial."

"Yes, of course, but perhaps Arthur couldn't bear to miss the spectacle of John Meares on trial."

"Some people have better hobbies -- like pulling the wings off flies."

She laughed warmly. There indeed was no love lost between Lewis and Meares. Besides the usual landlord-tenant antagonism, there was Lewis' intense jealousy of Meares' Old World money and aristocratic air. And it tore up Meares that after throwing all his millions into American real estate -- only to watch it melt away within a matter of months – low-class, deadbeat tenants like Arthur were turning profits now that the economy was humming. "Still, I need you to come over. We're going into conference in a few minutes -- an adjournment even before the trial starts -- and I'd like you in on it, particularly what you've found out on Lewis."

"A conference with Meares?" Miles had never met the man. He had cased his home in Cambridge, his properties in Bourne and Martha's Vineyard. He had checked his listing in the city census, driver's license and auto registrations. Even glimpsed a photo of him taken from an appeal at the Cambridge Rental Control Board. But face him?

WHAT IS YOUR DUTY?

"Yes, and I'd like you to bring that coin. It's inside a copy of a price guide in big file folder on my desk. Bring the whole thing. And you have a copy of your memo on said collectible?"

"Right here," said Miles.

"Okay, meet me outside the conference room on the 12th floor. It's the last room on the right after you exit the elevators. However, if you take the elevator to the 11th floor, you can walk up one flight directly to this room, never passing the courtroom or Arthur."

SHE IS USUALLY ONE STEP AHEAD OF YOU.

The McCormack Federal Court House and Post Office described as Clark Kent architecture. Big, bold, blue-suited, glasses. Twenty stories of U-shaped Art Deco complete with ̲ ̲ ̲gitcous 1940's-style eagles adorning the uppermost regions. Not so much a building as a throne looking out upon Post Office Square. And like the half-dozen elderly guards running the single metal detector at its only entrance, it was headed for retirement. Even the judges wanted a water view these days.

Miles placed the fat file folder on the conveyor belt. This overreaching security was getting ridiculous. Just beyond, up the stairs, was the central post office for downtown, meaning half the people passing through this bottleneck had no need to use the court facilities. Unfortunately, the paranoid security trend seemed to point towards putting metal detectors in all post offices. Crazy people.

He retrieved the briefcase on the other side, thankful that at least this machine never gave him any problems. Of all the metal detectors he encountered, the US Federal Courthouse had the least sensitive. Moreover, the crack team of gerontological sentries were none-too watchful of what passed by on the video screen. Unless it had something like UZI printed on it, or looked like a bowling ball with a long fuse attached, it was unlikely they'd recognize anything significant from the assorted junk people fill their personal packages with. Miles personally didn't care for the idea of the government X-raying his personal mail.

The doors to the elevator opened on the 13th floor. Miles stepped out.

Why walk up when I can walk down? Besides, he hated being predictable. The sign that greeted him across the hall read:

THIS FLOOR RESTRICTED

FEDERAL PERSONNEL ONLY

Miles glanced up and down the hallway. It wasn't the broad expanse of corridors like the floors below. He headed down the foreshortened passage to the right, to where he knew the other stairs should be. Instead, he bumped into a clean-cut, pale blue-shirted bureaucrat complete with idiot badge. "Can I help you, sir?"

Sir? Who's he kidding?

YOU DON'T BELONG HERE. YOU'RE GOING TO BE LATE. Miles tried to look like a lost pedestrian. "Just trying to find the stairs."

"Right down here." The bureaucrat frowned and pointed to the central staircase opposite the elevators. Marked plainly behind Miles was word STAIRS.

I don't want those stairs! I want the others at the end of the hall, you dolt!

YOU OBVIOUSLY CAN'T GO THAT WAY. SO JUST SHUT UP AND LEAVE.

The conflict inside him, along with the inability to explain quickly and reasonably why he needed the other stairs, caused Miles to blush. This just made the situation worse. *Get me outta here!*

Miles stammered a thanks and bolted through the doors to the central stairs.

YOU GOT CAUGHT. THAT'S HOW PEOPLE GET SENT AWAY. BEING IN THE WRONG PLACE AT THE WRONG TIME.

Fucking waste of time! On the 11th floor, Miles burst out of the central staircase doors, surprising some cleaning staff, turned and raced down to the end of the hall. He found the stairs and took them up two at a time.

Turning the corner, he ran smack into a man of almost equal stature, broader build and fifteen years his senior. The man flung himself back against the wall with a quick "Jesus!" Miles found himself the center of attention in the small anteroom lined by Lotta, the Brahmin Barrell, Meredith and the "Jesus!" freak, whom he recognized as John Meares.

HE IS NOTHING. DON'T REACT TO HIS PRESENCE OTHER THAN NORMAL. Miles tried to look innocent. "Gosh, I'm sorry 'bout that," and promptly turned to Lotta.

Lotta Coolidge was about half his height and twice his age. The graying short hair and conservative dress were even better presented than usual. But the absolute certainty, mental talent and legal sense were overflowing. This was not a woman to tangle with, nor an attorney to take on, lightly. She didn't miss a beat. Turning to the assembled, "And here he is, John Kendrick, apparently rushing here from his last concert for the Maharishi, wasn't it?"

He took in each person, not pausing extra-long on Meredith, saying "Actually --" he noticed Meredith had averted her eyes to fidget with some legal briefs, "-- it was the Dalai Lama." He smiled at the Brahmin and the Jesus Freak. They nodded and chuckled politely.

Lotta brought her hands together to signal the conclusion of the joking, adding quickly "Yes, tomAto, tomAHto. These are Joseph Barrell --"

Barrell smiled warmly and shook Miles' hand, "Mr. Kendrick and I have already had the pleasure."

This caught Lotta short, its intended effect, but only for a heartbeat.

"Oh?"

DEAL WITH THIS. Miles returned the feigned warmth equally. "Why, of course, when you sent me to return those files yesterday?"

"Mmm. Of course," she slid into sudden understanding.

The Brahmin gestured to the lovely beside him, "And you already know my assistant, Meredith Gray." She looked up from her fidgeting, but didn't offer her hand.

Miles smiled politely and nodded respectfully. "Yes."

Lotta regained control by stepping between Miles and the Brahmin. "And you know John Meares."

Meares was still taking in Miles, but slowly reached out his hand. Miles took it and shook with the old politician's handshake of firm and quick -- three times. Meares' grip was a little weak. Perhaps from bewilderment. "You're not what I pictured -- I mean from the times I've spoken with Lotta on the phone about you," Meares said with a faint English prep school accent. "Not really what I thought."

"*I never am.*" Miles scanned his eyes across the Brahmin (nothing), Meredith (half-rolling her eyes), and Lotta (grinning like a Cheshire cat).

Lotta led the way into the small conference furnished with a table and four chairs. Meredith, the Brahmin and Meares each took a seat. "Oh, dear...," Lotta cast about the room for a seat for Miles, "... perhaps in the next conference room?"

He nodded, but reached for the file folder, pulled out the coin and book and handed it to Lotta. The other three tried to contain their curiosity, Meares and Meredith failing. Miles walked across the hall and found the next conference room locked, taunting him through its small window with conspicuous chairs. He returned with a helpless expression. "Uh, it's locked."

Lotta was getting irritated with such a silly delay, but remained diplomatic. "Perhaps down the hall?" Miles hesitated. Arthur was down there.

The Brahmin jumped up. "Here, allow me." He brushed past Miles and down the hall. Miles tagged along. Barrell opened another door halfway down the hall. He smiled large yellow teeth, and pointed. Inside were a small desk and chair. "The bailiff's. He always sneaks one out. Back problems. Just don't let him catch you putting it back."

"Right." Miles and the Brahmin exchanged conspiratorial smiles. Two Yankees versus the Irish cops.

Barrell was already back at the conference room when Miles began to catch up with the bulky chair. No sign of Arthur. Barrell reached for the door handle and pushed. Miles thought it was strange the door was shut since he didn't remember closing it.

The force of the blast slammed the door back towards Barrell. The fractured glass from the window coated his suit and one side of his head, hanging like small cubes of ice. The flash occurred in the instant Miles had blinked. All he heard was a muffled concussion, then silence. A second later the fire alarm and sprinklers went off.

What the hell was that? Miles was dumbstruck. It took him a heartbeat to realize something had just exploded. Barrell slowly wiped the glass off his coat, and pausing, caught sight of Miles, still holding the chair. The artificial rain from the sprinklers mixed with the white smoke billowing from the blown-out window.

GO!

Simultaneously, Miles and the Brahmin headed through the door. It wasn't until he was through the door and enveloped in cloud that Miles caught himself.

PUT DOWN THE CHAIR, STUPID. He did. Where is everything?

OPEN THE WINDOW. Reaching out in front of him, Miles moved slowly to the edge of the room. A low groaning came from the opposite corner. Miles found the window. The glass hadn't been blown out, but it was cracked. He could feel the edges and a sting along his fingertips -- *Ow!*

The glass became sticky with his blood. His left hand found the latch and pushed it open. Puffs of white smoke breathed out and in as the door opened and closed again. Miles was choking and getting dizzy.

The door burst open with a dozen bailiffs and federal police. "Okay, c'mon!" barked a hulking, bristle-topped bailiff in a white shirt, who picked Miles up like a rag doll and carried him out through the door.

The only response Miles could manage was a slow, quiet "Don't step on Lotta," as he realized there was a great deal more blood on the glass than could have come from his finger.

CHAPTER FOUR

Polly

Wednesday, October 18, 1995

The darkness was disturbed. Some intruder. *Sleep.*

There was a shaking. Pressure on his shoulder. He refused to open his eyes. *It will go away. I can ignore it.*

From the foggy darkness hands reached out. "Mr. Kendrick. C'mon."

Leave me alone! Miles jerked away hard. Light had burst though the fog, threatening the peace. Still, there were muffled voices about him. He let go hard and sank further into the darkness.

A larger hand with a softer grip cupped his shoulder. But this time there was no shaking, but a slight, even squeeze. "Johnny?"

Someone familiar...

"Johnny."

OPEN YOUR EYES. Miles struggled against the surprising heaviness of the lids, as some faint crust had sealed them shut with crazy glue. But there he was -- *The Prince of Darkness.* Paulie's long black hair was drawn back, displaying the prominent widow's peak. Swarthy complexion. Black mustache with a small triangular tuft under the lower lip. Black eyebrows. And those large, round brown eyes, which opened wider upon seeing Miles' own. The Prince was pleased. The grin of white teeth expanded broadly across his face.

Miles rubbed the crust from his eyes. Without his contacts there was a lingering fog. He addressed the dark one. "Pa --" The word disappeared into a breath. *Something in my throat.* He cleared and tried again. It came out as a whisper: "Paulie."

What the hell is in my throat? He totally ignored Paulie and the nurse beside him, swung his legs off the bed and attempted to expel the clog in his throat. *I want to talk.* The forced coughs became increasingly violent.

Paulie and the nurse reached forward. "Whoa -- whoa. Take it easy, Johnny." Paulie put his arm around Miles' shoulders.

Now he'd impress this pretty nurse. Miles looked up at Paulie, subtly communicating the need for help with his eyes, and adding a slight leer.

Paulie spun around, grabbed a cup, picked up Miles' hand and placed the cup in it. Miles held it close to his face so that the nurse couldn't see. Unfortunately, the mass was too big to be gently spit out, and he had to force it out with the whole of his tongue. Expelling it required opening his mouth wide. It dropped into the cup with a dull *plop!*

The nurse had the good taste to turn away. She held a cup of water in front of Miles, which he hesitantly traded for the one with the greater treasure. She stared at its contents intently. "Hmmm... no blood...," she decided.

"No blood?" Paulie echoed. He almost sounded disappointed. "You sure?" He stepped over as she offered a look, but held onto the cup. He also took it in his hand, and peered intently. Then he raised his eyebrows and granted, "Well, that's right. No blood!"

The nurse laughed too. Miles grinned and re-cleared his throat. Paulie let go of the cup, and asked, "Do you need anything?"

Miles was heartened by his friend's charity. He downed the glass of water and coughed. Volume was coming back, but it was still hoarse. The nurse offered to get a Coke. The two males watched as she left. Miles raised his eyebrows at Paulie, who did a double-take at the now-empty door, leered and shook his head. Miles held up one hand, palm up and fingers lowly spreading wide. *"Yours."*

Paulie shook his head dramatically, in mock concern. "I don't know... I think she's pretty interested in you."

"She was more interested in that piece of chung I just birthed."

Paulie smiled broadly and began to laugh. Miles began to giggle. "Chung!" Paulie's laugh turned into a cackle. That was it. The laughing continued until Miles had to slump back onto the bed, red-faced and weeping. It abruptly ended when his coughing erupted again. Paulie was there instantly with another cup of water. What a perfect scene for the nurse returning with the can of soda.

"The doctor will be along shortly to check on you. Your breathing seems to be better." She tapped the side of the bed next to the control panel, "Just call if you need anything." Leaving, she smiled sweetly at Miles and a little more intently at Paulie.

Miles sipped from the can but continued to stare at the empty doorway. *"Yours."*

Paulie chuckled and paused. He looked down at Miles and exhaled. Waiting.

LET HIM WAIT. Miles looked up innocently. Paulie lowered his head in all seriousness.

This is fun! Miles cocked his head to one side. He smiled stupidly.

"OH, COME ON!" Paulie erupted, frustrated, but almost laughing in admiration at his friend's inscrutability.

I win. Miles leaned back against the raised bed and laid his folded hands on his stomach. Buddha or Confucius? No, neither of them were ever portrayed with a shit-eating grin.

YOU MAKE JOKES AFTER A TRAGEDY. His attitude darkened. He examined the texture of the blanket and the folds it made as it swept down to his feet, like baby blue snow drifts, or rounded waves on still water. "I don't know."

Paulie shook his head, walking away. "I told you, " he lunged back, "Didn't I tell you? I said one of these days you're gonna to get yourself killed."

"But I'm not dead." Miles held up his left hand in benediction. It stopped Paulie cold. Miles asked, "What happened?"

Paulie was shocked. "You don't *know?* You were there when it went off!"

"When what went off?"

Paulie fell silent, his arms at his sides. He took a seat in the bedside chair. "Wow. They said you were the first one in."

"All I know -- or all I remember is hearing a Ba-Doom in the conference room, running in, getting a face full of smoke, and opening a window. Then some big gorilla wrestled me out into the hall. After that it was all stretcher and needles." He looked contemptuously at the I.V. in his left hand. *Something metal in me. If I clench this fist tightly the needle might rip through the flesh on the back of my hand --*

DON'T DO THAT. But the thought fascinated him.

Miles looked up and realized Paulie looked pretty dragged out. His clothes were wrinkled and the hair frizzling up from his ponytail. "Paulie," Miles addressed his friend earnestly, "did you spend the night here?"

Paulie lowered his head and shook it slowly, "No --"

"Good --"

"-- I spent it with the FBI."

Miles face slowly froze into a stoic stare. *Nobody's spoken to me. Yet.*

FOCUS. He examined all his options. Stay. Go. Call for help. Who's paying for this hospital room? The state. Where is he? The view of the Charles River meant it was undoubtedly Massachusetts General. Ah --

Indigent Care. Good. No bills. Paperwork later. God bless the Commonwealth of Massachusetts!

The Commonwealth -- what about the State Police? "Paulie," Miles asked in an even, soft tone, "perhaps you can tell me if one of your new friends or their associates -- uniformed or otherwise -- are waiting outside?"

Paulie glanced at the door and nodded. "They brought me here."

Miles stopped. *I'm in trouble.*

YOU WILL BE IF YOU DON'T HANDLE THIS PERFECTLY.

Miles ripped the tape off, exposing the needle in his hand. The sight of the tube under his skin was too much. He looked up at Paulie, to whom he offered the rest of the task. It was done in a second, with Miles immediately re-affixing the tape. "Paulie," Miles placed his hand on his friend's shoulder, "where are my clothes?"

Miles insisted the door remain open. Any apparent change would have sent a signal prematurely. So he dressed in the bathroom. The bandage on his hand began to leak, and he had to repeatedly reapply it. Blood on his white shirt would not look good. Dirty, bloody people look suspicious. Guilty.

ALWAYS PROCEED AS IF TWELVE REASONABLE PEOPLE ARE LOOKING OVER YOUR SHOULDER. One day, they might be. Miles, in yesterday's hippie outfit, was still presentable. But, without the contacts, blind except for 10 feet in front of him.

Paulie brought him up to speed while Miles was showering and dressing in the tiny bathroom. Lotta was dead. Meares was dead. Meredith was in intensive care with some sort of facial injuries. The news reported her doctors hoped to save one of her eyes.

Miles forbade Paulie from turning on the television in the hospital room. The news reports were on every station. The media was having a feeding frenzy with their "Beantown Blast" and "Boston Court Bombing". But Miles didn't want his mind tainted by their conjecture, innuendo and sensationalism. He was meeting with the big boys.

WHAT IS YOUR DUTY? He was going to tell the truth. Be helpful. He must look innocent.

I am innocent.

THAT IS IRRELEVANT. YOU MUST APPEAR TO BE INNOCENT. He wished he had his glasses. BETTER NOT TO HAVE THEM. True. To close to the "hacker look". Feds hated that more than the bomb throwing nut. A bomb? He stopped. Why a bomb?

DON'T GET CAUGHT.

Right.

YOU'RE READY.

"Don't piss them off," Paulie warned.

"That's *your* job," said Miles.

Miles turned the corner and headed down the hall. Funny -- he couldn't remember coming in here, so he knew of no way out. Or at least any one quicker than any other. Paulie walked just ahead of him. Compared to Paulie, with his hair down and a day's worth of heavy black beard growth, Miles was the Jesus to Paulie's Satan. Down the hall were the Romans.

Walking, his mind was a cyclone of thoughts and images. Lotta. Blood. Meeting Meares. Meredith. That glass of Coke. Barrell the Brahmin. He wondered if the FDIC would proceed with the case against the Meares estate and if Barrell would handle the execution of the will. Did Lotta have a will? Who would handle that? Miles fancied himself the Executor of her Will. What a title!

YOU'RE BEING COLD. But it was all that he knew. It was another blow. In cold reality he was alive. The others were dead. Meredith was alive, but probably blind. What the hell was that, if not cold?

What's more, Paulie didn't seem to care either. Not about Meares, Lotta or Meredith -- Miles hadn't told anyone about that night with her. And, hell, Miles and Paulie never talked about women, so why start now? All Paulie would want to know was if she was good in bed. Ignorant of this, Paulie cared only about protecting Miles, and Miles protecting himself.

Entering the lounge corner with a shy gait, Miles squinted at the sun. Paulie introduced Miles to three men. Archer and Lambert from the FBI. In their thirties and forties, respectively. Lambert was black. Good. Maybe he'd champion the underdog. Taney, a Deputy US Marshall, was no older than 30 and clean-cut. The rest was a fog in his poor vision and the glare of the sun. But Taney seemed familiar. No women. Too bad. He related to them better. Miles dropped into the chair facing the sun, and immediately shrank back, like a dog from a beating. He tried to smile. Archer, obviously the senior, started: "Mr. Kendrick --"

STALL THEM. Miles held up one hand. "Excuse me." Archer stopped. With pleasant, pleading eyes, Miles coughed, and asked Paulie, "Could you get rid of that?" pointing to the sun. Paulie jumped up and drew the curtains. A movement of Miles' chin kept him standing at the window. Miles beamed, and slowly turned to the men. "I'm sorry. Please, sir, continue."

Archer didn't miss a beat. "Not a problem. Mr. Kendrick, we need to ask you a few questions about what happened yesterday. We understand you are under a lot of stress and appreciate your talking to us here and now. You understand this is a critically important investigation and we need to follow any leads before they grow cold."

Miles sat forward, trying not to dispel his mock-sickness with the action. He disguised it with a pained swallow. "You have leads already?"

Lambert affirmed: "Yes, but we need your help to conclude our investigation quickly."

They have no leads. "Shuhr!" He cleared his throat again for effect.

"Now..." Paulie spoke and all three Fed heads swung back to the windows, "don't be giving this guy the third degree 'cause he's just woke up after a night in an oxygen tent. I mean, you should seen the size of the thing he coughed up!" -- chung -- "And without a lawyer -- I don't know..." Paulie shook his head.

Archer returned to Miles. "Mr. Kendrick -- John -- all we want to ask are a few routine questions. There's no need for a lawyer. We realize you're not fully recovered, but time is definitely of the essence here. I also think this might be over sooner if Mr. Kimball excused himself." He shot a glance at Paulie, who glared back, and quickly caught Miles' eye.

Lambert added "I agree."

"No." Miles was all common sense now. He looked each man in the eye for a moment. "I am more than happy to give you gentlemen or anyone who asks all that I know. I want to help. My friend and client is dead. I have been injured physically for no reason. Another man, whom I'm sure didn't deserve it, is dead. And a young woman has been very badly hurt. This is wrong. I can help you by continuing to do my job, which is simply telling whatever I know."

Archer sighed "Well, we appreciate that -- "

Miles began coughing. First slowly, then suddenly quite violently. Archer stopped talking. All looked concerned, and Archer reached forward to offer assistance. Miles held up a hand, shaking it, refusing the help. *Lambert's wearing the wire. Archer's doing too much talking and Taney's not FBI.* His coughing stopped. Miles knew he was quite flushed now. He closed his eyes. "Offhand, I don't know why anyone would do this, unless they wanted to hurt John Meares for bad debts, but doesn't make sense to do it in a courthouse with others around." OPEN YOUR EYES. "But I am willing to go over every little detail with you gentlemen so long as you allow me some dignity of mourning. That means no lawyers will be called in, but I'd like to not feel so alone... okay?"

With their assent came a barrage of at first routine questions. Age -- 29. Residence -- he gave Beacon Hill. They'd check and find the Cape address.

Oh well. Occupation? Freelance researcher. From their reactions it was apparent they didn't like the "freelance" part. Length of employment -- Seven years. Marital status -- Divorced, four years. Her name and address? Justine, whereabouts probably in Texas. Prior difficulty with the law -- None.

These were all things they already knew -- they were double-checking their files. Prior history of mental illness? Miles waited half a second.

None of their damn business!

DON'T DELAY. Miles chuckled. "Mental *illness* ?" He shot a glance at Paulie, who, with the release in tension, laughed too. "No, nothing I've ever been committed for." Paulie didn't know. Why should he – he'd been studying in Spain and France that year. Miles had registered under the name Robert Hopkins. THEY WILL EVENTUALLY FIND OUT.

Only if they look real hard.

The questions continued. He found it all quite pleasant after while, as he loved answering questions and generally talking about himself. Then they got to the reconstruction of the events that took place just prior to the explosion. This was the best part as it allowed him to become the storyteller, setting the tone and the mood, creating a world out of whole cloth, having utter control over its events, and thus, his listeners. These men were attentive.

Miles had come to the part about taking the elevator up to the 13th floor when he realized he knew Taney. Leaning forward, the Deputy came into slightly clearer focus -- the bureaucrat from the 13th floor. TELL THE TRUTH.

That sounds so stupid!

Continuing, he compromised and edited. His unfocused eyes settled upon Lambert, his potential defender. "Lotta was concerned for my safety -"

Taney broke in, leaning closer, "Why is that?"

LOOK AT HIM. The visible anguish welled up inside Miles as he faced Taney. "There was a man there, Arthur Lewis, who owed Meares a great deal of money and I had just recently purchased some incriminating evidence from him. It was to be used in settlement negotiations with Meares. If Lewis saw me anywhere near the trial he'd know who I really was working for, and it would get tricky for me very fast."

"You have this evidence?" Archer asked.

"No, I gave it to Lotta."

"When?" asked Lambert.

"Tuesday. No -- wait -- yesterday. Wait. What day's it today?"

"Thursday," Paulie volunteered.

All three agents looked at Miles, emotionless. YOU'RE LOSING THEM. "See, I left it at her office Tuesday, with a memo. Then yesterday -- yesterday? -- yeah, I picked it up at her office after she called and told me to bring it over to the courthouse."

"As a researcher, you usually take part in privileged negotiations?" Archer had posed this question as innocently as possible, but there was no getting around its inherent incredulity.

"No."

"Then why were you there?"

DIMWIT! I just told you!

CONTROL. A cough deflated an outburst, and Miles tried a bland face. "As - I - said... this evidence was the subject of settlement negotiations, as was the nature of my acquiring it. My client asked me to be there and I would have been remiss in my duty to not go."

Taney jumped in: "Your *client*? Who -- Barrell?"

Aaaaah! They're so stupid!

HOLD ON. SHOWING ANGER WILL DESTROY THIS. A wave of calm seemed to descend upon Miles. He sank back into his chair, closing his eyes, and was blanketed by a spell of stillness. There was a moment of silence. Paulie cleared his throat. Miles took a deep breath. It was painful, but he let it out slowly, and opened his eyes.

"Gentlemen, I understand you have a job to perform. Please allow me some leeway. I'm told I inhaled a great deal of smoke yesterday, and it's a miracle I don't have any brain damage. Then again, perhaps I do." His pleasant face addressed each man's eyes so there was no mistaking his intent. It was Miles' prerogative to play the uncommunicative moron. "So, I ask you refrain from this lateral brand of questioning. I will tell you all I know --," WAIT, "-- save for those matters that are protected as attorney work-product."

Archer shifted uncomfortably in his chair, and all three exchanged worried looks. Attorney work-product is privileged information, just as any communications between attorney and client, or priest and confessor. Even a judge -- especially a judge -- would be loathe to compel Miles to violate that canon of law. If the FBI could force attorneys' employees and contractors to tell all, it would be as if the attorney herself was spilling the beans.

After pausing second, Miles went on: "I am a contractor. Lotta Coolidge was my main client. I have several others in and out of Boston. I can supply you with their names and addresses and they will attest to my honesty and professional abilities -- but you were asking about my day yesterday?"

Archer, sensing information flowing again, sat forward. "Yes, please go on."

"Lotta directed me to another floor and told me to take the stairwell to the twelfth floor conference room. Not knowing my way around, I tried the thirteenth and found no way to the far stairwell," and casually gesturing to the Deputy, "where Mr. Taney sent me back down the central staircase." Taney smiled sourly.

BE CAREFUL. "I'm sure I made a hell of an impression running down the stairs to the eleventh floor." Indeed, the FBI men were nodding tentatively. The cleaning personnel probably told of a long-haired crazy bursting through the hall, minutes before the explosion. "But I was running late -- the trial was being held up by the settlement negotiations and couldn't start without me and the evidence." Miles went on to describe the meeting, the confusion about the chairs and his leaving with Barrell.

"You left first?" Archer interjected.

"Yes."

"Then came back and got Barrell?"

"No, Barrell left, and I with him. I had no idea where he was going."

"So you stepped in the room, Barrell left and you with him?"

"Uh... I guess." *What's going on?*

Archer leaned forward again, with an earnest expression. "You see, John, we need to know where everyone was exactly before the blast. But there are gaps. Now, you say you were out of the room, alone, then in the room, then out of the room with Barrell."

DON'T BE CAGED. "Well, I..." He was at a loss.

"We just want to establish who left the room and in what order."

"*Why?*" It was Paulie, God bless him. Lambert and Taney jerked reflexively back to face him, an annoyed expression on his face. "I mean, why don't you just come out and tell us what you *think* happened. This is *our* government, right?" He pointed to Miles, and addressed Archer, "Here's a guy who works for the *Federal* Deposit Insurance Corporation, a part of the U.S. government as I understand it, he risks his life for a little money now and then, and you're giving him a hard time 'cause he got lost and couldn't find a chair to sit in?" Classic Kimball.

Taney, the least professional, struck back. "Listen, pal, you wanna to spend another night in our basement?"

"Hey, you got nuthin' on me!" Paulie had a target now. "Does that make you feel big? To be able to say things like that? To harass and intimidate people?" He turned to the FBI men, "Nice partner -- I *thought* I was in America." Then he turned his back on the room and peaked out a crack in the curtain. The sun's rays shot through and across the room, catching a swirl of dust. Archer stared at the floor, embarrassed. Lambert's fierce, cold stare froze Taney in his seat. Normally, the ultra-professional Federal Bureau of Investigations hated to have anything to do with the politicized U.S. Marshals -- here again was justification. The "partner" shot hit close to home.

"Paulie?" Miles ventured.

The brooding figure at the window barely stirred. "Yeah?"

"Could you please go find that doctor. I'd like to know how long they're going to keep me here." It was indelicate, but had to be done for the next move. Paulie stood up straight, turned on his heel, and with a nod to Miles and the FBI, he walked out of the lounge -- although there was distinct crack of his knuckles as he passed behind Taney.

Taney began to pump himself up a little bit.

DUMB PRIDE. "Mr. Taney," said Miles in a most gentle way as he stared down at the cheap Formica coffee table between them, "thank you. Your contribution has been most enlightening. I think you better go now."

Taney reacted as if slapped, "Wha--?", but was stopped by agreeing looks from Lambert and Archer. He left in a dark huff.

Miles waited for his footsteps to disappear down the hall. With his eyes closed he remembered that he was alone. Lotta was gone. It was all up to him. He tried to blink away a tear. The sigh that came out was more of a shudder. What faced the two Feds now was a different man, much more vulnerable. He gave a brave little smile. "Okay," he added, and the edge crept out of the room.

For all their professionalism, Archer and Lambert looked relieved too. Archer resumed in a more conciliatory manner. "John, when you left to look for a chair with Barrell, did you leave the room first or did he?"

"I don't remember." *Why are they asking me this?*

"Okay, forget that for the moment..." Archer continued with questions about what happened after that. Miles gave what little he could. Archer said the smoke had come from some sort of homemade explosive device, about the size of a softball, and it was the shrapnel that had torn apart the table. It appeared to be located in the center of the table, on top, so that no one particular person seated would have been any closer than any other.

Except me. They didn't show the accusation. He was the fifth wheel. The amount of damage received by each person was determined by a matter of how few inches they were from it -- or how they were posed at the table. Any one of them could have been the target. Or all. They hadn't found any fingerprints on the device's fragments. Its homespun manufacture was so simple that its components were not easily traced. But how did it get in there?

WHAT ARE THE POSSIBILITIES? Someone inside did it: Meares? Perhaps the debt was worse than anyone else knew, he felt suicidal and wanted to take Lotta down with him? But why include Meredith? Angry at his own ineffective representation? Then he should've waited for Barrell -- he was the real counsel. And why not wait for Miles to return, too, as it had been his research that drove everything. If he was going to take anyone, why not the sneaky investigator? No, Miles had walked too many steps down this same road. It made no sense.

Lotta?

What? She simply was not the suicidal type. Or the homicidal type. She had Meares where she wanted him, ready to settle after so many *years* of work. Anyway, a bomb wouldn't be her style. You'd know very well when Lotta was going to strike, and why. She made a point of alerting you.

Meredith?

Why? Why kill your client? And opposing counsel? This wasn't even her case. Miles had seen the memorandum and correspondence between the law offices. Meredith was never mentioned in even the most informal exchanges. Miles wasn't even aware of her involvement or employment with Barrell until the day before yesterday. So if Meares was going to lose the case or make a settlement, what big deal would that have been to Meredith? It was Barrell's case.

Barrell?

Barrell. Why would he want to kill his own client, opposing counsel and his own assistant? That would be pretty cold. And pretty ruthless. Lotta was offering a way out of the trial -- peace with honor, through an exposure of Lewis' hidden assets. Was there something Barrell wanted to keep quiet? Did he not want this settlement to go forward? Sure, he was getting paid regardless of whether he won or lost, but he was old money. In Boston the pursuit of money is a sure indication of your lacking it and breeding. No, the loss was nothing -- unless it was a point of pride. DON'T BE RIDICULOUS.

"Someone else?" In the millisecond of Miles' pondering all these possibilities, the Feds had been watching him. His hand on his goatee, leaning back sideways in the chair, looking searchingly off to one side -- he wondered how they would perceive it -- guilty? Perhaps trying to think up a new lie? Ready to sacrifice another for his own misdeeds?

"Go on...," Archer prompted.

"Speculation, really," Miles offered. YOU'RE NOT THE VULNERABLE SICK MAN NOW. "Someone could have thrown the bomb in after we left to get the chair."

NOW YOU'VE DONE IT. There was only a small gap of perhaps thirty seconds when Barrell and Miles were gone from the room. The bomber would've had to know where the settlement was taking place and accessed it via the back stairs. *The same way I did.*

IT WOULD BE SIMPLER TO JUST SAY IT WAS YOU ALL ALONG. "So you want to know whether Barrell or I left first *when he offered* to show me where the chair was --," GOOD, "-- because perhaps the last one out might've seen someone on the back staircase." VERY GOOD.

I hope the wire picked that up. On cue, Lambert furtively buttoned his suit jacket. Archer would play along. "Sure, that might be one possibility. Did you see anything?"

Nice try, but I'm not that dumb. "Well, I don't know, 'cause I'm not sure the order of things. I can't even tell you if I actually stepped into the room or not when I returned. But I don't recall seeing anyone in the hallway. Sorry."

"Okay, so when you closed the door, you saw nothing in the stairwell?"

"When I --" STOP. " I never closed the door." It had been one with a hydraulic mechanism. It kept closing by itself during all the smoke.

"So who did?"

"I don't know." This was serious. Whoever closed the door would have been localizing the blast. Miles recalled the shattering of glasslets onto Barrell -- certainly not the reaction of a man consciously expecting a blast. But Barrell must have been the last out, and so would have kicked out the door wedge holding it open.

Or maybe Lotta did, as she always preferred privacy in her conversations. But again, why would she have blown herself up? And again his mind ran the circuit of possibilities, all coming out the same. "So whoever shut the door also threw the bomb."

Archer and Lambert nodded tentatively. *Are they suspicious because I caught on so quickly?*

"Johnny." Paulie stood in the entrance of the lounge beside a middle-aged Asian woman sporting a white coat and stethoscope. The name tag read "Dr. Zhu." Her casual indifference became increasingly marked with annoyance at seeing her formerly unconscious patient now chatting in the lounge.

The interrogation was over.

CHAPTER FIVE

Captain Cook

Thursday, October 19, 1995

"Hello, John, this is Joe Barrell. I'd appreciate it if you'd give me a call. There are some details we need to discuss. The number here..."

Miles was hovering over the answering machine and phone, hesitating. Barrell? What does he want? PICK IT UP. "Hello, Mr. Barrell."

The cough had settled into an annoying producer of hard brown phlegm. There was still a chemical taste in his mouth, and he was always thirsty, but Miles coped. None of these were on his mind now as he plodded along the leaf-strewn side streets of Beacon Hill. Gone was the jogging pace. His stamina could not overcome his lungs. KEEP A STEADY PACE. DON'T SLACKEN. YOU DIDN'T EXERCISE THIS MORNING.

I'm sick.

NO, YOU'RE JUST TIRED. Tired from too much rest and too much thinking and too much time for both. He was disturbed. Disturbed because he still hadn't reacted to the deaths of Lotta and Meares and injuring of Meredith. Disturbed because he wasn't sure if he felt anything. Or if he did, it was one of amused resignation.

It's said that a mentally healthy person reacts to tragedy with sadness and grief, but a schizophrenic reacts with laughter. This was Miles' usual response to any sudden reversal -- to throw back his head and laugh heartily. Ah, what a joke! Of course -- I should have known! What a joke Life is, and what a joke I am for trying to think I can win this game. Good show, Life. Nice move. Well done.

Detached from reality, the schizophrenic views life as something to be accepted or not. Able to create alternative realities within and alternative selves without, he holds his trump card in reserve: simple removal from the game.

Miles stopped dead in the street and looked down at the cobblestones. The pressure was beginning to build. Normally he juggled quite a bit - finances, friends, duty to clients, duty to his father, duty his houses. Everything free came at a price.

The photos of him in the news were from eight years ago at the State House. Clean-shaven, pale with short hair and a three-piece charcoal pinstripe suit. Very Republican. He still had the suit, but wore it differently these days. The news had labeled him a victim. A survivor. They were harassing his father, offering money for interviews.

Ducking out of Mass. General's kitchen had worked up until breakfast this morning. The phone call was Archer -- remember to stick around... please. Miles had mentioned the media money and, of course, his total unwillingness to accept. Archer had sounded relieved.

"Buddy" Magee was at his security post, but gave Miles, in his brown leather jacket and gray jeans, a suspicious glance. The disguise worked. Or Buddy didn't remember.

This time the elevator went straight to the 25th floor. The conference room to the right looked out onto Boston Harbor. As he took a few steps along the burgundy with gold-trim carpeting, something seemed to hop about the skyline, just over the blue horizon. In his nigh-ill state, it proved terribly disorienting. *What is that?* It seemed to disappear within the mass of the twin spires of Harbor Towers as he stepped through the doorway of the glass-walled conference room.

A long mahogany table of some fifteen feet ran the length of the room. The chairs were brown leather with fine brass rivets. A faint relief of the firm's logo, BARRELL, BULFINCH & GRAY, sat in the wall opposite. The view of the water was meant to impress and impose. This was a commanding spot, a tower atop the famous "city on a hill". All that caught Miles' attention was the optical illusion. It wasn't outside. It was *in* the glass. Moving back and forth between the hall and the conference room, he saw there was something dead center of the glass wall. Something small.

"Mr. Kendrick."

Him.

DON'T BE SO JUMPY. Miles turned slowly, meeting the Brahmin face-to-face.

"I see you've found our medal," Joseph Barrell waved towards the fixture in the glass. Miles moved closer and discovered it was a coin, just a little larger than a half-dollar, and about the same color as an old nickel. The face on the conference room side read:

FITTED AT BOSTON, *N. AMERICA* FOR THE PACIFIC OCEAN
BY
J. BARRELL,
S. BROWN, C. BULFINCH,
J. DARBY, C. HATCH,
J.M. PINTARD.
1787.

"Hmmm..." Miles shot a glance at the Brahmin, "May I?"

"By all means." He was a man willing to appreciate those who appreciate. The opposite face of the coin, on the hall side, was more interesting. It presented a picture of two sailing vessels, one much larger than the other. Around it ran the words:

COLUMBIA AND WASHINGTON

COMMANDED BY J. KENDRICK

Barrell and Bulfinch -- facing inward. J. Kendrick -- facing outward.

Miles had heard the whole story about an ancient ancestor, Captain John Kendrick of Cape Cod, who, two hundred years ago, financed by Boston merchants, sailed to the Northwest in his ship *Columbia*. Along the way, he discovered the fabled great river of the west and named it after his ship. From thence lay the U.S. claims to Oregon and Washington. Manifest destiny and all that. So one of the merchants was a Barrell... and another a Bulfinch. Like the firm name. Then who was Gray?

HE IS WATCHING YOU. Miles stood up with a nod of approval. Sufficiently impressed. But Barrell wanted more. His lazy eyes had perked up a little bit. He was actually interested, Miles could see. LET HIM ASK.

"Well...?" The Brahmin was still pleasant but close to frowning.

Close enough. Miles clasped his hands behind him. "I think you're facing it the wrong way."

The Brahmin actually laughed -- a laugh that showed his vast array of yellow teeth. At least they were his own. They reminded Miles of wooden teeth. "I can see why Lotta appreciated you!" The smile faded as he offered

Miles a seat and took his own at the head of the table. Miles preferred one with its back to the window.

"You know, she used to work here." Barrell's tone was more somber. "After she got her law degree from Harvard. Very tough. A fighter. I was sorry to see her go."

From the firm or from the world? "As was I." Miles directed his eyes into the Brahmin's. Bad move. The dark eyes hardened with a blankness. Miles couldn't read this man. It was like looking into the eyes of a reptile -- cold, unblinking, waiting. *He wants to kill me.*

DON'T BE RIDICULOUS. The silence continued. As did the staring contest. The seconds passed. It was apparent they represented different things, but perhaps Barrell needed to get a reading of a man he had already once underestimated. Miles shrugged off the stare with a dopey grin. "I sure hope Meredith's doing better."

That broke the stare like an ice pick. "I'm afraid she will be in for a couple more weeks. They're transferring her soon to the Mass. Eye and Ear infirmary for surgery."

"I am terribly sorry." And Miles was.

But the Brahmin continued, unabated. "We hope to get her back home by Thanksgiving." He gestured over his shoulder at a gilt frame sitting on a small table behind him. Its photo showed a younger Meredith, all suntanned and bleached blonde, at the helm of a sailboat, surrounded by her more adult crew of six, including Barrell himself. A close-up from this picture had been used by the media in recent days to evoke sympathy for the other "victim", the more seriously wounded "survivor." "You know we have a little place down off Falmouth where the family comes and, well, it'll do her a world of good. You wouldn't happen to be from Wareham, would you?" Barrell asked.

"No." Miles' answer was a little too adamant. Cape Cod was everything east of the Cape Cod Canal, and Ware-ham, as he said it, was just on the mainland side. It had all the cranberry bogs and ticky-tack of the worst of the Cape, but none of the quaint charm or open-ocean beaches. It was the difference between being a Cape Codder and a Swamp Yankee.

Barrell's lineage probably ran through a dozen old families -- Cabots, Lodges, Winthrops -- founders of Boston and the Massachusetts Bay Colony in 1630. On that tiny peninsula surrounded by mud flats and their own posterity, they created first a theocracy, then an oligarchy that came to rule New England's religion, politics and business for well over three centuries. Sitting before Miles was the product of this well-heeled inbreeding.

Nothing but a late-comer. Ten years before the Puritans, a settlement had been planted south of Boston by a group of English settlers. Instead of pushing their beliefs on others, they had simply asked those who disagreed with their community to leave. Compared to most, their relations with the Indians had been cordial. All they wanted was to form their own little corners of the Plymouth Bay Colony. These true blue bloods, off the *Mayflower,* and their descendants settled the southeast of Massachusetts, preserving its rural nature for over 300 years. And always having to pay homage to the upstarts in Boston.

In the eyes of the Brahmins, these Swamp Yankees and Cape Codders were simple country cousins, amusing for their quaint local color and pleasant surroundings. The Bostonians would return to their city, teeming with Irish, Italians, Jews, Blacks, Hispanics and Asians, and look down from their ivory towers as fortunes passed from generation to generation. *But I'm not bitter.*

"No, I live on Beacon Hill." The old home turf of the Brahmins -- themselves now more likely to live in the leafy suburbs of Wellesley or Manchester – having divided up many of the Hill's townhouses into apartments and condos. "But I have a place down the Outer Cape. That's where my family's from."

The Brahmin's interest was piqued -- not a common occurrence, Miles guessed. A paralegal with a place on the Cape and Beacon Hill. And a blue-blood pedigree? It spoke of money. "Do you know if you're related to the Captain?" he swung his bifocals toward the coin.

Miles was indifferent. The tale went that before the first Captain John Kendrick left for the Pacific, he stopped and named his newborn nephew after himself. Auspicious, as the second Captain K went into the China trade. "Oh shurh, but all Cape Codders all related."

Barrell appeared to accept this with a smile. A cough changed his expression. "Well, we've had quite an episode, we two. You know, of course, that this firm is handling the settlement of the Meares estate. Fortunately, John had substantial life insurance coverage, so his family will be provided for... and I'm sure you'll be busy with the FDIC claim against the estate. It goes to probate court now, and as Executor, I shall have to retain my own help."

"Actually, uh, I'm not sure if I'm going to be on this case anymore."

"Oh?"

"Yes, you see, I'm freelance. The FDIC will simply have to find another outside counsel for this case, or turn it over to their own staff. I never had any direct contact with them, so short of tying up loose ends, I'm out of a job. Or a client, really."

The Brahmin was silent. He nodded. He did this well. *What!?! Stop staring at me! Out with it!*

PATIENCE. YOU CAN'T USE THAT STUPID SHRUG AGAIN.

"You have no other work." A statement, not a question. Repeated for emphasis, not response.

DON'T MOVE.

Let him think I'm helpless.

Even so, the Brahmin's observation, though flawed, was close to the mark. Landscaping and his few other clients could always keep him, just as landscaping alone had kept him before. But winter was coming, and with it, cold, lean times. He wouldn't be able to afford rent in Boston -- *the rent!*

The thought had been lurking in the back of his mind, waiting for a time to strike. Rent was due a few days ago, and he had forgotten about being reimbursed for purchasing the coin from Arthur. A call to the FDIC should... be very... bureaucratic. *Shit, I need money.*

The brush of anxiety was undoubtedly not missed by the Brahmin. His high forehead eased. But instead of pursuing this line, he, in one surprising burst of energy, brought his large frame up from the chair, and Miles up from his, without so much as a word. The movement was less physical and more commanding and irresistible for Miles -- one moment he was leisurely sitting, the next he was standing with Barrell's arm around his shoulder, before the coin in the glass.

"John, this medal was struck in 1787 by Paul Revere upon the commission of my great-great-Great-GREAT grandfather."

Family. Heritage. Miles knew the feeling well. He could sympathize. He let the man go on. "You've heard of Captain James Cook?"

A question? Miles was surprised -- he expected a monologue.

ANSWER. BE ATTENTIVE. "The British explorer -- killed in Hawaii -- say 1778? -- by the natives, right?" Miles cast his eyes up to meet Barrell's, though they were equally as tall.

It worked. The Brahmin smiled paternally, but kept his eyes riveted on the coin. "Ye-es. On Cook's third voyage to the Pacific he was charged by the British Crown to probe the extent of the Spanish claims -- they in turn having claimed that entire ocean and all lands bordering it. His track up the west coast of North America found no Spanish presence north of San Francisco -- and so kept away from the coast until forced by need of repairs into Nootka Sound on the west coast of Vancouver Island."

Miles nodded affirmatively. He had a talent for appearing to confirm people's own understanding of subjects when quite honestly he possessed no knowledge of it whatsoever. Not that he wouldn't normally find it mildly interesting, but he wasn't too keen on maritime history. It always depended so much on fleets that seemed to pop out of nowhere or get swamped by freak storms. He preferred vast, slow migrations of armies and peoples -- something easily predicted and tracked. Anyway, he found he could either *appear* to be attentive *or* actually listen. He could not possibly do both. Cook. Nootka. Vancouver. Yes, yes.

"Of course, by this time, Cook's poor sailors -- most of whom had been dragged out of any seaside pub by the Royal Navy press gang years before -- were wearing just the tattered remains of their cotton and woolen clothes and not enjoying the damp, cool weather of the Northwest too much." He chuckled, which Miles echoed. Cold, wet limeys. Yeah. Heh, heh.

"Now, you must understand the natives out there had probably never seen anything like the British men-o-war -- well, maybe the stray Spanish ship a year or two before. But when they paddled out in their massive canoes, they saw something on board they wanted, and as they were a trading people, seized the opportunity." He held up the lapel of Miles jacket near the collar. *He's going to hit me!*

STEADY. The Brahmin's eyes locked onto the collar. "Buttons. Brass buttons on the sailors coats and pants," shaking the collar for emphasis. "They had no metal or metalworking of their own -- and certainly nothing as pretty as these ornaments the shivering English sailors wore. And so the natives offered to trade the sea otter skins they wore for the sailors' buttons."

With that he let go of Miles' collar. Miles was sorely relieved for the distance and the extent to which he allowed the Brahmin a false sense of security.

"Cook left Nootka with his ships, *Discovery* and *Resolution*, with his crew draped in these huge, six-foot skins of magnificent beauty and warmth, and the natives paddled away, naked but with their prized jewelry. Everyone seemed pretty happy, right?"

Miles murmured skeptically. The yellow teeth of his host showed themselves. A fellow cynic.

"Right. The ships continued onto Kamchatka where the Russians had been trading for years --"

Kamchatka. Miles recognized it from RISK, a simple strategic wargame like monopoly but instead of buying Park Place, the object was to conquer the world. Kamchatka was an important province to take due to its position on the northeast coast of Asia -- a jumping-off point to Alaska, Japan or northern China.

"-- and a Russian trader caught sight of the otter skins the sailors wore. They gladly unloaded them for his price of seven Spanish dollars each. You can imagine how the sailors felt, what with getting more from a few buttons than perhaps their wages for the whole of the miserable voyage. The Russian was going to come back the next day for the rest of the lot, but the Brits were anxious to leave and sailed for China before the Russian could return. It was just as well for the men, too, because when they arrived at the Portuguese colony, Macao, at the mouth of the Pearl River, the Chinese offered them fifty dollars for each fur, knowing the upper classes couldn't get enough."

"Quite a haul." It was base, but Miles preferred the succinct sound of the statement.

"Indeed! The sailors who had shivered in the rain of the Northwest dressed in the finest silks. It surely irked the English sense of class in the officers, and there was a near-mutiny by those men wanting to return to Nootka for more furs. Who could blame them -- they had been wearing a king's ransom on their backs!"

Miles had now lost all pretense of *feigned* interest. The story of easy riches in days gone past pulled at his heartstrings.

"Before *Resolution* and *Discovery* sailed from Macao, two men disappeared in a long boat, apparently headed back across the Pacific for their fortunes." Barrell broke from the coin and wandered over to the head of the table, gripping the back of the seat with one hand. The question begged at Miles' mind. Did they make it? What happened to them? DON'T ASK IT.

"They disappeared." The Brahmin paused for another awkward moment at the chair. Slowly he brought his arms to rest across its head, followed by the lowering of his chin to his folded arms. In his peripheral vision, Miles could feel the lazy eyes upon him. FOCUS ON THE COIN -- J. BARRELL, S. BROWN, C. BULFINCH,...

"As you say," Barrell continued, "Cook was killed in the Sandwich Islands -- the name he gave to the Hawaiian Islands -- and his logs were ordered sealed by the British Board of Admiralty, for they contained a wealth of military and commercial knowledge. But as with all government secrets, there was a leak, in the form of a fanciful account by one of Cook's young officers, and it became a sensation in Europe and America."

FACE HIM. To Miles' surprise, the Brahmin was now at the window, taking in the harbor and beyond. "Joseph Barrell -- the one on the medal -- saw an opportunity. It was simple -- cheap trinkets like buttons and beads, and other assorted junk manufactured in New England to be traded for sea otter furs, then off to China, sell furs, and load up a cargo of silk, porcelain and tea for sale in Boston. Simple enough. Derby contributed the ship, and a sloop as its consort, and found two men to command them."

Ship. Sloop. Consort. Words to Miles. Nothing more. BE ATTENTIVE.

Barrell took a deep breath, and his expression hardened at the window. "They chose a young man of 30 years from Rhode Island to captain the sloop *Lady Washington* -- that's the smaller vessel you see on the medal -- Robert Gray. He was already working for Hatch and Brown, and *supposedly* had fought in the Revolution as a lieutenant or some such." The Brahmin waved his hand dismissively. "The commander of the expedition, and the flagship *Columbia Rediviva*, was only 47 years old -- but an old man in those times -- and a successful privateer and navigator."

With this, he turned to face Miles and proceeded to sit down in his head chair. From his vest pocket he produced a checkbook and as he wrote he spoke the name: "John Kendrick."

REMAIN STANDING WHERE YOU ARE. The check was torn out in a swift rip that stung at Miles. *Money!* The Brahmin slid it in Miles' direction. The hand remained on it for a moment as the lazy eyes rolled up to Miles. Miles, however, simply focused on the hand, and as it withdrew, the check. From this distance he couldn't make out the amount, but it had at least three zeroes and a comma before the decimal point. WHAT IS YOUR DUTY?

Oh, forget that -- he's trying to buy me. No one owns me!

"In the end," Barrell slipped the checkbook back into his coat, "Kendrick proved himself of service to my family... and his country as well." The last was an afterthought, as if it were redundant. "And you?"

I am incorruptible. What was the money for? On the face of it, Miles felt like he was being honored for an accident of kinship more than anything else. If so, it was flattering, and perhaps more than about time, and he was certainly never shy about free money --

BE RATIONAL. HE WANTS SOMETHING.

My complicity. In the weeks before the trial, Lotta had sent Miles bustling through the U.S. District Court Law Library searching for case after case that in one way or another set precedent for her own legal argument. But that's all the law was -- precedent upon precedent -- quoting scripture to suit your purposes. He had happened upon a recent federal decision in Louisiana concerning privileged information held by employees of attorneys. While a judge or a bar association in a jurisdiction are powerless to discipline a non-attorney, it is the duty of a law firm to screen out such employees to prevent any possible conflicts of interest.

The difference was Barrell was trying to screen Miles in. And as soon as other attorneys discovered this, they'd screen Miles out. YOU'LL BE LEFT WITH ONE CLIENT. AND BE COMPLETELY AT HIS MERCY.

They're aren't nearly enough zeroes on that check for me then.

NEVER MIND YOUR BETRAYAL OF LOTTA.

I'd become one of Them. Miles hadn't moved from his position next to the coin in the glass. He was tired of being on the defensive, being passive, waiting for others to tell him one thing or another. Better to head off further efforts with a demonstration of *my powers*.

He squatted down, resting on his toes, to examine the medal. He exclaimed a satisfactory "Huh!" Just as deliberately, he rose and, ignoring the check, walked to the door and to the other side of the glass to squat and ponder its face. For a moment he almost lost his concentration, thinking of his ancestor taking the two delicate-looking vessels all around the world in search of riches.

COLUMBIA AND WASHINGTON

COMMANDED BY J. KENDRICK

A brave man. The thought shook him back to reality. "Huh!", and from his balanced toes he peered over at the Brahmin. "Nickel?"

Without so much as a flinch, Barrell replied, "They minted twelve silver, maybe fifty copper. The rest, some 300 like that one, were pewter."

"Still rare, though." Miles rested his elbows on his knees, and his chin on his folded hands. He knew, from weeding, he could stay like this for hours. *I could smash this glass and take the coin. How's that sound for a pay-off?*

SOUNDS LIKE YOU'D END UP IN JAIL PRETTY QUICK.

Still, he is now trying to figure out if I want more money.. or the coin. Or... more?

DATA. ALL THIS IS DATA. GOOD. BAD. TRUE. FALSE. All to be weighed and absorbed in its own context and relation to all other data. It is –

"Priceless," Miles announced to the coin. He rose effortlessly to full height. He looked at the Brahmin, who now regarded Miles with a hint of curiosity and perhaps amusement. "Truly priceless," Miles said with surprising calmness to the attorney. Thereupon, he turned and walked casually through the door to the fire exit.

CHAPTER SIX

Hope

Friday, October 20, 1995

He could lose this woman.

And think of the money, power and prestige if we were married.

WHAT IS YOUR DUTY? Miles stiffened, pulling upright and poised in the chair, all the while keeping Meredith's image in the mirror within view. The old man in the hospital bed next to him snored gently. Seated in the room across the hall, Miles had a perfect view of Meredith asleep -- he guessed -- who could tell with the bandages swaddling her eyes?

Hers was a private room, cascading with bouquets and other well-wishes. He imagined the smell must be overpowering, what with her lack of sight. But better the cloying smell of roses than the disinfected urine smell inherent in any hospital. *I hate these places.*

Miles looked down at his newfound "grandpa" with compassion. No one had come to visit him for the past week, the nurse had said upon dropping in a few minutes ago. Thankfully, this was different wing of Mass. General than Miles had been in, so there was little chance he'd be recognized by the staff. And now he was in a hell of lot better shape, with clean hair pulled back. Wearing his white union shirt and white jeans lent him a half-institutional, half-religious appearance. *I am pure.*

WHEN YOU LISTEN.

Who was this old man? His thin limbs and shriveled face were so delicate. It was hard to believe that time had done this to a once-vibrant human being. He was either Italian or Portuguese from the hint of olive complexion in his pale cheeks, and the remnants of a few black streaks in his thinning hair. Perhaps he had been an engineer, had built great projects in Boston, or in the Second World War constructing an airstrip on some isolated atoll. Now to end his days here in a bright, quiet closet after a final attempt to replace yet another failing organ. A wave of satisfaction swept over Miles. YOU ARE DOING GOOD.

This old man didn't know Miles was here, but the pained expression on the sleeping face had slowly been replaced with one of, if not contentment, peaceful recognition. Another was here with him, he sensed. No longer alone.

This accident of charity grew out of Miles' need to see Meredith. Not so much to talk to her -- no, she was too vulnerable, too captive. DON'T MAKE HER HATE YOU.

I must go to her. She was the survivor. She was his only connection to this greater world which had invaded his own -- one he had no apparent control over. If he could just lay eyes upon her, see that she did indeed bear evidence, through her wounds, to the blast, it would be easier to accept. If he hadn't felt that he could have fallen in love with her, he would have never even kissed her. Or made love to her. There was a vulnerability there, and perhaps a hidden respect as well, within her eyes. Intimacy. He got the idea she may never have experienced it.

Lotta was simply gone. Just not there anymore. No calls for getting copies at the Bankruptcy Court. No creative interpretations of judicial decisions. *No work for me. No money.*

More than that, though. Just gone. Lotta's body, he had seen on the news, had been shipped back to the Midwest for burial tomorrow. The paralegal is always the last to know.

And Meares, well -- so what? He had achieved near-mythical status to Miles -- *The Legend of John Meares and the Missing Millions.* Tracked him for years, but again, so what? Miles might have simply met an actor playing Meares for this one scene ("Yeah, I've been in *Bomblast in Boston.* I played the deadbeat real estate tycoon.")

The only other connection, Barrell, was a mystery Miles wasn't sure he wanted to tackle. Besides shifting from patrician to sphinx, the attorney had attempted to bribe Miles into... what? Working for Barrell, Bulfinch & Gray? Providing copies of privileged communication between Lotta and the FDIC? Or to simply have a Kendrick in the employ of a Barrell -- again? Whatever it was, it was unethical, in appearance, if not in substance.

APPEARANCE IS EVERYTHING. But it doesn't pay the rent. A call to Barbara Fletcher, senior attorney for litigation at the FDIC, had not elicited an immediate and sympathetic response. In fact, there was no response at all. His was just another pink message slip on her desk. He had another few days, but the landlord wouldn't hop-to so quick for repairs to their crumbling ceiling. *My crumbling world.*

WHAT IS YOUR DUTY? Miles took a sharp breath in, and looked

over at the mirror, at Meredith. Her room was dark in the autumn twilight but for the television casting flickers of color upon her. Now white, now pale blue, then a shock of yellow and orange, now a dark pause and whiteness again. Glare. *I can save her.*

WHAT ABOUT YOURSELF? He knew he was nothing. His happiness insignificant, unimportant. His frequent attempts at achieving it ludicrous. Unattainable. But he could make others happy. *That is my duty.*

She was all alone. No other man had come to share supper. As Miles would have. Where were the loved ones -- with their expensive gestures -- now, while the one who could truly cure sat across the hall, imparting kind company to a fragile, unknown old soul? YOU COULD STAY HERE AND NURSE HER BACK TO HEALTH.

That might work. Or, more likely, she would come to feel trapped and smothered in her bed by this too-sweet, strange man. It would retard her recovery. YOU CAN'T ALLOW THAT ABOVE ALL THINGS.

I can't operate here -- not in these surroundings. Whatever magical spell he could cast over her, as healer, he knew it would not work here, in the presence of real healers. All it would take was one handsome doctor to sideline Miles. *No!*

FOCUS. WHAT CAN YOU DO TO HELP? What could he do that no one else could?

I am an instrument of God.

WHAT IS YOUR DUTY?

To do good and make things right.

HOW WILL YOU DO THIS?

I will discover the truth.

YOU KNOW THAT IS NOT ENOUGH.

And I will show everyone in such a manner that no one can deny I am right.

Miles found himself up at the doorway of Meredith's room. He did not remember getting up and walking here. It was unnerving -- who had seen him? What if he had fallen over someone in a wheelchair? More unnerving, however, was the sight of Meredith's hand upon the television remote. Her fingers moved across it to mute the sound.

Idiot! He saw that his shadow, cast by the hall lights, hovered upon her face. The change in light must have caught her attention. Her face turned towards the door. The mouth and cheeks appeared to have an expectant or perhaps apprehensive look. *Damn it!*

DON'T MOVE. Miles shadow cast half across her face, darkening one side and not the other. As he was leaning forward on his toes, this pose was now hard to keep. But it was obvious that any movement on his part would be sensed by her. YOU HAVE TO GO.

He knew he couldn't be caught staring like an idiot into her room. It was too late to simply go in casually and say hello. She wasn't stupid. She'd know he'd been here a while. The nurse could confirm his visit to grandpa across the hall. Typical obsessive-compulsive behavior. From there it would be a short jump to pinning the explosion on him. *They'd all love to blame me. It's so easy.*

DON'T GET CAUGHT.

A single gurney laden with a recovering patient passed by in the hall and Miles jumped in step with it. The synchronization of its passing with his disappearance was pretty close. Close enough. It had to be.

The window display caught his eye with an outrageous sign screaming:

CREATE YOUR OWN WORLDS!

I do.

GO HOME. DON'T STOP HERE. Figuring he had a minute to spare from his self-appointed tasks, on a whim, he stepped inside the software store. Straight into the back where the games were. YOU'RE NOT BUYING ANYTHING.

I just want to see... The program allowing its user to start at critical moments in history, and alter them, and thus the future, sold for only $39.95 on CD-ROM. Two weeks' meals. Turning on his heel, he saw the large figure intently studying the interactive multimedia CD for the group *Queen.* Glasses, and almost as tall, but much broader and undefined. *Has he seen me?*

GO TALK TO HIM. Why not? "Thad."

He was too big to fully startle. "Oh, Johnny," Thad held out his hand.

"What's up?" Miles asked.

Thad rubbed his jaw, "Wa-el, just trying to figure out if this CD is worth it or simply another attempt by big record companies to milk a man's death by tempting my curiosity."

"Or both?"

"That was my idea."

"You know you're going to buy it anyway...," said Miles.

"This is true. But I don't want to necessarily give them the satisfaction of an early sale." Thad held it up, "It came out yesterday."

"So wait 'til tomorrow."

"Can't. Going to Portland tonight for the weekend, and if I don't buy this now... I'll forget."

"And never waste your money. I see your point." Miles tried to be nonchalant. "What's in Oregon?"

"Uh, a trade show."

"Mm." BE CIVIL. He nodded stiffly. "Mm-hmm."

"Saw you caught in some serious action at the courthouse. You okay to be walking around?"

"Yeah." PUT AN END TO THIS NOW. BE MAGNANIMOUS. "You know, it gave me a chance to think. Maybe it might be time to resurrect a program that's been gathering dust on the shelf -- before it becomes obsolete."

"What program is that?" asked Thad.

"*SEXTANT*."

"Oh... we've already started distribution. A couple days ago we started free shipping to private PC owners. In another week it will be downloadable at our Web site."

What!?!

CONTROL.

My idea? My program!?!

FOCUS. WHERE ARE YOU?

I could kill him right now --

NO. NOT HERE. OTHERS WOULD GET HURT IN THIS STORE.

Right through the plate glass window --

HE'S BIG.

I'm fast and have nothing to lose.

YES, YOU DO. Meredith.

Shit. "Oh."

"So, how's Paulie?"

"Pretty good."

CHAPTER SEVEN

Three Brothers

Saturday, October 21, 1995

The ship was saved. The Captain had lost his trusted First Officer in the bargain. Even the crotchety Ship's Surgeon betrayed emotion. But this vessel's explorations in uncharted regions, its discoveries of new life and new civilizations, and confrontations with rival empires were far from over. The three young men watched as the *Enterprise* cruised slowly out view. Miles hit the rewind button and hunted around for the third movie in the series. Still five movies to go in this marathon.

Retiring to the kitchen, Seth pulled out the plates and Miles the glasses as Paulie went down to pay the pizza boy. "Kendrick," the Professor called from the pantry, "you knew about your connection to John Meares, didn't you?"

What? The clinking of the glasses in the kitchen stopped. Miles froze in thought. Connection? Potential conflict of interest all along? Maybe he should've taken the check from Barrell, if so. NO, YOU WERE RIGHT NOT TO.

What does he know that I don't?

"Miles?" Seth poked his head around the corner.

A commotion outside grabbed their attention. It sounded like a dogfight. Down on street level were the sounds of angry, young male voices. Up at the window, Seth and Miles could not identify anything -- simply shadows between the gaslights and parked cars.

Paulie came stalking out of the shadows, a large, white flat box in his hands. Behind him, in the dimness, two red tail lights flicked on like the eyes of a chastened dragon. The high roar of the engine revving was followed by the car's defiant and sudden race from its curbside spot and out of sight.

After a minute of waiting in silence before empty plastic plates, the door finally re-opened. Its slam was followed by a heavy tread. Paulie emerged into the living room with a large pizza box, pissed. He opened the lid, lifted an edge of the pie, and dropped it with disgust. "And fuckin' *cold*, too!" Then he dug into his pocket, "Oh, here," and returned Miles and Seth five dollars each -- their original contributions to the cost of the pizza. He proceeded into the kitchen, leaving the two in the living room in mutual puzzlement.

"Uh, Paulie...?" Miles ventured as he stood up and approached the oven. Paulie shoved the pizza inside and closed the door with those jerky movements that betray forced restraint and controlled fury. The sounds were crisp, not harsh, but definitely not those of a man pleased with the present.

He held up the spatula he had used to shove the pizza. "*You* -- I knew this sort of thing would happen," pointing at Miles. "I said I didn't want any part of this. And now, here it is, right in front of my home -- these fuckin' assholes poking their noses into here, snappin' their pictures --"

"Chilling your pizza," Miles added.

"-- Chilling my pizza." Paulie let loose a quick smile and a laugh before shaking them away. It was funny to see Paulie like this. It was so rare. Miles knew how to turn the anger and frustration into laughter. Paulie wanted to be mad -- never mind the reason -- but it all became comical. So he appealed to a higher authority. "Seth, you know what I'm saying!"

Smothered in blasé, the Professor replied, "Haven't the foggiest, but you're probably right --"

"Hey!" Miles swung around to meet this flank attack.

"-- but I gather it has something to do with this place being under surveillance." He smirked when the shocked look on Miles' face confirmed that only he himself had possessed this knowledge until just recently.

"*WHAT!?!*" Miles strode to the window, opening the large old frame so fast it nearly broke, and cast the entire upper half of his body out. His eyes wide and searching swept the dark cobblestone alley, brick sidewalks and the street. He frowned at the many darkened upscale imports and sport utility vehicles parked curbside. *Nothing!*

From inside, a million miles away from his focus, came Seth's question to Paulie, "You chased them away?" That didn't seem right. The FBI wasn't likely to run, and the U.S. Marshals would just as soon shoot Paulie than put up with him.

"Some reporter -- hah! Not even that. Just some guy with a camera."

Miles turned back to the two still entirely inside the building. None of this squared with professional, effective surveillance. With squinted eyes he asked "Heh?"

"Kendrick, close the window or jump out of it," Seth offered, "and we'll take this into the kitchen. Pizza done?"

The first slices were polished off before Paulie began. "Well, I go down to the front door and there's this guy there with the pizza and he asks 'John

Kendrick?' and I say yeah. I thought it was kinda funny 'cause this guy wasn't carrying the pizza box in one of those big mitt sleeves to keep it warm. And I go to give him the fifteen bucks and he shoves the pizza at me. So, y'know, I just smile -- trying to be pleasant. Then he swings around and pulls up what I fuckin' swear I thought must've been some big-ass magnum and my jaw just drops. All I could think of is that this is some kinda mob hit on *you*!" Paulie looked accusingly at a sheepish Miles.

Seth roared. "The Pizza Gunman! I love it!"

"I nearly peed my pants, " Paulie continued, "until I saw it was just a camera with a huge flash. It goes *BAAM!* And I'm just about blinded -- fuckin' amateur..." He hunted for another slice and took a disgusted bite out of one. For a photographer like Paulie, who took great pride in his ability to capture great impromptu shots of people in the city, such slipshod work was the hallmark of tabloid newspapers. The difference between a hack and an artist.

"You're going to come out looking all washed out," Miles observed.

"Well, this guy obviously doesn't give a fuck, and -- get this -- he says 'Thanks' and gives a little wave as he runs back to his car. So I follow him --"

"With the pizza box," Miles interjected.

"Shit, yeah. I don't want to leave it out on the street for some bum to steal -- not after all this. And as I catch up to him I can see he's fumbling in the dark with his keys, and he's looking all guilty 'cause he knows he's been caught." The thought of Paulie emerging from the shadows, full of vengeance and purpose, would be pretty damn intimidating. The pizza box, rather than rendering the whole scene ridiculous, probably added the element of some sort of weapon to smite the guilty.

"But I just walk very calmly up to the car, set the box down on the hood and I say 'You know, that wasn't very nice. I try to respect people's privacy and hope they will respect mine.' And he starts getting all, y'know, 'Well, the public has a right to know!' and shit, but all the time backing away. So I very calmly ask him to give me the roll of film, which, of course, he refuses. Then I say, 'Look, can I at least have my fifteen bucks back? -- the pizza's stone-cold by now', and he figures he's getting off easy and relaxes and reaches into his pocket. When he does, I grab the flash off his camera."

Very nice. For a quick man it would be about as easy as taking someone else's glasses off their face. For a hack photographer, a good flash is pretty hard to come by. "You had his attention, then," Miles observed.

Paulie grinned wickedly, followed in a low voice by, "Yes. And his respect. We came," he fished a roll of film out of his shirt pocket, "*to an understanding*."

CHAPTER EIGHT

Imperial Eagle

Sunday, October 22, 1995

5:00 A.M. "I'm goin' to bed," Paulie murmured, crunching a step dead into the center of the pizza box on the floor, and knocking a few empty Coke bottles aside like bowling pins.

In the chill of the morning, Seth and Miles made their way down the dew-slicked brick sidewalks of Beacon Hill. The Federal townhouses seemed their most authentic at this hour, as if it would be more appropriate to see a frock-coated Samuel Adams emerge from one of the narrow doorways and make his way down the granite steps, past the cast-iron boot-scraper and subterranean servant's door, to a waiting carriage. As it was, the late-model Volvos and Toyotas lining each side were quite out of place, and only served to narrow the tight street even more.

"You ever hear of the Nootka Sound Incident?" the Professor began.

"'The Incident'? No. The Sound itself, yes. The other day I was at Barrell's office and he showed me some coin they had there -- pretty neat. They had it set in the glass -- and he told me that Cook had put into Nootka and discovered it wasn't a bad place for fur trading."

"No, it was *the* place for fur trading," Seth explained. "In 1787 the Spanish got wind the Russians, who were trading all along the Alaskan coast, were planning on setting up a trading post in Nootka Sound. The Spanish governor at San Blas, Mexico decided to send a few warships to reassert His Catholic Majesty's claims. Now, what no one knew was that John Meares, an English naval reservist, had been bringing ships over from Macao for years. Over the winter of... 1787-88 I think it was, he'd even built a small schooner at Nootka -- right next to the house he was supposed to have put up."

"He was following the published reports of Cook's voyages," Miles observed.

"Exactly," Seth said, "they'd bring over trinkets from England, trade them to the natives in the Northwest for furs, and sell those furs for an *obscene* profit back in China. Meares' financial partners included the Portuguese governor in Macao, so you can be sure Meares got good treatment when he brought in his haul."

"Pretty nice operation."

"Oh, it was small-time, but Meares had it mostly to himself, and was preparing to enlarge it substantially --," he stopped at the curb at Charles Street and shot a look directly at Miles, "-- until *your* ancestor came along and screwed it up."

"*My* ancestor?!" Miles yelled at Seth as he crossed the commercial street of Boston's most exclusive neighborhood. Miles followed at a slower pace across, and into the convenience store. "Hey, pal, we're from the same shallow and very tight gene pool --" and pointing back up the hill, "-- not to mention our acolyte!"

The Professor was examining the bagels with a discerning eye, "Yes, but you're the one named after him."

"True." As Miles had been told further back than he could remember, his first name came from ancestor Captain John Kendrick, the nineteenth schooner captain, who, in turn, had been named after his uncle, the first "Nor'westman". "More or less," he admitted.

"Whaddya say -- onion or garlic?" Seth held two tongs with a bagel in each.

"Both. How much bacon you want?"

"None! You shouldn't either. That stuff's no good for you."

Miles fished a bright red plastic package of pink-red meat strips from the freezer case, twirling it about as he approached the register. "It's for Paulie. Anyway, we leaner strain of Cape Codders aren't the ones who have to worry about longevity."

Seth sighed as he placed his bagels and coffee on the counter. "My point. He's broader of beam like me, and I worry for the man. He smokes, too. Java?" His tone turned snide, "Oh, yes, that's right -- your addiction of choice is sugar."

Miles handed the coffee to him as they headed out the store. "I told you -- this stuff doesn't effect me -- unless it has about three sugars."

"Gack! Kendrick, you won't being dying of lung cancer, heart disease or cirrhosis, but diabetes is definitely in your cards -- Oh my." Seth had stopped at the stack of the *Boston Sunday Herald* near the door.

On the front page of the tabloid, below the advertisement for the latest *Million-Dollar Wingo* contest, was a familiar face in an unfamiliar pose. Paulie, washed-out from a brilliant flash, stood open-mouthed and gaping in the foyer of their townhouse, holding a pizza box. The caption was headlined:

KENDRICK CAUGHT RED-HANDED

Plucky Courthouse Bombing Survivor John Kendrick returned to his Beacon Hill townhouse over the weekend, apparently starved for that Best of Boston thin-crust pie.

Paulie would not be happy. "But better him than me," said Miles.

They continued down Charles Street, past the real estate offices advertising loft studios atop five-floor walk-ups for $700 per month, and the various specialty antique shops. Miles wondered if Arthur Lewis might have considered this area to lease once he moved out of his waterfront warehouse -- *Arthur!*

DON'T GET CAUGHT. Miles whipped around instinctively.

He'll want to kill me! This concern had been trying to shoulder aside rent worries in the back of his mind. The media had earlier mentioned the name "John Kendrick" along with "other FDIC personnel". Maybe with Paulie being misidentified as Miles in the paper, it would buy another week of safety. But Arthur wasn't stupid. And no one cares about the injured anymore -- or the guilty, for that matter. It's the suspects that keep everyone's attention.

A hand caught his shoulder, and he turned to see Seth nodding down in front of them. "You should be more careful." A pothole just off the curb lay in wait for his ankle.

"Yo, jeez, thanks," Miles shuddered. He did not need to be sidelined with a stupid injury now. The sugar buzz from last night was wearing off in the fresh mid-autumn air. Miles was entering a dreamy state as they navigated the switchbacks of the pedestrian overpass crossing Charles Circle. On the opposite side of Storrow Drive and the leafless trees of Esplanade, the Charles River began to glow as crew boats from Harvard, MIT, Northeastern, and Boston University sliced though its glassiness. The two men found a bench down by the Longfellow Bridge and broke out the bagels. The onion smell in Miles' nostrils was harsh against the sweet muskiness off the river. Now he could listen and absorb.

The Professor leaned forward, tipped his beaten baseball cap back with the one hand not holding his coffee cup, and tracked the progress of the crew boats. "Pantywaists…," he muttered. "When Kendrick arrived in Nootka about a year after sailing from Boston, he figured they'd have the whole coast to themselves. But instead they found Meares in his vessel *Felice Adventurer*, accompanied by William Douglas in the *Iphigenia Nubiana*, with the schooner they had built there, *Northwest America*. This set the Americans off quite a bit, especially when the English all told them there were no furs around so they might as well go back home."

"Gotta love those English merchantmen," added Miles.

"Well, you should keep in mind this was 1788. Only five years after these guys finished shooting at each other in the Revolutionary War. Apparently Kendrick's men gave some letters to Meares to deliver to their American business agents in China. A few hours after Meares left the Coast, Douglas returned the letters to the American... with the feeble excuse that Meares wasn't sure if he'd be able to do so."

"But wasn't Meares headed to China?" Miles asked

"That's not the point. There was no post office in Nootka. It was a matter of maritime courtesy, but Meares snuck out and left his employee Douglas to do the dirty work of returning them."

"Very honorable."

"Meares didn't want anyone getting in on his gravy train," Seth said. "He also took most of Douglas' supplies. So Kendrick, figuring the sooner these English left the better, took his own supplies out of *Columbia* and had them sent on board the *Iphigenia*. After the last English ship left, the natives came out of hiding and helped the Americans winter over until the spring of 1789. Douglas returned in May with the *Iphigenia* and *Northwest America*, but by then the Spanish had arrived to set up their fort, and were wondering what everyone else was doing on *their* coast."

"So," Miles mused, "instead of finding Russians they found two English and two American ships."

"Nuh-uh," the Professor corrected, "Meares' ships weren't even flying English colors. They were of Portuguese registry."

"Wait -- oh -- right." Miles stumbled with comprehension. "Macao is the Portuguese colony in China, and the governor there was a partner of Meares --"

"No, it was more than that." Seth turned and took a quick sip from his coffee. "See England and most of Europe didn't have the same kind of economic system like we did -- they still really don't. We've got all this 'Cowboy Capitalism'. You see an opportunity, so exploit it and for Chrissakes, keep the government out of the way."

Miles nodded. "Like, you're in Boston and you hear that if you ship brass buttons off to the Northwest you can get furs to sell in China for tea you can sell back in Boston and make a mint -- maybe."

"Maybe," Seth added. "But that's the risk. In England, however, the Crown granted the right to one company -- benefiting the King, mostly -- and then backed up their operations through their seventy-four gun warships."

"Not like we had any kind of a navy back then," said Miles.

"Exactly. So from the southern tip of Africa to India the only company with the right to any maritime commerce in England was the British East India Company. In the Pacific it was the British South Sea Company. Meares, like a lot of Brits, either had to buy an expensive license from them or sail under another country's flag."

"It was probably cheaper to bribe the Governor of Macao," said Miles.

"Sure," Seth admitted, "but things really got interesting when two more of Meares ships arrived in July. See, the Spanish Commandant, Martinez, asked the Americans for their papers and what the hell they were doing in Spanish waters. Kendrick said they were on a voyage of discovery and had to stay the winter in Nootka because of repairs."

"'I got a flat tire'," Miles joked. "Good answer."

"The English weren't so astute. When Martinez questioned Douglas, the answer was that they had been trading there for a year, had built the *Northwest America* in Nootka, and were headed to China to sell their furs."

"That famous English diplomacy."

"Yeah, and Martinez seized *Northwest America* as a prize since she had been built on Spanish territory, and renamed her *Santa Gertrudis*."

"That name is a crime in itself."

"It gets better. The third and fourth ships of Meares, *Argonaut* and *Princess Royal*, had been sent to build a trading post, complete with supplies, Chinese carpenters and artisans -- the works. So that's what Colnett, their captain, told the Spanish."

"Smart move," Miles shook his head. "I'm sneaking into your house with a large black bag over my shoulder. You greet me with a .44 magnum and ask what I'm doing. And I say 'I've come to steal your stereo, of course.'"

"And I blow your head off," Seth agreed. "Or, in this case, the Spanish seized the ships. Of course, it didn't help any that Colnett's papers from the Governor of Macao gave him the power to seize any ship that fired upon them -- in the translation from Portuguese to Spanish, Martinez took it to mean Colnett could take any ship he encountered."

"Oops!"

"Yeah, and the Brits, in their infinite wisdom, blamed Kendrick, figuring since he spoke to Martinez first and got away scot-free, that he must've poisoned the Spanish against them."

Miles rolled his eyes wide. "No -- no, it couldn't possibly have had *anything* to do with their blatant attempt to set up their own illegal colony."

Seth shook his head. "Nah. Naw, it's those pesky Americans teaming up with a Catholic country against us. Never mind we've been robbing the natives blind of their furs and lining our pockets with the proceeds."

Miles jumped up off the bench. "Oh, forget that! Hell, they wouldn't even deliver our mail!"

"Probably felt they had been justified after the whole Nootka Sound incident."

BE CAREFUL OF NEUROTIC PEOPLE. "Yeah...," Miles lost his train of thought somewhere beyond the banks of the river, "... people assume their faults are shared by the world, and end up treating everyone they encounter like the shit they themselves feel like."

The sun had poked its head over the horizon by now, on the opposite side of Beacon Hill and the Financial District. Seth launched himself from the bench. "Ready to go?"

Miles floated away from the river back to the sidewalk. "Yeah, sure. So that's it? That's the whole deal on Kendrick and Meares?"

"Just about. Or at least what I studied in grad school. Except," the Professor said, "when Douglas arrived back early in Macao and told his boss what had happened, Meares sailed straight back to England and petitioned Parliament, claiming Spain had seized the lands he purchased from the natives --"

"Land*s*? Plural. I thought you said it was a just lean-to."

Seth preceded Miles up the overpass and spread his arms wide. "Like anyone knew any different. Meares could've claimed the whole of Vancouver Island. The point is, it was in the commercial interest of Britain to make this seem like a big deal, so Prime Minister William Pitt decided to build a fleet and threaten Spain with war unless Meares was compensated, and his ships and lands returned."

"Did they?"

"Yeah, they paid him $200,000 and there were a couple different treaties that eventually led to Spain relinquishing its claims to western Canada."

"So Meares made out like a bandit, the Brits got British Columbia and Kendrick got...?" Miles asked.

"-- Footnote status as the man who opened the Pacific to American influence," the Professor said. "Think about this: after he arrived in 1788, of thirty vessels trading in the Northwest up until 1795, fifteen were from Boston. Within ten years, only a couple of the Brits were left to compete with scores of Americans. But the natives made only one distinction between the white men they saw. If they were English, they called them 'Kintshautsh Men' -- meaning 'King George's Men'.

"And if they were American?"

"Boston Men."

Miles stopped atop the overpass, searching the rooftops as they crept up Beacon Hill. Two hundred years ago Paul Revere and his sons had scraped off the hill's steep sides and began to build what were then suburban homes. They had also constructed the dome on the "new" Massachusetts State House. For one hundred years after, the golden dome, designated center of Boston, was the tallest point in the city. But the laying of its cornerstone had still been eight years away when Captain John Kendrick sailed out of Boston on the *Columbia*. He smiled. "Ah, to be a Bostonian then... or, even better, a Cape Codder commanding the ship of one."

"Bostonian! Hah!" Seth spat. "That's some dainty Victorian label coined about fifty years after all this. Naw, if you were a sailor shipping out from here, you weren't a friggin' 'Bostonian'. You were a Bostoner."

CHAPTER NINE

Discovery

Monday, October 23, 1995

It was an exercise in patience.

"Whom shall I say is calling?"

"John Kendrick." It was his "telephone voice" -- deep, yet clear, slightly louder than usual and authoritative. It was difficult to maintain, however, in the face of repeated holds and transfers. YOU MUST GET THROUGH.

"Litigation Division."

An answer. Miles sat up in the conference room chair. "Barbara Fletcher, please."

"Whom shall I say is calling?"

"This is John Kendrick from Lotta Coolidge's office."

"Just a moment and I'll see if she's in."

"This is Barbara Fletcher."

Thank God! "Ah, Ms. Fletcher, this is John Kendrick. I've been trying to get a hold of you for some time now."

"Yes, I've gotten your messages, but I've had my hands full with the Meares case." The voice was a little husky, but refined. Black? Thirties. Perhaps tired and preoccupied. Lotta had mentioned Barbara's looks to Miles in the past -- stunning. In a male Irish Catholic environment like the Boston legal system, the going in the court houses must be tough.

BE PROFESSIONAL. SHE WILL APPRECIATE IT. "Yes, I understand that the FDIC transferred the case from Lotta to you." A practical move -- outside counsel dies just prior to settlement, so proceed with your own in-house staff lawyers. It would take some time for her to catch up, but it was just mopping up.

"Mmm-hmm."

She's not paying attention to me.

LET HER KNOW. "So I was just sitting here in Lotta's office, sifting through her various files...," Miles leaned back in his chair and took a look at the empty conference room table, his voice taking on a much more cavalier tone,"... and I thought perhaps you could direct me to the procedure for reimbursement on evidence."

Silence. For a heartbeat. "C-can I call you back?"

"Certainly," he replied with a touch of velvet, "I'll be here for another fifteen minutes."

"Are you okay?"

Miles jumped at the voice from the door, as he hung up.

Jennifer stood there with a mixture of concern and puzzlement on her face. The sweatshirt, jeans, ponytail and glasses gave her a homey look.

"Yeah, I'm fine."

She sighed in relief. "Well, y'know, I wasn't sure after everything and the news said you were in the hospital -- and then that picture in the *Herald* yesterday -- I said to my brothers, 'Hey, that's definitely not the John Kendrick I know' --"

"My roommate. He's not real happy about it."

"Yeah, but he *is* cute -- and God, those guys from the FBI were just everywhere, trying to get into everything -- and NO, I didn't let them," she said. She'd make a terrific mother. "Which didn't make 'em too happy, but I didn't spend the last three years working for Lotta just to --" She bit her lip as the moisture quickly collected on her eyes. "And you were there! You saw it all!" The tears began in earnest. Her grief touched his heart. "And now you're here, able to deal with it all and go back to work..."

Miles tried to pass by her in the doorway to where Lotta kept the tissues, but Jennifer misinterpreted his slight touch on her shoulder. She fell into his arms, sobbing sweetly. No, no, not like this.

HOLD HER. Awkwardly, he put his arms about her shoulders.

"I'm sorry," she looked up at him, then buried her face in his shoulder. Her breasts, hidden by the sweatshirt, pressed into his ribcage.

Someone in the hall -- Miles whipped his eyes left quick enough to catch Bill Connor through the glass entrance to the law office. Bill was already leaving with a grin on his face. *Shit! What the hell's he doing up here?*

The ringing desk phone saved him. While Jennifer answered it, he ducked into the conference room to hide -- or brainstorm. As he turned around, she was back. "It's for you. Barbara Fletcher from the FDIC."

"I really can't help you if you lost it," Barbara Fletcher began.

"I DIDN'T LOSE IT. I delivered it to Lotta Coolidge, *your* legal counsel, who, as *my* client, authorized the purchase. If the coin is lost, that is not my problem -- it's *yours*."

"*Mister* Kendrick, the federal authorities performed an exhaustive search of the room and apparently found nothing --"

"*Ms.* Fletcher, they were looking for evidence of a bomb, not a coin -- unless, of course, you know something about this coin that I do not, like, say, Its explosive qualities -- is that it?" DON'T PUSH TOO HARD.

There was a sigh at the other end. She was getting pissed, but maintaining control. *I'll crack her any minute.* "Look," she tried, "you're in Lotta's office -- correct?"

"Yes."

"And are you familiar with her files?"

Miles look at the conference room table stacked to the ceiling with paperwork. "Of course. I'm the one who put them in order in the first place."

"Well, then... it shouldn't be too hard for you to find Lotta's authorization for your purchase of the evidence."

The load of stress rose like a cloud. The FDIC would pay. No bounced rent check. No anger from roommates at having pulled a stupid stunt at the wrong time. All would be well in the long run.

FIND THE MEMO.

"Noon," Jennifer answered as she headed out to lunch. She had spent the morning consolidating her desk and could afford to take a break. Lotta's estate was paying her salary for the next week.

The conference room was a firetrap. The maple table was moved to one side, littered with papers, and each of Lotta's stacks had been dissected down to each and every file folder. And still nothing. But Miles enjoyed himself. It reminded him of years ago, when his then-wife, Justine, and he would set aside a day in February and do their taxes. One year it fell on Valentine's day. That romantic scene drifted over into the present. Out of nowhere, Miles imagined himself married to Jennifer.

Alone now in the conference room, he thought about Jennifer. If they were no longer working together, it would be safe to date. Like always, just when Life had set him back, along came another opportunity. He had become the king of the rebound, but it always demanded a price. No expectations meant no dreams.

Even so...

FIND THE MEMO. The memo. Money. He snapped-to and searched the room. But there was little use in looking. His attention was destroyed. Where had he been looking, anyway? The piles in the corner of the room were all in neat stacks, and he couldn't tell the searched from the unsearched. Among the unsorted piles on the table were a stack of faxes loosely with a sticky note reading "Meares Corr./Discovery" in Lotta's scrawl. Horrible handwriting, to be sure. "Shoulda been a doctor instead," Miles murmured. She'd also be alive.

The thought of her absence from life was sobering. He picked up the file case and slumped onto the floor. JUST IN CASE.

Anyway, Meares' stuff was always interesting. Unlike most plaintiffs, John Meares refused to let his attorney handle all communication. He regularly sent faxes and letters to Lotta about the state of litigation, which, to be fair, sprang from the limited degree of cooperation he and the FDIC enjoyed in pursuing his own non-performing debts. Like Arthur Lewis.

But whereas Lotta considered Meares, for the most part, simply a means to an end -- John Meares saw himself as an equal player in the game, and chose to comment quite colorfully. Meares painted himself as someone lured by a greedy bank into taking out all sorts of loans in a hot real estate market. Then he was left holding the bag when both the market and his tenants went belly-up, and subsequently, the bank, too. Why couldn't the FDIC accept that "these things happen"? Instead, they held him personally responsible on the flimsy reasoning he had signed some notes. How very noble.

When all this wrangling began, he faxed a short note to Lotta that held with this "go away" tone. Miles loved the one line:

How to proceed? No doubt, discovery is a farce of little use to all.

Discovery is a farce. "Discovery" was a concept that made Miles' job superfluous. It meant supplying opposing counsel with just about anything they requested of you as long as it wasn't privileged. But Lotta liked to see what was there before she asked for it. No surprises. Miles' job.

Discovery is a farce. Yes, when you have nothing to hide. He read on:

> *Perhaps the coat off my back and the fillings from my dear mother's teeth are not enough for you? Financial statements would simply show the obvious, unless you want to include the esoteric -- the John Singleton Copley painting donated to the Museum of Fine Arts, or perhaps the one-thirtieth interest in Meares Island in British Columbia. I understand they will be logging Mt. Colnett there soon, so the FDIC may want a share if they speak up before the province signs the papers.*

Meares Island -- ? -- Mt. Colnett -- ? The speed and force of his tightening grip on the slick, thin fax paper nearly tore it. He read it again. A one-thirtieth interest in Meares Island. The rest of the letter was rubbish. Meaning it gave no more forthcoming expansion on what Meares had alluded to.

John Meares, the English trader 200 years ago Seth had mentioned yesterday. John Meares who started a crisis between nations over a hut on the edge of nowhere, and complicated by an American named John Kendrick. Today's Meares was now dead. He had, off-handedly, mentioned a possible asset worth... well,... *something*, if it could be proven.

DON'T BE RIDICULOUS. NO ONE WOULD TAKE THIS SERIOUSLY.

I would.

"You dog," Charlie Connor answered his phone, "left alone for five minutes and you put the moves on the secretary."

"Oh, and what were you doing up on that floor -- waiting to pick up Lotta's old clients? Don't you have enough ambulances to chase?" Miles was too focused to be kind. "I'll forgive the spying. I gotta go to Salem -- soon. Whaddya guys need in Essex South?"

CHAPTER TEN

Essex

Tuesday, October 24, 1995

Neither of the guards recognized him as Seth Jones. Miles handed a scrap of paper to the middle-aged Hispanic woman. She looked at it as if there might just be someone manufacturing false receipts for pocketknives down the hall. He attempted a smile. Neither of the guards cared. This was metal detector duty at the Essex County South Courthouse in Salem. How much lower can you get?

The younger of the two, a jarhead of most definitely Irish extraction (what -- did they breed these guys just for this duty?) handed over the knife. Miles had only jumped into the Registry of Probate for fifteen minutes, but the two guards showed no glimmer of recognition. He almost forgot he had used the Seth's name when leaving his knife with them. Why alarm anyone? Perhaps this extra security was related to the bombing at the courthouse in Boston. If so, then somebody in the state courts was being a little paranoid. *Bombs are for pathetic cowards, anyway.*

The Boys at Connor & Vanzetti had sent Miles here to get a copy of a will -- to search for a dead man, really -- and then see if any of his heirs had deeded out their interests in his estate. A musical theater on the North Shore was looking to expand parking, and had been negotiating with several neighbors for their houses. Simple.

The most willing seller had died without a will, and his brother claimed ownership. So all that was required was to prove this brother was the sole heir, and the sale could go through. Downstairs was quite different. Whereas a Registry of Probate is populated with divorce lawyers and women seeking restraining orders, a Registry of Deeds is full of books.

No Registry of Deeds ever had enough space. Holding copies of all the deeds recorded since the creation of the county, they are the first resort for determining Who owns What Where. Want to sell your house? A buyer wants to see your deed -- recorded here. Want to take out a mortgage? The bank will want to see a full chain of title traveling back at least fifty years. Only then can you insure that your title to your real estate is secure -- provided all the previous mortgages have been discharged -- all recorded here.

The independent title examiners working at any Registry of Deeds tend towards the female and the middle-aged. A typical title search can pay $75. A good examiner can perform four or more in a day -- work provided by an attorney, bank, realtor, or even certain companies that specialize in such work. Eight hours a day checking through thousands of deed books to make sure Joseph and Libby Lazaro actually have a free and clear title to grant to Daniel Thompson, Trustee of North Shore Development Trust, on their house at 93 Ridge Road, Beverly, County of Essex, recorded in the Essex South Registry of Deed Book 8970, Page...

Good money, but the slavish attention to mundane detail was just too much for Miles. Tedium would foster mistakes.

Just half an hour -- Miles had one question answered. No, our dead friend hadn't deeded out his property or encumbered it with any sort of mortgage BUT he had been married when he bought it. The computer index in Essex didn't show the wife's name, either, for transfers, but a jump back up to Probate found no will for her either.

Was she alive? If so, why wasn't she involved in this proposed sale? More than likely, she had predeceased her husband and left no will -- thus hubby got the property. Miles called the Boys, but neither were in the office to confirm any of this. It was time to leave, with the resources of the Essex Registry exhausted.

"May I see some picture identification, please?" The tall, bookish Assistant Curator was simply going through the motions. No big deal when you're dealing with original manuscripts. Why should the Peabody Essex Museum not take such a precaution?

Miles tried not to smile as he passed his drivers license over to Mags. A gentleman who appeared to be her superior was absorbed in assisting another researcher in the dark mahogany-paneled reading room. "Thank you, Mr. Jones," she said in a stage whisper.

Now this was a library. The room, 10 by 20 feet, was but the entryway to an invaluable resource. The shelves that lined each wall and reached up to the ceiling were filled with genealogical volumes on practically each of the 351 cities and towns that comprised the Commonwealth of Massachusetts. Many other books traced the roots of some of the great and first families.

But neither subject was what brought Miles here. It was the archives that lay beyond these simple oak tables.

Salem actually preceded Boston's founding in 1630, and served a short time as the original capital of the Massachusetts Bay Colony. Of the two cities, Salem possessed the better natural harbor. But Boston was at the center of the great Massachusetts Bay. So just as Boston overcame its more laconic neighbor to the south, Plymouth, Salem proved simply too far north for geography, too treacherous for shipping, too cold for swimming, and too hot for heresy. In short, Salem was just too... Salem. And yet, still the capital of northeastern Massachusetts.

The literature plopped on the space on the table next to him. He smiled sweetly at Mags, thanking her for yet again letting him use the Professor's membership. "I think I know what I'm getting you for Christmas..." she murmured from her desk and began writing something down on her message pad. Her bobbed hair had grown out a little longer he noticed, and her long legs showed just a little from the corner of her desk. *Not what I want.*

She looked up at him. Miles couldn't help but blush as he focused on his work. Before him lay an assortment of articles, books and papers. Practically the entire card catalog's listing for the topics "Kendrick" and "*Columbia*". Miles had first looked up "Meares" and found nothing. That said something.

He decided to start slow. One little tome about some county in Oregon mentioned Captain Robert Gray of *Columbia* (where was Kendrick?) meeting George Vancouver's expedition towards the end of April 1792. The British commander congratulated Gray on his reputed circumnavigation of what was to become Vancouver Island -- much to the surprise of the American.

Apparently, Meares' reported to Parliament that the commander of *Washington* had performed the feat when the Spanish began seizing ships in 1789. Gray had to admit that he had not done so. Had Kendrick? Eventually Vancouver would perform the feat himself. But Meares gave *Kendrick* the credit -- not what you would expect from an enemy.

Gray told Vancouver he was heading south from Nootka to investigate what looked to be the mouth of a great river at 46° 10' North latitude, perhaps the much sought-after Great River of the West. Vancouver, heading north, advised Gray not to bother, as he found it not of much importance -- as had John Meares years earlier when he named a spit of land near it Cape Disappointment. Gray, undaunted, sailed on into what indeed was the Great River of the West, and named it after his ship -- the Columbia. From here lay the basis of the American claims in the Northwest. Not too shabby.

Another document, secured in an old manila envelope tied with tattered red ribbon, next caught Miles' attention. The brown parchment was brittle in his hands, and he took care lest it shatter like a wafer. United States 32nd Congress, First Session, 1852-53.

The shape of legislative documents hadn't changed in 150 years. It was a report accompanying a senate bill to compensate the heirs of Kendrick, Gray and the financial backers of the *Columbia* missions which left Boston in the autumns of 1787 (under John Kendrick) and 1790 (under Robert Gray). The heirs were seeking a grant of land from the United States following the treaty establishing the 49° North latitude as the border between British Columbia and the U.S. Northwest.

Up until 1848, the U.S. had argued for a claim to all land up to the Russian territory of Alaska at 54° 40' North -- including all of British Columbia and Vancouver Island. This would have meant no Pacific coast at all for Canada, a prospect the British Empire did not care for following their expeditions of discovery under Cook and Vancouver.

The rallying cry of the hawks in the U.S. Congress was *54° 40' or Fight!* But cooler heads prevailed. President Polk had successfully concluded the war with Mexico, and so doubled the territory of the U.S., but the British still had the largest navy in the world. And beyond the Rocky Mountains, naval power was what determined who owned what.

Before noon, Mags dropped off the last massive volume. *Voyages of the Columbia to the Northwest*, edited by F.W. Howay in 1935. Miles sat back in his chair, flipping through the collection of logs from various officers serving on both voyages -- Haswell, Hoskins and Boit. Raw data. Too much to absorb. Hundreds of pages of misspellings and astronomic observations. Mags was great, but the museum would never allow him to check the book out.

With raised eyebrows, the Assistant Curator measured the thickness of the book with her fingers. "Read fast -- we close at nine."

Dusk.

I gotta get outta here. There was too much information in his head. With a near jump from the table, causing the normally-immobile gaggle of researchers to break their concentrations long enough to notice, Miles dashed from the room.

Down the marble steps out the library, past the front desk of the museum and, in a final desperate plunge, through the heavy wooden doors. The granite steps barely acknowledged. He slowed his run down Essex Street to a quick stride, then to a careless dash across Hawthorne Boulevard. The red sedan with Pennsylvania plates caught its anti-lock brakes in time. There was no honk, but Miles caught the fury in the husband's eyes behind the wheel.

BE CAREFUL. Still, he ran down past the park in front of the cathedral and the statue of Nathaniel Hawthorne. Miles needed water. At end of Derby Wharf he finally stopped. Looking over Salem Harbor, with its remnants of a shipping past, now just filled with sailboats and lined with waterfront condos and restaurants.

Having taken full measure of the data, he had discovered nothing relevant. This aspect of history, 3,000 miles away on the other side of the continent, based upon the advance of the trade -- not the steady encroachment of populations -- was too new for Miles. Besides, there was a whole element of science to it -- navigation -- and lore -- different kinds of vessels and their components -- which was worse than trying to read another language. It was a whole different culture. Worse, even, it was a culture seemingly more advanced than himself. How could he begin to pull the pieces together when he didn't even know what the pieces were?

WHAT WERE YOU TRYING TO FIND?

Sitting down on a wooden piling, staring down at the sloshing of the sea, Miles remembered his original purpose for coming to Salem -- if there was a connection between Meares and this land, it was a motive to kill him. And kill anyone else who might know -- his attorneys, Barrell and Meredith, as well as opposing counsel, Lotta. Anyone, no, *everyone*, in that room should have reasonably possessed knowledge of a connection. How better to deal with the problem than to kill them all at once?

DON'T BE RIDICULOUS. There were better ways to deal with this than murder, or at least cleaner ways to kill. But it depends upon the motives of the murderer. A bomb is more than a way of eliminating someone...

It's a demonstration of power. My scream at the world -- "Hey, look what I can do!" The placement within a protected United States federal courthouse, no less, doubled the sense of power. *No one, nowhere, is safe from me.*

So if Meares was killed for his claim to land in the Northwest, the bomber wanted to shut up anyone else who might know (his lawyers) or would inherit from his estate (his family). All based upon a thin assertion obviously meant as a melodramatic joke.

Yes, in the cold objective, rational world. But there can always be an element of truth in all jokes. And some people have been known to take jokes all-too seriously so as to rationalize any action or behavior. *I should know.*

An irrational act? BUT WHOEVER DID THIS WAS CAREFUL AND CALCULATING.

A seagull landed on the pier nearby. Miles cocked his head to imitate the bird. Neither had anything for the other. But, to be sure, the bird sidled closer.

Whoever said one couldn't be both irrational and organized?

YOU SHOULD KNOW. But no, it opened the door too wide to begin to allow for consideration of irrational motives. One of the security guards could have wanted to kill Lotta for not smiling at him one day. Or Barrell for dropping a candy wrapper on the ground. Who knows? Miles simply didn't have enough information to begin such sort of extrapolation.

The seagull, having returned to piling, ruffled his feathers in classic pose. It was apparent that this human had no food, so perhaps flying over so eagerly was a mistake, but, then again, why leave? Since this was as good a place as any at the end of the day, why not stick around and see if anything better showed up?

"Hey-ho, " Miles sing-songed to the gull, "whaddya-know?"

The bird blinked back at the human, then returned to his survey of the harbor. Gulls always appeared to be so downy white and clean, but Miles had grown up knowing them as "dump chickens" -- filthy and certainly not worth eating. Lazy scavengers of the coasts. And yet this one appeared so aloof right now.

The politics of it. That was it. Miles sprang to his feet. The gull took wing at the sudden movement of the human.

Pacing the end of the wharf, Miles knew there was no way he could begin to comprehend the workings of navigation and merchant sail 200 years ago -- at least, not immediately. But behind the officers' logs lay those men who set the events in motion. Men on shore. Men who gave the orders.

This, Miles could wrap his mind around readily.

King George

November 19th, 1790
London

"He *is* a bit of a prig," Banks answered, "but, then again, that is to be expected from one of Captain Cook's 'boys'". The implication was not an unwelcome one. Especially coming from a gentleman supposedly dedicated to science, as the President of the influential Royal Society, Joseph Banks, was. Through the indulgence of His Majesty King George III, Banks had inaugurated the now-flourishing Royal Botanical Gardens at Kew. Expeditions such as Cook's had led to wealth of knowledge of the globe, its cultures, as well as its flora and fauna.

Nevertheless, of the other two gentlemen, both in their thirties, seated in the dim study this evening, one soured at Banks' faint praise of the subject at hand. Old men, near fifty, usually cared not whom they offend.

So thought the Earl of Chatham, John Pitt, First Lord of the Admiralty and, by small coincidence, elder brother of the Prime Minister, William Pitt. "HOWEVER," he began, catching the attention of the old 'King's Friend', as well as the other young gentleman, "you, yourself, Mr. Banks, also attended Captain Cook upon his first voyage to the Pacific. Back when he was young and vibrant --"

Banks gasped at the affront.

"-- I mean, dear sir, before his untimely death at the hands of the natives of the Sandwich Islands in the Year of Our Lord 1778?"

Such was typical of exchanges between Tory and Whig, with Baron William Grenville caught in the middle. Conservative Tories, supporting the power of the Crown and its exclusive trading companies battling the progressive Whigs. With the loss of the American colonies in 1783, and William Pitt's appointment as PM while still in his twenties, the monarchy increasingly saw its hands tied by the Whigs in Parliament. But Grenville had agreed to serve as Foreign Secretary of State in the cabinet of William, his cousin. And so with his cousin, the Earl of Chatham.

"Precisely my point!" Banks thumped the arm of his ornately embroidered wing chair so hard the dust flew up from his white wig. "We must not have any shenanigans like those which led to the loss of a great navigator like Cook. If it is not the murderous savages of Hawaii, as they call it, it's the amorous girls of Tahiti!" Chatham's face became even more wooden while Grenville tried to suppress a sly grin. "... Or," the old naturalist continued, "the Spanish on the coast."

"Which is precisely why our Lieutenant Vancouver came so highly recommended. In the Caribbean, he was noted for a high degree of discipline and meticulousness, which, no doubt, should please you, sir, your institution, your sovereign, and his Board of Admiralty." Meaning myself, Chatham might as well have added.

Banks shifted in his chair, seemingly uncomfortable. This late in the autumn, windows to this room were tightly sealed against London's damp cold. For Chatham and Grenville, the atmosphere had become intolerable as they realized how Banks managed to keep all those tropical plants in his greenhouses so warm. "Very well," he grumbled, as if he alone had any real authority, "show the boy in."

"The boy", a short, pale and puffy round man of thirty-four years, strutted stiffly and painfully into the salon. As he came closer, his illness became more apparent. Yellowed hair and skin. Glassy, swollen eyes. A distended chest and throat. It was reported he became much worse with the onset of the cold. A temperamental element supposedly accompanied the condition. Better to send George Vancouver back to warmer climes to be of any use at all.

He was dressed in full British Naval uniform of a Lieutenant, with black bicorne hat, white waistcoat and pants, and blue great coat. He nodded in order of rank and peerage to the Earl, Baron, and gentleman. Catching a look of discountenance -- cold from Chatham, warm from Banks -- Grenville interceded. "Lieutenant Vancouver, this is a rather informal, preliminary interview. We felt it best that the full Board of Admiralty need not be bothered yet. Sit down."

The ball-shaped Vancouver was able to sit comfortably bolt upright. "Sir Alan sends his regards from the *Courageux*, sir," he addressed Chatham, then added to Grenville and Banks, "to all of you." Chatham, displaying the worst snobbery of the Whigs, barely nodded acknowledgment. But liberals are always the best aristocrats.

"It must be comforting being under the Admiral again," Banks cast out. Sir Alan, following his sterling service in the *Europa* off Jamaica, had recently been promoted Admiral. When the building of the *Discovery* was commissioned earlier this year, he had sponsored his young lieutenant as second-in-command to the expedition. Included was heavy emphasis on Vancouver's experience in the South Seas with Captain Cook. But when reports of seizures at Nootka arrived in London, Prime Minister Pitt called for the so-called "Spanish Armament" in March, scattering the new *Discovery*'s crew amongst the assembling English armada. Admiral Gardner commanding the warship *Courageux*, took George Vancouver as his first officer again.

"Yes, sir," Vancouver piped at Banks, "although there is some concern as to our current status." The Nootka Convention had been signed in Madrid three weeks prior, effectively settling the dispute in England's favor. Vancouver hoped to get back on track with the *Discovery* expedition, though much had changed over the summer.

"One issue at a time, dear fellow," Chatham offered with all the cold smoothness of an ice flow. "First, the Board finds itself wishing to alter the nature of the expedition -- mind you," shooting a calming glance at Banks, "discovery, both scientific and geographic are of utmost significance. But there is an added element with particular... nuances. They lend themselves to a reconsideration of the command of the expedition."

"Yes, Your Grace," Vancouver responded instantly.

"You are familiar with Lieutenant Bligh's plight on the *Bounty*, sir?" Grenville asked.

"Yes, my lord." The story of the successful mutiny on a British ship of war off Tahiti competed for space in the papers with the news of Mr. Meares' seized ships, and an expedition had been sent out in the *Pandora* a fortnight ago in search of the mutineers.

"You served with Mr. Bligh, is that correct?" Banks pursued.

"Yes, sir, though not directly, sir. During Captain Cook's final voyage, Mr. Bligh was master of *Resolution*." Of the two vessels under Cook's command on his third voyage, *Resolution* was the junior member, *Discovery* the flagship. "I was a midshipman on *Discovery* at that time. My service aboard the *Resolution* was simply as an able bodied seaman on the second voyage."

"You do realize, Lieutenant," Grenville intoned, "that the Admiralty is most concerned with the ramifications of the act of piracy by the officers and crew of the *Bounty*."

"Indeed, sir. And may I say so, sir, that I did express my sincere desire to serve aboard the *Pandora*."

All three gentlemen nodded in solemn agreement and approval. For there would have been no mutiny had not Fletcher Christian, the first officer, and other officers, been involved. British naval policy kept the crew of their vessels ignorant of such matters as navigation -- or even swimming. Cook had kept his officers in the dark as to their journey's missions, save for "discovery and exploration." Bligh's mistake had been allowing the crew of *Bounty* to gain too intimate a knowledge of his plans.... and of Tahitian comforts.

"The *Bounty* left our shores at Falmouth December 28, 1787 bound for Tahiti by way of Cape Horn," Grenville expounded. "Did you know that a ship and her consort left Boston, Massachusetts Bay, just three months earlier and found themselves about Cape Horn at the same time as the *Bounty*?"

Vancouver's cheerful attentiveness faded into a quizzical air. Bligh had found himself in the following March unable to round Cape Horn, where the South Pacific screams into the South Atlantic, amid icebergs at the onset of winter. Traditionally, English ships bound for the Pacific made the easier journey by way of the Cape of Good Hope and India. But Bligh had attempted to markedly shorten the trip to Tahiti. With headwinds incessantly blowing against his square-rigged vessel, he gained only 85 miles in 31 days. So failing, he turned *Bounty* east to the south of Africa. How could Americans merchants have made it where the British Navy had not? "My Lord Baron, I must admit this sounds rather incredible..."

Banks harumphed his satisfaction, challenging Chatham.

"The ship was the merchant ship *Columbia*, commanded by Mr. Kendrick," Chatham explained. "Mr. Bank's man in Boston confirms this is the same Kendrick who spent some time in our Dartmoor prison during the war with the colonies -- but not before he had done us a bit of damage in command of three privateers. The vessel in company appears to be the sloop *Washington*, under a Mr. Gray, and intended as a tender to the ship in its pursuit of the Northwest fur trade."

Lieutenant Vancouver blinked once, expression changing from attentive to comprehension. "Mr. Meares' Americans."

"Quite," blurted Banks.

"Have your read Mr. Meares' accounts, Lieutenant?" Grenville asked.

"Yes, my lord. I considered it most prudent for any officer to avail himself of the causes of the Spanish effrontery -- not that an officer of His Majesty's Royal Navy requires any explanation for his orders." All in the room was quiet for the moment, save for Banks' occasional shifts and winces. Grenville wondered if a pretty girl could be brought back from Malacca for the specific purpose of fanning the air of any room Banks stepped into. No, such duty was too cruel, even for savages.

As in so many interviews, the present one seemed to have no real course Vancouver could discern. Cook. Bligh. Americans. Meares. He hoped it would come to him eventually. Patience would persevere.

"According to Mr. Meares," Grenville explained, "the sloop *Washington* circumnavigated the area around Nootka, finding it to be an island of some size, and, so doing, discovered a passage to the Atlantic." It was a testament to desperation and greed that even at this late date hope was still held out for a direct waterway from Europe to the Orient. "You have been to Nootka. What sir, is your opinion?"

George Vancouver stiffened upright as all three gentlemen leaned their eyes forward. When in doubt, he chose to be precise. "I apologize, my lord, but could you be more specific? Do you refer to Mr. Meares, or the ability of the American sloop to perform such a task, or the supposition that such terrain exists around Nootka Sound?"

Banks arched his brow up into his wig. "You doubt Mr. Meares' claims?"

"Yes, sir, I do."

"On what grounds," Chatham inquired, "do you impugn the character of a fellow officer of the Royal Navy?"

Vancouver remained calm. "Your Grace, by public record. Firstly, in his prior voyage, Mr. Meares endangered his ship and crew by taking shelter in Russian America. Secondly, his last voyage was completely outside the law of British Admiralty and of exclusive commercial licenses granted to the East India and South Sea Companies by the Crown."

Touché, thought Banks. But he laid into Vancouver: "That is not the point, sir! We are now concerned with the events surrounding the seizures of his ships at Nootka!"

Are we? Vancouver sensed a thread.

Banks continued: "Need I remind you that Mr. Meares was and still is a Lieutenant on half pay with the British Navy?"

"Indeed, sir, and my point precisely. If so, why were two of his vessels flying under Portuguese flags?"

The point, indeed. If Meares had been a simple civilian, the British would not have been able to blow this whole legal seizure into a near-war. But he was an officer, reserve or not. That he had chosen to skirt British commercial law by offering a partnership to the Portuguese governor at Macao was overlooked. On his last trip, he had finally secured the expensive licenses from the royal monopolies, and thus royal protection.

Grenville, attempted to skirt the issue, "British ships. British officers... British interests."

"Yes, my lord, but, if you please, you did solicit my opinion. British interests were at heart, sir. Mr. Meares decided to bend the rules, and he ought to suffer the consequences of his greed. I am quite sure the Spanish would have acted otherwise if the Union Jack was flying from *all* of Mr. Meares ships."

Chatham interceded. "Yes, yes, Lieutenant. Rest assured, Mr. Meares shall follow the rules. In fact, I believe Mr. Banks, here, is more intimately aware of his affairs of late...?"

Banks, for once, stopped squirming in his seat, took his eyes off Vancouver, and settled them upon Chatham. "Ye-es," he acknowledged.

"Richard Etches, a dear friend of mine, joined with Mr. Meares in sending out the two *British* ships the Spanish seized in July of last year."

Too coy for his own good, Banks was more than good friends with Etches. Since the reports of fortunes to be made sending Northwest sea otter fur to Macao and Canton, Etches and Banks had worked to send out trading vessels. With the merging of the Etches and Meares companies into Associated Merchants in early 1789, Banks became Meares' greatest ally and patron -- in London. The seizures had been a blow. Of the $200,000 Spain agreed in the Nootka Convention to compensate Meares, how much would end up in Banks' pockets?

Chatham, having quieted Banks, became a great deal more serious. "You are familiar with Mr. James Johnstone?"

Vancouver, with a chance to respond again, did so attentively. "Yes, my Lord Admiral. We served together aboard *Discovery* on Captain Cook's final voyage."

"And your opinion of him as an officer?" Grenville chanced.

"I am sorry, my lord, but we only served as midshipmen -- but I have heard he acquitted himself quite admirably with Mr. Etches." Johnstone had sailed as an officer on the initial voyage of Etches' *Prince of Wales* to the Coast in 1787. From China, the ship was entrusted to Johnstone's command for return to London.

"Doctor Menzies speaks quite highly of him," Banks threw in. It was a barb. As first officer of the newly-built *Discovery*, Vancouver oversaw the construction and provisioning of the ship. This duty included care of a small greenhouse on the quarter-deck for specimens collected by the botanist sent by Banks' own Royal Society, Archibald Menzies. Captain Cook had found these men of science a bothersome lot on board -- Banks apparently the model. They not only took up valuable space, but time as well, with their insistence upon visiting some God-forsaken islet to collect seashells. The only benefit of being away from *Discovery* all these months for Vancouver was the understanding that he would be far away from the meddling Doctor Menzies.

"Oh?" Vancouver was polite, not caring what opinion Menzies had of any naval officer.

"Yes, they both served aboard the *Prince of Wales*." Banks was again trying to impress upon this impudent officer that this disdained scientist *already* had experience in Northwest America. Perhaps more.

"But you know Mr. Colnett, too, yes?" Grenville asked.

"Yes, my lord. We served on *Resolution* on Captain Cook's second voyage." The elusive theme began to emerge with this arch back to Nootka. Of all of Cook's boys, James Colnett was the most renowned, but for the wrong reasons.

It was Colnett whom the Meares-Etches (-Banks?) Associated Merchants had hired to command the *Argonaut*. It was Colnett who set sail under British flag in the *Argonaut* in the company of Mr. Duncan's *Princess Royal*, with over twenty Chinese artisans, from Macao in February 1789. It was Colnett who, the day after arrival at Nootka, informed Spanish Commandant Martinez of how he came to be there -- to establish a British trading post and British colony -- based upon Meares' purchase of land and agreement of exclusive trading rights from the native chief Maquinna. And it was Colnett whom Martinez slapped in irons as a prisoner for violating Spanish territory.

"Colnett's account of events, along with that of Mr. Douglas, describe not a small degree of duplicity by the American commander, Mr. Kendrick, with the Spanish Commandant," Banks observed, adding, "They seemed rather chummy. Of course, it is entirely unnecessary, I am sure, to prevail upon you how troublesome this American intrusion is."

Grenville took his turn to shift uncomfortably. A champion of free trade, he had incurred the wrath of the Crown and its monopolies. Held at such a competitive disadvantage by the entrepreneurial Americans, British merchant shipping -- and thus, influence -- would begin to wane. The Spanish were on the Coast first, coming up from California. The Russians were encroaching from Alaska. But the American traders answered to no government for their trading... or support, for now. Perhaps it was time to enlighten the Lieutenant. "Sir, are you familiar with a John Ledyard who served as a corporal of Marines on board *Resolution* on Captain Cook's final voyage?"

"Yes, m'lord. Indeed, as I recall, he was with Captain Cook when he was murdered." Cook's attempt to punish the Sandwich Islanders' thievery by using his compliment of marines to kidnap a local chief ended with the explorers' face in the surf and a knife between his shoulder blades. The ignominious British withdrawal from the islands was marked pointedly by the marines frantic splashing back to *Resolution*.

"An American. From Connecticut, I've been told," Banks announced, condemning the whole nation, and that state in particular. "Upon his return, Ledyard made quite a nuisance of himself, on both sides of the Atlantic and in France. He most strenuously desired to induce some entity to finance not only a trading expedition, but establish a *colony* at Nootka."

Banks knew this all too well, having funded Ledyard's aborted walk to Nootka across Russia.

Grenville explained, "Apparently he died two years ago of some stomach upset outside Cairo, having given up on one dream, but not before he gained the ear of the Marquis de Lafayette and the present American Secretary of State, Thomas Jefferson. At present we hear of at least one French ship and half a dozen American vessels outfitting for cruises to the Northwest Coast."

"That is why we have called you here, Lieutenant Vancouver," the Earl of Chatham revealed. "Your familiarity of not only the geography, but the gentlemen involved in these events are a testament to your aptitude for such a mission. Moreover, your precision is duly noted by your commanders *and* the Royal Society."

Vancouver displayed both surprise and humility in his silent thanks to Banks. It was returned by a severe aversion of the old botanist's eyes and a clearing of the throat.

"Tomorrow you will meet with the full Board of Admiralty. Tonight we will give you an opportunity to prepare yourself. Your mission shall be two-fold. Firstly, in keeping with the original scope of your mission, you are to proceed to the Northwest Coast of America, making a comprehensive survey thereof from 30° latitude north to 60° latitude."

The goal was staggering. A coastline stretching from Cook Inlet in Russian Alaska to Lower California in Spanish Mexico. Thousands of miles multiplied by the number craggy fjords north of the Strait of Juan De Fuca. It could take years for *Discovery*'s 100-man crew.

"You will be accompanied by a smaller vessel bearing the name *Chatham*," Grenville added as the Earl (of Chatham) stared impassively, "of thirty men and officers, commanded by Lieutenant William Broughton, first officer Lieutenant James Hanson, and master *Lieutenant James Johnstone*. In the summer of 1792 you are to rendezvous with your supply ship, *Daedalus*, at Nootka. It will carry the details as to how you are to proceed with the second element in your mission."

"Which is -- ?" Vancouver sat even straighter if such a thing were possible.

"A mission of state. Article Five of the Nootka Convention empowers you to receive back from the Spanish Commandant the buildings and tracts of land at both at Nootka and southerly at Clayoquot Sound. Subjects of Britain and Spain are to be equally free to trade and establish posts anywhere north of the areas already occupied by Spain."

"And that point of Spanish occupation is exactly where, m'lord?"

"Your survey of the coast should easily determine that, but as Mr. Meares will be interviewed soon by the House of Commons, such information shall be sent in the *Daedalus*."

Chatham intervened. "You will be promoted to Captain and take command. You will have the choice of your own officers on *Discovery*, but it is my sincerest hope," the serpentine First Lord of the Admiralty breathed, "that you will accept my young nephew, Thomas, as a midshipman."

Again, staggering. From second-in-command aboard a warship to command of two on a voyage of indefinite length, treading in the footsteps of such great names as Magellan, Drake and Cook. The "request" for the boy was a small thing. "Yes, m'lord," Vancouver assented.

"Doctor Menzies also wishes to be taken on as surgeon aboard *Discovery*," Banks murmured. "He believes he can spare time from his duties there for observations for the Royal Society."

"No..., sir"

Shocked at the impertinence, Banks merely asked, "Do you object to Doctor Menzies' presence aboard your ship?"

"No, sir," Vancouver replied dutifully, "Doctor Menzies is aboard as a representative of the Royal Society. But the officers and men under my command shall be under my command, my Ship's Surgeon included. Discipline must be maintained. It cannot if a man is serving two masters."

"Lieutenant, we also cannot impress upon you enough the urgency of your mission. Such information shall be of great value to His Majesty's subjects in the fur trade and whale fisheries." Grenville leveled his eyes upon Vancouver, "We must not lose our current advantages."

"M'lord, do you believe the Americans pose any grave threat? Their navy, what there is of it, consists mostly of privateers and small frigates."

Banks pounced: "Lieutenant, do you recall a man serving aboard Captain Cook's *Discovery* by the name of Simeon Woodruffe?"

"Well, sir, it was possible -- yes, there was a seaman by that name. He would be about your age, sir."

Banks took in a long, deep breath. "That man served as First Officer aboard Mr. Kendrick's ship *Columbia* -- that is, he did as far as the Cape Verde islands. The ship and its sloop continued 'round voyage Cape Horn, to Nootka, thence onto China. Presently, it has left Boston on a *second* voyage. Sir," Banks let out a grimace, "those two vessels had not a man who had ever ventured below the equator, never mind to Nootka, yet managed to circumnavigate the globe. And with one month's time to refit in Boston this past August, set out to do it again."

As the soon-to-be Captain Vancouver was escorted by Baron Grenville to a carriage, Chatham and Banks stood at the now blessedly-open door of the salon. "I recall you mentioned the sloop *Washington* has yet to return to Boston," Chatham sighed.

"It hasn't. Queer thing, as *Columbia* arrived under the command of Mr. Gray. Under orders of Mr. Kendrick, they had exchanged vessels in the Northwest and were to rendezvous at Macao, which they reportedly did."

"The old American must have lost the sloop in a storm. It is a rather long and arduous journey for a such a tiny vessel."

"Yes, with any luck...," Banks mused, "... it is unfortunate about my last man, Woodruffe. Not my best choice -- too clumsy. Kendrick sensed mischief afoot. In any event... hmmm." The Tory faded, caring not to give too much away to the Prime Minister's brother.

Silence persisted for a moment, broken at last by Chatham, "You have placed another aboard *Columbia* for its second voyage? Perhaps the man who dispatched poor Ledyard?"

Banks tapped his walking stick on the floor. "Your Grace, you must sometime come visit His Majesty's Royal Botanical Gardens. We have the most fascinating species there, and we take care to cultivate and experiment with various surroundings. Now *your* happy little Captain Vancouver shall go off to Nootka with all the formalities and power of *your* government behind him, and by the grace of the Almighty, shall forward its interests. But I have already planted a seed to duplicate the ends, if not the means, of your grand expedition." With that Banks took his leave, "Oh, I must speak to that impertinent young Captain of ours before he departs."

The problem with monarchs, Chatham reasoned, was that they possess an innate tendency to operate outside the government. Likewise their "friends". He called to Banks, "Your man in Boston can do so much?"

"*My* man in Boston?" Banks busied himself down the long hallway, "*I* have no man in Boston ... at the present."

CHAPTER ELEVEN

L'Emilie

Wednesday, October 25, 1995

She had written each of the names on the back of Miles' business cards, and handed his notes back to him. "You've got the easy job," Mags said, "*you've* only got the ships to do."

A single light illuminated the small apartment above the witchcraft store. Miles hunched over the card table and scribbled on the backs of old library cards. First *Bounty*, then *King George* and *Queen Charlotte*, and so forth. "Done!" he announced, and cut and recut the deck in one hand.

Such cocky displays had only marginal effect on Margaret Skinner. Her reply was a humor-the-boy smile and a "Well, put it down" gesture towards the table.

This tall and pretty young woman with the endearing awkwardness had once answered his ad for a roommate two summers back (Seth having gone for a season teaching marine archaeology at Mystic Seaport). During his impromptu interview, Miles had learned she was leaving public relations to study post-colonial art and antiquities at Emerson College. With his cursory understanding of Cape Cod genealogy to trade for hers in New England history, they had gone out several times, culminating in their trip to Salem this past spring for an exhibit at the Peabody Essex Museum.

Her classes had been finishing up, so the offer to take over for the Assistant Curator on maternity leave was like a clean entry onto her new path. Miles had originally been the one to broach the subject with the all-too-obviously pregnant Assistant Curator, but it disturbed him. He had known it was his duty to ask. In doing, he became the man to help with Mag's life. It was just too perfect. Too well-timed. That familiar feeling he was Life's pawn.

Mags hadn't take the room for that semester, a house-sitting deal she found was too good to pass up. There was doubt in his mind, though, that a motivating factor for her not moving into his Mount Vernon Street apartment was his single romantic gesture after their third date -- a half-dozen salmon roses and a heartfelt note from the shy to the shy.

Miles found the taller the woman, the less self confident -- and Mags could practically look him straight in the eye. Was that his main attraction to her? No, but the thought was intriguing, no doubt about it, with all its nuances. But he had always been a perfect gentleman, and nothing romantic ever occurred before or since. IF NOT, YOU WOULDN'T BE HERE NOW.

Most likely.

"That's nice. What is it -- a kimono?"" he nodded at her silk robe.

Her attention off him and the cards, she plucked at a sleeve. "Oh, you like it? No, it's from India" She stood up to model the back, displaying the fanged and many-armed god, Shiva the Destroyer.

His eyes wandered up her back to her shoulders, draped in deep green and gold, down the design, to her black leggings and back up. "Very nice," as he gathered the cards together.

A frown brushed across her face, and she sat down forthrightly. "Now you concentrate on the cards -- what's the first name on those little ones?"

"Captain James Cook."

"Okay, place it anywhere on the table." Mags had explained this was an easy exercise in understanding the interconnectedness of people in history. When the library began to close down for the evening, Miles had come to her in despair -- all these names and dates and ships -- how could he make sense of it all? Mags had suggested a game of cards.

It was simply a matter of finding a common event or place to begin to understand history in a visual sense. Maritime history was easy to translate with the cards since a ship acted as both place and event -- a common connection.

"And what ship did Cook command?" asked Mags.

Miles looked at his notes. "Uh, lets see, well, there were a couple of voyages and different ships..."

"No," Mags said, "it doesn't matter. Put them both down, but on either side of his card. See? As commander of both *Resolution* and *Discovery*, he connects both events. So, now, who else served on board?"

Miles read off the names: Vancouver, Colnett, Bligh, Ledyard, Dixon, Banks, and Woodruffe. As he did so, she dealt out the cards with their names, placing them all about the two vessels on which they served. The design they formed looked like a pair of spectacles with James Cook at the center. "Now *that*," Miles sighed with relief, "I can understand."

"And when Cook was killed on that last voyage," Mags plucked the card out of the center, "all these guys who served under him lost their center. It was a traumatic experience. But it also made their careers. Every one of those men you see here got a leg up because they had served with legendary Captain James Cook."

"And," Miles observed, "like graduates from an exclusive prep school, they kept bumping into each other from then on." The revelation was refreshing. *I understand.*

"Okay, what's going on?" Mags demanded. "Is there something you want to tell me?" Earlier, even before he was allowed to sit down, Mags had grilled him on the events surrounding the explosion at the courthouse. Like everyone else he knew and had encountered since, she had read the papers, seen the footage of the smoke billowing from the twelfth floor windows and heard the latest reports of various underground groups claiming sympathy, if not responsibility, for the aims of the bomber.

But other, even more esoteric news had eventually edged the story away from the media's attention. Only the wonderful splash of Paulie on the front page of the *Herald* had revived some scant interest, and that had only served Miles' purposes further -- first, by mistakenly identifying his swarthy roommate as John Kendrick, and secondly, by the sheer lack of taste of the photo and its use, had relegated the regional celebrity of the whole affair to quirky folklore, to be reminisced along with the Blizzard of '78 and Dukakis '88. A subject to identify Bay Staters at parties and quickly discard over chit-chat.

Miles was coy, "Whatever do you mean, my dear Margaret? I came here, seeking a little information -- that's all. These cards are a great system. Ever think of selling the idea?"

"Hmm. Okay. Well, we can get back to this, but --" she shook the deck of cards at him, " -- John Miles Kendrick, don't think you're leaving here without an explanation."

Indeed. He nodded quickly, smirking, "Mm-hmm."

"Okay, now let's go to the next step. What ships did they serve on afterwards?"

Miles continued with the placing his larger ship cards next to the various names of the class of 1778. *Bounty* next to William Bligh. *Prince of Wales* next to James Johnstone. *King George* next to George Dixon. Each man spinning off to become his own link. From there, it was simply a matter of checking Miles' notes to see who else had served on their new ships. Archibald Menzies on the *Prince of Wales*...

"Wait," Miles held the card in his hand, "Menzies also served on Vancouver's ship *Discovery*. Which do I place him on?"

"Ah...," Mags smiled, and took Miles hand just long enough to place the Doctor between the two ships he had served on, "now do you see what's happening?"

It was a network. More ideally, a web. The outer rings of names began to connect in broader and broader circles. "And Menzies," Miles drew an arrow on the card, "worked for Joseph Banks and the Royal Society."

"John – hello?" Mags laughed, "Banks *was* the Royal Society. Didn't you know he was the richest man in England at the time? He was the one who thought up making Australia into a penal colony."

THINGS YOU DON'T KNOW.

"He was also a friend of the King," she went on, "and could get whatever license he needed to trade from the English East India and South Sea Companies. He wasn't just collecting plants for the sake of science. It was exploration in the name of exploitation."

Miles began placing more of the smaller cards down and drawing arrows here and there. Ledyard to Banks. Dixon and Colnett on the *King George* saving Meares in the *Nootka*. Later Meares and Colnett on the *Argonaut*. Then Miles stopped at Simeon Woodruffe -- and made up a new ship card -- *Columbia*. He placed it next to the man's name.

*"I can **do** this..."* Miles breathed heavily as he drew a line to Meares and Colnett, and another from Meares to Banks. And another to a new card with the name King George III.

"I think you're getting too into this, John," Mags said with more than a hint of concern. "I know your boss was killed --"

He straightened up. "I have no boss. I have clients."

"-- Whatever. You're not thinking about playing detective, 'cause if you are --"

"No!" he shook his head, trying to rid his skull of the detached amusement. "No, this is just really interesting. It makes history so... personal. It makes the actors so accessible. I just wish I could go back and meet them."

I could go to Nootka.

?

YOU CAN'T EVEN FIND IT ON A MAP, LET ALONE AFFORD THE TRIP. YOU SHOULDN'T GO UNTIL THE INVESTIGATION IS CONCLUDED. DON'T BE RIDICULOUS.

She took a deep breath and looked at her watch. "Oh, jeez, I gotta meet somebody in ten minutes --"

"Midnight? Not another blood sacrifice with the warlock-du-jour, I hope."

She laughed, "No. No, just somebody I met at Monserrat College of Art who teaches a night class in classic portraiture."

Mags, as far as she told Miles, either went out with her "girlfriends" or on dates with "somebodies" and "someones". Never "a guy" or "a man". Or, if she did, it was always past-tense, like "there was this guy I was seeing up until last week" or "I had been thinking of asking this man out, but..." It was wonderfully careful way of letting Miles know she was busy. But not necessarily committed. So go away for now -- but not too far -- just in case.

Heading down the back staircase, Mags handed Miles the trash to throw in the dumpster. He was reviewing his cards in his head. He walked her over to her car, and she slid into the clean red Jetta. "Call me when you're back here, okay?" She shut the door and drove off to oil paint-bliss.

It was a short walk back up Hawthorn Boulevard to the Peabody Essex museum. Repassing the statue of Nathaniel Hawthorn, he paused and considered. The crescent moon hung behind the bald contemplative author of sin and redemption.

A web -- a conspiracy?

DON'T BE RIDICULOUS.

Melcher Street. With a perverse exhilaration Miles moved down it like a security robot on patrol, head scanning back and forth, movements forcibly loose. The black bandanna tied around the top of his skull; leather jacket, wrap-around sunglasses, black tee shirt and jeans helped too.

Passing by the alley near Arthur Lewis' stash was the hardest part. Miles ached to see if the Audi was parked down there, but didn't want to give even the remotest impression he was interested. Interest begets interest, and Arthur Lewis was an expert at discerning frauds from the genuine article.

When the tiny door to the tiny elevator opened, Miles pulled back the wire cage and stepped into the studio. Giant sheets of lead paint dangled precipitously from the ceiling, waiting to lower the IQ of dozens of toddlers. The walls were streaked dull red with the rust that dripped from the old steel beams and pillars. The grime of the last industrial age covered the six foot-high sash windows. At least Paulie had found someone to sweep up.

In the center of the room a woman in a black velvet bathrobe was picking up one of many huge piles of dust and paint dandruff gathered on the floor. Both the dustpan and her attire were below the tasks required, and Miles tried not to stare. *Lovely.*

SHE'S A PROFESSIONAL. DON'T GAWK. "Good morning," he said.

She walked over to the overflowing, battered garbage can and tried her best to keep the erupting dust storm out of her huge, round brown eyes and long sandy-brown hair. Then she turned and held the dustpan and broom apart. "Âllo."

Woman is French?

Woman is not happy. On the other side of the pillar, the velvet voice of Paulie could be heard schmoozing someone over the phone. Beyond, the photo lighting and tripod were set up, directed at a giant cardboard model of a six foot-high wood screw. One distinctive element was missing -- the model.

Woman is not happy. Somehow, Paulie had not only been able to get this woman from another country to pose nude for him for free, but to help him clean up his new temporary studio in time for his show two days from now.

Miles caught Paulie's eye, and it was only another fifteen minutes before the click of the phone and accompanying shudder signaled the end of the electronic ordeal. In the mean time, Miles helped Emilie -- the name managed with remnants of his high school French -- fill a bucket with hot water and ammonia.

"Oh, you don't have to do that!" Paulie good-naturedly grabbed the mop out of Emilie's hands. She smiled an evil look at him. "Entendes," Paulie soothed her. From what Miles could make out, the photographer soothed his bristling model with something like: *"I'm sorry, but that was an agent I've been trying for weeks to come to the show and he called, so I had take it, but he just kept talking and talking -- but, listen, he's coming and I told him what you're doing here today with the screw, and he really wants to see it!"*

She lit up. "C'est vrai?!" Then she caught a glance at Miles, and bit her lip. "We work... later?"

"Oh, yeah, this is -- this is my roommate Johnny, but I guess you already met. I gotta have a cigarette. Emilie, *why don't you meet me back here in half an hour and we'll finish up, okay?"* He took out his wallet and handed her a ten dollar bill. *"You're probably hungry maybe get something to eat at the sandwich shop around the corner?"*

Woman is placated.

Out on the roof overlooking Fort Point Channel, Paulie lit up his last generic-brand cigarette, taking a long, heavy drag. "Fu-uck."

"Ten bucks for lunch. That's pretty good," Miles commented.

Paulie shook his head and held out his empty wallet. "That's the last of it. I hope she enjoys it. I can't afford to lose her now -- those shots I'm taking of her are a major -- I mean *major* -- part of my show. This better fuckin' pan out."

"Don't worry. You'll get some attention. Half the city's coming from what I hear." Miles held up his index finger, "All you have to do is sell *one*. Then the feeding frenzy will begin."

Paulie tried to blow off his anxiety with a laugh, then he remembered something. "Hey, *great* news!" He grabbed Miles by the shoulders and shook him smiling victoriously. Great news from Paulie could be either good for Miles personally or for their cadre at large. "Bella's coming!" The Prince of Darkness released his compatriot and took a happy toke on his death-stick. "Friday -- she'll be here for the show. Her fiancé's covering the secession referendum in Quebec for the past couple weeks, and brought her along as his assistant. They're coming down here catching the President's fund-raiser at the Copley Plaza and have a couple hours before their red-eye flight back to Montreal."

"Fiancé?" Miles sighed. "How fiancéd is she?"

Paulie sympathetic sigh was followed by, "Yes, but that chick -- my model, Emilie? How do you think I got her -- it's his sister!" he cackled. "She's over from France and Bella steered her to me!"

Isabella Quimper, the little firecracker from San Sebastian, Spain, had herself attracted the attention of many a man during frequent summers on the Cape. And while neither Paulie or Miles had ever quite succeeded with her, it was a matter of sincere interest between them. Perhaps it was the way in which it had all developed -- from Paulie's discovery of a young woman in need in his home town, only able to speak rudimentary English. Not three hours later did he bring her back to *Nautilus* to meet Miles, who could only communicate, not knowing Spanish, in his pidgin French. She had instantly expressed interest in all the maps on his walls.

"She told me she'd marry me if I bought *Nautilus*," Miles reminded Paulie. It was a joke, they both knew, but she had fallen in love with the dilapidated old house instantly.

"Shit, I was thinking about this just last night when you didn't come home 'til late-late!" Paulie was adamant: "You're *not* going to solve this case."

"Don't say that."

"Fuckin', you're not. You're going to get yourself hurt, and I'm going to end up having to spoon-feed you tapioca for life!" His humor was meant to emphasize, but it still sent a wave of giggles through Miles. "I'm serious! Jesus!" Paulie turned and flicked the retired butt down onto the emptiness of Melcher Street.

"You catch the news this morning?" Miles glanced sideways, "The FBI announced a $100,000 reward for information leading to the capture of the Boston Bomber..."

Paulie hung his head and glared at Miles.

"...And the Barrell family offered to match it," Miles added.

"No."

"$200,000."

"No."

"Two-hundred-*thousand*-dollars."

"Do you know," asked Paulie, "I've had to show my license to half a dozen people in the last week. I can't even cash a check in this town 'cause all the fuckin' tellers think *I'm* John Kendrick."

Miles tried to swallow his smile. "I'm sorry. I really am."

"You know, you do this and I'm catching all the shit. First the FBI grilling me, then this cocksucker dick from the *Herald* -- you know I fucking *HATE* that picture!"

"I know. I'm sorry. But I *need* to succeed on my own like this. And if it works out, we're all set. You know that -- it's like our lottery ticket. -- Hey, I don't think I've got anything anyway -- just a thought. It's nothing anyone else couldn't do and it's all *legal*. I'm heading down to the Cape today to check something out right now. I can still come to the show, right?"

"Yeah! I want you there. Just no bombs or cops, okay?"

"Don't worry," Miles patted the man on the back, only partially accomplishing reassurance, "AND we'll figure out a way to make those guys who've burned you pay -- and pay dearly."

The Prince of Darkness glanced quickly at Miles. "Yeah, well, forget about it." He suppressed a smoker's cough, spat something down onto the street, and said, "It's all in the past."

The Sturgis Library is located in the home of the late Captain William Sturgis in the village of Barnstable, in the Town of Barnstable, in the County of Barnstable in the Commonwealth of Massachusetts. Besides the

Sturgis' small lending library there is the Genealogy room. For information on *Mayflower* or Cape Cod families, it is a heck of lot more efficient than running to each of the 13 Town Clerks all over Barnstable County. In this room Miles had discovered an unknown heir and thus saved a client $10,000 in lawyer's fees and court costs a few years back. But this time he had come to Sturgis for their other collection.

"Yes," the librarian turned to greet his patience with a smile, "would you like to use the genealogy collection?"

"No, I'd --"

"Oh, you want to use the Kittredge Room."

Just off the narrow genealogy section was another room, much more open, with white walls and two old red leather wing chairs. Opposite, in front of the window, was a model of the ship *Eliza*, in a glass case. Young William Sturgis had signed onto her at age sixteen in 1798, and had wisely learned enough of the Nootkan language to become his captain's liaison to the local tribes. Later, he returned to the coast as master of his own vessel, and eventually commanded fleets of others in the opening of a worldwide trading center based in Boston, crewed by Cape Codders.

So said *Shipmasters of Cape Cod*, authored by none other than Henry C. Kittredge. The book's examination of the Northwest fur trade devoted practically an entire chapter to Captain Sturgis of Barnstable's economic success that followed in the wake of the groundbreaking voyages under the command of that other Cape Cod captain, John Kendrick of Orleans. The other book Miles simply hadn't had time to dive into was the enormous tome of Frederick Howay's *Voyages of the Columbia*. Peabody Essex had noted only a couple libraries in the state had copies, one being at Harvard, the other Sturgis. And he could borrow this copy.

Miles thanked the pleasant librarian and gently sat down in one of the antique-feeling chairs to re-examine the book, as she went to search for Howay's work. There had been one piece of information that had intrigued Miles, setting him off in this direction. With all his reading of about the Nootka Sound incident, it wasn't settled in his mind whether Meares had a valid claim. Supposedly, the Spanish had returned the land to the English after numerous treaties and struggles, and that had of course resulted in the British claim to Pacific Canada.

His call to Provincial Archives in British Columbia had prompted a search of their own records. But, they said, the British Crown had granted exclusive rights to the Hudson Bay Company colonize and trade on there in 1849 in an effort to forestall the Americans along the Pacific coast. But hadn't that all been settled in a treaty the previous year establishing the U.S.-Canadian border at 49° north?

Even so, what happened to the Meares claim? Clayoquot Sound, to the south of Nootka, where Meares also claimed to have purchased land, looked to be safely British, too. In any case, the staff at the Provincial Archives agreed that all the area around Nootka and Clayoquot were what they called "Crown Lands." In the U.S. the closest equivalent were federal lands.

"The main difference is that the President of the Untied States doesn't personally own the entire country except for those portions he's deeded out to others -- like the Hudson Bay Company," Miles observed.

"Well, I wouldn't put it that simply," the Archivist on the phone had said. "The Queen only symbolically owns the land. It's really held by our Province."

"Only because she and her predecessors gave them the power in the first place."

Still, some monarch of England -- George III, IV or Victoria or the government -- had somehow assumed title to Captain John Meares' private property -- the seizure of which initially by the Spanish had nearly caused a war. Meares *must* have been compensated. Unfortunately, Miles knew he was handicapped -- the British at that time were not renowned for their sympathy for due process. IT'S NOT RIGHT, THOUGH.

It wasn't, even if the late (or later) John Meares of Boston was less than above-boards. England had recognized Captain Meares' claim. His heirs -- unless they deeded out the land -- had *prior* and thus, *superior*, claim to the land. Even the Nootka Convention had settled the right of individuals to buy land from the natives.

Miles could understand how someone else could interpret Meares' joke about inheriting land in Nootka. Judging from international conventions and treaties, it sure looked -- on the surface -- as if Meares might have a point there. And that's all an American lawyer needs to build a case -- reasonable doubt, or a reasonable suspicion. *Or a paranoid mind.*

DON'T BE RIDICULOUS.

It was true, though. For someone to go to the lengths of planting a bomb in a federal courthouse based simply upon a suspicious Meares claim, they'd have to be either desperate, greedy, or irrational. In any case, Miles had stumbled onto a tangent, and figured since it involved an ancestor, Captain Kendrick might be interesting to pursue. The perspective of an American bit-player who prompted this rush of Anglo-Iberian diplomacy might prove illuminating.

Kittredge provided a basic outline: Captain John Kendrick, "the Navigator" had been born in a part of the Town of Harwich, now part of South Orleans, around 1740. His father commanded whaleships off Greenland, which his son -- instead of attending any sort of schooling -- shipped out on several, serving with a mixed crew of Inuit, Indians and blacks. As a young man, he moved to Vineyard Haven on the island of Martha's Vineyard, where he married and had a few kids. During the Revolutionary War, he commanded a couple of privateers in the English Channel, and afterwards built a house in Wareham. Off-Cape. Miles could understand moving to the Vineyard, but off-Cape?

On October 1 of 1787 he had left Boston in command of *Columbia*, accompanied by Captain Robert Gray of Tiverton, Rhode Island, in the sloop *Lady Washington*.

Yeah, yeah, I know this already. On board were two of Kendrick's sons, John, Jr. serving as fifth mate, and young Solomon, as a lowly seaman. Junior eventually joined with the Spanish at Nootka.

Oh? Miles sat up in his chair as the librarian brought over the copy of *Voyages of the Columbia*. "Thank you."

Captain Kendrick surprised the British explorer George Vancouver at Hawaii, telling him of the wealth of sandalwood in nearby Kauai --

-- So they met --

-- And was later killed in an accident December of 1794 by a cannon blast fired by the British merchantman *Jackal* in Pearl Harbor attempting to salute Kendrick.

Miles read it again.

"Accident."

"British... attempting to salute."

"Blast."

Explosion.

John Kendrick. John Meares. Robert Gray.

An irrational person -- a truly paranoid person -- might think --

DON'T --

They were trying to kill me!

Two hundred years ago. Or a week ago.

CHAPTER TWELVE

Nautilus

Thursday, October 26, 1995

Salt air.

That was the first thing that hit.

Not some cold, clammy murk of a waft, but a gentle coolness, fresh from the breakers out on the bars, sent spinning up to the bluffs onshore. Smells travel farther in warm weather, but in the midst of autumn, who could tell whether it was going to be a hot or cold day? The wind would tell. And the ocean.

His walls were covered with maps. Mostly from cross-country treks and get-aways that might-have-been. The nook above his head held the map and its mates spanning the entire U.S. and southern Canada. His eyes followed the interior of the dormered roofline down past the "Army Corps of Engineers Map of the Alaskan Coast", to the "Official Virginia Map" just below the two front windows. Roads. Patterns. Beltways. He had gone to school in D.C. He saw where Interstate 395 passed into the city, by the Pentagon. He had studied politics, until as a sophomore, he realized that no person in that profession should ever spend more than two years in the nation's capital.

Above, the windows were cracked and peeling. Geriatric caulking somehow held the panes in place. Facing directly upon the ocean, taking the east wind of the Atlantic in the eyes, these windows had seen ship captains, widows, tourists, and centuries pass.

GET UP.

A street separated the house from the sea and guaranteed that the location would not be its downfall. Across the street and down the bluff were a few larger, more sustained houses whose wealthy owners had invested heavily in their restorations-- and then watched as the ocean began to chew away at their foundations. Sea walls were the answer... for now.

Besides, the Town government would not allow this street running parallel to the coast to fall in. Not yet. Not until the next one hundred and thirty year cycle kicks in and claws this white-washed village of second homes into the breakers and the mist.

He'd be dead by then. Ninety, ninety five, a hundred years -- that was the typical life-span of the Cape Cod genetic stock, borne out of successive generations whose infant mortality necessitated the births of eight to ten children per mother. Small pox in the mid-1700's. Bitter cold and damp temperatures. Poor nutrition. If you lived past four you were just as likely to live to ninety. Do that for successive generations -- say, eleven -- and you produce a group of long-lived people. They also tended to poor eyesight and bad posture. But this all began to change with the influx of newcomers and implementation of modern medicine.

At 16 weeks old he was rushed to the hospital with pneumonia. Two hundred years ago this would have been a death sentence. Two hundred years ago penicillin was simply a fungus on a fruit found a couple thousand miles away. Or he'd live to be one hundred.

Normally he'd do his sit-ups until the music was done -- *Long Train Running* by the Doobie Brothers. But there was no music here. Nowhere in the house. The electricity had gone out in August. Paulie had turned on the broiler and flames shot out of the wall. He had jumped back in disbelief and declared "*No fucking way!*" When Paulie did call the fire department, he asked if sending the trucks would cost anything. Learning that his taxes paid for this service, he told the dispatcher to send all the trucks they had -- *spare no effort!* They came and shut off all the power.

Miles, Seth and Paulie had lived like this for the next month, because it was free. "Dear Mrs. Marston," his letter had begun, "I am writing concerning your house on Lower Main Street." As it turned out, Mrs. Marston was in a nursing home and her niece was acting as Conservator. And no one had the money to repair this old boarding house. A local builder said it would be as much a restoration as a resurrection. Miles called it a lottery ticket. But the faded letters above the front door read *Nautilus*.

Emerging from the shower, he looked in the mirror and remembered eleven days ago. Back before his beard had begun to grow in and surround his goatee in scruff. When his brown arms had enveloped the soft white torso of Meredith, and she lay her head, eyes closings in restful peace, back against his shoulder.

Every woman who stepped across the threshold fell in love with *Nautilus*. Seth called it VNI -- "Visible Nesting Instinct". But Meredith's reaction was more profound. She had lingered on every loving word Miles had used to describe the house, and when they arrived she had hardly waited for the end of the tour before her lips were on his.

Having *Nautilus* meant having Meredith. Seeing that peace he could provide to her. He would do anything to get that back again.

Miles pulled his six year-old Mazda into the yard full of elder trucks in various states of disrepair. He parked in his usual spot -- under the trees in the corner -- right where his old Hyundai had been kept until six months ago, before it took up a better residence in the barn behind *Nautilus*. "That car doesn't owe you a red cent," Seth had noted upon its internment. It was true. Hyundai's were never made to go over 150,000 miles -- hard miles, too, 'round and across the country many times. Its royal blue had been slowly replaced with red primer. The plastic grill long since gone, it reminded Miles of a gapped-tooth hockey player with a rash.

In athletes, they say the knees go first. With the Hyundai it was the front wheel bearing -- same thing, really. Five hundred dollars to repair. Instead, he bought a $600 car that had been mashed in on one side by a truck. Unsellable. Perfect for the city. The two usually sat nose-to-nose in the shade of the barn, nearly identical, save for the difference in colors -- burgundy for the Mazda, blue with creeping red for the Hyundai.

Tim came up to the Mazda. It was still "summer" so his face was clean-shaven and his hair crew-cut short. "John," Tim called him by his first name, as did Miles' father and the rest of the family, "whaddya suppose the Army Corps of Engineers is doing down at the Fish Pier?"

"I dunno, Tim," Miles said as he got out of the car. "Catchin' fish?"

Tim grinned. "No. I think they're getting ready to dredge the channel again."

Miles started walking past the trucks, "Again?" Ben, a rounder, lion-y sort of fellow, jumped out of his battered little pickup. The stocking cap on his head and three layers of shirts told his morning's story. Miles asked, "Ben, when's the tide?"

Ben scratched his head. "Well, it should be around eleven. I figured I'd ask your dad if I could work a coupla hours and catch the tide at ten "

Tim added: "The bank near the north jog of the pier is going to fall in pretty soon. The channel's undermining the toe-stones of the sea wall."

"Hello, Bart!", Miles yelled far too loudly.

A grizzled face looked up from the tailgate of the big dump truck. He had been lying there, on the end of it. Bart always reminded Miles of what Santa Claus might have looked like if he had fallen out of his sleigh over Toledo in the late sixties and never made it back to the North Pole. Bart smiled through his new teeth, and growled "Hello, John. Lovely morning."

As Miles passed the tool truck (so named because it was the oldest of the fleet and had come to serve as a storage area for shovels, rakes, hoes, etc.), he wondered if he could bring the Hyundai back here to become "the tool car" (for storing smaller things like hand-clippers, chain saws, motor oil and pesticides).

NO. GET RID OF THE EXCESS BAGGAGE.

"Bart, you look so peaceful there, why don't you just stay here all morning and get some beauty sleep?"

"Thank you, John, I think I will."

"It's too late for that!" Tim yelled as Miles crossed the lawn to the dormered Cape Cod cottage.

GET THE PAPER FOR YOUR FATHER. Miles stopped, walked over to the plastic newspaper tube marked with a faded "Cape Cod Times", and pulled out the rolled broadsheet. He met his father on his way out. Seth had remarked recently, upon meeting Miles' father again after a twenty-year hiatus, that he was getting the look of an elder statesman in the administration of John Quincy Adams. Miles pictured Alfred John Kendrick in a black frock coat and top hat instead of faded jeans, sweatshirt, turtleneck, denim work coat and faded plaid wool cap. Maybe it was the sideburns. Or the prominent hawk-nose. Save for a dash of Irish from 100 years ago, he was old-line Cape Codder stock -- looked it and dressed it.

"Wa-el..." Usually this word was as much a greeting as anything. A warning that something might follow it, or simply an acknowledgment to begin a conversation. His father peered over at the trucks "... Who's here?"

"Tim. Bart. Ben. Ben wants to catch the tide at ten." Their eyes never quite met. Cape Codders usually don't shake hands or look each other in the eye. No need.

"Well... I told him I don't want anybody leaving unless they work the whole morning."

"Mmm... yeah. I think he wants to go quahaugging. He said the tide's at eleven." Shellfishing had always been the final resort for those wanting a short work day and quick cash. The round, hard-shell clams were best dug out of the mud at low tide.

"I think he's just making noises in case we don't do anything fun," his father said.

Fun.

What was fun? Working for Alfred J. Kendrick, Jr. Landscaping wasn't fun. Funny, yes. Fun, no. Miles' uncle Nat, his father's brother, had called it the worst job on Cape Cod. It was lawn mowing. And as his father said, "Any moron can push a lawn mower." This was Miles' other job. It allowed him to keep his clients in Boston -- what other job was flexible enough for him to leave at any time and not come back for a week? The only time he was required to work was before Memorial Day and the Fourth of July. For the tourists, mostly, coming back to their summer homes.

"O-kay...," he pulled at a postcard taped above the sink, "there's a postcard from Nancy and the kid. Says every afternoon she takes him here for a walk under this bridge and ice cream."

As his father shut the door, Miles studied the card from his eldest sister. After she and her husband had adopted Will, they had moved north from Seattle, across the border to Canada. The photo on the reverse showed a suspension bridge with two enormous stone lions guarding the entrance. Miles carefully replaced the tape and put it back next to his father's various mysterious bottles of supplements, extracts and prescriptions.

He offered the paper to his father, now seated with his coffee. "Oh, that's okay. You can take a look at it... Um, did you feel like doing anything today?"

That meant work, not that there was much this time of year. Planting a tree here or there, if they were lucky. Four guys to plant one tree. As Ben summed up the job: "We pretend to work and Alf pretends to pay us." But what else did these guys have?

Miles headed into the living room. "Naw, I'm still not quite up to snuff. I got some research to do, anyway, in Plymouth and Boston."

"Oh, you're heading up?" came the voice from the kitchen table.

"Yuh," Miles turned the second page of the paper, catching yet another photo of a mangled car in Falmouth.

"Well, uh, what about that house down by the lighthouse?" Miles' father was never one for names of places.

"*Nautilus*?"

"Um, uh, yeah, I guess. You should have someone down there to shut off the water soon."

"Feet Eldredge is coming this weekend. Paulie already called him."

"Oh," the question had already been dealt with, "good... Are they planning -- I mean -- are they going to be doing anything with that place? Uh, fix it up or sell it?"

"I honestly don't know. I don't think so. If they did, I don't think I could've gotten in it for these past few summers in the first place."

"Oh." Here it comes. Miles braced himself. "You know, you COULD offer to show it for them, or talk to some real estate brokers and split the commission with them."

Yes, that was reasonable, Miles knew. It not only made a lot of sense, but it was an opportunity to get his foot in the door of the real estate business -- always a viable way for one to support oneself reasonably here year-round. YOU SHOULD THINK ABOUT IT.

I have. But the Marstons weren't interested in selling. And they weren't financially in a position to fix it up. They were on the verge of retirement and the house had sentimental value. It was too good to lose and too bad to fix. Selling was simply pointless to pursue.

And even though he felt an incredible obligation to his own family to move to independence from their continued charity, it just couldn't be this. Not sales. Poverty meant never having to be nice to anyone again.

YOU HAVE AN OBLIGATION. THEY HAVE SUCH HIGH HOPES. DON'T DISAPPOINT --

"*Aah--!* " Miles jerked in his chair, the paper tearing in his grip as he caught and stifled the attack. He quickly covered it with a coughing fit.

"You okay?" the voice from the kitchen asked.

The attacks had been pretty consistent, but rarely occurred in the presence of others. Lately, however, they began to eat at him more, but were as quickly quieted. No one had ever seen one, or at least recognized it for what it truly was. The lung problem temporarily provided an easy cover. Still, there was no telling what train of thought would lead to one. "Yuh, I'm fine... tore the paper a little," Miles walked into the kitchen, clearing his throat, and grabbed a quick glass of water.

"Oh," his father examined the picture of the wrecked Firebird, "that's okay. Um..." he waited for Miles to finish his glass of water, "if you're up in Barnstable sometime you might want to check out that road problem for me so I can sign some sort of release."

The terms of his parents final divorce decree had never taken into account the road that led to "the house." Originally the way leading to the salt water inlet had been one giant lot, and over the years his parents had subdivided it to pay off the mortgage. A year ago the town wanted to install water mains, and found that the private road itself was a separate lot, still jointly owned by both parents. What's a road worth? Nothing. A half-interest in a road? Half of nothing -- unless you considered the liability if someone were injured on it. Ownership of the full length simply carried the financial responsibility of repair, and negotiating power should anyone else want to use it. Someday.

"Yeah, I'll stop at the Registry on my way back to Boston. It'll take two seconds. No problem."

The post office box wasn't much, but for the past seven years it had been Miles' one permanent address. There, in the 3"x 5"x 6" metal box, was his home. That and the larger metal box of his car. Besides, it was just up the road from his father's.

Most people in town still received their mail by P.O. box rather than having it delivered. The concept of someone delivering his mail had always bothered him. Better to receive your mail right off the truck in the morning, fresh like bread. Twelve dollars a year for peace of mind.

Sometimes mail direct from Boston took only a day to come down, but it wasn't the previous day's postmark that caught his eye this morning. Nor the lack of proper street address. "John Kendrick" and the town were all that was written on the front of the envelope.

Written. Tightly controlled writing, but flourishing -- as if great care was taken in the work of art. Masculine, he guessed. On a fine cream envelope with no return address. The postmark simply read "BOSTON -- Oct 24 -- 021". The central post office had received this yesterday and shipped it to its smaller neighbor. Miles could get his mail anywhere in town, regardless of address. Whether he wanted it or not. YOU SHOULDN'T HAVE OPENED THIS.

How the hell was I supposed to know what's in it? Nicely wrapped within a single blank sheet of linen paper was the check for $2,000 from BARRELL, BULFINCH & GRAY. No signature, per se, but the name Joseph Barrell was preprinted at the lower right hand corner.

What is this?

The money would be nice, but it was unethical. And counterproductive. The more Miles was pushed, the more resistant he became.

YOU WILL NOT, UNDER ANY CIRCUMSTANCE, CASH THIS CHECK. YOU ARE INCORRUPTIBLE.

I am incorruptible.

THROW AWAY THE CHECK. Sitting in his car just outside the post office, he paused.

No. It would mean getting out of the car. He didn't feel like it. *I'll keep it. It's my evidence against him.* Miles slipped the envelope into his briefcase. Better to hold onto it just in case -- wouldn't the Massachusetts Board of Bar Overseers be curious to see this? More importantly, there was no mention of the check's purpose. Postal regulations are pretty clear -- *Anything I get in the mail unsolicited is mine. Unconditionally.*

YOU JUST CAN'T CASH IT. Yeah. He grabbed the envelope out of the briefcase, stared hard at it and started the car. WHAT DOES THIS TELL YOU?

He's persistent. He's desperate? No official stationery. *He didn't want it thrown out before I looked inside.*

That glimpse of the check would have a stalling effect on any initial rash impulse of throwing it out straight away. No note. No letter. No indication of what the two grand was for. Vague. Could be interpreted six ways 'til Tuesday. In a match of equals that excuse might hold... but what about a pillar of the legal profession versus a quasi-paralegal?

He remembered correcting the Brahmin as to where he lived on the Cape, but not specifying the town. There were only six on the Outer Cape. The Brahmin had faith. He didn't know where Miles lived.

Nobody knows where I live.

NOT NECESSARILY. Finding people is easier than it should be. It's just that until recently no one had ever cared to find *him* before.

A couple of years ago, Terry Eldridge, Licensed Surveyor, explained to Miles and Gibby Borthwick, Surveyor of Highways for the Town, the concept of property transfer. "Let's say John here deeds a piece of property to you. Then he deeds the same piece of property to me. Who owns the property?"

Gibby, in his sea captain's beard and worn blue Highway Department uniform, looked straight back at Terry. "Me."

"Right. But let's say that John deeds the property to you, then deeds same property to me, and I in turn, deed it to...," he searched around his conference table, finding only his Skye Terrier waddling atop the far end, and pointed, "my dog."

Gibby laughed. Miles raised his eyebrows with a grin.

"Who owns the property?" Terry asked again.

"Me." Gibby was firm.

Terry waved his finger, and pointed, "No. My dog. You see, it's intent to defraud. John here may have intended to defraud you, me, or both of us, but I never tried to defraud my dog. If Skippy shows up at the Barnstable County Registry with his deed in his jaws before you can record yours, the Supreme Judicial Court of the Commonwealth of Massachusetts says he holds title," Terry shifted his finger from canine to municipal administrator, "not you."

With such guidance, Miles had begun his first assignment in the world of property title research, determining what roads the Town did or did not own. What a mess.

Unless, of course, you went to Land Court. Every Registry of Deeds in every county of the Commonwealth has a split personality. On the one side there is "recorded land" where deeds are recorded in the order in which they are received, copied, bound in volumes of 500 pages each, and dogs end up owning Main Street.

On the other side is Registered Land -- Land Court -- the attempt by the state once and for all to settle the question of who owns what. If a person is willing to put upwards of $10,000 and wait three years for the state Land Court to determine what, if any, interest a person holds in a specific piece of real property, they would receive an inviolate title that the Registered Land office would keep track of for them, including mortgages, attachments and, ultimately, sales. In so doing, the Court hears *all* appeals -- slowing the process. On the other hand, short of proving fraud within the court, it is nearly impossible to appeal a Land Court Judgment. The government is infallible.

The morning had turned warm on the north side of the Cape, and Miles wandered out the Registered Land Office and around to the front of the old Barnstable County Superior Courthouse. He took up position sitting on this knoll overlooking tiny Barnstable Village, the marsh, and Cape Cod Bay beyond.

The gloomy gray granite columns and eighteenth-century cannon somehow brightened the quaint landscape of proliferating stone walls along Route 6A -- the north side's main route, also known as the Old King's Highway. From this building James Otis had led his attacks against British injustice in the 1760's and '70's. A generation later, young William Sturgis had watched ships head out from Boston, Plymouth, and even Barnstable Harbor from here. Quite likely he saw *Columbia* and *Washington* leave at about this time two hundred years ago.

The Land Court Certificate rolled into a tube flipped about in the gentle breeze. For three dollars, proof that his father owned a half interest in a property not even worth that. Miles would probably come to inherit it through his mother -- well, perhaps splitting it with his siblings.

My legacy. Perhaps the house on Oyster Pond as well, also held jointly. And Grammy Kendrick's house outside town which his father lived in. It was always there for him, he knew. Like a well-raised net below the trapeze. Not so far to fall, but less distance from which to bounce back.

YOU SHOULD HAVE YOUR OWN.

Nautilus. A goal. Earned by his own skill and talents. It had been eating at him since the mere possibility of cash reward was dangled in front of his face. *I can do this. I can have this.*

BUT SHOULD YOU? YOU'RE WASTING TIME AND MONEY.

GET BACK TO WORK.

I owe my soul to CitiBank. The thin margin that kept him from defaulting on a lifetime's work of accidental debt had been exposed by the FDIC's threat not to reimburse. The hundred-dollar unemployment check would offset it, when it came, probably Thursday, but these risks simply caused stress. He could be making more money.

I do what I want.

AND WHO PAYS?

At *Nautilus* he paid no rent. The situation in Boston -- its boarding house status protected by an ancient statute -- came from his on-again, off-again living with his middle sister, Eleanor, who was on extended vacation, leaving him sole tenant. The agreement Miles hammered out with the landlord was an extension of dirt-cheap rent in exchange for the entire unfinished top floor of the building. The workmen on the other floors would be gone soon, replaced by new upscale condominium owners, or, more likely, their upscale tenants. Hence their apartment's designation by Paulie as *Terminus.*

And Miles' living expenses were negligible. It was amazing what it allowed him to do.

NOTHING. That was what he feared. The $2,000 check from Barrell, Bulfinch and Gray therefore was nothing. What could it do -- pay off one credit card? There was plenty of debt to swallow it up. No, he needed far more than that to be free and clear.

Barrell wants me to do something.

The thought caused him to jump up. It possessed him.

WHAT?

He needs me.

WHY WOULD HE WANT YOUR HELP?

No explanation. Nothing firm.

He's afraid.

OF WHOM?

Miles was pacing now, back and forth in front of the great white doors. If this wasn't the place for such debate and examination, where was?

Someone irrational. Someone who doesn't attack in the standard way. The bomb -- it had shaken up the Brahmin's world. His cool exterior was simply a mask for the torment inside. His client dead. Opposing counsel dead. His assistant badly injured. They never covered this in Harvard Law School thirty years ago.

How could I have been so dense!?! Barrell couldn't come out and say it. Yet another Bostonian coming to a Cape Codder for his expertise. The Brahmin felt a connection, somehow, through the name John Kendrick.

What about Meredith? Was that why Barrell had hired her -- because her last name was Gray? Was there a connection to her, too?

WHERE ARE YOU GOING?

Miles found his hand on his car door, and himself getting in. It had happened again. But it often occurred when he was obsessing over something. Sometimes he would realize he had driven the last twenty miles of narrow, winding roads and have no recollection. Like anesthesia -- a blank spot on the memory tape when the serious work had been done. One minute they're sticking a needle in your arm, the next you have cotton mouth and a nurse prodding you mercilessly.

At least on an operating table Miles knew who was in control.

Data. I need more data.

The stack of books from the Sturgis Library filled up the back seat of his car. Stopping at the McDonalds at the Sagamore Rotary for a quick burger, he took two seconds to open the envelope of photocopies sent down from Peabody Essex. Mags didn't waste any time, he had to admit, but it wasn't cheap. Nearly twenty bucks for copies. There goes food for next week.

It was the Congressional Report that first caught his attention. There again was the dry language of the law, unchanged since 1852. Perhaps all writing had once been like this, and only the law had remained stuck in the time of its founding. Whatever the case, this report had never been acted upon.

> The Committee to whom was referred the memorial of George Barrell... and other heirs of the owner of the ship Columbia, and sloop Washington, and the heirs of Captain John Kendrick and Martha Gray, widow of Captain Robert Gray, praying the confirmation of their title to certain lands purchased of the Indian tribes in 1791, on the northwest coast of America; or such compensation as Congress shall deem just and proper for their explorations and discoveries in those regions...

The report that followed was a jingoistic synopsis of the adventures of Captains Gray and Kendrick, funded by Joseph Barrell. Apparently their heirs felt they were due some sort of compensation by the U.S. government, and in past sessions of Congress had petitioned for attention to their plight. With this latest report in 1852, the urgency seemed compounded following the treaty delineating the 49th parallel as the U.S.-Canadian border. First and foremost of the claims was the discovery of the Columbia River by Gray in 1792 while on his second voyage, and his erection of Fort Defiance the prior winter in Clayoquot. Doubtless, the basis of American negotiating points with British diplomats in 1848.

The Kendrick case was more curious, and immediately aroused Miles' attention. Apparently, Captain Kendrick had been directed by Barrell, "*to be sure to purchase the soil of the natives... in the name of the owners*" if a piece of land appeared desirable. Of course, there was also the mention of the establishment of Fort Washington in Nootka in 1788 during the first voyage. But after swapping vessels with Gray, Kendrick "the Navigator" had set up another Fort Washington, this time in Clayoquot. And this time, he got deeds.

At the back of the stapled photocopies were four deeds from different native chiefs on the east coast of Vancouver Island. A fifth deed had been mentioned, but was not listed with the rest. Kendrick sent attested copies directly to then-Secretary of State Thomas Jefferson -- the best excuse for a land registry Miles could imagine.

Interesting, but the deeds were from the chiefs into John Kendrick personally, not Barrell and the other Owners. Even more so was the assertion that the deed to the fifth tract, which was seen by many contemporaries in the Pacific, was never recovered. The report claimed it encompassed four degrees of latitude, two hundred and forty square miles or six million acres.

The call to the Harvard Maritime History Office was urgent.

"Kendrick! Where the hell have you been, sir?"

"Seth, how big is four degrees of latitude?"

"That's like asking how cold 32° of Fahrenheit is! What are you trying to measure?"

"Acreage."

"How about square miles?"

"Fine -- is it 240 -- or six million square acres?"

"Latitude only measures one way -- what's the longitude?"

"Uh, west coast."

"Of America, I assume."

"Of North America."

"Kendrick, you don't measure land by longitude and latitude."

"Well, *guess*, can't you? Isn't that what historians do when faced with gaps?"

"Okay, lets see here... you know, you're way off on your acreage... in square miles it'd be... the State of Washington, maybe half of Oregon, too."

"Okay, flip it the other way -- north of the border."

"That's 49° North -- wait, you should count that southern jog Vancouver Island takes south of that line --"

"Forget that."

"Forget that? Okay, then it's 49° plus 4° equals, well lookee here -- I wasn't even using my calculator and I got 53°! Want me to re-check my math?"

"No, but your parents must be proud. Where is that?"

"Queen Charlotte Islands --more than two-thirds of the way up the British Columbia coast. Remember, Alaska starts at 54°40'. Why do you want to know all this?"

Miles stopped, recalling the radio reports concerning the latest international monetary fluctuations. "Isn't Quebec voting to secede next week?"

The six million-acre figure came from the Senate report's inclusion of a letter from the controlling partner of the *Columbia* and *Washington* ventures. Joseph Barrell had empowered his brother in London, Colburn Barrell, to act as sales agent for this particular amount of land "*on the northwest coast of America, better land and better climate than Kentucky.*" It was dated December 1, 1794. Captain Kendrick's "accidental" death came just less than two weeks later. The original deeds were never forthcoming to Barrell from a John Howel, the man who took possession of *Washington* following the "accident".

Even so, a circular in four different languages went out from London, advertising the land bought by the Navigator on behalf of Barrell and company. John Box Hoskins, an agent of Barrell's, who had accompanied Gray on the second of *Columbia*'s voyages, attested upon return from France that Kendrick bought "*a tract of which he took formal possession of in the name of the United States.*"

All Gray did was sail up a river. That thought ate at Miles as he parked next to the Plymouth Cemetery. Torn between purpose and perspective, he finally walked up the hill between the ancient tombstones overlooking the town and Plymouth Harbor. 1794? What was that -- last week? No, the Kendricks were latecomers into the Plymouth Bay Colony, compared to his mother's family. That perspective, along with the fresh air, humbled him.

"All probate cases before 1881 are now at the State Archives on Columbia Point in Boston," the clerk in Plymouth had told him. He was encountering some familiar names.

But "Huldah"? Sometimes old names come back into style. Miles hoped never to read the name "Huldah Kendrick" again, except in relation to the Navigator's wife.

She also served as Administratrix of the Estate of Captain John Kendrick. Well, why not? Miles squinted at the faint projection from the microfilm. The guy left her when he was 47 and never came back. She was left with the house, "*1 cow + 1 swine... and Crow.*"

?

"*Crow bar.*" Oh. God, this handwriting was atrocious! The sum total of the estate of the Navigator, cash and property, amounted to a whopping $1,206.49 -- most of which was the house in Wareham. The rest came from little things like pewter plates, china cups, wine glasses and crow bars. Notably absent was the subject of Miles' research -- any mention at all of land in the Northwest. Nothing anywhere. Because of whopping debts, the estate was rendered insolvent, and Huldah had to subsequently sell the house.

Funny, but she waited until 1799 to administer the estate. Kendrick had been killed four years earlier, and while news traveled slower in those days, it seems even old Joe Barrell had heard tell of the accident in Hawaii by late 1795. Was she holding out some vain hope?

The lady at the Orleans Historical Society had told Miles on the phone that the Captain and Huldah had six kids -- John, Jr., Solomon, Benjamin, Alfred, Joseph, and, of course, another Huldah (a Cape Cod tradition of naming a daughter after the mother). John, Jr. had joined the Spanish at Nootka. Solomon and Benjamin were lost at sea. Alfred died in Dartmoor prison, a British prisoner during the War of 1812. Joseph drowned when the whaler *Essex* was stove by a whale. And Huldah (Jr.?) married and moved to first Maine, then Nova Scotia. No word on her.

If John Kendrick's lands in the Northwest were never probated, and all his kids died childless, then it passed to... his nephew. Who Alf Kendrick referred to as "Great-grandpa John."

The light from the machine was getting to him, and he flicked it off. For all the people using it, the Massachusetts Archives are as quiet as grave. Leaning back, he caught sight of a map of Boston, 1796 -- a hodge-podge of wharves pointing off of a thin spit. He wondered if it was for sale.

The City of Boston, that was. Although the map was nice, too.

CHAPTER THIRTEEN

North-West America

Friday, October 27, 1995

The Professor was struggling. "You own Vancouver Island?"

"Yes" Miles answered.

"And most of British Columbia?"

"That's right."

Setting down his plastic cup of gin and tonic on the once-gritty sill of the studio, Seth's eyebrows raised even more. In his Harris tweed blazer, kilt and wire-rim glasses, he put Miles' own "professor-outfit" to shame. "You realize, of course, the Trade and Non-Intercourse Act of 1790 forbade the purchase of land from Indians -- you had to buy it directly from the government."

Miles' shit-eating grin grew toothier, and he glanced about the studio at all the beautiful people admiring Paulie's work. The show was a success. A throng of people clustered about the thrilled creator and the evocative photos of Emilie and Monster Screw. Neither of his two roommates were in their element, though, despite Miles' appearance -- charcoal suit, black silk shirt with banded collar, and the same Indian-print vest. Slicked back hair and closely-trimmed goatee finished off his Great American Sleaze look.

I own the world. Catching then discarding the eye of an almond-eyed dusky minx in a tight black dress, he focused again on Seth. "That Act, my learned friend, only applied to territory *within* the bounds of the United States. When my ancestor purchased these lands in 1791, the territory was held by Spain -- and English Crown nearly went to war over John Meares' right to buy that same land from the natives. Now, you're not telling me the United States was forbidding *all* Americans from buying *any* land from *all* Indians everywhere, are you? Hell, apparently one of the deeds was made expressly in the name of the United States government."

"Kendrick, you know this is ridiculous. And pointless. You just said

Meares bought the same lands at Nootka and Clayoquot first -- right? Sounds to me like the natives there gave out deeds left and right."

Dog deeds. The Professor was a great one for poking his finger through the veneer of theory. All that concerned him, like any good cynic, was the truth. To keep his respect, Miles had to work on the same level. "I don't know the history of this period as well as you, but I do know property law, which hasn't changed much in 200 years."

"First, Meares never produced a deed, not to the Spanish and not to the British Parliament. Even so, the Spanish paid $200,000 in reparations, and the land at Nootka was eventually turned over to -- I think it was to Vancouver -- but I read that the final agreement between Spain and England stated that north of a certain point the Coast would be open to people in both their countries --"

"But not the U.S." Seth countered.

"No. In fact, it said they'd defend each other against the claims of outsiders."

"And that's why you think the British killed Captain Kendrick?"

"Shuhr! They had assembled a whole fleet to sail against Spain over the seizure of Meares' half-acre at Nootka. You think they'd do any less against an old man in a sloop who claimed to have bought practically the entire coast? Hey, by the way -- what's a sloop?"

"A sloop is a single-masted square-rigged vessel," Seth explained.

"One mast."

"Right."

"Square-rigged -- you mean square sails rather than triangular, like what we're used to these days."

"Right. Triangular sails are for schooners and the like."

"Why the difference?"

"A schooner can sail at much closer angles into the wind, . A square-rigged vessel against a headwind has to beat at right angles to it -- first one way, then the other."

"Then why the hell would you ever have a square-rigged ship?"

"Lots of reasons. Sometimes speed isn't important -- they're good on fat cargo ships. Also a square-rig under full sail with the right wind can move a fat boat faster than a schooner. There's a bit of danger there, too, since there's more tilting of the ship when those triangular sails catch a cross wind -- imagine having a heavy load shift below decks --"

"That was my favorite part of sailing your sailfish -- tipping over -- remember?"

"Yes. You became quite adept," Seth snarled, "even when there was little wind. ANYWAY, you can imagine that dealing with several small sheets of canvas running up a mast as easier than one big triangular -- gives you more control in variable, unknown conditions."

"I think it's ugly."

"You would."

Miles had read that Kendrick's flagship, *Columbia*, was a *ship* of 212 tons, accompanied by the sloop *Washington*, of 65 feet. To him that was like saying a dog of 100 pounds was accompanied by a puppy ten months old. DON'T BE ARROGANT.

Checking out the refreshments table, Seth grabbed a Sam Adams from the two cases he had donated to the effort. As he popped the top off, he said, "I don't know -- I think you have an uphill fight against reclaiming that land from the Queen. She's a pretty tough biddy when it comes to her property, I'll have you know." During his sojourn at Saint Andrews University in Scotland, the Professor had been invited to a private reception following the fire at Windsor Castle. On the suggestion that She use her vast fortune rather than tax moneys for rebuilding, Seth had found She was not amused.

"True. However, I have pre-existing deeds held in the archives of the Department of State," countered Miles.

"The United States Department of State? Like I said yesterday, wasn't this settled back in 1848 with that treaty?"

"The treaty delineating the U.S.-Canada border allowed for British subjects in the U.S. to retain their property rights after the boundary was fixed. So shouldn't the reverse hold true?"

"Except the treaty doesn't explicitly say that it does," Seth asked, "does it?"

"No." Damn him.

There was no place to sit, save for the few folding chairs Paulie had improvised as a stand for one frame. It almost looked intentional, Miles thought. Paulie had a way of making a pathetic fuck-up seem like a daring innovation. Miles steered Seth around the edges of the studio. "But a U.S. Court might be persuaded to see things more fairly." They stopped in front of a photo of lovely Emilie, partially clad in an old shower curtain, lying within a tangle of twisted metal.

"Wait --" Seth grabbed Miles' arm, looking at him with all seriousness, "what you said yesterday about Quebec seceding --"

"Exactly. You know the scenario." Miles swigged hard back on his cup, crunching triumphantly on the remaining two ice cubes.

Indeed, the Professor was familiar with the scheme for the partition of Canada. The seemingly-imminent vote in favor of secession by the French-speaking Quebecois would divide a country two-hundred thousand square miles larger than the United States, but with one-tenth its population. The province of Quebec sits above the U.S. Northeast. To the east are the maritime provinces of Nova Scotia, Newfoundland and Labrador, with their pervasive unemployment and struggling fishing industry. The eastern Canadians had the most to lose from the Quebecois leaving the federation, and probably could be easily induced to join the United States -- if their richer southern cousins would have them.

Central Canada -- Ontario and Manitoba -- on the other hand, held the heart of the country along with its capital and breadbasket. No doubt about it, they'd remain independent of U.S. entreaties. But it was the question of the western provinces...

British Columbia and its neighbor across the Rockies, Saskatchewan, possessed abundant natural resources -- minerals and lumber, as well as scenic attraction for tourism. The *city* of Vancouver, on the mainland across the Georgia strait from the *island* of Vancouver, and the provincial capital at Victoria, had in the past fifteen years come long ways from being sleepy little burgs just north of the U.S. border. The influx of wealthy Hong Kong businessmen fleeing the 1997 reunification with China had sent the population and real estate market of B.C soaring. Strategically located on the Pacific rim, it was Vancouver, not Seattle, that was the world-class city in the region.

Talk had been bandied about lately of these two western provinces either being welcomed into the U.S. with open arms, or becoming totally independent free-trade models along the lines of Singapore. The nationalist in Miles wanted *54° 40' or Fight!* -- a non-stop U.S. border from Baja to Prudhoe Bay -- but would western Canadians want to give up their free healthcare, strict guns laws and low crime rates?

"You've got to be kidding," Seth answered. "How many 'ifs' are you counting on? Let's see -- IF Quebec secedes, then MAYBE Canada will disintegrate, and IF that happens then MAYBE British Columbia will become the 51st state, and IF that happens MAYBE you can bring some suit for that land in the newly-established U.S. district court. What happens to the people who've been living on that land there for what -- 150 years now?"

Miles was reasonable. "Oh, well, one of the deeds at Nootka allows the native tribe to continue use of the land, so I'd have no problem with them remaining --"

"HAH!" Seth loved the pure bluster.

"-- the same with anyone else out there. I mean, they do have some sort of squatter's rights -- I can afford to be generous. No, confining myself just to Vancouver island, it pretty much seems to be open public land, and that's all I'd want back. I don't want to displace anyone."

"Except the mining and lumber companies."

"Hey, it's not *their* land," said Miles. "Of course, I'd have to review all their leases allowing them to extract natural resources."

"Old man, that'd get them!" Like any old-line Yankee, the Professor was a conservative and conservationist at heart. And, as partially-baked as this all sounded, the idea of twisting the tail of any entity lining their pockets by destroying the unreplaceable delighted him to no end. "Even the thought of having to deal with you -- AHA!"

Miles held his hands in front of his face, staring down at the pyramid they formed. He nodded.

Seth drew himself alongside Miles, and looked down at the dark alleys below. The change in his tone became more direct. "You think YOU were the target of the bomb. You think someone with an interest in maintaining the status quo out there was afraid if B.C. became part of the U.S. you might try to claim half the Coast. You realize, of course, that everything you've just explained is an entirely preposterous proposition. You've explained before that, even after a hundred years, inheritance cannot be extinguished -- there is always an heir -- so what good would killing you do?"

"It was a bomb," said Miles. "Not poison. Not a bullet in the head or a knife on the back. It was... a display of power."

"You have it figured out?"

The Brahmin. "No doubt about it -- Barrell," said Miles. "He had seen that memo to Lotta from Meares about the land. Probably even brought it up in a subsequent consultation with his client. So like Meares, Lotta had to go, based simply on her knowledge of the memo. Meredith...," Miles had to stop and finally shook his head, "... damn, what a waste."

"Probably included in the negotiations, since she was Barrell's assistant," Seth said, "but what was her last name again -- GRAY? Like Captain Robert GRAY who discovered the Columbia River and whose widow petitioned Congress along with Barrell's heir for some sort of settlement?"

"Yes, yes, I know," Miles waved his hands. "But, any claims by the Gray family would be groundless. There's no record Captain Gray bought one square inch of land from anyone in the Northwest. And if his simple claim is based upon discovery, then you, I and the evil photographer we are here to support," he gestured towards Paulie, "own Boston."

"Or the heirs of Christopher Columbus in Genoa," Seth added.

"Right. But here's something I can take to the FBI. Joseph Barrell had a motive -- greed -- a little irrational, sure, but justified by the magnitude of the gain. Then there's his actions -- ducking out of the room just before the explosion.

"Just like you."

"Hmm. Heh, heh," Miles parried the straw man around, "but I know I didn't do it. It's just not my way." *I reserve violence for my enemies alone.*

"But does the FBI know this?" Seth asked.

"I figure I'll take tomorrow off and write it all up for them in a way even a lawyer can understand it. As in politics, all I have to do is make my charge *first*, then suggest a check of Barrell's calls and air travel to the Northwest in the past couple years. That'd cinch it."

"And if he's already said the same thing about you?"

"Then I'd already be in jail. Hell, they've only questioned me once -- lightweight treatment at that -- and ignored you altogether. No, to them," Miles sighed, "I'm just a victim...," he smiled, "... who very soon is going to collect on some well-earned reward money."

"You're pretty sure of yourself," Seth observed.

"Nothing to worry about," Miles tossed his cup into a nearby trash can. "Don't be ridiculous."

"Two hundred years ago we would have been underwater." Here, atop Melcher Street, the view of Boston was magical, with the twinkling lights of the office buildings and hotels. There was no rhyme or reason to the placement of the buildings, no long boulevards to catch sight down. Between the narrow streets that separated them was -- yet another building.

Thirty degree angles are the norm for intersections in Boston, leading to vast confusion for those unaccustomed to the way affairs are conducted here. There always seems to be another "square" -- Post Office Square, Liberty Square, Dewey Square -- in the shape of a triangle, to be sure, directing you further and further towards the center, the Hub.

It had been an island at one time. Or, to be more precise, at two times. Daily. The tides of Boston Harbor would every twelve hours creep up and over the narrow causeway of Washington Street -- and the city would, for the better part of an hour, be inaccessible. By land.

Like that mattered. Along the rough and pitted roads of Post-Revolutionary America, any mode of land travel then made as much sense as *walking* would today. Railroads were decades off. Water, cheapest of all transportation, was the undisputed ruler.

This was evident in spite of the shallowness of Boston Harbor. Movement in and out of the Hub wasn't nearly so much halted by high tide as it was by low. With the only power sources being godly winds and human backs, there was a limit to how close a ship could approach the waterfront during an ebb tide.

In the late 1700's, the Town of Boston was ringed with a ganglia of wharves, grasping out into deeper water for commerce. The jumble of cobblestoned cowpaths led into a warren of wooden and brick buildings surrounding the three hills -- the "Tri-mountain" or "Tremont" -- jutting up from the water to form the Shawmut peninsula. Corn Hill, on the northeast and the oldest, housed the better families of the likes of Paul Revere then, and the Italian North End now. Fort Hill, on the southeast was the yin to the Corn Hill's yang -- upstart and more open, it would get its own by falling into industrial use.

Beyond, in the sticks, was the largest -- Beacon Hill. Its steep western slope shaved down to accommodate a State House designed by Charles Bulfinch, and charming federal townhouses on subdivisions created by Paul Revere. From such schemes, the mud flats were filled.

If the first remedy to shallow water were piers like Long Wharf, extending State Street a quarter-mile out like a frog's tongue, the second remedy was more direct. You have both hills and shallow water. If you can't bring the channel closer to land, then extend the land to the channel. Thus, the in-between of wharves were filled, then pushed further and further out. Offices and warehouses came to be built on top of the old wharves, and the process repeated. A rule of thumb for Boston is, if you can drive more than two blocks in a straight line, you're on landfill. The Dorchester Heights had been almost a mile south across the mud flats, but with fill, nineteenth-century man created a verdant industrial plain. Only the tumid Fort Point Channel separated twenty-first century downtown Boston from its past.

Seth's pea coat kept the draft up his kilt at bay while he leaned against the yellow brick and cement sill. With the remnants of the harbor behind him, it looked to Miles as if the historian was resting against the rail of a ship coming into port in the dead of night. The were both quiet for a steady, long time as they absorbed the innate heritage -- the only difference being the Professor's general intent stare opposed to Miles random casting about on fixed points. *Damn! Born at the wrong time.*

Paulie's show had exhibited every sign of going well, and neither of his room-mates were going to be heading home until it was all put to bed. If the measure of success was the time at which one could leave, 2:14 AM signified public nigh-adoration. It was a testament to their exhaustion that neither heard the trap door swing up and the subsequent skittering footsteps across the gritty surface until it was too late. Two arms wrapped around Miles' midsection. *What the --*

"Hey!" The force of him whipping around nearly flung her off the roof, and he caught her waist full in his arms. The crystal-blue eyes rolled wide with the thrill, then broke into a smile amidst the tangle of red curls. "Johnny!" the Spanish coiled spring lunged at him, kissing both cheeks, "hey!"

"Bella!" After such an introduction, Miles was more than a little hesitant to release his grip -- *now that I've got her* -- but beyond he saw the Prince of Darkness emerge from the trap door with an evil grin, followed by lovely Emilie and a very large, very broad Gallic gentlemen. In the darkness Miles couldn't make out an expression, but a few seconds more embrace could not be healthy.

LET HER GO. SHE'S NOT YOURS. Flying right back out of his arms, Bella grabbed Miles' hands and led him over to the Big Frog. In her heavy Spanish accent she announced: "This is Robért, my fiancé".

Lucky man. Robért held out his hand and flashed a winning and genuine smile across the GQ face. "Allô."

Die.

SMILE. BE GRACIOUS. At his most diplomatic, Miles nodded positively, catching Paulie's eye with an amused expression, and finding the only thing he could think to do was introduce Seth. Emilie, Seth and Robért acted carefree because only they were.

"Where in France?" Seth asked.

"Paris, or my family is from Bordeaux." Robért's English was stilted. Phrases came out connected by random conjunctions like so many people speaking a new language. Hello, my name is Fred *but* I live in Dayton *so* I need to use your bathroom.

Paulie wandered downwind to split a pack of French cigarettes with Robért and Emilie, while Miles chose to re-acquaint Bella with Seth, and reminisce about previous summers by the sea at Nautilus. It was terrific to see her again, as she was so full of life and absolutely brazen. Some of the first words in English were taught to her by a mischievous Paulie, and even now her speech was peppered with enough profanities to make a sailor blush. Seth just laughed.

"Yo, Johnny!" beckoned Paulie, holding up something silhouetted against the harbor. "Check this out!"

The two groups of three rejoined as Miles took the plastic something-or-other in his hand. It was about the size of a playing card and had a long string of metal beads running through it. The memory caused him to recoil. *Idiot tag.*

"Oh, here," Paulie held up his brass Zippo lighter, "get a load of this."

In the flickering of the flame, Miles caught enough French printing below Robért's photo to see it was a press pass. He nearly burned his eyebrows off when he lunged forward to catch the faint computer printing. *Robért Hoskins.*

It wouldn't have caught his attention any more than normally except for the similarity to the name -- Robert Hopkins – the alias he used three years ago checking into Pocasset. And besides, that distinctively Anglo-Saxon last name for a man struggling to speak English... a few obscure blocks of the previous week fell together.

Miles jumped back, throwing the ID down on the roof. He had to pick it up again, just to make sure. It was even possible a seizure might hit.

GET A HOLD OF YOURSELF. In the darkness, Miles knew his general movements would convey some sort of alarm, but the jerks and creeping of his hands across his chest still might not be seen.

"What the fuck? Johnny --," Paulie began.

"*NO!*" Miles yelled back. TOO LOUD. "I'm okay," Miles explained. "Hold on. Gimme a minute." He paced off to the far corner of the roof in an attempt to dissipate the bolt of energy thrown into his system.

This sort of thing had happened on occasion. More so since his fall into depression a few years back. There was no rational explanation for it, save coincidence.

F.W. Howay's *Voyages of the Columbia* was mainly a collection of the logs of officers on both expeditions, supported by letters and ship's papers. Strangely, both Captain's logs were lost, as well as that of Kendrick's First Officer, Joseph Ingraham -- traditionally the official report to the owners. Miles' reading of Howay clearly showed the editor's predisposition against a lazy and borderline-piratical Captain Kendrick. Those same charges could be leveled against Miles should he be cut down before presenting his accomplishments to the world.

While that connection pranced about his mind the past few days, he had pretty much forgotten about John Box Hoskins. Apparently dissatisfied by the performance of the clerk on the first voyage, old Joseph Barrell assigned his most trusted ward, the son of a departed associate, to act as his direct agent and accountant (a/k/a "Supercargo") to accompany the second voyage. *"Except for Mr. Hoskins I hardly ever saw a man in your N.W. employ who was not either fool or Rogue,"* wrote the subsequent owner of *Washington*, John Howel, to Barrell. Those words were fixed in Miles' skull. The dutiful servant. Hoskins' account included in *Voyages* wasn't a log per se, but rather a narrative taken down some years later when retired with his new family. In France. Bordeaux? Miles wasn't sure, but by this point it didn't matter.

I have to know. Striding steadily across the roof, Miles delivered the press pass back to Robért, with a "Merci" and weak smile. Then Miles grabbed Seth. "C'mon -- this is important."

As they rushed down the stairs, Seth acknowledged Miles' description of John Hoskins connection to events on the second voyage, as well as his connection to Kendrick's purchases. Desperately fiddling with the keys, Miles nearly broke the car door lock, and reached inside for his knapsack. The contents spilled out onto the dark muddy ground of the empty lot, but he managed to catch the object of his pursuit in midair. Rifling through the pages he presented the passage to Seth.

WAIT. DON'T SAY ANYTHING. LET HIM ABSORB WITHOUT ANY MORE BIAS. Faced with the historical record of Howay, the Professor sat himself in the passenger seat of the car, reading intently the short biography of John Hoskins. Then he flipped to Hoskin's narrative itself. "Huh. You haven't read this, have you? You really should, you know."

"Okay, well, I'm going to check it all out when I actually read the damn thing in its entirety -- but from what I gather, Hoskins was just an employee on the second voyage. He had no financial interest, no ownership in either Kendrick's or Gray's adventures -- or purchases."

"Except that by helping his employer --"

"Barrell."

"-- yes -- he helped himself." DUTY. "So his heirs in France...," Miles started.

Seth raised himself out of the car and handed the book back to Miles. "Wait just a minute. You have no basis to assume that these are the same family. Even if they are, so what? Hoskins was just an employee. This was a case between Barrell, Meares and Kendrick. Don't confuse the issue by dragging people into this that don't matter. A better use of your time is to stay focused."

Miles, heading back to the stairs, laughed and turned back to face Seth. "Did you just hear an echo?"

"Allô, Papa?"

The tension surrounding the corner payphone was greasy-thick. Under the streetlamp near the pizza and sub shop at 3:15 AM a tall Frenchman hunched over a less traceable form of communication than the studio phone. This call to six hours and 3,000 miles hence would run Miles' calling card a bit more, but when would he get another chance to play a hunch?

"As-tu son nômbre?"

Seth, Emilie and Miles hung back while Paulie and Bella flanked Robért, tandemly translating the more complex French of the father and son exchange. A few anxious stares at Paulie --

Now.

-- and Robért cut short the pleasantries. "À bientôt."

He looked first to Bella for reassurance. Paulie laid his hand upon his shoulder. "Maintenant (*now*)," said his smooth, firm voice, "s'il-te-plaît (*please*)."

As Robért punched in the codes and numbers again, Bella gripped her beau's arm firmly and whispered loudly, "His uncle, you know, they are not so close. But his father thinks he is not in his office so he works... uh... going to Eastern Europe and Russia for his bank."

"Monsieur Hoskins," Robért addressed the phone. French culture had still not fully adapted to the electronic age of voice mail extensions. Robért only had to ask a half-dozen more times, as he fiddled with an unlit cigarette and cursed.

"They think he just left the building," Paulie threw over his shoulder before asking Robért, "*Can they find him? C'est vraiment important.*"

Now.

Robért's expression changed to disgust and he hung up the phone.

Eyes wide, Miles took half a step forward. Robert backed away, and an exchange ensued involving him, Bella, Paulie. Then it ended with Bella picking up the phone, grabbing the phone card and dialing herself, all the while waving to Emilie to come. Robért stood by, rather put out. Between her waiting to connect to various departments, Bella noticed Miles' angry bewilderment, and smiled. Paulie did more, "It's okay. He just got disconnected. It was making him nuts, that's all."

Miles slowly turned his eyes on Robért, who lit his cigarette and affected Parisian detachment with only a hint of guilt. BE NICE. HE'S HELPING YOU. Without going too soft, Miles nodded, adding, "Merci." Robert replied with an exhale of smoke and a half-grin.

"Emilie! Vite!" Bella grabbed her arm, pulling her to the phone.

"Âllo? Oui, c'est moi," She nodded nervously. It was her uncle, Jean-Pierre Hoskins. Paulie waited for his cue. Apparently, from Emilie's decreased fidgeting and occasional relieved laughs, "Uncle John" was a pretty cool dude, quite pleasantly surprised by this abrupt overseas call from his errant niece.

Emilie reached the purpose of the whole call with a purely French "Euh..." and a searching look to Paulie. *Get to it...*

LEAVE THEM ALONE. Miles had felt terribly conspicuous here, especially so close to Arthur Lewis' digs, and he tapped Seth's arm. "C'mon. I feel like a vulture. Lets give 'em some room to work."

"Not a bad idea."

Miles had already written everything out on a sheet of paper -- the phone card number and the simple questions for Emilie Hoskins to ask Jean-Pierre Hoskins:

1) *Are we related to John Box Hoskins who came to France from Boston around 1800?*

2) *Has a Joseph Barrell of Boston tried in any way to contact you, and, if so,*

3) *What did he want?*

Miles had clipped his business card to the top of the sheet for quick reference of address.

From across the intersection, deep in a dark doorway, Seth caught the answer to the first question. Paulie snapped his fingers and gave a thumbs-up sign.

I'm right!

The Professor nodded, "Wa-el done, sir. Well done."

Miles, too anxious about the second and third questions, simply nodded quickly. "Had to be done. Had to be *now*. Their flight's in less'n an hour. Even one minute more..."

The exchange on the phone became more intense. Long pauses followed by imperative statements and questions abruptly cut off. Bella and Paulie tried to intercede as Emilie shared the receiver with Robért. There was another element, too. "Sounded like she said your name," Seth observed, "a couple of times."

"Yeah," Miles was not comforted by this, "wait a minute," he began to cross the street.

Seth grabbed his shoulder, "Kendrick, let 'em sort this out."

Miles could see Robért now looking directly back at him with a fearful, puzzled expression as he listened with a more focused Emilie to the phone. *What's going on?!*

Miles held back. Robért mumbled something quickly to Bella, and Miles saw incredulity spread across her to Paulie. Both echoed back, "Non, il n'est pas Johnny." When Paulie took over the phone, Miles was beside himself.

"Don't look. Don't even face that way," the Professor counseled. Miles sat down on the steps and started counting the number of window panes in each window across the street. Let's see, five wide and four high is twenty panes. And there are, hmmm, twelve windows on each floor, so that's 240. And five stories is 1200. And four sides is 4800 panes of glass in this building. Less on the side with the old loading docks. Oh, and doors.

Arithmetic, geometry and algebra had always been high points for him in standardized tests, but the grades in class almost kept him from graduating from first high school, then college. What fascinated him most was that the answer to any problem would come to him before he tried to reason it out. Since school taught it was the METHOD that was the goal, he had learned to discount and even distrust what his mind told him. Process over product. Ideology over pragmatism. Or intuition?

The click of the phone hanging up brought him back. Paulie headed across the street with his head down, eyebrows up. Bella, Emilie and Robért were gone. "Yeah?" Miles stepped out of the doorway, arms apart.

Paulie walked over to the car and opened the driver-side door. He smiled, stuck a new cigarette in his mouth and shook his head. "Let's go."

CHAPTER FOURTEEN

Pandora

Saturday October 28, 1995

Paulie wound down the window and carefully expelled a cloud. "Let me know if this is getting to you, okay?"

"No problem," replied Seth from the back seat. Miles had cranked up the heat to compensate. Better fresh cold air than warm smoke.

They crossed the Northern Avenue Bridge into Downtown and easily slid onto the most accident-prone section of interstate highway in the country, Boston's elevated Central Artery. In ten years this would all go underground, and be covered with parks, Miles reminded himself. "Well!" Paulie announced the beginning as they hit the highway. "It's pretty good." Old Joshua Nickerson wrote once that the highest praise a Cape Codder can bestow is "Not Bad." Just below this is "Pretty Good," meaning all right, but not good enough to be "Not Bad."

"Uh-huh," Seth prodded from the back. Miles waited for Paulie to talk the whole thing out.

"Okay, #1, you were right -- they are descended from John Hoskins of Boston through his only son. They became bankers in Bordeaux for the nineteenth and most of this century. He's a pretty sharp guy, I guess, which explains why he was anywhere near the office on a Saturday."

"And... #2?"

"Yeah, okay, well, here's the thing," Paulie shifted in his seat, turned to flick the ash out the window, "No, Barrell hasn't gotten in touch with him --"

Seth and Miles began to deflate.

"-- *but* -- get this -- he got silent when Emilie told him who asked her to call."

Miles pulled onto the Storrow Drive off-ramp high above the

Bulfinch Triangle. This set of blocks had been Boston's first major reclamation from the sea, designed by the famous architect of the U.S. Capitol and Massachusetts State House, Charles Bulfinch. A/k/a the not-so-famous financier of a Northwest fur trading expedition, Charles Bulfinch. Later he claimed architecture was a poor field to enter into, guessing that he had built all the great buildings necessary.

"Me?" Miles reacted.

"John Kendrick," Paulie corrected him.

"What did you say to him?" Seth asked.

Paulie spun around in his seat. "Yeah, you saw that? Shit, it was all Bella and I could do to keep fucking Robért from hanging up again. So I figured I'd get on the phone and introduce myself as you."

"John Kendrick," Miles said.

"Right. It would be less confusing than translating and, you know. And this guys asks, well, wait a minute --" Paulie grabbed Miles' arms as they came up from the underpass near the Museum of Science and approached the S-curve near the Arthur Fiedler footbridge, "-- did you know this guy?"

"Me?" Miles shook his head deliberately, "No. I mean, I had a hint about Robért and the name Hoskins from... well, anyway, Old John Hoskins was on the second *Columbia* voyage, but that's it. Why?"

"'Cause he said -- I mean after a lot of dead air on his end and a lot of massaging on mine -- that he knows who I -- you -- are. And -- listen here -- *he has my letters.*"

Only second of silence passed by before Miles quite sincerely asked, "What?"

"He claims," Paulie continued, now a little more at ease from Miles ignorance, "that somebody's been sending him letters over the past couple years and signing them 'John Kendrick, Commander'."

The pull-off into the Hatch Memorial Shell was a great deal more abrupt than the two passengers anticipated. Miles shifted into Park and demanded, "Letters?"

"Yeah. No return address, but postmarked from Boston."

All was quiet for another five seconds before Paulie lit a new cigarette and Miles pulled back into traffic. "So," Paulie began again, "he's sending a copy of one of them. Pretty weird after he got them translated. I mean, he speaks English, but still he thought it was best when they didn't make any sense to him. Bad spelling, poor handwriting. But-but-but," he patted Miles on the shoulder, "the last one arrived *yesterday*."

"Is that the one he's sending?"

"Yeah, 'cause it was there in his desk. The rest are in a safe deposit box in Paris. He was heading to Prague for three weeks that second, and is sending the rest when he comes back."

"To where? Here at *Terminus* ?"

"Yeah, that's the address on the card you gave me."

"Oh, good," Seth cracked from behind them, "that means the FBI will see them, too. Did I tell you I found some of our mail had been opened and resealed?"

Both heads whipped back, "*WHAT!?!*"

"Yuh, pretty amateur, too. Still don't know why they haven't questioned me. Probably got all they needed from Harvard -- you know, the university, for all their high values, rolls over when the Feds step in. Protect the endowment *Uber alles*. Anyway, they're probably doing a sloppy job of surveillance just to let us know they're watching."

"Yeah...," Miles said distantly as they passed along the Charles River towards that most vaunted institute of higher learning, Harvard. *Sloppy... or they've already gotten to Seth.*

DON'T BE RIDICULOUS.

Paulie finished his second butt and rolled up the window. The car became a great deal more quiet with its airtight seal in place. Seth broke the silence. "What did the letters say?"

"He said they all sounded very cryptic," Paulie said. "But all ended with something like, 'Your faithful friend and servant, John Kendrick, Commander, *Lady Washington*,' and a P.S. saying that no matter what he heard, he, John Hoskins, was in no danger."

"Oh, yes, I'd be terribly comforted by that," Miles commented.

"Right. But you'll see. He's faxing a copy," Paulie said.

"Good man!," Miles applauded as they sped past the Harvard boathouse. Drives like this had no destination, save sorting things out.

"So it'll be waiting for us back at *Terminus*?" Seth asked. "You realize, of course, our phones are probably tapped and faxes can be intercepted by other fax machines as well."

Miles began to slow down the car as his eyes opened widely. "If they --"

"No problem," the Prince of Darkness went from alarm over the thought of a phone tap to sweet, sinister victory. "I gave him the fax number on your card."

"Which is where," Seth wondered, "*Nautilus?*"

Miles veered off into the tangles of roads that splices Storrow Drive into Soldiers Field Road near Harvard Stadium. Ignoring the traffic lights that at this hour stopped no traffic, he headed into Brighton. If he caught the Mass. Pike --

Miles caught sight of Seth in the rearview bracing himself against the swerves, likewise in his peripheral with Paulie. "No. It's Lotta's office."

It was an office building with lawyers in it, so even on a Saturday it would be open at the ungodly hour of 6:00 AM. Miles had dropped Paulie off at the 24-hour copy and computer shop across Congress Street for first watch at 4:30 while Seth and he headed back to *Terminus.*

Jeans, sweatshirt, glasses -- the contacts needed a rest. Heading down State Street, pizza box in hand, Miles looked much the part of the still slightly-funky law student on the way to the weekend law clerk grind. Thank God for the Haymarket being open even at 5:45 AM, with its vendors of fresh produce and the best, cheapest pizza known to man in Boston. It gave him both a prop and breakfast for only two bucks.

Passing by the copy shop, he caught Paulie's eye as he sat at a rented terminal, manipulating some photograph or another. The watcher's eyes told him no one had gone in the building opposite and the coast was clear. Then they registered on the pizza box as Miles flauntingly brought it up to his nose for a whiff. Hunger.

As the security guard inside unlocked the front door for Miles, Paulie emerged from the copy shop, and made no small haste in the direction of the Haymarket. "Must've been a late night for him, huh?" the white-haired guard chuckled.

"Yeah," Miles feigned catching the scene for the first time, mirroring the old man's amusement, "some guys have all the luck."

"Oh, sure, but some day you'll be a high-priced attorney and that character'll be driving you around."

As Miles stepped into the elevator across from the front deck, he forced himself to smile agreeably. *Then where would I be?*

Perhaps the most beautiful act of nature is the way a wave will crest and strike the shore at an angle, sending a successive roll of liquid crystal turquoise crashing down the line where land meets sea. Not the fantastically huge "surf's up" pipelines of California, and not even the storm-driven breakers that were so great for bodysurfing here. It was the gentle rhythm of the ocean, demonstrating its consistency -- I shall always be here. I have power... but need not use it today.

His steps were plodding and whimsical. Having been driven to this walk -- the plumber, Feet Eldredge, would be by "around two", meaning sometime this afternoon -- Miles simply left *Nautilus* unlocked and headed reluctantly to the Great Beach. Only the ocean could help him now.

There had been no sleep since -- what? -- yesterday? What day was it? What *was* day? Or night? It was all one long blur. Many hours ago he was gleefully telling the Professor tales of redemption and reward. As is their nature, their promise was quickly jeopardized by something as small as the slick paper folded in his pocket.

If there was anything John Miles Kendrick felt was truly his, it was this tenuous scab of sand that had broken off from the barrier beach, then reattached itself to the mainland half a mile to the south a couple years later. Dismissed by the harbormaster as fleeting, it had endured and broadened, just as Miles had predicted. Of course, it was fleeting. The entire beach would be nothing in another 50 to 75 years, overtaken by its creator, the all-powerful Atlantic. *Like me.*

His boots traced the high-water marks of the waves, occasionally darting above the grasping reach of yet another surge. What was the tide -- rising or falling? He didn't know. YOU CAN TELL ON YOUR WALK BACK. YOUR FOOTPRINTS WILL BE WASHED AWAY.

How far was he going? The beach stretched for four miles to the south, like a finger hanging down from a fist. On semi-soft sand in late October it was one hell of a hike, never mind his near-depleted reserves.

Out of sight of the lighthouse and its surrounding cluster of weathered-shingle and white-wash dwellings, there was only the broad, flat expanse of the ocean on one side, and the high, curving slope of the Great Beach of Cape Cod on the other. It had looked like this since the glacier created it 10,000 years ago -- but three miles further east before erosion and sea level immediately set to work. Settlers from the west found they could go no further east maybe 6,000 years ago. Settlers from the east found their ship could not round the dangerous shoals to the south almost 400 years ago. The face of the land had changed and yet appeared to remain the same.

His pace slowed to a few forced steps and finally a tired halt. "That's it," he shook his head, very tired, very overcome. "No more."

Down where the water drew back to gather strength for another wave, stones had gathered. The force of the hastily retreating water sent them cracking into each other like chattering teeth in the mouth of some broad-mouthed beast. The strength of the oncoming wave could be judged simply by listening to how long and low the chattering continued. It was possible to walk the beach, eyes closed, and avoid the waves by simply listening.

Darting in at the last moment, he grabbed a black stone from the maw before it sent out its chilly tongue. With something to catch his attention, Miles could continue.

Worn smooth by eons of crashing waves, the dark gray stone was about the size of a partially-flattened goose egg. Probably pulled off some mountaintop in Maine during the last glacial invasion. Granite, maybe. A band of white shot through the center like a lightning bolt. Good luck, his sisters had told him, to find any stone with a circle that ran fully around.

He dried it by rubbing it between his hands and on the rough wool coat. The darkness faded to something like gray flannel, and its texture, though solid as hell, was surprisingly soft. It was a good thing to occupy his hands as he continued more steadily down the shore. Tossing it up and around like a juggler, there was that burning temptation to throw it off into the sea. *Wonder how many times I could make it skip?*

But it felt so right in his hand -- just heavy enough and not too large -- well, once thrown it would be gone. And he didn't feel like getting his feet wet looking for another so pleasant.

This late in the fall, it still wasn't that cold, even down by the ocean. Because of the ocean. It never got cold here until Halloween, or snow until Christmas, and by the time the ocean water had absorbed the winter chill, it was March. Miles never understood how people could say spring only lasted for two weeks in June. They had no sense of moderation.

Slowly, he found himself driven higher up the bank by the waves. Turning around, he caught sight of just the last fifty yards of footprints, arcing ever-so-slightly up as the water consumed those farthest away. The tide was coming in.

At the crest of the slope he found the line of dried eelgrass and other seaweed demarcating the line of the highest storm surge. Beyond lay the soft sand of the dunes, perhaps another hundred yards or more, dotted with it long shards of grass, stretching to the calm, warmer waters of Nantucket Sound. Houses on the opposite shore were protected by this thin elastic of sand.

KEEP GOING.

He was well-beyond the halfway point now. There was no good reason for turning around even if he was tired. *I can walk forever.*

YOU HAVE TO WORK THIS OUT. His run had slowed down to a quick stride. Might as well get this over with.

He should have been writing today, save for the message brought to him through Bella and Robért. Lovely Emilie had taken off to New York for interviews with modeling agencies, Paulie's photos in hand. Thus, circumstances had made it impractical for Miles to thank them for their help. Except for a big loose thread, all would be wrapped up. A big loose French thread connected to Jean-Pierre Hoskins. Or John Box Hoskins. *I should be done by now!*

YOU COULD STILL WRITE YOUR REPORT. It was only slightly far-fetched, and quite rational. It made sense. The Hoskins letter was a red herring.

Such faith...

OR DON'T DO ANYTHING AT ALL. THERE IS NOTHING THEY CAN FIND.

I can't let this go.

PROTECT YOURSELF. GIVE YOURSELF TIME TO REGROUP. There had been something disturbingly familiar in the fax of the letter Jean-Pierre Hoskins had sent. Miles dug his hand into his coat pocket. The stone was there, still warm from his hand. Next to it was the folded letter, and he pulled it out. There was no need to open it yet -- the breeze sweeping along the beach might tear the thin paper and it was his only copy -- he saw no need to risk duplicates falling into the wrong hands. So he held it in his own for comfort.

The angle of the slope became steeper, the height shorter as the shoreline began to bend off to the right, to the west. A low rumble was audible from over the top of the bank, and Miles slogged his way up though the soft, wet sand.

And here he was. Fingers of sandbars ran off in every direction from the end of the beach. The continuous cross-rip where separate Atlantic and Harbor currents fought for their share of water at the tip produced a dizzying effect with its rumble. Wave met wave at angles equal to the angle they each met this point of sand, in a triangulation of Force, Force and Inertia. He could go no further.

Well back from the rising tide and wind, safe within the dunes, Miles sat down cross-legged and hunched over the letter. Its wide arcs and poor spelling were familiar to him -- definitely eighteenth century.

Boston, Oct. 17, 1995

John Hoskins Esq.

Deare Sir:

I am afrade no longer. Deare friend and loyel supporter, this old sailer has not forgotten your lasting contribution to his defense, as they but bare witness to the perseverence of my Just cause. Those deserving of a violent fate out of trechery, insolence, faithlessness, ignorence, greede, Lust, etc, have been brought Lo by the guiding hand of the *Avenger.*

By the date of your receipt of this correspondence my mission shall have met its conclusn. My best expectatn therefore leads but to a time of blessed release and rest from my laybors, though I do perform the duty of restoring equity, albeit delayd. While those most directly responsibel for my delivery into destruction lye long deade, others equaly culpabel yet remaind, and you possess the testimony in my clerk's own hand in prior letters.

From those who abandond me, outright falsehouds markd their own deceit, and fed two centuries of prideful lies and half-truths. It is not for myself I have brought these tormentors Lo but for the memory of the Tender child, now lost and long forgotten. Their progeny payd for their fathers' sins for having nursed at the breast made round by my diligence. Two of the most deserving have payd. But three more shall come this morning Just, hence you may render this vessel's books balancd and my duty exectutd.

Only you understand the twisting of history and perversn of this commander's name. My first desire to destroy the messenger proven pointless not three years ago, I recognize for its want of determinatn, yet I presently hold confidence you possess the insights to, once and for all, correct the record, for which I shall remayne, most humbly, yours to command,

Lady Washington   John Kendrick, Commander

Shocking. Dreadful. Miles blinked hard and stared intently at the letter again. Horrendous. He jumped up quickly and waved the paper back and forth at the surrounding waters. "What the fuck does this mean!?!"

Another yell of pure frustration sat him back down hard on the sand, glaring angrily at the letter. Except for the date, it might as well have been written 200 years ago by Captain Kendrick himself, flourishing signature and all. It was that date that concerned him, too. The 17th was the date "three more shall come this morning", which wasn't too hard to figure out -- the bomb went off killing two and injuring one severely. The rest, though, was clear as mud.

There were all these allusions to unnamed people -- "the Tender child", "two of the most deserving", "the messenger". YOU NEED MORE DATA. THE PREVIOUS LETTERS --

I don't have time! Jean-Pierre Hoskins wouldn't be back for three weeks. A solid case of confusions could be built against Miles by the Feds in less time.

THEN GO TO THE FBI NOW. THEY WILL APPRECIATE YOUR HELP.

My name's signed to it!

DON'T BE RIDICULOUS. YOU WOULD HAVE TO BE CRAZY --

If they find out -- No. Miles gripped the letter firmly again. "There is nothing in the dark that isn't there in the light. All I need I already have. What is this really saying?"

He looked beyond the words, the grammar, the spelling. Something resonated. He read it aloud. It sounded different as he strained to be heard above the roar of the waves.

VENGEANCE!

ALL WILL PAY.

The list of all possible conspirators against Captain Kendrick had a shocking mortality rate. To have been connected to Captain John Kendrick and his voyages seemed a sure path to an early grave.

Gray died of yellow fever off South Carolina in 1806. Robert Haswell, insolent Second, and later First, Officer of *Columbia*, set sail from Boston on August 1, 1801 as captain of the *Louisa*, bound for the Northwest coast, and was never heard from again. Joseph Ingraham, First Officer after Simeon Woodruffe left *Columbia* at Cape Verde, was sent out by Barrell's commercial rivals and became the most successful at trading furs on the Coast, in his little brig, *Hope*. Later commissioned as a lieutenant in the U.S. Navy, he served aboard the brig *Pickering*, which sailed from Newcastle,

Delaware on August 20, 1800 -- likewise, was lost at sea.

Solomon Kendrick did return home from the first voyage of *Columbia*, but set sail again as Third Officer of the ship *Jefferson*. Aboard its tender, the schooner *Resolution*, he was lost near Queen Charlotte Islands. William Douglas, Scottish captain of the first English vessel the Spanish seized at Nootka, *Iphigenia Nubiana*, became a creditor of Captain Kendrick's. In Macao, Douglas lured away the *Washington*'s First Officer, Davis Coolidge, for similar service aboard his schooner *Grace*. Douglas died on the return trip from the Coast to China.

The most inspiring deaths were those of the commanders of the English vessels responsible for "accidentally" blowing up Captain Kendrick. Captain Gordon of the sloop *Prince Lee Boo* and Captain Brown of the schooner *Jackal* were killed by the natives of Oahu, just a week after the accident.

Even George Vancouver didn't escape. After his five-year mission, the intrepid commander of *Discovery* only had enough time home in England to finish the government-imposed writing of his *Voyages* before dying of a strange thyroid ailment, myxedema.

John Howel, who, by vague authority, "assumed command" of *Washington* after Kendrick's death in Oahu, set sail before the natives' capture of *Prince Lee Boo* and *Jackal*. Still, Howel died of a violent fever in Bengal, India, not soon after losing the brig in the Malacca Straits off Singapore. And so *Lady Washington* herself was lost.

More telling was who lived. Barrell. Bulfinch. Except for Pintard, the New Yorker, who went bankrupt, all the owners stayed in the comfort of their featherbeds in Boston while their hirelings encircled the globe, finding new dangers at every turn.

Meares got his $200,000 from Spain, received a promotion to Commander in the Royal Navy, and was never heard from again. Old Simeon Woodruffe, incompetent First Officer of *Columbia*, returned to Connecticut and lived there at least another twenty-five years. Doctor Roberts also returned to Boston, as reported in some private letters, but no first name to work with left Miles with a chore, indeed.

Davis Coolidge, after Captain Douglas died aboard *Grace*, became the schooner's master, and continued to trade for a few more years on the coast. Most interestingly, though, was that his cousin, Joseph Coolidge III, married Eliza Bulfinch, sister of the great architect and original financier of *Columbia*. Thus two lines combined into one. And again when Charlotte Bulfinch married Peter Coolidge, becoming Lotta Coolidge? She made a doubly-good target.

John Kendrick, Jr., who left his father's service at Nootka and joined the Spanish, later was discharged from His Catholic Majesty's Navy, and apparently commanded vessels along the coast. But no records ever show him coming home. Huh.

John Box Hoskins? As supercargo of *Columbia* on Gray's voyage, he had said nice things about Kendrick to Barrell. He returned home, moved to the south of France, made money, had a family, and died a happy man. The contrast was striking. *Cross Captain Kendrick and you will pay.*

The addendum, added recently, sounded like: *Or your descendants will.*

The sand had gotten in his ears and between his lips, but the glasses had stopped most of windblown assault from reaching his eyes. Curled up behind the dune, he could see the sun starting to kiss the blue-red horizon. It would be dark in half an hour.

Shit. Jumping to his feet, Miles saw that the water had risen to its highest extent a mere ten yards away. There were two ways to get out of here. Facing north he ignored the ocean and headed directly into the dunes, up the spine of the Great Beach. There was a steady purpose to his stride. Running up and down the hillocks of soft sand would simply exhaust him, and probably twist an ankle.

DON'T GET CAUGHT. So he marched to the rhythm of his thoughts.

I can't get back soon enough. The motivation. It wasn't greed. It was far simpler. Something Miles understood far too well. *Revenge.*

His own inability to reconcile his pain to the realities and restrictions of life, and control his desire for some kind of payback to those who had stolen both his affections and prized creations years ago had led him to the institution in Pocasset in the first place. That time-out had given him the chance to find a way to avoid madness, day-by-day, by promising revenge through material success. Only now, years later, that success eluding him time after time, began to matter less and less. He had just stopped caring.

But another person had allowed their own *Rogue* to take over, and use the discipline of the PRIEST to satisfy their paranoid desires. Miles had read between the lines of the various accounts of Captain John Kendrick. His officers abandoned him. His own ship and its owners had forsaken him in a hostile lands. Blazing the way into the uncharted Columbia River, his second-in-command, Gray, received all the glory. Kendrick's duty to his employers and his country had been twisted by historians like Howay, to render him the bumbling fool. But the only people who really mattered at the time -- the British -- did take him seriously. So much so, they killed him.

When they met in the conference room, there had been something in Barrell's eyes that surprised Miles. The Brahmin had taken the time to explain the importance of the *first* voyage of *Columbia*, led by Kendrick, but not the second, more historically significant voyage, led by Gray. He had tried to buy Miles, but upon reflection, it seemed more like a gift. Restitution.

"*..three more shall come this morning...*"

Meares. Gray. Coolidge. *But not me. Not John Kendrick.*

Meares and Gray, in the eyes of conspiracy-minded paranoid, would be perfectly sculpted enemies of the Captain. Lotta Coolidge? It didn't fit, but she was an adversary. Miles would have to check it out. Also the first "*Two of the most deserving*". That was it, Miles knew. He's have to construct a list of all the enemies of Captain John Kendrick.

YOU DON'T KNOW HE HAD ANY. NO AMOUNT OF RESEARCH WILL TELL YOU THAT.

That wasn't the point. Truth, hard fact, was not important. It was perception. The way someone would find victims to justify lashing out. *Like I would.*

But there was something more. The letter was signed "*John Kendrick, Commander*". It wasn't just Barrell making up for the failures of his Bostonian ancestor, from whom all the inherited wealth and power flowed. Something had triggered guilt or shame in him to cast off that cloak. The look in his eyes that day was of familiarity. And envy.

A POWERFUL ATTORNEY ENVIOUS OF YOU?

A fraud envious of an original. The Bostonian envious of the Bostoner. Joseph Barrell had become John Kendrick. *I am John Kendrick.*

But someone else had adopted the persona of the old Bostoner sea captain -- and a couple centuries later was back to settle the old accounts of the voyages of the *Columbia*.

THAT HAS NO BASIS IN REALITY.

The paranoid schizophrenic rarely does. *He'll want to kill me, then.* Eventually. The Brahmin's kindness had been rejected twice. Miles stood in the path of the delusion.

The sun was down now and the shadows began to melt into each other along the dunes. KEEP GOING.

CHAPTER FIFTEEN

Felice Adventurer

Sunday, October 29, 1995

Sand and clay. That's all Cape Cod was. A sand bar on a monumental scale. Low, but not flat. Hilly, but not ragged. It was bumpy.

When French explorer Samuel de Champlain cruised around in 1606 he found huge stands of white pines, like the coast of Maine. As the Cape was settled, the massive, straight trees were taken down to become the masts of His Majesty's ships -- as well as all sorts of houses. But the biggest export of the colonial period was far more mundane: charcoal.

Charcoal to run forges. Forges to create tools of iron. Tools to build an empire. When the last of the primeval forest was cut in the early 1800's, the bumps in the land not only became appreciably more noticeable, but people noticed the bumps began to move. Into their fields. And houses.

The first reforestation project in the country began on the elbow of Cape Cod when the Great Hill, devoid of its protective toupee of vegetation, threatened to engulf the town in sand. One specie of quick growing pitch pine took to the acid soil better than the native scrubby oaks. Within thirty years a forest of these ugly weeds would stand thirty feet high.

They were lucky to get even that tall. Desperate for heat in damp, windy and often deadly winters, Cape Codders kept cutting down these new trees for firewood. Coal from Wales or Pennsylvania cost good money, having to be imported by sea or rail. A woodlot of "ten acres scrub land" might have sold for $100 at any time in the nineteenth century. Send out your six sons for a week to cut, split and haul it back (why else did you have them?) and your winter would be warm in perpetuity. Without wood, the land -- sterile soil and all -- was worthless.

It wasn't until after World War II that these woodlots -- in some forgotten part of town -- fell into disuse. The widespread introduction of home heating oil and installation of gas lines, combined with the new booming tourist economy spelled convenience and prosperity for a corner of the country that had never known either. Over the next fifty years, the lots were subdivided for cottage colonies, second homes, industrial parks and golf courses. Meanwhile the trees remained, by and large, untouched, and grew to levels never anticipated by those who first planted them.

As Miles drove along the spine of the peninsula, tracing the high ridge that separated the north from the south side of Cape Cod, all he saw were ugly, scrub oak and ugly scrub pine, uniformly 25 feet tall. To him, all they meant was *sand*.

The villages originally settled here by the English and their descendants were far and few between. Some fertile areas might support a few cows or sheep, perhaps a crop of corn. The moisture locked in this densely-packed earth allowed fine red cedar and elm to thrive, and the village centers, buildings huddled closely, were lined with these indicators of *clay*.

When Miles' parents were trying to grade the rear slope of the house on the Oyster Pond, the front-end loader had attempted to scoop up a load. The earth fought back. And, instead, the hydraulics of the scoop lifted the rear of the machine off the ground, its load so heavy and dense. It was clay.

Sand was the Cape Cod of the last fifty years of development and prosperity. It was seafood shacks, go-carts and miniature golf, strip development, retirees from New Jersey, cineplexes, summer traffic, and endless cul-de-sacs of Cape Cod Cottage clones with attached two-car garages.

Clay was the previous 300 years of poverty. It was split rail fences, white-washed Greek Revival and cedar-shingled rose covered cottages built out of the timbers of shipwrecks, strollable downtowns, clam flats and knowing your neighbor (but not *having* to like them).

Sand blows in the wind, and flows *like* water. Clay stays where it is, and disperses in water. And unprotected, sand covers the clay, hiding the beauty with an ugly skin. Until the ocean comes along and consumes it all.

It was enough to drive a man to the sea. Generations of men.

In the rearview, Miles caught site of the stubble forming around his goatee. God, it would have looked better if he didn't have the stupid thing at all -- at least then it would all be even. Munching on the slice of apple-rhubarb pie from his father's icebox, he steered the car over the Sagamore Bridge, and down the Cape Cod Canal road that was more like an elongated roller coaster. Instead of heading directly to Boston he was chancing a side trip to Wareham.

If Barrell -- or whomever the Bostoner was -- adopted the personae of some historical figure, he would have poured over the historical record, become a patron of societies striving to preserve "the true story". He would have visited every site in the subject's life, no matter how insignificant. *I would.*

There was a great deal of meaning in the old cliché of somebody's crazy uncle Harry having the delusion of being Napoleon. Despite unsurpassed charisma and talent, the great French Emperor was brought down by the incompetence of his lieutenants and sheer bad luck (so the myth goes). Uncle Harry, after losing his job, his wife and his dog, and having to come live with relatives, could identify with Napoleon. Some day, Uncle Harry might, too, return from Elba. And this time, Waterloo might just go his way.

It created unreal hope in an unfair world.

Miles couldn't miss the place as he pulled next to the public dock on the Wareham River. He had passed by the old seafood restaurant and over the river into the old center of town. Stretching up the hill were the buildings of Toby Hospital. Three houses down stood an old yellow mansard-roofed structure. The Captain John Kendrick House was purchased in 1778 when he moved from Martha's Vineyard with Huldah and their six kids.

A little Honda wagon then drove into the spot across the street behind the Kendrick House. Well, there would be plenty of cars going into the driveway, as it was shared with an adjacent professional building and the hospital above on the hill. Luck. *If I hadn't come here at this exact moment...*

RUN. Rounding the corner he found a late middle-aged woman wearing a blue raincoat on the rear step working the door lock. "Hello!"

Startled, she turned to see a tall man with a goatee, slick-backed ponytail and a leather jacket. He smiled and clasped his hands behind him. KEEP YOUR DISTANCE, HERE, BELOW HER. "Is the house open?"

She had an intelligent face. "Not Sundays. But here, let me find the key..." As she fiddled with the lock, she said, "I'm just here to make sure all the doors inside are closed. Our gas bill is atrocious in the winter. You know old houses never have any insulation -- there!" The door swung open.

A map. Before he noticed the display on Captain Kendrick's visit to Japan, the photo of the two faces of the Columbia Medal, or the rough-hewn beams in the ceilings and the crooked angles of the door frames, Miles saw the map.

A *National Geographic* map of the world had been posted inside the door and criss-crossed with lines of yarn to note where the *Columbia* and *Washington* had traveled. Here it was. From Boston east to the Cape Verde Islands off Africa. Then straight south to the Falklands off Argentina. 'Round Cape Horn, with one stop at the San Fernandes Islands off the west coast of South America before hitting the North American coast somewhere near the state of Washington. No hugging the coast -- just long stretches of open ocean, from island to island, none of which had ever been visited by any of the crew.

His host shook rain from her coat. "I'm sorry we can't give you a complete tour today, but it really is too dark for you to appreciate everything here. Was there something specific you wanted to see?"

"Oh, uh," Miles tore his eyes from the map, "not specifically, no. I'm terribly sorry to intrude," his sheepish eyes grew wider, "it's just that I'm a descendant and was driving by and figured I'll take a look at the outside and well, here you are."

"Oh, you're *descendant*? Of Captain Kendrick's?" It was as if she had found a unicorn grazing in her vegetable garden. "I suppose I can show you a few rooms -- could you come back some other time as well? Which child are you descended from? I'm sorry, I didn't catch your last name."

He held out his hand most courteously. "My name is Kendrick. I can't remember the whole family genealogy, but I think it comes though his nephew."

"Oh yes," this caretaker understood, " Of course, we're always curious about direct descendants -- from the Captain's own children."

"I guess that would be pretty difficult what with the two eldest, John, Jr. joining the Spanish at Nootka, and Solomon lost --"

"Murdered," she corrected. "Solomon and the crew of his vessel were scalped by the Indians on a subsequent voyage."

A family torn apart in the service of others.

As they moved from room to room, Miles was shocked how much like *Nautilus* this house was, from its open fireplace in the kitchen to its "good morning staircase" in the front hall -- leading up half a flight, then branching off both left and right to separate sides of the house. From the outside, they appeared wildly different. But inside, except for small touches like wallpaper, the rooms, the light from the windows -- the atmosphere of the two -- were eerily similar.

"Oh, here we are." In the front bedroom facing south stood a coat rack holding a white powdered wig and several pieces of highly ornate period clothing. "We're hoping to get actors to play certain parts when we open in the spring." She reached into a nearby closet and pulled out a long navy blue frock coat. "We just received this last fall -- a replica of the Captain's coat."

"Good Lord," Miles held the coarse, many-buttoned coat in his arms, "It weighs a ton. Bet it's bullet-proof. But don't you think it's a little out of scale? I mean, 200 years ago poor nutrition and all that meant shorter people," he pointed to the five and a half-foot doorways and six-foot ceilings.

"Yes, that's what a number of our members asked," she took the coat and began folding it into its box, "but when Captain Kendrick landed at Kashinoura, Japan, the physicians had never seen an American you know, and he allowed them to take extensive measurements and cast of his hands and face and whatnot that still exist. According to the casts, he was over six feet tall, a real giant to the Japanese then." She sized up Miles and smiled, "They also hadn't seen anyone with red hair or beard before. And you know every year they celebrate the Festival of the Red-haired Barbarian."

The Rogue.

"This coat must have cost a pretty penny, then. Where did you have it made?"

"Now that's a funny thing," she stopped trying to fold the enormous garment back into its box, and Miles reached forward to try, "it was donated anonymously. Sometimes we receive a certain donation from an estate or some persons attic and they don't wish their names to be made public --"

"Since other family members might squawk over losing a part of their inheritance," Miles observed.

"Right," she laughed. This young man was savvy beyond his years. "But this coat is quite obviously brand new and tailor-made -- see the buttons?"

The pause he took magnified as he drew the coat quickly to his face. The coin. "I-I've seen this before," he murmured.

"Oh, yes, downstairs" she indicated the two vessels depicted, the ship *Columbia* and sloop *Washington*, "They're exact replicas of the Columbia Medal."

"No, I mean the coin itself. Actually, it was a pewter version... um...

Would you mind?"

"No, by all means," she gestured, "be my guest. It should fit you. Now, where did you say you saw this?"

"In--" STOP. DON'T GIVE THE WHOLE GAME AWAY.

She could I.D. me. Miles covered his pause with a struggle with the coat. The height was right, but it had been made for a man much broader of beam. It hung abut him like the skin of a starving elephant. "Not quite, huh? The medal -- yes, I think I saw it in an old family collection. Pretty valuable, I suppose."

I like this coat. Used to overly-large clothes that worked to hide his lanky frame, Miles decided it only needed some gathering in the waist to make it useful. A tailored coat like this, complete with buttons would cost plenty, and his search found no labels or country of origin. The number of pockets inside and out made it perfect.

She was beginning to look a little anxious. "Yes, well, it's not a perfect fit."

"Too bad. Yes." Miles fidgeted about, looking as if something were not quite right with the coat. "If it did, maybe I could've played Captain Kendrick next summer, but -- *there!* -- of course, he was much older."

He slid the coat off and managed to fold it just so into the box. DON'T GET CAUGHT. "Thank you so very much. I truly do not want to keep you in this dusty, damp house one minute longer. Perhaps some time in April I can have a better look."

She couldn't have been more agreeable. On his way out the back door, she urged, "Don't forget to sign our guest book. A 'John Kendrick' would look quite nice there."

YOU FOOL.

Aw, fuck! "No problem."

"You'll be the only entry since, my goodness," she pointed to the dates above his, "August."

There, most beautifully exposed in the line above, Miles saw the first piece of solid connection in scrawled handwriting. He had seen it many times before in Lotta's correspondence files, on a letter from opposing counsel -- Joseph Barrell. Miles' blowing his own cover was worth finding this. Soon it wouldn't matter. *Victory!*

CAREFUL. "O-oh," Miles struggled with his glee, "M-Mr. Barrell. Joseph Barrell. What a coincidence."

"He's been a wonderful patron. Silently, of course. You remember like I said upstairs? In fact, he donated, quietly, this piece here --" She reached under the table and slid out a narrow cherry box three feet in length. "You know him?"

"Not really." Miles stood far back as she flipped up the latches. "No. Just funny to see those two names – his, above mine -- considering the historical connection..."

I know what's in the box. She flipped the lid back and slowly pulled back the red velvet wrapping to expose the tempered steel. Miles could make out the cross of St. George on the hilt. She explained, "It was the sword of a commander in the British Navy. Mr. Barrell tells us it is definitely from the reign of George III."

"Why –" Miles tried not to sound incredulous, "why isn't it better protected? I mean, in a safe-deposit box. I can see you don't have the facilities to display it here safely year-round."

She held up the hilt. The metal didn't look quite right. "It's been reconstructed here along the grip. Perhaps only twenty-five years ago. Shoddy job." Miles could see the glob of molten solder. Probably lead. "Only the blade itself is definitely original. See -- it's even cracked here," she traced a gap running down the handle. "It won't be worth too much until it's fully and accurately restored." She dropped the lid shut and slid it back under the table. "Even so, it's been here for a year and nobody knows, so it's safe, right?" she winked.

"Absolutely," Miles agreed.

Buttons.

Having successfully restrained himself from *running* across the street to the Mazda, Miles was less so in racing up Interstate 495. Now he could examine the small package he had maneuvered out of an interior pocket in the massive Kendrick coat. It was a crumpled yellow envelope used to hold buttons. He flipped it open and spread the contents out on the dash.

Buttons. At least two were. One was a large white plastic pearlescent button about the size of a nickel. Another was much smaller, just a little ball covered with burnt-orange fabric. Another at first looked simply like a peg, but then he recognized it as the kind of wooden button used in terribly preppy wool parkas. The last was covered in white lace that was yellowed with age and had a dark gray smudge on one side. From its back, a small bit of lace string or cord still remained attached. It had a pungent, smoky smell. *I just stole something worthless.*

WORSE, YOU JUMPED OUT BEFORE YOU GOT ANY

SOLID INFORMATION.

Wrong. All information, right or wrong, is good information. Data. He had learned quite a bit. This *was* a sacred spot. *I was right.*

The Brahmin was in the habit of making anonymous donations to a museum dedicated to preserving the memory of Captain John Kendrick. The sword -- a British Naval officer's sword -- it was as if Barrell had captured it from those who destroyed the commander of *Washington*, and had brought it home as a prize. A demonstration of power. Unlike other schizophrenics, Barrell, as the Bostoner, could indulge his fantasy in plain sight and receive thanks for it. He might not even be aware of his actions.

WAIT. The car began to slow down -- he had turned onto Route 24 North to Boston. More so, though, as Miles turned into the rest area. He was only concerned by that last thought.

"Doctor Ormand, please." The payphone at the rest area Burger King was bad enough without the roar of the truckers downshifting, "it's Miles."

"Miles! Good to hear your voice," came the energetic but still-detached Southern-drawled echoes of Lisa Ormand. As a grad student she had been assigned to run a series of experiments on random symbols, which Miles couldn't get enough of during his "time away."

"Sorry to bother you, babe, but got a quick question. Psych-like."

"Okay, quick. We're just gettin' the horses checked out and I'm runnin' late to pick up the vet."

"Lisa, I know all the stories and myths, but I gotta hear it from someone in the field: Is it possible to be schizophrenic and do things in one personality and have no memory of it in another?"

"Shuhr."

"And have it direct or guide the actions of the individual in ordinary life so as to justify its actions? You know, like my suppressed, gluttony side needs to know when the ice cream store is open, so gets the good part of me to stop at the store for directions or a glass of water, in order to rationalize gathering the information. Then, the glutton, in control, comes back later, totally breaks my diet, and I wake up the next morning wondering how I've gained five pounds?"

"You should write textbooks. Why -- you start findin' ballerina tutus in your closet?" she teased.

"Yeah, and I'm savin' them all for you, darlin'."

"I'll stick with my horses."

"For once I have some healthy competition."

"Goodbye!" she emphasized.

"Bye, sweetheart. Dream of me." Lisa was just great. That beaming thought stayed with him another thirty miles. It was only occasionally interrupted by an even more potent thought than the woman in the Plains. *I'm right.*

"What the fuck!?!" he pounded on the steering wheel. *"It's a Sunday, for cryin' out loud!"*

Looking over at the dashboard clock reading 5:15, he wondered if this was regular weekend traffic back from the Cape or if the Southeast Expressway held an unavoidable delight ahead like a jackknifed tractor-trailer.

TURN ON THE RADIO. The switch to the AM band sounded as clean as filleting with a blender. Having missed the tail-end of the last radio report, he knew he'd have to wait through another, what, ten minutes of crackly reception, debasing commercials and hundred mile-an-hour weather reports on this "all news" station.

Just past the Columbia Point off-ramp, he heard: "At twenty-two minutes past four we're just one minute away from Bernie in the 'copter, but first this word from Beano --"

4:22? He looked at his watch. 5:22. He looked as the dashboard clock. 5:22. DAYLIGHT SAVINGS TIME ENDED THIS MORNING.

He'd dropped an hour behind the times, completely ignorant. There was no way out of the traffic since all exits would simply shuttle him off to endless traffic lights. The ramp to Chinatown, the first of the downtown exits, was another half-mile away, and the traffic wasn't so bad. He reached for the switch to cut off the announcer: *"Recapping our top story, Channel 7 is reporting a break in the investigation into the bomb --"* Click.

Realizing what he just did, Miles flicked the tiny knob the other way, unknowingly increasing the volume.

*"-- courthouse. **Law enforcement sources are reported to be focusing on one of the victims of the blast that killed two and injured three others. John Kendrick was said to be lurking on a restricted floor just minutes before the blast, and along with recently uncovered reports of his institutionalization for mental***

illness, it is widely expected that police will soon make an arrest..."

Numb.

I can't listen to this. Miles fumbled to turn off the radio.

DON'T TURN IT OFF. YOU HAVE TO KNOW WHAT THEY'RE SAYING.

Numb. The control of the car seemed to float away from him. *No, no. I can't move this car. It's too heavy uphill. I gotta get outta here.* He tried the door, and the noise of the outside brought him back.

NO. DON'T.

He was in the left lane, his exit was coming up, but a wave of apprehension overcame him. Not wanting to do anything to capture any attention, Miles found himself sitting bolt upright, moving in sync with the traffic speeds, and looking straight ahead. *They're probably broadcasting a description of me.*

Slowly, Miles reached behind him, found the bandanna and, as inconspicuously as he could, tied it around his head, skull-cap fashion. The sunglasses, despite the encroaching dusk, went back on. He rubbed his palm against his lightly stubbled cheeks -- if only the beard could grow in faster -- like *now!*

There was no running away. He was stuck in the Dewey Square Tunnel, moving ten miles an hour. The pace would pick up further down as the Central Artery headed north out of town, but that would be way past his last possible exit. *Unless I kept going...*

Interstate 93 North veered off to the Northwest to Vermont, hooked up with I-89 on the west bank of the Connecticut River, and then it was clear all the way to Montreal. If he made it across the border. The other option was northeast on U.S. Route 1 to I-95, then deep into the Maine woods. Perhaps a small rowboat across to New Brunswick... *Escape.*

DON'T BE RIDICULOUS. THE ROAD IS THE WORST PLACE TO BE. Canada had an extradition treaty with the U.S., too. A mad bomber didn't have the same cachet as a peaceful draft dodger. RUN AWAY AND YOU JUSTIFY THEIR SUSPICIONS.

Everyone's. *Shit.* In one minute he had gone from living life on his own terms to being branded a psychotic outlaw. *They're all happy I finally got caught.*

The steering wheel was firmly set on its column, but even so, it suffered a pounding never meant by its designers. The thrashing only lasted a couple seconds.

FOCUS.

YOU CAN'T BE SEEN LIKE THIS. Image is everything. GO HOME.

Miles parked his car along Joy Street, grabbed his backpack and books, and headed towards the throng of reporters perched on his stoop. They'd remember the insect sunglasses, the black bandanna, the brown leather jacket and the goatee. Without them, he was invisible. BE PLEASANT. YOU HAVE TO FOOL THEM.

I can fool them all. There was nothing beyond the view of his dark sunglasses. It narrowed to a tunnel leading directly to the door. He adopted a gentle firmness. A man going home. Moving his head just a little way first to the left, then to the right. Behind his masks he stayed on track for the door, but to those viewing it would look like acknowledgment. He was ignoring them and they didn't even know it. The babble of their questions were simply blocked-out -- he knew they would teeter and careen into the ridiculous, and answering them would only make it worse. *I will choose the manner of my confrontations. I allow no one to do it for me.*

The jostling didn't bother him. Nothing worse than the subway at rush hour. They were just doing their job. In the thick of it, he was overwhelmed with warmth. It felt like one big hug. *They want me!*

FOCUS. Only eight steps up, he pulled out his key, but the door opened by itself. The Professor. He said nothing. A few tried to follow him inside. Seth spoke: "No, sorry. Better watch your fingers. Oops, watch it. There we go."

Upstairs, the two walked in silence. Miles went up to the TV in the living room, screwed in the antenna, and clicked on the remote. The picture on Channel 7 showed its reporter on the street below, then replaying a length of tape showing Miles entering the townhouse, then to a picture of Paulie in the *Herald*. Miles sat and fixed his eyes upon the screen. "He home?"

"Negative. Some chick at the studio said he'd be back soon."

"So," Miles stood, slowly pulled off his bandanna and sunglasses, and ventured just close enough to the window to catch the scene below through the curtains, "I'm trapped."

CHAPTER SIXTEEN

Globe

Monday, October 30, 1995

1:00 AM. "You better stay there," the voice on the phone advised, followed by a click.

Miles had used the fax line -- listed in Seth's name -- to call his family and advise them to say nothing to any reporter, nor provide any photos. That wouldn't be difficult. Perhaps a total of five had been taken of him in the past ten years.

The beep of "Call Annoying" prompted Miles to thank his father again before switching to the new call. The background rumble, combined with the late hour indicated either a hospital or a police station. The voice, young, male and street-tough, sounded sincere.

"Mr. Kendrick. John Kendrick, please."

"I'm sorry, you must have the wrong number," Miles answered.

"Ya, right. Listen, you don' know me. I don' really know you. But I just got word from my -- from inside -- that the Feds don't have shit on you. They already did a search of your place and found nuthin'."

"Oh, without a search warrant?"

"Who says they didn', ya know? Figured they'd only flash it if anyone was home, but if not, why tip you off? The judge's --" There was an exchange of voices, male and female, then a muffling of the phone for over a minute, and a more hushed back and forth. Pure Southie accents. "Yeah, so I just wanted to tell you -- you better stay there."

"Why?"

"'Cause the Feds and that Barrell guy got the whole division so riled, I mean, you so much as walk through a red light, you're gettin' hauled in for life."

"Barrell?" So that's who was pushing this. "Great. Sure. Say, what's it to you, anyway?"

"Listen, we're like so far up shit creek if this gets out I might as well join ya in prison. But my -- we -- I saw -- I know, okay? Ya didn't do it, okay? I know. Anyway," he snorted, "you lived in Southie, right? I mean, they said it on the news, right?"

For nine long months. Back in the days of marriage and politics. Thirty thousand fourth-generation Irish in one neighborhood and not a single bookstore. "Yeah. Gotta love it."

Paulie wouldn't have any trouble not coming back tonight. Hell, what's a better excuse to remain with a model? "My roommate's suspected of murder. I -- we -- could stay here..."

Although the tip from the Southie Boy -- most likely tapped if not enough time to trace -- was interesting, it was nothing Miles hadn't heard already from his own family, Seth or THE PRIEST. Nobody from the FBI, Boston Police or even the gas company had stopped by -- strange, if he was such a wanted man. The call brought it all together. Barrell wants to pin this thing on me.

Money and power talked in Boston, the older the better. The Yankee power structure was still firmly in place, and, frankly, it reflected poorly on the city that this whole episode hadn't been wrapped up already, what with a suitable scapegoat and all. Tourism, a major industry in this historic town, might suffer if conventioneers from Des Moines and German tourists thought twice about this new "terror campaign."

Uncovering his stint at Pocasset was a piece of work, Miles had to admit. Must've done a search by social security number to find the Medicaid claim. That and some pretty heavy pressure on the hospital staff to release the records. 'Course, it was the only way the Feds could contrive a motive.

Nothing made sense, so try the nonsensical. That idea was what led Miles where he was in his own research. Too bad they had been coached by Barrell, or they might have taken it one step further. I'm not crazy. The whole world is. The cry of the schizophrenic. And that guy on the phone. He saw. He knew. What did he see?

FOCUS. DO WHAT YOU CAN WHILE YOU CAN. There was no sleep. All that was left for Miles, in his solitary confinement, were his books and his research.

Howay was a judge, and, to his discredit, wrote as such. To be charitable, his coming of age in the late Victorian and Edwardian eras, even in Canada, must have warped his point of view. Upright and unforgiving to failure, his prime importance was placed upon events, and not their context.

Pre-eminent in his field 150 years after history, Howay was able to compile the exhaustive lists of details other historians came to depend upon in their theses.

The damage he inflicted was almost irretrievable. *The fool!*

Judge Frederic W. Howay, the authority on the Northwest fur trade, splayed across Miles' living room floor. Lists of vessels that operated during the crucial opening years of 1783 and 1800, articles on "John Kendrick and his sons," "Later Affairs of Kendrick", and the now-infamous *Voyages of the Columbia* spread about, illuminated by the desk lamp placed in their center. At low volume, Mozart's Requiem played on the stereo, Miles having consulted the Professor's collection for music circa 1790.

The Canadian judge, writing in the 1920's and 30's, had been pretty harsh with John Kendrick. Old Captain K was simply not up to the task. At 47, his energy had been spent in privateering a decade earlier. The owners of *Columbia* and *Washington* found this out too late.

John Kendrick was a lazy, overly cautious and unambitious commander. Refusing to put on more sail, the expedition made a slow first leg of the voyage, from Boston to the Cape Verde Islands, in the fall of 1787. Then, Howay citing Captain Gray's letter to Joseph Barrell, Kendrick stayed over a month, where only five days were necessary. Before rounding Cape Horn, he proposed wintering on the treeless Falkland Islands, only to be overruled by his junior officers. In total, the passage from Boston the Coast took a ten days less than a year. Once at Nootka, Kendrick kept *Columbia* at anchor, sending its consort, *Washington*, to cruise the coast for furs, himself afraid to venture into unknown inlets in the larger vessel.

John Kendrick was a poor commander. At Cape Verde he alienated First Officer Simeon Woodruffe -- the only man in the whole expedition to have been to the Coast -- and the ship's surgeon, Doctor Roberts, losing both their valuable services not two months out of Boston. His indulgence of "the men" (the crew, rather than the officers) by generous rations of rum created a lackluster performance. He undermined the command structure with violent outbursts against his officers. Worst of all, he allowed Gray to take command of *Columbia*, the flagship of the expedition, so that *Washington* could continue to collect furs under Kendrick's personal command. Such actions defied all sense of the contemporary naval protocol.

Worst of all, John Kendrick failed in his duty to his employers. His slow trip from Boston to Nootka should have taken only eight months. Losing the entire fur-trading summer season of 1788, he was forced to winter over to await the next. He refused to send *Columbia* cruising the coast for furs, forcing Gray in the 90-ton *Washington* to fill the hold of her 220-ton flagship - - creating even more delay. No matter his feeble attempt to gather a few more furs into Washington by trading vessels with Gray at the end of the 1789 season.

Gray had sailed to China via Hawaii, and proceeded from the Portuguese trading colony at Macao up the Pearl River to Canton. Barrell's agent in China, Thomas Randall, told of recent Chinese prohibition on the importation of sea otter furs. Prices at Canton, the only port open to foreigners in China, were low since all trade was illicit. Gray bought the only cargo available for his small return, poor quality green tea. Word then arrived that Captain Kendrick had arrived at Macao and planned on coming up to Canton. Randall and Gray wisely counseled otherwise.

Gray returned *Columbia* to Boston in August of 1790, and told how he had tried to pay a visit to Captain Kendrick before leaving Macao, to advise him against selling the *Washington*'s cargo of furs at Canton. But a gale blew up in the harbor, making such a visit impractical, so *Columbia* continued on around the globe to New England.

Kendrick, after selling his furs, never returned. His letter to Barrell afterwards defended his actions, stating if Gray had stopped on his way out of Macao, "something handsome might have been sent you from me." Such a vague and empty promise was pitiful.

Selling his furs, Kendrick indulged his private fantasy of adding a second mast to *Washington*, converting it from a sloop to a brigantine. For two years he watched from his private house in Macao as the money ran out, then finally set sail for another cruise along the Coast in 1791. His flights of fancy took the form of an illegal stop in the closed nation of Japan. All for naught because, according to Kendrick, the Japanese "*knew not the use*" of furs, considering the wearing of dead animals barbaric.

Over the next three years Kendrick plied the Pacific fur trade, with the requisite stops in Hawaii for his own pleasure and indulgence, all the time sending *Washington* further and further into debt to creditors in China, fellow captains, and eventually his own clerk, John Howel. On the captain's death, Howel assumed command and ownership of *Washington*, eventually making an extensive accounting to Barrell of the debts attached to the brigantine.

The only return Barrell & Company ever saw on their investment in Kendrick and *Washington* were notarized copies of deeds to land in the Northwest, Howel explained might be worth something by the turn of the millennium. But all had been signed over to Kendrick personally.

Kendrick had even advanced most of his wages before leaving Boston in 1787, so the owners didn't even have the satisfaction of holding that sum for remuneration.

Judge Howay juxtaposed his portrayal of John Kendrick in contrast to his junior commander, Robert Gray. It was Gray who demanded they leave the Falklands immediately and 'round Cape Horn, rather than dawdling in the barren Falklands. When the two vessels became separated thereafter, Gray made great haste in *Washington* to Nootka, arriving a week before *Columbia*. When taking command of the larger ship, he again wasted little time in either China or Hawaii.

Upon his return to Boston, *Columbia* required only a month in the shipyards before heading back out for the second voyage. Gray was not only in command this time, but had risked his own money to become a full partner in the venture. A tight schedule and discipline were kept, a point of pride to show the difference from the first voyage's commander. *Columbia* stayed on the Coast long enough for one season of collecting furs, a subsequent winter at Clayoquot to construct a small sloop, *Adventure*, and then another season to again collect furs.

This was the historic voyage of *Columbia*. Gray headed south, first entering a wide harbor along the Washington coast -- Gray's Harbor, the crew naming it after their commander -- and eschewing the advice of Captain George Vancouver, proceeded across a treacherous bar into the mouth of what turned out to be the legendary "Great River of the West," named it after his ship -- Columbia's River -- and took possession of the surrounding lands for the United States by right of discovery.

A nice story.

It was 5:15 AM and Miles couldn't contain himself. The Coke and doughnuts had drenched his arteries with his drug of choice -- sugar -- and the anger just couldn't be limited to his chair. Pacing back and forth, it was maddening. *I've got to tell someone!* Reaching for the front door, he got as far as one foot across the threshold.

STOP. "WHERE ARE YOU GOING?" THE PRIEST asked out loud.

Damn! Damn! Damn! Nowhere. There was no *where* to go. Only a *when*. And that time was long past. The people involved had long since all died. No one cared.

I care. What's more, he knew in the mind of madness, someone else could care. It was hard to read Howay and not become slanted against Captain Kendrick. It was hard to know the rest of the story and not become angry with everyone else. Howay. Barrell. Gray...

Meredith. He had to succeed. The hands gripped at each side of the doorway as the tremors of rage hit. The old woodwork gave a bit of a groan, then quieted as the fury passed.

"Your grasp of history, now like your grasp of reality, is, at best, tenuous."

Miles coughed, looked across the kitchen table at Seth drinking his java, and replied: "I'm right."

"Look," Seth shifted in his chair, "we both know historians, especially amateurs from the turn of the century, probably did more harm than good by perpetuating myths and reinforcing stereotypes. But what you're claiming," he leaned forward, "is that Howay skewed the historic record so badly that some psychotic --"

"Paranoid schizophrenic," Miles corrected.

"Oh, yes, that's right," Seth smiled with a hint of bile, "I forgot. You're the expert on the subject." He opened his mouth to drive the point further, but caught Miles' round, open eyes and stopped. "Sorry. I'm sorry. That was out of line. You should have told me about Pocasset before this, though. It wouldn't have mattered."

"Then it wouldn't have mattered," Miles observed. "Besides, you were sailing around the Arctic with the Navy back then, and I needed to do something on my own, to show myself I still had some control --"

"A demonstration of power," the Professor murmured into his coffee cup.

Surprised only a second, Miles nodded firmly at the revelation. "Exactly."

It was a small door, just a wooden panel with two finger holes in it. Beyond was an iron door hinged to the brick foundation. Many houses on Beacon Hill were connected this way. Some had been built with the luxury of separate servants entrance next to the front door, and others interconnected with their neighbors.

As many of the finest houses were converted to condos and apartments, the servant's entrances, usually only four and one-half feet high, became the front door to basement apartments. But not too many people cared to investigate the door just off their building's laundry room -- that is, if the last contractor hadn't forgot to plaster it over.

Miles felt around the hinges. The re-wiring hadn't been started yet down here, so all was dark, save the tiny flashlight Seth aimed at the hole in the wall. It looked like a utility room. Miles crawled through the entrance, four feet off the floor, two feet high and two wide. As he felt around in the shadows with his feet, there seemed to be a ledge. He set his weight upon it and went tumbling down, twisting his ankle. "*God--!*"

QUIET. Flat on his back, in the dark, staring up at the light from the hole through which Seth frowned, Miles bit his lip. The bucket still held his right foot, twisted, and the slop had spilt out, drenching his back. CONTROL.

The rage was wordless. Quite carefully and quietly, he spoke. "Ow." Then, "I'm okay. Ow." He shook himself from the bucket -- *Let go of me!* -- and proceeded to take his backpack from Seth. "I'm-fine," said Miles. It was a lie.

The high-top hiking boots which normally protected his battered ankles were part of his old outfit -- the look that the media pinned on him. Today he wore his running shoes, and immediately paid for it. Without armor, you get stabbed.

"Call back at noon or...," Seth began.

Miles slipped the iron door closed, "Or what? Send out the Marines? I think they're the only one's not looking for me. Don't worry."

"Don't get caught."

The reporters had assembled again at 5:45 AM in preparation of the morning newscast. They'd been interviewing people in neighboring buildings -- all of whom jealously guarded their privacy.

From the maintenance room, he crossed the hall to the laundry room, finding another door in the wall, and so forth, until he was at the end of the block -- he figured. Anyway, that's where the door ended. Just a hop up the stairs -- the ankle was starting to swell, so he grabbed a pair of pantyhose out of a washer to improvise as an ace bandage -- and out the back door. He was safely outside.

Cold. Rain. The cobblestones and brick were slick, and the last of the fallen leaves brown and gooey, so he had to be careful. With his hair up in his baseball cap, olive slicker, khaki jeans and shirt, he resembled some sort of uniformed government worker -- not quite a National Parks ranger, nor the municipal sanitation worker (although the backpack worn underneath the slicker gave him a line-backer appearance). No matter -- he looked official, and thus, non-suspect. *I'm invisible.*

"Barrell, Bulfinch & Gray."

"Good morning. I'm calling from the *Dayton Daily News*, doing a follow-up on the bombing there. Can you confirm if the woman killed, Lotta Coolidge, ever worked for your firm?" The trick to not being cut off was saying it fast.

"Did you mean Meredith? She -- oh, hold on." The receptionist hadn't put him on hold, the standard practice, but was simply asking a passerby. "Uh-huh. Oh?" he heard her say. The other voice she had asked was distinct. "Sir?"

"Yes?"

"I'm sorry. Yes, Ms. Coolidge began her practice here upon graduation from Harvard School of Law in 1978."

"Under her father?" A shot in the dark.

"No." There was another conference. The other voice sounded quite low --

-- the Brahmin.

The receptionist came back. "No, her father died in 1975. She worked under the direction of Mr. Barrell. He's right here. Would you like to speak with him?"

"No," Miles' pitch was a little high. "No, no. Got all I need. Sorry to keep you." Miles ran from the phone as if it had turned into a tarantula, as if Barrell himself could crawl through the line, with an army of police carrying straightjackets. FEAR IS A HORRIBLE THING.

I'm not afraid.

"The first twenty minutes are free, then it's $3.00 an hour after that," the bored clerk had repeated the familiar script an hour ago, and pointed to a clipboard, "sign here."

The Professor's identity came in handy yet again. Miles had caught a glance at the morning's *Herald* at the sign-in desk, and this time it really was John Kendrick on the cover. Looked like a cross between a wrestling promoter and an outlaw biker. The hint of a grin didn't help. YOU LOOK INSANE.

That's not me. It didn't look like him. Maybe the nose and the mouth, but the camera flash had virtually defoliated all but the thickest of his chin hair. In reality, the beard was now filling in his cheeks, even covering the faint scar across his throat. The guy at the counter of the Massachusetts Vital Records Office hadn't given him a second look.

If he could figure the whole thing out, he could collect the reward money -- well, probably not the amount offered by Barrell -- and Meredith would be so grateful -- now there's a motivation.

A whirlwind of thought had sent him to the payphone. Too many familiar names related to each other. The greatest revelation of the morning was that Meredith was Barrell's niece. Of course, since she was his assistant, just like Lotta had been.

As he rested the writing tablet on the shelf, he scratched out a quick genealogy:

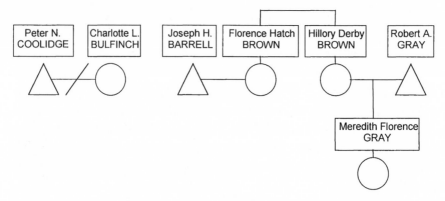

Lotta Bulfinch Coolidge, descendant of Charles Bulfinch, murdered by a bomb. Meredith Gray, descendant of Robert Gray, injured in the same explosion. John Meares, another descendant of a Kendrick tormentor, also dead.

Enemies. Mags' system was better. Sitting on the stairs of the emergency exit, he tore the names out of his genealogy and placed the pieces of paper on the floor. All he had to was find the connector.

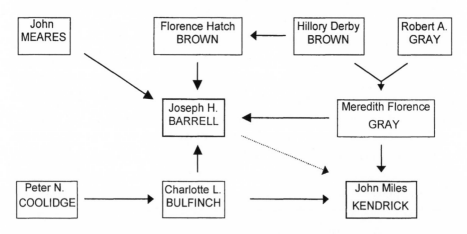

It wasn't that far of a shift from schizophrenic to *paranoid* schizophrenic.

Through *The Rogue*'s eyes, Miles imagined he'd see threats everywhere. Conspiracies. Add a dash of psychosis and you gave wing to the gulag of your mind. Any perceived slight or rejection is a wounding insult. Repressed, it festers. It didn't matter if the actions of others were disconnected -- a mind, the more brilliant, the more powerful and capable, could weave the most fantastic of plots arrayed against it. *I am powerful, as shown by the powerful plot against me.*

YOU'RE REACHING...

Like, Lotta thought she was better than the firm -- *Better than me. Hah! The only reason she was here was because her father never had any sons. He wasn't such a great jurist or senior partner here, himself. It's in the blood, though. Disloyal. Egotistical. Look all around this city. Everywhere. Building's with "Bulfinch" written on them. I can't stand it.*

YOU DON'T KNOW THAT. It was a guess, sure, but it fit. Meredith assumed the same role in Barrell's eyes. Gray would be the real villain as seen though his -- Barrell's Bostoner Kendrick -- eyes. And Meares? Oh, the name and lineage were perfect. His attitude was even consistent -- have the government pay the price for my misdeeds. It all connected to just one incident -- the bombing.

It seemed too big to be a first act of someone so committed. If Barrell were this Bostoner, he had let himself come precipitously close to his own destruction. If Miles hadn't asked for the chair, he and Barrell most likely would have been blown up, too. *Me.* The pretender.

Staying there himself was not just exhilarating for the Bostoner -- it was the classic cry for help, the need for self-destruction. *I know I'm bad and I can't help myself.* By asking for the help, Miles had allowed the Bostoner, the Barrell's dark side, to escape. *Fuck! I should have stayed.*

YOU'D ALSO BE DEAD.

But so would Barrell. The true key would be to find prior acts. There hadn't been any prior bombing in Boston or the case would be closed by now. Nor any series of multiple killings, he guessed. But what about people Barrell already knew somehow. Or had found. *It's in the blood.*

"You got a call. Some lawyer," said Seth's voice on the phone.

"Bill Connor?"

"Don't know. Maybe. Said he needs a plan picked up at the Suffolk Registry of Deeds. Guess he doesn't watch the news."

"He knows I need the money, God bless him," said Miles. "He's got faith. Probably an excuse to talk when I drop it on by his office. If he calls back, tell him I'll be there before one."

Miles still had two dollars left over as he walked down Atlantic Avenue and crossed the surface artery beneath the elevated Central Artery. Here in the shadows he was less conspicuous. *I'm invisible.*

YOU'RE LATE. He hoped whatever he was picking up for Connor & Vanzetti wasn't too time-sensitive. Forced to walk the back alleys and side streets, he came up behind their building -- Lotta's building -- but decided at last not to step in. It was the one sure place he'd be recognized.

The guards. The building super. Jennifer?

From this angle on the street, he could pick out the windows of Lotta's office. All dark. How sad. Something could have developed with Jennifer, but then he became so caught up in this case... and now couldn't even call her because the office was closed and his home phone tapped. He found he had stopped in the middle of the square. *They'll spot me.*

YOU HAVE DONE NOTHING WRONG.

That doesn't matter. They all want to kill me.

Kill?

Kill... no, that wasn't quite right. Arrest, yes. But *kill?* Where did that come from?

The Commonwealth Library in the Massachusetts State House still was in desperate need of renovation. Back in the Dukakis administration the plan to repaint the ceiling began with chipping away the old layers. But when ornate designs were discovered on the original surface, all work had stopped for lack of funds for their tedious preservation. Only a small rectangle of the brown ceiling showed a faint golf fleur-de-lis against a blue background.

Avoiding the marble steps, Miles had taken the elevators from the sub-basement at the rear of the building near Hancock Street -- chancing a walk past the State Police office -- up to the fourth floor for a simple purpose. *The Boston Globe* on microfilm.

January 2, 1993. Poor Simon Woodruffe. Miles found his obituary pretty quick. There was no need to check genealogies anymore. Miles had faith in the Bostoner's research. Age at death: 72. Cause: Hypothermia. Place: Boston Harbor.

The newspaper told him something more -- Woodruffe was a quiet man. A caretaker of old lighthouses. No family to speak of, but there was a picture of him there on the New England section of the Sunday *Globe.* Taken just a week before the Christmas party for the Chelsea Sailors Home, helping to shovel snow, God bless him.

Woodruffe had been found floating in a rowboat beyond Boston Light, naked and frozen to death, New Year's Day. Authorities guessed the old sailor had indulged a wee too much, and decided to face the elements by borrowing a longboat from the Charlestown Navy Yard.

Winter 1993. Miles remembered that winter. The cold blasted in right after Christmas and kept the region in near-zero temperatures for weeks on end. It had been *evil*. Boston Harbor had nearly frozen shut, save for the work of the Coast Guard ice breakers.

Salt water can freeze at 28° but, with tides and currents, doesn't like to unless it's much colder. In short, old Simon Woodruffe needed more than liquor to get him out into the water, and more help than the weak currents of Boston Harbor. God, what a horrible way to die, especially when you're old.

The only other names of potential targets of the Bostoner's vengeance were John Kendrick, Jr. and Doctor Roberts. It wasn't a stretch to imagine Junior's historical slight to his father -- abandonment at Nootka for the Spanish. But there was no need to check the *Globe* index this time. *I am John Kendrick.*

In the Bostoner's eyes, Miles was a boy. Young enough. Could be the man's son. And Miles had spurned his offer of employment before and after the explosion. Not much more damaging to an ego than rejection. No wonder Barrell was throttling the Feds to pin it on Miles.

Roberts -- jeez, what a name. No first name, either. There were hundreds just in the obituary sections of the last year alone, but he narrowed it down. First, it probably took place in Boston. Second, it was probably male, Lotta and Meredith not withstanding. Third, the name would be like those 200 years ago -- John, Joseph, or Daniel, not Brandon or Mustafa.

Before leaving the Vital Records Office, Miles had checked for the name "Roberts". Four of the men were black. Didn't quite fit the picture of the same doctor in the late eighteenth century. Only three were doctors. One died of cardiac arrest at his home. The other from lung cancer -- a doctor. Nice work.

The last led Miles to an article on page one of the second section of the *Globe* for May 5, 1994.

Doctor Stabbed Outside Clinic
Police seek Pro-Life Connection

Funny thing, Samuel Roberts was killed in Lawrence, an old industrial city twenty-five miles north of Boston. But his residence was a condo in Charlestown. Semi-retired, the doctor worked one day a week at Planned Parenthood, helping with family planning counseling to immigrants from Southeast Asia and Central America. Crime was no stranger to those streets, but Lawrence Police found no cash missing from his wallet and his car door ajar -- miracle of miracles.

That's when attention turned to anti-abortion forces -- especially after a couple calls to local talk radio shows hinted *"he got what he deserved."* Stabbing an unsuspecting abortionist, to the Lawrence Police, was a lot more symbolic than the now-traditional shooting. And precisely why Miles knew it didn't work out so simply.

Arthur

There was one other way into the Suffolk County Courthouse. Off the front entrance a door leads down to the Office of the Docket Clerk. Just inside the wall he passed the bored guard at the desk. "Where you going?" she asked.

"Upstairs," he pulled an old docket sheet from his slicker, "they said in the Docket Room I gotta go back up to the first floor to pay for this."

"Oh. Okay, go ahead."

The beauty of the Suffolk County Courthouse was its complete disconnection with any sort of efficiency. Look at a court case on the first floor. Get a copy of its docket in the basement. Pay for it back on the first. To understand and avoid security, you had to understand how this building functioned, and that pretty much assumed you belonged there anyway. *Or in the nuthouse.*

Marble steps. Painful. The short walk just a block from the State House included many steps of densely-formed natural rock -- granite, marble, slate. The stairwells of Suffolk were extremely horrible since they curved, so that going up, all pressure was placed on a small area around the toes. On his right ankle. YOU SHOULD HAVE TAKEN THE OTHER STAIRWAY. THOSE STEPS GO IN THE REVERSE DIRECTION.

Too far. I'm here now.

Ow. One step at a time. These were late nineteenth-century stories: twenty foot ceilings. The Plan Room at Registry of Deeds was on the fifth floor, and the second floor had a mezzanine level as well.

Ow. Halfway up the third, he rested. Nobody *ever* took the stairs. The curving staircase meant constant vigilance for the person descending, especially near the windows. Looking down onto the paved courtyard at the center of the courthouse on the basement level, several Cadillacs and Lincolns, belonging to judges and various Registrars of Deeds, Probate and Indifference, beckoned to Miles through the thin, tall window adjacent to the steps.

Today, being rainy, some genius had decided it was also going to be cold, and so turned the furnace on. The stairways acted like a giant heat shaft, and combined with his lack of sleep, swollen ankle and persistent cough, began to make Miles feel dizzy. The windows easily lifted up and he stuck his head out. A hundred feet up, he guessed. Nice drop onto a car hood. *If I angle my neck just right --*

WAKE UP. The fresh oxygen in his blood hit his brain. Better. He started up the stairs again, but stopped at the fourth floor. An actual wooden phone booth existed on this floor. It was another break from spiraling up those marble steps, too.

"Peabody Essex Library."

"Yes, is Mags there, please?"

The voice of the man on the other end of the line hesitated and wavered. "I'm sorry, who do you want?"

Oh, right, he realized. "Margaret Skinner. Is she there today?"

"Who?"

"Mags. The Assistant Curator? Is she not in?"

The man was unsteady. "I-I'm sorry, we have curators here, but I don't recall anyone here by that name. Perhaps if you left your name, and number --"

"NO. Listen, I know she works there. I saw her last Wednesday night. Tall, blond, kinda self-conscious... are you new there?"

There was a pause, then a very controlled length of speech. "I'm the Curator, and I know who works here and who doesn't, sir. I don't know what you think or who you spoke to, but you have the wrong place and wrong person. Good-bye."

The line went dead.

? -- Miles stared at the phone, its dial tone shocking him as much as the conversation. Was it a different part of the library? ARE YOU SURE?

Yes, I'm sure! I brought her there in the first place! What the fuck!?! He reached to dial the number again.

YOU BETTER MAKE SURE. He stopped, called directory

assistance, and confirmed the library's number and address. It was right.

Stupid priest -- don't second-guess me! Maybe it was Tuesday night. Maybe it was a new Curator, and he resented Miles' impertinence. Maybe he didn't like Mags, and this was academic jealousy...

The options flew like arrows out of the darkness of his mind as he walked to the stairwell. The fourth floor had been designed like a camel's hump, and so required him to go down six steps to get to the stairwell. But he wanted to go up one more flight to the fifth. He had earned those six steps already, and didn't want to pay for them again. DON'T BE LAZY.

Stupid priest. I'm in pain. Does it make any sense to make it worse? There was the back staircase on the far end of the Registered Land Office on this floor, just behind him. It was a longer walk, but no steps.

As he cantered along through Registered Land, his mind was distracted from the pain of every other step. Maybe Mags got fired. Maybe she was supposed to be working late that night. Maybe... *I'm right.*

"ANDREW MACINNIS -- LINE ONE. ANDREW MACINNIS," the P.A. beckoned a title examiner to one of the public phone lines.

The middle-aged, rotund man in suspenders and bow tie was seated at his desk in the Plan Room, just off the far end of the great hall holding the Registry of Deeds. Making an entrance from the adjacent fire stairs, Miles simply turned the corner and winced a smirk.

"What can I do for you, sir?" the clerk tapped his fingers on the desk as if it were a piano.

"I've been told," Miles began, "that I'm to pick up a plan for Connor & Vanzetti."

The man looked beyond Miles, out into the Registry, and held up one finger. "One moment, Cynthia, my dear."

"It can wait, Jack," came the response behind Miles.

Jack lowered his glasses from his silver coif and check about his desk. "Hmmm. Nope. You say it was a plan? Did you order it, or was it called in?" Getting up, he walked over to a file cabinet.

"JENNIFER CHASE -- LINE ONE. JEN CHASE."

Miles propped himself up against the door. "Sorry. Don't know. I was just told to stop by. Figured it was supposed to be ready an hour ago."

Jack sorted through the tubes of rolled paper on his desk. "Huh, nuthin' here. Say, maybe it's under your name. Ya think?"

No, that would be stupid. "I doubt it. It was ordered before they knew I could get it."

"Even so..."

"Okay. 'Seth Jones.' Anything?"

Jack looked again. "Nope... Nope... Bernstein... Ropes & Gray... Nope... Kendrick -- naw, that's something else..."

!

"... Sherburne, Powers & Needham... Nope. Connolly -- Connolly?" He looked up.

"Connor," Miles said, preoccupied by the mention of the name Kendrick.

Jack flipped them back down again. "Sorry, sir. Are you sure it was here a Recorded Land, and not downstairs at Registered Land?"

Kendrick. The name still resonated in his head. From what Miles could see, it wasn't a plan, but an envelope on Jack's desk. This man didn't know Miles to be a Kendrick, never mind *the* Kendrick whose face adorned the cover of Jack's *Herald* open -- thank God -- to the sports section.

Still, there were other people in the world named Kendrick. "Maybe it is downstairs. Sorry to disturb you."

What the hell!? The least Bill could have done was to say it was down on the fourth floor. The prospect of facing the stairs, after climbing that extra flight for nothing, only raised his growing fever. The rain coat was unbreathable, trapping heat, and he could feel the unmistakable trickling of sweat from his armpits down his ribs, and the prickliness building from the base of his spine up to the back of his neck. He was at the payphones in the center of the Registry of Deeds before he knew it. CALL.

Shedding his raincoat and cap on a nearby chair, he slumped into the old wooden booth and slid the door closed. Rest.

"ATTORNEY ZWEIMAN, LINE TWO. ATTORNEY ZWEIMAN."

It was good to sit, finally, although his legs were curled up like a pretzel in the tiny space. His injured ankle, favored when he was standing, was now pinched against the door. He retrieved a dime out of his pocket.

Nothing. Both Bill and Frankie were not only out of the office, but in court here in Suffolk. Why would they pay Miles to pick up something they could easily retrieve themselves? Fucking waste of time. It wasn't that much out of the way from home, though. Just those stairs...

GO HOME. ICE YOUR ANKLE. YOU'RE NO GOOD CRIPPLED. Miles grabbed the payphone to haul himself up and stopped before cracking the door. Another dime into the phone.

"Suffolk Registry."

"Plan Room, please." Miles looked out the glass of the booth door, and saw Jack answer his desk phone.

"Plan Room."

"Hello, I'm calling from Brooke, Bradley & Kendrick. Is there an envelope there for Mr. Kendrick?"

"Hold on --" Jack went immediately over to his file cabinet, stopped, and picked the letter off his desk. "Yes, here it is."

"I'm terribly sorry to bother you, but can you tell me who it's from?"

"Well, I don't see any return address."

"I don't suppose you can open it?"

"No, I'm sorry. Maybe you should send a courier over to get it. It was here when I came back from lunch."

"You're right --"

"JOHN KENDRICK, LINE ONE. JOHN KENDRICK."

"Oh," Jack leaned forward, "they're paging your guy now. It's John Kendrick, right? That's what this envelope reads. Is he here?"

"No. He's in Europe. Thank you anyway. We'll send someone over."

Who the fuck is paging me?

His name blaring over the P.A., what with all the press of late, was bound to attract attention in the hall. He began to feel conspicuous, despite his "disguise" and despite the shielding wooden box of a telephone booth. He waited for another five minutes, then nonchalantly opened the door and easily made his way through the broad tables, cases of deed books, and scurrying examiners, to the plan room. PAIN IS SIMPLY AN INDICATOR. YOU CAN OVERCOME IT.

My body is simply a tool -- despite the pain. It receded into just a red blinking light in the control room of his brain.

Jack looked up. "Any luck?"

"Naw," Miles shook his head, "but I got a page telling me to pick up something from Brooke, Bradley & Kendrick."

Jack's eyes went up, "Oh yeah." He handed the thin gold envelope to Miles. "Hey, could you tell the front desk to stop paging this Kendrick guy? Guess he's outta town, and they've been calling him for the past hour."

Shit. Miles tucked the envelope in his slicker. He nodded, "Sure," and brushed by the center bookcase heading to the front desk in the heart of the great hall. At the end of the bookcase, Miles was about to turn to approach the front desk when he saw Arthur Lewis there. Miles spun around behind the bookcase and made his way back to the Plan Room.

"JOHN KENDRICK, LINE ONE. JOHN KENDRICK."

Jack caught his eye. Miles shook his head. The two men in the doorway at the Plan Room turned around. He could see Jack had just said something like: "The fella just left --" YOU'RE NOT INVISIBLE.

I know these guys -- how? They were big. Not taller than him, but broader. One maybe forty at most, the other maybe half that. They were dressed better than Miles, the older in a barn coat over a Greek sweater; the younger, a Bruins jacket and yellow silk shirt. Dark pants. Curly hair, although the older's had gone half-gray. They didn't smile. They didn't frown. They simply walked toward Miles. One on each side of the central bookcase.

RUN.

They can't hurt me here. Miles was already turning when he bumped into one of the shelving clerks, and knocked his cart sideways into the aisle. "Hey!" the clerk yelled.

"Sorry." The cart wouldn't move out of his way. *Dammit!* It wheels jammed in different directions, Miles pushed futilely against the cart. The older man was but five yards away now. His direct expression hadn't changed.

"Hold it," the clerk complained, trying to straighten the cart, "you have to pull it towards you --"

GO.

"Get out of my way."

"What?"

"NOW." Miles pushed the cart over, spilling its contents down onto the clerk--

"Wha-?"

-- and launched himself out of the gate on its frame. With enough momentum --

By the time Miles reached the end of the bookcase, he had met the younger tough, and veered right, leaping up onto the nearest examiner's table. Cap flying off his head, momentum propelled him onto the next table. In the corner of his eye he caught Arthur saying something. No sound was coming in, though.

Leaps from table to table to table to table -- all four feet apart -- the force propelled him. The exit at the far corner, his focus. Lucky not to hit any examiners, their papers went flying. Stopping would be the problem, and some guy just stepped out from --

Shit. Another one.

On the slope of the last table, Miles' weak ankle caught the plastic cover of an open deed book. His feet flew out from under him, and he went sliding down at the door in a tuck-and-roll. If Miles had been any heavier, the force would have broken at least one of the guy's shins. As it was, Miles' cannonball sent the big man face down on top of him.

GET AWAY FROM HERE. This new guy in a blue jacket was resilient, having already wrapped his meaty hands around the rain slicker. But Miles was already on his feet while the guy on the floor held onto the slicker like a leash. The sight of Arthur & company changed Miles' mind. He jammed his foot down onto the guy's wrist, wriggled free of the coat and ran into the maze of side corridors to the fire stairs.

After what sounded like a fleet of buses passed by, Miles emerged from the women's cloak room, backpack still in hand. Arthur met him at the top of the stairs.

"Arthur, I'm sorry --"

There was blood in Arthur's eyes. Miles rebounded against the opposing wall. The springboard effect sent him backwards into Arthur, and they went flying down the long flight of concrete stairs.

"Oh! You bastard!" Arthur clutched at his shoulder. The landing was only halfway down, but it was enough for Miles. He had caught his cheek on the last few steps, but was able to evade Arthur's weak grasp from the floor. Not so, Blue Jacket flying up the stairs.

Miles never was a brawler. Nor a fighter. He knew one punch was usually the length of most fights, so he evaded. DON'T LET HIM HIT YOU. USE YOUR OWN STRENGTHS. Here in this confined stairwell, there wasn't much for a praying mantis like Miles to do against this bunch of beetles. The crash against the railing in front of the window would've knocked the wind out of Miles if he hadn't been unconsciously holding his breath.

Gripping onto the railing behind him, he allowed Blue Jacket to push his chest forward, and feeling the balance shift, gave a hard shove against the wall in back with one foot. Blue Jacket, balance lost, staggered back, and almost recovered -- if Arthur hadn't tried to get up. As it was, a backwards trip followed by Miles' head-butt to the chest sent Blue Jacket crashing through the window.

WHAT ARE YOU DOING?

Arthur rolled over, "Huh?" with enough time to see his man rolling six feet below on the asphalt causeway between new and old courthouses.

Down.

Miles grasped the handrails of the stairs, taking a dozen stairs in one swing.

Fourth floor. Where can I go? He shot out the door. Registered Land Plan

Room. The main hall to his left was clear. As he ascended the marble steps to the middle of the camel's hump of the floor, he began to slow. The pain in his ankle was back. *I can ignore the pain.*

BUT PAIN IS A WARNING. It was tightening up. It simply wasn't working right. Turning around, he caught the side staircase with its narrow circular stairs. Easier to go down. More people on the third floor.

The steps became treacherous hops. Twenty of them. He could see the hall below crawling with bailiffs, cops, defendants and their lawyers. Good. Out of the stairwell doors, down the hall and onto the mezzanine, he almost ran for the elevators.

No -- no enclosed spaces. Just as the doors opened, he saw the Bruins jacket, and dashed down the mezzanine. The crowd of people entering the elevator slowed his pursuer, and Miles had time to duck around the corner. Ignoring the back staircase, he went straight down the narrow side hallway to the men's room. Dead end. It was tiny. One open stall. No urinal. No lock. *Fuck!* But the ceiling over the toilet reached up pretty high. Old, dark paneling leading up ten feet to -- windows! It was a vent.

The kid in the Bruins jacket burst into the bathroom just as Miles found that the hinges up there opened only so far. Braced against the walls of the cupola, Miles almost fell backwards down into the toilet as he threw his feet into the frosted glass.

The kid's ferocious grab at the straps of the backpack only yielded the tails of Miles' khaki shirt. He landed on the porcelain below with a thud and a crash. Miles rolled out onto the asphalt of the roof, scraping the exposed skin of his lower back. Back up on the causeway, he looked up to see an old foe. "Oh no," he groaned at Blue Jacket, now leering for an impromptu rematch. *Why the hell am I back up here?*

Behind Miles were the broken windows of the fourth floor of the "new" courthouse, none of which were open on this cold, rainy day. The only window to the old courthouse was blocked by Arthur. And his approaching friend. Miles backed up to the vent, and heard the kid trying to jump up again. Staying away from the exposed side, he edged around it, trying to keep the cupola between him and Blue Jacket. All this time, they were saying something, but the words didn't register. Or were irrelevant.

Dodging back and forth around the vent was ridiculous. Eventually someone in the offices would notice. Unless they weren't looking. The windows were either filthy or filled with air conditioners. THERE IS NO HELP FOR YOU.

On the opposite side, he could see Blue Jacket disappear. The words

"Give me your hand," came through sharply.

He's ignoring me! He actually thinks I'm such a little threat he can help the kid up! Two against one. That's not fair. *Fine --*

Miles swung himself around the cupola as the kid was halfway out, and dropped himself on Blue Jacket. The kid went flying down into the toilet again. Blue Jacket grabbed Miles and threw him face down onto the asphalt. The man grabbed around under Miles to trap a wrist, but Miles had clenched them both together under his chest. Miles rolled away from the grasp until he felt his head get jerked back violently.

"Ah--!" his mouth flew open. Every muscle from his shoulders up the back of skull froze in place. They all seemed to terminate in the strands of hair the guy had gripped. YOUR VAIN PONYTAIL.

"Let-go-of-my-hair."

The response was a laugh, which Miles thought very unprofessional, just before his face slammed into the asphalt. A quick blast of white, a spot of light in the dark cleared enough for him to feel broad, dull pain around his mouth turn into a sharp sting around his lower lip, and to notice the roof rush up at him again. And again.

TAKE IT IN THE FOREHEAD. He leaned forward. He could feel the grit, stone and tar tear away at his eyebrows, and become embedded in his skin. Brain cells, he could lose. Teeth and blood, no. One more, and through the dizziness Miles was getting angry. What was the point of this?

To kill me and leave me up here on the roof of the courthouse? Is Arthur that stupid? Or that angry? These men were stupid. They weren't even men. They were animals dressed up in clothes.

YOU ARE SOMETHING MORE.

They're wasting my time. As Blue Jacket wound up for his next hit, Miles drew up on his knees, and threw himself backward. Blue Jacket surged forward, and Miles caught the man's teeth in the back of the skull. Ow.

Miles tumbled up onto his feet, swung the backpack around like a centrifuge, and landed knees-first on Blue Jacket's shoulder blades. If there was a yell, Miles didn't hear. He was already up and at the window on the near side of the roof.

The office was dark, and someone had left the window ajar, probably during summer. Stepping into the murk, he turned to glower at Arthur -- *How dare you!* -- but Arthur was gone.

Out of this office, and onto the fifth floor of the new courthouse, Miles knew he was a mess. He could taste the blood on his lip, which felt like it had swollen up to cover his top teeth. He brushed his forehead for blood, but only asphalt came down in a shower on the floor. It was embedded in his scalp, too.

As he headed down the staircase, he began to fume again. No sleep. No food. Bad lungs. Bad ankle. Walking all over town. Mags not being where he *knew* she was supposed to be. Sprinting across desks. Getting beat up. It was getting to be too much.

Even the hops down each step were fraught with danger. Not for four more flights. At the bottom of the this stairwell were a lobby full of guards who would be mighty curious about his messed-up face -- if they hadn't been alerted to the disturbance at the Registry already.

He got off at the -- what? -- fourth floor. What floor was it? What day was it? Monday? Tuesday? It wasn't Sunday, he thought as he tagged behind a crowd of what must have been family of a defendant on their way back into the old courthouse, too confused and self-involved to notice him just behind.

As they approached the courtroom, Miles jumped into the court clerk's office, and down the stairs he knew led to the judges' chambers. On the third floor – no -- second mezzanine level he emerged into the hall and calmly passed down the hall to the back stairs. That draft was from the tatters of his shirt, and he attempted to tuck in what was left.

JUST GET TO AN UNGUARDED EXIT. The south staircase led to the Superior Court's old files and certain smaller courtrooms. The stairs were dirty and dark, but wider, and Miles felt more comfortable hippedy-hopping down them. At the bottom, in the basement, he found an empty hallway. To the left, six stairs led up to the main entrance. No. But he could head back down the hallway to -- an alarmed door. *Let me out!*

NO.

He lurched at the handle. ALARM WILL SOUND, it read.

I gotta get outta here. The cold steel of the handle didn't give way immediately. No play in it.

DON'T GET CAUGHT.

Shit.

Back at the base of the steps up, a door marked "AUTHORIZED ACCESS ONLY" swung aside as a middle-aged well-dressed woman emerged from the door. She looked behind her, and held the door for a moment, then shrugged and let it shut. Miles grabbed the edge of the door before it closed. WAIT.

Somebody's waiting for me on the other side of this door. How dare they! Miles swung the door open wide and jumped back. Nothing. He peeked around the corner. Nothing. The stairs led down to the garage and courtyards through a set of doors.

DON'T BE PARANOID. JUST GET OUT OF HERE QUICKLY AND QUIETLY. Quickly. Hop. And quietly. Hop. Quick. Hop. Quiet. Hop. The door closed behind him. Quickly. Hop. Quietly. Hop. Halfway down the stairs the shadow moved at the top of the stairs.

The man in the barn coat. He reached into his pocket.

Hippedy. Quickly.

He can't have a gun.

Hoppity. Quietly --

Oh, fuck that.

Hippedy.

Miles saw the man start down the stairs, pulling out something small and dark.

Six stairs left, Miles jumped. Hoppity.

The overhead light fixture held for all of two seconds, which was about three seconds longer than Miles thought, but one more than he needed. Wrapping himself up in the pipes and rafters, he saw the lamp spark and crackle to blackness.

Through the windows of the garage some light seeped through. Miles could see the man just below him on the stairs, looking up. Another few seconds and Barn Coat would see into the rafters. The backpack caught him on the back of the head, the force of the deed books inside sending Barn Coat sailing down the steps to the granite landing below. Without the burden grabbed off the Registry cart, Miles moved more nimbly.

Barn Coat had landed on all fours, saving his face, but killing his knees. The impact of 175 pounds of human dropped from ten feet sent all four limbs out from under him. Miles wasn't much, but dead weight is still dead weight.

Miles peered out into the garage. The entrance beyond the courtyard held a transport van and some State Police. *No, not quite.*

Stamping on the wrist that still held what appeared to be a blackjack -- lead weight wrapped in leather with a short handle -- Miles retrieved the weapon and threw it into the driveway. Up the stairs, he scowled at the prone figure beneath him -- "SHAME ON YOU," -- and let the door close behind him.

How dare they! More indignant than frightened or angry, Miles headed down the hall to the alarmed door. *"How dare they!"* he repeated.

ALARM WILL SOUND. He glared at the door, the street painfully close through the glass. *"Fine,"* he sneered, and shoved the door.

Nothing happened.

"Nice fuckin' safe courthouse," he muttered, emerging onto the brick steps below the One Beacon Street office tower. He shook his head again, stopped, took the books out of his backpack and placed them next to a concrete planter.

"How dare they," he repeated as he limped purposely back over Beacon Hill.

"Salathiel."

The barrel of the 9mm was a wholly unfamiliar sight for Miles. More so upon entering his own home. Having violently ignored the traffic, pedestrians and camera crews set up for God-knows-what on the State House front steps along Beacon Street, Miles had re-entered the building on the corner of Walnut and Mount Vernon Streets. Perfect timing. *Oh, yes, very funny. Joke's on me again.*

Heaving through one laundry room after another, focusing only on the lusciously cold ice bath awaiting his ankle, Miles was more than a little surprised to see the Professor waiting at the their building's hole upon returning. With a gun.

But after he lifted himself back into his own cellar with one hand from Seth, Miles began to laugh. *Oh, yes. Too perfect. But who to my wondering eyes should appear --*

Arthur Lewis.

"Kendrick, may I introduce you to our new landlord --," Seth began, clicking the safety on his pistol.

"Huh," Miles rubbed his forehead, and as a few asphalt remnants crumbled out, "heh, heh. Yes," he laughed and shook his head, "Oh, yeah." Too perfect. He lifted himself onto the washer. "Talk."

Arthur opened his mouth, "I --," but Miles cut him off, pointing to Seth.

"You first, sir."

Seth's realization began to gel. "Aaaaoohh," and holding the butt towards Arthur, said, "Got another call on the fax line after you did, from the same guy wondering about that pickup at the Registry, and gave him the message about you being there at 1:00. Then at 1:15 he called again, really anxious about you showing up, and got very cagey when I asked for his name. What did you say -- Monahan?"

Arthur shrugged, mumbling something, finishing off with an attempt at a smile.

"So I set up a vigil down here in case you popped up again. And he comes through there," Seth pointed to the rear cellar door, "which *you* said was always locked. And have a gander at this --"

It was the envelope from Miles' lost rain slicker. The paper inside was a familiar shape. Legal-size photocopy folded four times. The gothic lettering spelled "Quitclaim Deed," and below the typewritten words: "Edmund F. Burgess to Arthur P. Lewis, Trustee." The date read October 17, 1995. The day of the bombing. Funny. Life was playing a great big joke on Miles.

"I'm... I'm *very* tired," Miles closed his eyes and began to slowly rock back and forth to the rhythm of his own pulse. "Arthur, your keys, please."

"What? Hey, I own this --"

Miles opened his eyes wide. "Arthur!"

Arthur stopped, half a sentence still dangling from his mouth.

Drawing his legs up onto the washer painfully, Miles continued in a low voice, "I understand." He drew in a breath for strength. "I understand everything."

"You *are* nuts," Arthur's eyes grew round.

One of Miles' eyebrows lifted, then settled down to a placid face. He continued. "I understand you own this building -- your new gallery and warehouse? I understand you had no idea of who lived here. Probably the former owner told you about our little agreement, but not our names specifically. Otherwise you would have paid us a visit a little sooner, correct? Or your friends? Very convenient to use your construction crew to pick me up -- they couldn't get any work done in the building, anyway, what with all the news people. But you didn't even know about me until you saw the news, huh?"

Arthur nodded, "Yeah."

"I also understand you are concerned about something. About my former client. You are upset because I was not entirely above-board with you on a customer level. For that all I can do is repeat what I said a little while ago -- I'm sorry. I honestly enjoyed talking with you. You're a nice guy. But please don't squawk at me when you're caught with your hand in the cookie jar."

"You're just a weasel. A sneak out for your own --"

"I SEEK THE TRUTH!" Miles jumped down off the washer, "and that is all. It's people like you who fuck up the whole system, by eating the corners off of everything and excuse it by saying 'It won't be missed,' or 'Everybody does it.' Well, take comfort in this: If you behaved yourself, I'd be makin' an honest ten bucks an hour diggin' ditches in the rain!"

The Professor looked up at Miles with an Are-you-done-yet? expression, and cleared his throat. Arthur shifted his eyes to the pistol. Miles sat back down on the washer. "Sorry. Well, as I said, I understand. I understand you wouldn't have pulled such a ridiculous stunt at the courthouse just now if you weren't truly desperate. You're scared, Arthur, aren't you?"

Silence for a moment. The tension in Miles was tremendous. The adrenaline was still pumping in him, but it was all in his brain now, firing all twelve cylinders. It was a gamble. *I'm right. I know it.*

Arthur blinked once. Recognition. Understanding. "Listen, you don't know," Arthur said, "I got a business -- a family. I didn't blow up anybody. I can handle the money for the lawsuit, but I'm not going to jail."

Miles grinned broadly, "You won't if I don't," and held a finger to his lips. "Keys, please."

CHAPTER SEVENTEEN

Constitution

Tuesday, October 31, 1995

Sleep had brought him from early afternoon to early morning. On the street, Miles saw the reporters had withdrawn from their stoop-side vigil. Even so, there were a few unfamiliar cars, bespeckled with bright orange parking tickets. The die-hards. The hungry. Desperate enough to spend the night alone in a car, window cracked open to let out the exhaled smoke. Afraid to leave for fear of missing their one chance.

A fever had woken Miles with a leather tongue. He laughed to himself as he drew aside the curtain. Come! *Here's your chance -- look at me!*

Nothing.

Propped against the sill, he elevated his ankle to keep the bloodflow to a minimum. The ice packs from earlier in the day were now just so many wet rags. The swelling had rendered the end of his right leg a single immobile unit. Black and blue traveled up his shin, but it was the yellow fringe around it all that bothered him.

From the comfort of his bay window, he heaved up his copy of Howay's *Voyages of the Columbia*. Eight hours regeneration complete, his racing mind demanded -- *Data. I need more data.*

It looked raw outside. Couldn't be comfortable. A man outside. All night. All alone.

Porto da Praia Bay, Cape Verde Islands
December 8th, 1787

"Still alive, I see."

"You needn't have done so, sir," the grayed and sawed-off *former*

First Officer tried to hold himself erect before the Commander's table. The smell of the fresh eggs and bacon drew water to his eyes. No food, save for what scraps the young Third -- no, Second -- Officer, Robert Haswell, had smuggled to him since the forenoon watch. Then this charade began.

"I have lost faith," Captain John Kendrick said between bites, "the men so, too." He was a bear of a man. Seated, he was as tall as Simeon Woodruffe was standing before him. On board ship, the average crewman measured only 5'9" -- even better for this former gunner's mate, Woodruffe, for dodging below decks. And yet this behemoth seated before him troubled with the minutest details down below -- a place a captain had no business being.

Woodruffe began, "The officers --"

"Are under my command!" the Commander pounded the table with a ham-sized fist, the pewter plates and flatware jumping up for a moment. "My command. My mission. My responsibility. You, Woodruffe," not dignifying him with an officer's title of *Mister*, "failed me."

Water casks. This was all about the wretched water casks. As First Officer, Woodruffe's duty was to oversee the placement of cargo and provisions before *Columbia* had left Boston. After six weeks of sailing, too long from his experience, the drinking water in the hold had predictably begun to turn rancid, and the Commander ordered them refilled on shore here at Cape Verde. It was then he learned that the casks had been placed in the further depths of the hold. Removing them meant removing the entire contents onto the shore.

Woodruffe strained to remain respectful. "You should have allowed more sail to be used in crossing the Atlantic. Using but one mast when three avail you on this ship --"

"-- Is my decision," the Commander growled. He hated having been driven to anger by this man. But it was the last straw. By virtue of Woodruffe's voyage with Captain Cook , he was appointed second-in-command of *Columbia*, and thus, second in line, after Captain Gray in *Washington*, of this whole expedition. Without that precious piece of experience, the former First Officer was no more than a tired, old sailor. It was the new First Officer, Joseph Ingraham, who had read an illicit account of Captain Cook's travels, and found no mention of an *officer* by the name of Woodruffe -- exposing the man as a fraud not two days ago.

Regardless, the Commander found his contemporary of little use at sea.

At age twenty Kendrick had led long boats from whaleships crewed by Inuit, American Indians and Africans off Greenland -- years before Woodruffe could dream of powdering Captain Cook's cannon. This runt knew little of the weather cycle of the North Atlantic during the hurricane season. Being dismasted by carrying too much canvas would doom the voyage to the Northwest before it even began. "I carry as much or as little sail as I see fit. The officers, the Owners, and God Almighty may differ, but that is my prerogative and my power."

"That may be so, Captain, but must you refill *all* the casks? You should be able to move a few about to get what is necessary."

The Commander pulled his napkin from under his chin and wiped the egg from his thick rusty beard, puzzled. "Am I to understand, *Professor* Woodruffe, that some water goes bad before others? When, learned sir, did such intelligence reach your ears, and why was it not immediately brought to my attention?"

Woodruffe gritted what few teeth he had left. The Commander just wouldn't let it go. "Water, like all provisions, Captain, can be made to last if you are strict with the men."

"I am to poison them," the Commander nodded gravely. "Our next possible landing is the Falkland Islands, some four thousand miles and several *months* sail hence, and I am to allow -- to expect -- the men to drink rancid green scum because YOU ARE AN INCOMPETENT FIRST OFFICER!?!" The Commander stood and stalked around the table. No doubt, a bear, his long red hair unkempt and falling about his shoulders. He came at Woodruffe, sending the little man up against the door.

There was little point resisting, and Woodruffe eventually found the Commander's hold slackening, then release. As the Bear's fury subsided, Woodruffe sank slowly, carefully to the floor. "Your indulgence of the crew's welfare is wholly out of proportion to duty to the ship and the Owners", he said before the Commander threw open the door to the companionway.

"I have given you a chance to stay on, and see me proven right or wrong."

Woodruffe drew himself up. "You wish to disgrace me." The Commander might have as easily thrown Woodruffe overboard --

preferable to the offer of employment as assistant to the cook. It meant removal of his gear to the very front of below decks -- the foc'sle, where the pounding of the waves against the bow of the *Columbia* would combine with the delighted torment of the crew.

"There is no disgrace in earning your keep. Refuse, and I'll not suffer you cluttering my deck another night with your miserable form. I'll need every man soon. Because of your delay, I think it best the ship be hauled out on shore and repaired."

"Good lord, Captain -- haul out the ship? Here? Our man Boyd is no great carpenter. You don't mean to hire out these islanders? They're not much better than their Portuguese masters."

"No need, Woodruffe," the Bear turned playful, "no need. We have the tools, and I have seen myself where the keel needs repair. It shall not be the first time I've had to --"

"You?" Woodruffe was baffled. "You propose yourself to take up hammer and saw?"

It was Kendrick's turn to question. "You think me incapable? Why, as a boy I repaired my father's whaling ships, in a fashion. It's simply a matter of attending to weak spots before they break. Would you have me continue south in such a state?"

"As Captain, you should not even bother yourself with leaving this quarter-deck." Tradition held that the Commander of a vessel concern himself only with the voyage as a whole, rarely showing himself beyond his small, comfortable quarters at the very rear of the ship. "To perform work yourself... and what would you have of the officers?"

"Push or get out of the way," the Commander replied with a nod and a grin. "I note your disapproval."

This was not the way of a ship, Woodruffe knew. Disaster could only be hastened by a captain's flouting of maritime doctrine -- holding himself no higher than the crew! Besides, Woodruffe hadn't endured the miserable conditions, the floggings and other cruel disciplines all those years at sea to now become First Officer of a rabble ship, mutiny-bound. "Captain Gray has offered me service on *Washington*." He found himself quite quickly steered out of the Commander's cabin, past his own former quarters, and to the open door of the quarter-deck. "Wi-with your leave, Captain, I will serve at his pleasure," he tried to finish.

"No. I don't know *how* Captain Gray could have communicated such a ridiculous message to you," said the Commander. "I ordered no man to approach or aid you so as to give you time to reflect upon your actions. In Boston you took a heavy advance on your wages as First Officer -- more than you could make in your service in my galley or under Captain Gray's command." They stepped out into the glare of the tropical sun, reflecting off the azure blue of the bay. "I find his urgency admirable, but questionable... No, I will not have it. It's the foc'sle or the shore." The Commander turned to the rail, catching sight of the fair weather clouds to the Northwest.

"You are mad." Woodruffe allowed at last. "You need me."

"I need these men more," the Commander cast over his shoulder.

When the sounds of Woodruffe's steps indicated his passage halfway down the steps to the main deck, Captain Kendrick called out: "Mr. Ingraham! Take Woodruffe ashore in the next boat!"

"Yessir," came the response from the tall, fair-haired young man in shirt sleeves directing the unloading from the hold.

"Oh, and Woodruffe?" Kendrick still hadn't turned his face to face the man, "Your fare, before you leave. Passage to this port, I set at ten dollars. Lieutenant Howe has already taken the payment from your gear." He added with a laugh, "Not an otter in sight, but tell Old Joe Barrell we're already making money!"

Sao Tiago, Cape Verde Islands
December 11th, 1787

"You cannot force me against my will, sir!" Roberts was frightened, even more so by the apparent indifference of the stocky, dark-skinned Cape Verdeans passing by this fracas in the market.

Looking down the straight, thin sword point, the Commander, dressed unusually well in his blue coat and red pants, was in an altogether vicious mood. "I -- disagree, Doctor," Kendrick's tone was measured, as if the words in which to fit his rage had to be chosen carefully. "Recall, I can be very dangerous when pushed too far. I do not handle disloyalty with the casual indifference of most men. Consider me as a patient -- what remedy would you prescribe?"

Roberts hesitated. He simply wanted out. With the ungraceful dismissal of Mr. Woodruffe, the fate of the mission had become clear, quite clear. The Commander had hauled out the ship, and began to repair her hull himself, to the disdain of the officers. Their refusal to assist him had not met with the traditional punishment of the sea -- flogging by the Cat-o-Nine Tails -- but with the inhumanity of assisting the cook with the men's meals. Young Mr. Haswell had been the worst of the trouble, with his impertinent remarks.

Worse, though, was the insistence that the Doctor himself stand a regular watch, like any member of the crew. Roberts had attended Harvard and traveled through many of the coastal towns of New England, earning a reputation (if not much money) as a physician whose patients appeared, on the whole, to benefit from his serums, tonics and bleedings. If being treated no better than the men was to be the best expected this early on, who could guess his fate once on the other side of the Americas? So, under the pretext of purchasing some native root, he had gone ashore and sought asylum from the Portuguese Governor.

The Commander, as he returned from protesting the local government's harboring of a deserter, surely knew this. Driven to desperation, he had pulled his sword at this chance encounter with his former Ship's Surgeon on the street. "I need you, Doctor," the Commander implored as he edged them both to the side of the narrow dirt path. "Surely, I will lose men on such a long voyage without your presence. Where is the compassion?"

He knew the cards to play. Roberts also knew that a journey 'round the world would seal his fortune in the scientific and medical realms of America. After that, the courts of Europe. Perhaps even an appointment to the Royal Society -- they could learn a great deal from him. But at what price?

"Captain," Roberts bit his lip as a wisp of dull brown hair escaped from his tricorne. Wasn't anyone going to summon help? "My concern -- my apprehension -- is, most certainly, for your welfare and that of the mission. What you do to the officers undermines discipline. Yes, a firm hand must be kept on the men, but I hazard to guess who shall be next? Captain Gray...?"

Kendrick caught the line of reasoning. He pressed the sword point to the surgeon's throat, backing him against a rain barrel. "You? You want me to give you my word you won't be flogged?"

"For desertion, sir," Roberts assured him, "just this infraction. Have I ever given cause before? You shall have none hence. You have my assurance."

"Until you leave me again?" Kendrick pressed the flat of the sword against the Doctor's cheek. "No, if there is no punishment for disloyalty, what offense *can* be punished? You abandoned me, Doctor. No one will forget that."

"You would have me, though I am disloyal? Could you ever trust me on your ship, even at your bedside when you take ill?" Roberts tried.

Kendrick, enraged at the thought the man could so easily slip from his grasp, centered the point of the sword directly upon the Doctor's chest. "You know I don't make idle threats. I can't do what you do. I need your help. If you don't go to the ship now, I will run you through -- without guilt."

Roberts trembled a moment, then relaxed. Amidst the hordes of Cape Verdeans, white uniforms of the soldiers appeared, intent on the large Yankee captain. Kendrick, for all his ferocity, could not allow himself to be arrested. Such would be to end the mission, which he had just been laboring to avoid. At the sound of their approach, he did not even turn, but sheathed his sword, hung his head, and departed.

The ship was rocking. Not that you could feel it. Still, through the porthole beyond the three-ton cannons, the dock could be seen slowly heaving up and down, and Charlestown is not on a fault line.

"It's too big," Miles declared.

"Oh, for Chrissakes, Kendrick," Seth whispered in exasperation. "This is the oldest ship in active service in the U.S. Navy. Too big! It's only 175 feet. Aircraft carriers are over ten times that."

They stood on the broad gun deck lined with dozens of the huge cannon in their carriages. The clearance was just enough to let Miles pass. Towards the stern, a pimply-faced sailor in Navy pea coat and white cap directed the tour of the Commander's expansive quarters. During the summer months, these guides wore traditional mid-nineteenth century uniforms, which made them the darlings of the myriad of foreign tourists. But God and the *U.S.S. Constitution* help these sailors if some off-duty Marines ran into them.

"*Columbia* was half that. *Washington* even smaller." Miles observed.

"First of all," Seth peered out from under the wide, round brim of the black felt hat, as he led the way to back to the hatch, "they were merchant ships. Second, the *Constitution* was the biggest thing that had ever left an American shipyard in 1797. *Columbia* was some leftover from the pre-Revolution days -- what was that about its fate? -- what did it say? -- wasn't it '*1803 - ript to* pieces'?"

As they passed the guardhouse on the main deck, the two other sailors tried to smile pleasantly. They knew the Professor, but this tall guy who looked like the Phantom of the Opera... *I scare them.*

"Happy Halloween," one offered as Miles and Seth descended the gangplank. Their attempt to stifle their snickering was admirable. It was the *only way* to be on the *only day*. Miles' lip, cheek and forehead were bruised. Going out in public looking normal was not going to work. YOU'RE NOT INVISIBLE.

He had first tried some powder, then some easy-cover makeup some woman or another had left behind. Then it occurred to him to use the body paint that had mysteriously shown up on Paulie's dresser one day. Mixed with some white, the blue hid most of the spots on his face not covered by hair. Brushed out, his long hair hung about his shoulders like a deep auburn hood. The limp helped his disguise, too, he thought as they crossed the wharf towards the museum. The effect was striking, memorable and dramatic. *But I don't look like me.*

Against Paulie's and Seth's advice, Miles insisted on going to the one resource in Boston he knew would have period artifacts -- not dusty tomes and sketchy maps, but the items sailors 200 years ago used every day. The Bostoner would have come here, he guessed, to connect with them. To draw power from them. He guessed. *Constitution* had slid down into Boston Harbor in October of 1797, only ten years after *Columbia's* first voyage and three years after Captain Kendrick was blown up.

"You should have dressed like Quasimodo," Seth glanced back at the huge black three-masted warship. "What are you -- some kind of Zombie Victorian fop?"

Miles held the door open against the chill breeze blowing out of a milky southern sky. "Whoever heard of a six foot-three hunchback? Anyway, the hump wouldn't've fit through the cellar hatch."

"Yeah, I thought about that. Hey, did you know Beacon Hill was the major center for the Underground Railroad?"

"Well, I knew the Abolition movement had a lot of support in Boston --"

"No -- think. The hill itself was a major stop bringing southern slaves up to Canada. You have all these interconnected cellars in which to hide people and move them about."

"Jesus, the system could go on forever. I'm surprised Arthur came in through the back door."

"Probably didn't know. By the way," Seth steered Miles into a dark, uncrowded room showing a film tour of *Constitution*, taking two seats in the back, "you better hope the FBI doesn't check out your dad's place."

"Hm. Heh, heh, heh," the thought was too good. "Funny. Funny man." Miles began to rock back and forth. "Pity them if they try. I think it'd be the first time in fifty years anyone's tried to make sense out of that collection of odds and ends. Hell, *you* could do a doctorate on it."

The Professor frowned at Miles lack of concern. "Pass. Antique Yankee tool, paint and spare part collections are not my area of expertise."

"I thought that's all archaeology was," Miles grinned.

After Arthur had handed over his all-important keys yesterday, Seth had about ten minutes with which to grill Miles before the latter's complete physical collapse. Arthur hadn't been as concerned about discovering Miles' duplicity as about the explosion so soon after the sale of a genuine explosive device -- the cannister thrown in as part of the deal with the Moldova coin. Miles had explained to Seth the cannister was safely down in one of the sheds behind his father's.

Being the supplier of a bomb used against the courts of the United States was a sure route to a prolonged stay at some Midwestern hi-security prison. Arthur killing Miles wouldn't have done any good, especially if the Feds already had been tipped off -- it would look like a conspiracy caving in on itself. Arthur certainly had motive to see Barrell, Meares and Lotta out of commission. But no, only fear and desperation had driven Arthur to confront Miles.

It was the waiting that had done it, no doubt. Arthur's tormentors conveniently out of the way all in one blow. The FBI had come only once for a simple preliminary interview -- same as Miles. It began with: Do you know John Kendrick? He had said no, yes, well, not as such. He'd never known Kendrick except as a customer who bought a coin, and that was probably coincidence. Had he bought anything else? No, Arthur had replied. That was the truth. The cannister had been a gift.

Then they had left. And never come back. The press, meanwhile, pinned the whole thing on Kendrick, but the FBI was still mum. It was obvious they didn't want to move too quickly. Kendrick was just the delivery boy. They wanted the man behind him. It was just a matter of time before Arthur slipped up.

Arthur had simply wanted to find Miles as quickly as possible and... talk. He probably hadn't slept in the past week himself, and the pressure had driven him to bring the construction crew along to frighten Miles. A demonstration of power. *Now I have him in my power and his keys to the building.*

"Sorry to hear about losing your empire," Seth said.

"Yeah, well, hope springs eternal in the crazed mind -- or is that conspiracy? Conspiracy springs eternal in the mind of the paranoid. Yes, much better. Glad I'm not paranoid."

"Or delusional."

"Yeah... what?"

The news said it plain enough. Yesterday the Quebecois had voted, yet again, by a wafer-thin majority, to remain part of Canada. British Columbia would not become part of the United States, at least not for another ten years until the next inevitable referendum.

But Miles had already abandoned greed as the true motivation of the Bostoner, sealed with the coffin nails of Simon Woodruffe and Doctor Roberts. There was no profit to be had in the deaths of deserters.

Fifty years after *Columbia* had been the first American vessel to circumnavigate the globe, *Constitution* was sent out on a voyage of discovery and diplomacy. Fifty years too late. The display in the museum told of relations in Africa, Southeast Asia, China, Mexico and South America.

"A reverse course of *Columbia*, " Miles pointed to the Plexiglas map of the 1844-46 voyage," west to east. Like what the English favored."

"It was easier. The boys from Salem liked that route, too," Seth noted, tapping the Cape of Good Hope at South Africa, then drawing a line west to the southern tip of South America. "Cape Horn is a lot closer to Antarctica."

Miles checked the latitude lines of the map. Around 55° down there corresponded in the northern hemisphere to Greenland. "Icebergs?"

"Oh, worse than that. See, this far south it's just one continuous ocean east to west all around. No land to break up the currents, so you'd normally have seas 40 feet high. From what you've told me of *Washington*, she was only 70 feet tall at her main mast -- imagine what it was like being all the way up in the rigging, hanging onto a yardarm, and having one of those monster waves hit you *in the face*. You'd better hope there was something still holding you up after that," said Seth.

"So it would have been okay if they'd been going west to east," asked Miles, "from the Pacific into the Atlantic?"

"Yeah, but barely. That was what the crew on the *Bounty* didn't understand. Captain Bligh wanted to take the ship from Tahiti in the Pacific to Jamaica in the Caribbean. The time of year was right, but they had gotten the piss knocked out of them trying to do it the other way a year before." The Professor shook his head, disgusted, "But you still never know. Even without the winds, the currents are nutty down there -- here, look --," he pointed to the small passage between Antarctica and Cape Horn, "you've got this small opening where deep down the whole Atlantic is shooting into the Pacific -- a whole ocean. The wind stops you going west --"

"Wait, wait, wait," Miles insisted. That doesn't make any sense. I *do* remember my oceanography classes -- don't winds usually go in the same direction as water currents?"

"Ah, but you're forgetting the earth spins on its axis from east to west. Remember, the sun rises in the east and sets in the west? Don't you think that affects all this water on the surface of the earth?"

"Oh, right!" Miles understood, "Like, fill an ice cube tray and fling it to quickly in the freezer -- the water stays where it is, and the tray moves."

"Exactly. The water slides up on the eastern shelf of every continent -- Asia, Africa, North and South America -- and off the western. That's why Cape Cod is forever being eaten away -- it's on the wrong side of the ocean."

"Or the continent," Miles sighed, "as long as the earth continues to turn."

Swords. Cutlasses. Dirks. Pistols. Grenades. The display case was full of them. Bores of the pistols like massive hand-held shotguns. One shot of lead about the size of good marble was their capacity. Not that they were too accurate, but God help you if you got in their way.

Most of the collection was from *Constitution*'s birth, and roughly fitting the period Captain Kendrick sailed the Pacific. The naval dirks were simply short, flat swords or long daggers given to junior officers, more to enforce discipline than to fight. The traditional cutlasses were more for leading boarding parties ship-to-ship -- à la pirate sagas. But the swords captured Miles' attention.

Highly ornate, carved ivory handles, usually some engraving on the sheath itself, long, thin -- truly a thing of beauty. A kill with one was quick, clean and efficient. Surgical. Only the highest officers could carry -- or afford -- such a weapon. Such a display of power.

"The Bostoner would have seen this sword, or another like it, and wanted one for his own," Miles whispered, "it's one thing to leave an old man out in a boat to freeze to death, but another to possess this... implement, to know how to use it, and to do so. I'll bet you that the coroner's report says Doctor Roberts had just one wound."

"Kendrick...?" Seth hushed.

"One-single-fatal-wound," Miles repeated, nodding. "And then put the sword on display – down in Wareham? How tacky."

Seth tugged the cape. "Shut up. You want to see this."

"Oh," Miles stopped. "Neat! How much?" The small brass cannon looked about the size of a leg of lamb, complete with tapered end -- the handle. It rotated on a swivel to aim its four inch-wide mouth in any direction.

"Swivel gun," Seth labeled it. "Keep a few on the rails of the ship for close action. You could stuff anything in there, like nails, with a charge of powder behind it. Not a pretty sight afterwards."

"Like cannister."

Seth shot him a warning look. "Yeah. But they hadn't gotten as advanced as putting the whole thing together in one charge -- see?"

On the shelf next to the swivel gun was a grenade, something like the stereotypical bomb. Black, round, about the size of a softball, with a fat wick sticking out of its iron shell. A cutaway version next to it showed its center filled with black gunpowder. Just roll it down the muzzle of the swivel, light the charge and ba-doom! It would go flying maybe twenty yards before the wick burnt down to its own charge and exploded, sending shell fragments everywhere.

"You think--?" the Professor mused.

"Naw. I mean, look at it. On the metal detectors, it would so obviously look like a --" Miles stopped himself before saying "bomb" out loud. The museum staff didn't need to overhear talk about such things. "Well, the function's right, but the package is..." A word printed on the display had tugged at Miles' brain. "Cannister." But it wasn't a cannister. Not a *can* in the least. He had taken it as some sort of petrified sea life at first glance. But the wooden disk on one side threw him.

"Hm? What do you see?" Seth asked cautiously, keeping one eye on the hallway, the other on Miles, down on his haunches, practically kissing the display case.

"I...," Miles tapped the glass, where inside was a small canvas tube about six inches long fixed with two wooden disks sealing each end, "... I know." He turned his excited eyes up at Seth, the round white surrounded by the blue skin seeming to scream out of the darkness, "I got it!"

Wood. Canvas. *I've been so stupid!*

CONTROL. Seth practically dragged Miles into the stairwell, the intellectual adrenaline surge from revelation being almost too much for him to overcome.

"Did you see it? I can't believe it!" Miles gasped in whispers. "No wonder it didn't show up on the metal detectors -- a wood and canvas bag -- oh, sure, its silhouette would've appeared on the X-ray, but so what? Even the gunpowder --"

"How do you explain the ammunition, then?" Seth tried to keep Miles sitting still on the landing. "A bag full of gun powder is fine, but without something to shoot out -- wasn't Meares' face taken off by the flying shrapnel? That couldn't have come from the table. It had to be something metal."

"Metal," Miles seized upon the word, "metal." He rose slowly and began walking up the stairs.

"You know, like lead shot, ball bearings, nails -- that sort of thing," said Seth. "Where *are* you going?"

"Walk," Miles ascended past the plaques in the brick wall honoring corporate sponsors, "gotta walk. Metal. What would be metal that wouldn't look suspicious? Nails?" He shook his head as the list of names engraved in the brass, above which were the words "CHARITABLE PLANK." Miles screwed up his face, unable to answer his own hard question, and so asked an easy one: "What the hell is a Charitable Plank?"

Seth was not following, but nodded at wall decorations, "Oh, a fundraising scheme. They're rebuilding *Constitution* -- again -- for its 200th birthday, and you can supposedly pay X-amount of dollars for a specific plank of wood on it."

Miles scanned the various engravings. Bank of Boston. Massachusetts Port Authority. John Hancock Insurance. The usual suspects.

"Nails. No," Miles came slowly down the stairs, "not nails," he added, passing Seth on the landing.

"Now where are you going?"

"Water. I need to be near water to get my answers," Miles responded absently as he headed past the swivel gun and towards the front doors.

Dust.

"You should put these on," Seth handed over the safety glasses. "Bob, uh, c'mere."

A ruddy, middle-aged man with gray beard and curly hair set a wide plank against a lathe, and ambled over with a smile as Miles ducked around the corner, out of sight. The wind had picked up, and it was difficult to make out what was being said inside. He took the glasses off and tried to work out the dust that hit eyes upon entering the woodshop on the docks. The last of the saws shut off, and as it wound down he could begin to pick up more of the exchange.

"They probably make their own. Just for display purposes and souvenirs," Bob could heard saying. "All very pretty. Back then, they'd use anything cheap and handy. Glass if nothing else. But lead was preferable."

Glass? The thought of glass exploding just a couple feet from his face made Miles shudder. Poor Meredith, to have survived. The pain must've been incredible. In sympathy, the sawdust found its way under his contacts again, and he was forced to wipe some saliva into his eyes. He stifled a painful growl. *Not now! I need my sight.*

Glass would explain the large amount of blood. Was it, combined with the powder explosive, enough to kill two people instantly? Maybe.

Lead. He thought of cannon balls. And the brass cannon. Brass is mostly copper.

Copper. The sword hung above the swivel gun was gleaming steel. Shining. Like silver.

Lead. Copper. Silver.

Coins.

"Lead coins?" Seth asked. "What denomination is that?"

Miles capered around the plodding Professor as they headed down Third Street to the bus stop. The wind at his back threw Miles' cape about him, often covering his face. "Not really lead. Pewter. The Columbia Medal. The commemorative coin -- like the thing the original Barrell commissioned and supplied both ships with in 1787. Kendrick, Gray and each of the owners got the few silver versions minted. A bunch of copper and a ton of lead ones -- sorry, pewter -- were sent on board. And get this -- Captain Kendrick sent his silver one to George Washington."

"What a kiss-ass," Seth sneered.

"And *our* Barrell has a lead version set in the glass wall of his offices. Has all the names right there: Barrell, Bulfinch, etc., and on the other, 'Commanded by J. Kendrick' -- oh, come on, Seth. It's too good!" *Money. Victory! Mine!* Miles could hardly contain his excitement. When they got home, he'd call the FBI and tell them the whole thing. All he'd have to do is connect the coins in the wall with those in the bomb --

Seth asked, "You think Barrell actually went to the trouble of collecting all these rare medals --

"Or had new ones minted."

"That's one expensive bomb. Don't you think that's rather blatant?" Seth argued.

"Who says he didn't want to get caught, even a small part of him?"

"'Stop me before I kill again?'" Seth raised his eyebrows. "Yeah, sounds like you're sympathizing."

"*Only* me," Miles grinned broadly. It all made sense. Finally. The relief was intoxicating. He couldn't wait to get home to call the Feds, and revel in his triumph. *Now.* "Payphone," he whipped around, searching. "I need a payphone."

"You can wait 'til we get home, can't you?"

"Fuck it. Let 'em pick us up in a stretch limo for all the help I'm giving them." Miles rubbed his eyes fiercely. "Payphone, payphone -- ah!" spotting one around the corner.

Maybe they've been waiting for me to solve this all along. Oh, typical client. I do all the work and they get the credit. Well, not this time. I'm gonna milk this thing and it'll all have been worth it.

The betrayals. The heartbreaks. The pain. The poverty. The suffering. The anxiety. The complete loss of pride. Even the events in the past few weeks, too. "Special Agent Lambert, please," Miles asked in his most official voice, despite his breathless excitement.

Seth, nonchalantly catching up to Miles at the phone, almost seemed relieved. "Then you won't be interested in what Bob had to say about the *Lady Washington?*

"*Lady* Washington? Oh, right. That was the complete name. Sounds so formal, though. What?"

The receptionist came back on, "I'm sorry, he's in a meeting. Can I take a message?"

"Just that he was asked to help out on the construction," Seth answered.

"Huh?" Miles stopped, then into the phone said, "Perhaps you should interrupt his meeting. He'll want to take this call." He again faced Seth, quizzical.

The Professor saw he had captured Miles attention. "That sloop of *Columbia's* -- the one Kendrick turned into a brigantine in China."

"So, whom shall I say is calling?" the FBI receptionist demanded.

"John -- uh -- hold on --"

"Sir, I have other calls waiting."

"Fine! John Kendrick, okay!?!" he yelled into the phone, and turned to Seth politely. "Come again?"

"Bob said he had to turn down a job working on *Lady Washington* to take this one restoring *Constitution*. But --"

Miles dropped the phone. What was going on? New data. *I don't need this.* IT'S EXTRANEOUS. IT'S TOO LATE.

"Special Agent Lambert," the voice on the phone said as Miles hung it up. Quite uncontrollably, he grabbed the lapels of Seth's jacket, pleadingly, and looked directly into his eyes: "No. She sank. *Washington* sank. After Kendrick was killed by the British in Hawaii, John Howel assumed command," Miles gasped. "I don't know legally how, but he did, and-and took her all over the Pacific until sinking her in the Malacca Straits off Singapore." He ended by firmly stating, "They couldn't have raised her. Not after 200 years."

Seth removed Miles' hands from his lapels. "No, don't be ridiculous. It's a reproduction. Pretty good job, Bob said. They built the whole thing true to form -- two masts, cannon, everything." He stared at the hands now grasping his shoulders firmly.

"Where?" Miles asked in an overly-controlled voice.

"Gray --"

"Hold it!" The dark blue car came to a screeching halt just inches behind Seth. "Take your hands off him, sir!"

He wasn't a cop. The light blue uniform and massive shoulder badge identified him as something more dangerous. As Miles swung his head around, he noticed the gold lettering on the car. Out of this another silver-haired guard emerged.

MASSACHUSETTS GENERAL HOSPITAL. It matched the lettering on the shuttle bus and the building across the street. Hell, everybody had branch offices in the old Charlestown Navy Yard. As Miles turned to face the one behind him, a wind blew back the long hair, exposing his face. The guard switched his hand from his billy club to his gun. There was a glimmer of recognition.

No.

Seth intervened with his detached manner. "Nothing's going on," he said to the guard stepping out the car, "nothing. Just calm down, okay?"

"Step away from the other gentleman, sir, and place your hands against the car," the guard nearest Miles ordered, edging closer.

Miles slowly drew himself up to full height, and answered quite unemotionally, "No."

Did this security guard really not want any trouble? Just to have Miles get into the car and take him in -- *in* where?

There was nothing that could be done, Miles knew. *Talk my way out of it? They don't want to talk -- they're not cops. There're plenty around here -- federal, state, city. If they'd been following and wanted to pick me up, they'd be the one's descending on me, not these two doughnut hounds.* Once in their custody, anything could happen on the *loooong* ride to the closest police precinct house. Or to police headquarters in the Back Bay. Or who knows where they'd parade their prize? Miles could see the $200,000 in reward money reflected in their eyes.

DON'T GET CAUGHT. It was inevitable. Thanks to Barrell, once into the system, anything could be contrived to keep Miles there. It was too convenient. Miles' leverage, what there was of it, lay with the Feds, not the city. It was all a matter where he was picked up. And on what charge.

The pink, beefy hand reached out to grab Miles' shoulder, "Look--"

GO. Miles whipped the cape into the guard's face, rolled over the back of the car, and began to run back down the block.

"Son of a bitch -- hey, get the hell out of the way!" Miles caught sight of Seth dodging in front of the guard trying to take aim. The dash around the corner saved his friend from further such duty, but the squeal of tires wasn't an encouraging sound.

Heading towards the tip of the waterfront with its decorative concrete obstacles would keep the car from running him down. But it turned the two blocks Miles had to run into four.

The air splint was meant to keep the ankle from twisting, not repair it entirely. Miles' initial sprint kept up from the first block and settled into a painful run. 'Round between condo courtyards and offices reconstructed from ancient naval storehouses, he slid into one building. *They'll never find me.*

UNTIL YOU COME OUT. Chancing an exit on the other side, he burst onto the sidewalk right after the guard's car sped by. Across the park he heard its brakes lock and transmission shift into reverse. Only one and a half more blocks.

As he rounded the corner to the museum, the siren screamed from the opposite direction. Coming down Third Street was the unmistakable white and blue of a City of Boston Police cruiser. Miles hooked to the left at the dry-dock and raced down the pier. With any luck, there'd be no one on the gangway.

Shit! A family of four was meandering down from *Constitution*. Miles focused on the 200 foot masts. Rigging. There were three of them -- sailors, not masts. Shit.

The cruiser slid between the buildings at the end of the wharf directly in front of him. Too late. These boys work fast.

KEEP GOING. YOU'RE ALMOST THERE. With a leap he launched himself off a pile of construction debris on the edge of the dock, catching the rail of *Constitution*. Hoisting himself up with one leg, he rolled over the top rail, landing on his back on the main deck six feet below.

I guess that was the whole reason for high rails.

The sailors at midships ran forward from the guardhouse. Miles jumped into the rigging, and began to climb up the ratlines of the main mast. It was only a matter of seconds -- these sailors were trained for this. *But I have a head start.*

The rope ladders leading to the foretop -- a platform halfway up the mast -- gave Miles a half second to evaluate the situation. Two sailors coming up the ratlines behind him. Another on deck yelling at the state police to keep the city police from firing into the rigging, and another green cruiser just arriving closest to them.

Federal Park Police. *My heroes.*

Miles pulled on the closest line, got enough momentum, and prayed it wouldn't be a deck of Georgia Pine that next met him. *I'm glad this tux ain't rented. What a --*

Nothing.

Floating.

Darkness.

        *   *   *

Poke.

"Hey. Hey!"

Stop it.

Poke.

"Hey, you awake?"

Poke. Poke. Shake.

Head tries to move. Pain. Head won't move. Neck broken? Pain. Head can move. But pain.

"Hey, wake up."

No.

Poke. Shake.

Pain. Lots of it.

Cold.

"Whaddya think? He still out of it?"

"Naw," poke, poke, "fakin' it. I can tell. He's started squirming around just now. Look--" Poke. Shake.

The tormentor's hand instantly becomes caught in the vice-like grip of his victim. Murky blue eyes open. They shake barely as the tormentor tries to free himself.

A breath tickles in the back of the victim's throat, then travels down into the lungs. The coughing fit sets the tormentor free.

"Heh, heh! Nice try, pal. Next time, don't go swimming in Boston Harbor. If the fall didn't kill ya, all the shit in the water will."

Cough. Cough. Pain.

Neck stiff. Muscles one solid band from shoulders back up to forehead.

"Ah--!"

Breath. Slow breath.

Less pain.

Eyes open. Uniforms. Different colors. Cough. Close eyes. Pain. "It's -- it's not the water."

Why aren't I in the hospital? Clothes are wet and cold. Nearby, coffee is brewing.

"Oh, yeah. Pretty boy like you. Bet you were a real hit down in Provincetown, huh?" Laughter. Stupid laughter.

"Hey, hey, careful."

"Ya never know. I mean, if I'd been suckin' it back and takin' it up the ass all these years, I'd probably swan dive into the harbor myself -- or blow up my pals. Hey," poke, poke, "is that it?"

Breath. Breath. Dope.

"Shit. Yeah," poke, "I better not turn my back on you." Laughter.

"You're fuckin' paranoid. You think everybody who ain't got a size 30 neck has AIDS."

"Hey, ya never know."

Breath.

Stop.

Smile. "Huh." Broader smile. "Heh, heh!" Eyes open. "You're right."

The two uniform faces go from gentle surprise at the mere fact this speech to guarded alarm.

The green eyes that look back glare right through their skulls.

"Trick or treat."

PART TWO

Rogue

Hell is paved with priests' skulls.
-- St. John Chrysostom

CHAPTER EIGHTEEN

Daedalus

Wednesday, November 1, 1995

"Do you object to the use of a video camera in this proceeding?"

I am stoic.

"If you object to the use of a video camera, please signal now."

I say nothing. I do nothing.

"... and have been advised of these rights. For the record..."

How am I going to proceed? Questions flying.

"What do you know about explosives?"

The oily taste has gotten worse with the lack of fluids since this afternoon. No one ever offered anything. The best part about being dehydrated is not having to go to the bathroom.

"What did you have against John Meares?"

"Why in the courthouse?"

"How well do you know Arthur Lewis?"

"Have you ever been attracted, romantically or otherwise, to Meredith Gray?"

Something caught in my teeth? Tongue can't seem to get it out. Not enough saliva to force between my teeth. Should've had that cavity filled, dammit.

"What was your relationship with Charlotte Coolidge?"

Lambert asks the questions. Archer's hung back, pacing. The younger man is pretty good. Very cool. Doesn't stay on one topic too long. Changes at the right moment. But Archer is doing the reading.

"You were involved in a disturbance yesterday at the Suffolk County Courthouse. Now what was that all about?"

Someone isn't wearing deodorant and desperately needs to.

"Is that where you got those cuts and bruises?"

Nice rings. What was that big one -- Duke? Business school, probably. The new FBI.

"Why did you attack your friend, Seth Jones, this afternoon?"

Cough. The lurch forward is painful. Some tendon locked in my head from the fall. Turning it, to any degree, is not possible. Back and forth is better.

"Get'm some water," Archer mumbles. Lambert looks down at his own glass, hesitates, then grabs a paper cup from the water cooler, fills it, and sets it in the middle of the table.

He's not sure.

"Why did you run away from police officers at the Navy Yard this afternoon?"

Most people don't understand threats. So many are made because so many people are weak and gullible. Other time, threats aren't believed because they are simply unbelievable. That is why displays of power are so necessary. Your big belt buckle don't mean a thing less'n your Kenilworth blows by the rest of the traffic. A wedding vow only matters when a husband's old college buddy, fresh from the shower, clad only in a towel, surprises a married woman. An alcoholic is "recovering" only after leaving a bar without indulging.

Having come to understand this absurdity, Life has become one sad, repetitive joke. Wham! Learn the lesson yet? WAAM! How 'bout now? WHACK!! Don't you get it?!

Yes. I understand perfectly. But I don't have to like it.

Endurance was the thing. Strength came slowly. Agility was a dream. But staying power -- that's how to do it. Let the fools display their power. Get yourself a good look at it. Understand how it works. Is that the best they got?

Let them see me take it full in the face. Then hit 'em hard.

"Why did you tell Officer Sullivan you had AIDS?"

To create doubt. It worked.

Archer casually fishes in his pocket for something. Change, keys, whatever, begins to jingle around. He flips a square of plastic foil on the table.

A condom? The plastic is clear. The round gold disk inside shines brightly. It isn't latex. "What," Archer stops pacing and leans over the table, "can you tell us about this coin?"

I pick it up. I smile quite innocently. The word "Moldova" is printed on one side, and a profile of John Kennedy on the other. "I believe this is the property of the Federal Depository Insurance Corporation, and is, or was to be, submitted as evidence in a civil suit in the First District Court of the

United States."

They attempt to appear unfazed. Neither look at each other. Archer clears his throat.

I take a sip of the water. "Thank you. Now I can get properly reimbursed. You know, the FDIC gave me a hassle since they couldn't find it. I had given it to Lotta but, well, I guess I'm still bound by my duty to my client, so I shouldn't say anymore, especially on tape, even if we are on the same side. By the way," I cross my legs and sit forward, most sincerely, "where ever did you find it?"

"On the floor of the conference room where -- where the explosion occurred," Lambert replies.

From behind, Archer adds, "Along with about a hundred quarters."

"Quarters?" Hmm. Metal. Disks. Silver and copper mixed. Eagle on the back. Washington on the front. Of course. Quarters! "Turn that off," I say. "Now." They haven't begun to deflate. "Also, I'd like to see my attorney." But that did it, along with, "And what, precisely, is the reason I'm here?"

Lambert clears his throat. "The charge is criminal trespass on federal property --"

"Jumping on the *Constitution*," I interpret.

"-- and resisting arrest."

"And jumping off the *Constitution*." This isn't my world anymore. It is far too poetic. Or maybe I am the only poetic person in it. That is my gift to them. I hope they appreciate it. Nodding at the camera, I become quite firm. *"NOW."*

It is hard to stifle my glee. Three centurions have taken the field of battle in my name, and are winning. The entire legal staff of Connor & Vanzetti in conjunction with Paulie are playing good cop-bad cop with the Feds. Or "Kinda Reasonable And Compassionate Lawyer" (Bill), "Indignant Lawyer" (Frankie), and "Attack-Dog Roommate That Everyone's Guessing Must Be My Lover" (Paulie). I can't laugh, though, 'cause I know if Paulie sees, he'll start, too, and the spell will be broken.

"You've got a man here, sitting *how many hours* in wet clothes, probably with pneumonia and my God -- where the hell did he get those cuts all over his face!?!" Frankie demands.

"Did you do this?" adds Paulie, not to be outdone. "Sick sonofabitch, bet you had a lot of fun!"

Meanwhile, Bill has knelt down by my chair, and whispers, "so, what's this about your -- uh -- bad cold?" He mouths the letters H-I-V?

I cough. "Who knows? Let 'em brew. I just needed them to be afraid of me at a very vulnerable time. But, hey, a couple weeks ago I wasn't exactly safe --" Bill raises his eyebrows, "-- with a *woman*. Just the way it turned out. So, I could be telling the truth as far as I know. Or I could just be paranoid."

"Yeah, well, just don't wig out yet, okay? Your pal here's going for the gold right now."

Paulie is pounding the table, "*I-want-answers* -- hey! What the *fuck* is that?" he points at the camera. "Is that *on*?"

Frankie's demeanor is darker. "You guys better enroll yourselves in the Witness Protection Program like now. The Bureau will have you mopping floors pulling that shit."

Archer lit into Paulie, "Hey, now -- that's federal evidence and federal property, son --"

Paulie pulls back, his hands up by his shoulders. "Calm down, man," his look of concern for the agent apparent, "You're supposed to be the good guys, remember?"

Perhaps we should all take this down to the processing desk," Lambert tries to inject an element of calm, "Mr. Kendrick will go before a judge in the morning --"

"No."

Lambert looks across at me. "John, you've broken Federal law. A criminal law and there are criminal penalties. Even if there's bail, the judge --"

"No." I am quite serious. "I won't spend one minute in jail. I have done nothing wrong." Then I consider, "'Cept, maybe, be a little anxious to use the correct entrance for a naval vessel."

"Our hands are tied," Lambert sighs.

"Well, untie them!" Paulie argues.

"Listen, let's cut the bullshit," Frankie says, "You guys want to hold him in connection with the bombing. I know it. The press knows it. So charge him and get on with it or forget this candy-ass charge and let him go."

"Your client has been extremely uncooperative." Archer pulls back to professionalism, "Now, there's something he's not telling us."

"What -- that I'm a Taurus?"

Archer ignores it. Lambert looks out the window. Bill lays a hand on my shoulder, giving a firm squeeze. Paulie simply steps out of the room.

Frankie jumps in, "Hey, I worked in the D.A.'s office. I know how you guys operate. The FBI doesn't move until it has a rock-solid case." He points to me, "Now, here you spoke to him once in the hospital, hoping fresh memory or maybe a slip might lead you somewhere. Then nothing. You think you got something, but you let it simmer with this guy Lewis. You take John's name to the press to make Lewis feel the heat's off him, and maybe take some off yourselves -- but Lewis goes after John in a public place, and now you begin to think, hey, maybe there's a connection? I mean, so soon after Lewis bought John's building. This kid's never been rich, so maybe he pulled a deal with Lewis to make a risky delivery against his own boss. Right?"

"You know the Bureau doesn't comment on ongoing investigations, counselor," Archer answers.

"So you want to hold John on this trespassing charge in the hopes you can flush out Lewis again, is that it?"

"Or until John cracks," Bill adds.

"I could die first," I say in a soft, low voice, and look at each, even Paulie as he re-enters. "I really, *really* mean it." Taking a breath, "So how's this: I won't hold the city, state, Mass. General or the federal government responsible for these injuries," gesturing to my face.

"You had those when you came in," Lambert objects. "Lewis probably did that yesterday."

"You weren't there when they fished me out. And you weren't there yesterday protecting me from Lewis, so you don't know. No one in the press knows. But if I walk out of here or show up in a courtroom all beat up, sick, barely able to walk, and *not* charged with the bombing, what do you think the public reaction *could* -- not would -- but *could* be?"

Lambert draws in a deep breath, and looks at Archer, who simply shakes his head. "Mr. Kendrick, do you have any idea who orchestrated the bombing, then?"

I lie.

"No."

"John Kendrick is not a subject of this investigation at this time," the FBI spokesperson states. "John Kendrick clearly was not capable of such an act." From the look on her face, anyone can see she is uncomfortable reading from copy not her own, especially such a subjectively-worded statement. "John Kendrick had no motive -- clearly the record indicates nothing but a history of good relations between him and John Meares, Coolidge and Barrell, Bulfinch and Gray."

The Professor turns up the volume on the set. "You're being very tricky, here, Kendrick."

She continues, "Meanwhile, we understand that Mr. Kendrick has fallen ill. Following complications related to his injuries suffered in the explosion, so the Bureau asks that you all in the press community respect his privacy from here on."

"It's rumored," a reporter shouts, "that John Kendrick admitted to suffering from AIDS while in police custody late last night. Can you confirm those reports?"

"I am sorry," the spokesperson answers automatically, "I cannot confirm or deny that. Mr. Kendrick was never held in custody since he was never a suspect. It is true he fell into the harbor in Charlestown yesterday, and was pulled out by federal personnel, and held until they thought him well enough to leave, but no, that is all. Thank you, that's all the time we have."

Seth plops the remote into my lap. "You need anything?"

"Naw." I click the set off.

"How you holding up?"

"Horrible. I wish I could just get sick once and either die or survive. I mean, what's the point of being sick if all I'm going to do is recover, only to face it again and again? Better to get hit by a bus."

"That's the spirit." Seth refills my water glass and heads down for the mail.

It is so stupid. Incapacitated. The physical injuries like the ankle and the neck, they are understandable. The machine has been pushed beyond its limit. Driven too far on a flat tire and the steering cable has worn out. I can accept that -- penalties -- limits.

The fever is something else. I don't like feeling like an invalid. Fluid in my lungs. Burning eyes. A heavy head that wants to loll, but can't because of the extreme pain of the whiplash. And the heat. Pervasive. Every cell boiling over. What's going on? Nothing's working right. Flood the reactor core!

The temperature of my skull makes it impossible to recognize any one clear thought. Even the heavy black envelope with the return address of a west coast software developer Seth sets at my elbow. Dazzling graphics scream out "*SEXTANT Version 2.0!!!*"

So here it is. Yip-

Yip-

Yippedy-doo-da.

There is too much to think about. Too many questions. Too much data in my head, and not enough connected. With the help of the Professor's CD of Haydn's *Surprise Symphony*, I begin sinking into the late eighteenth century. Clues begin to emerge, but how many more am I missing? Looking in this envelope and using the floppy disk it held would only tear me off track, dredging up memories and passions better overlooked.

"Seth?" I call out, hoarsely. Where's he gone?

"Yessir," he calls from the kitchen.

"What --" I have to stop again, clear out a cough, and begin again as Seth emerges, "What about *Lady Washington*?"

"You sure you don't want to get a shot or something?"

"No medical insurance. You know that."

"And you know that doesn't matter. Hell, I'll pay for it, if that's all that matters. Anybody who falls into that harbor should get a tetanus shot at least, and some penicillin wouldn't be a bad idea, either. You've probably got some sort of bacterial infection."

"Oh, just let sleeping dogs die," I moan. "The ship?"

"You mean the brigantine?"

"Whatever." The world is dying and he's arguing syntax.

He explains that Bob had indeed been asked a few years back to work on constructing a replica of the consort to *Columbia. Lady Washington* was to be as faithful in design as allowed by Coast Guard regulations. With two masts to make it as it would have appeared after Kendrick modified her in Macao in 1790, and continued around the Pacific for another four years. "Where?" I ask.

"Out in Aberdeen, Washington. They sail it up and down the Coast -- San Diego to Vancouver, B.C. Like a floating museum, and some charters to boot. You'll get to see her, too -- that is, if you don't kick off in the next week."

"Oh?" I take a long draught from the water glass. The ice cubes fall onto my face, cold, and I hold them it there a moment. "Do tell."

"Bob said that since the resurrection of *Constitution* was more prestigious, he jumped at it, even though completely building a Revolutionary-era vessel from scratch was more interesting. But," Seth refills the water glass, "*Constitution* will be 200 years old in 1997, and they want to sail *Lady Washington* here for the birthday party."

"*They?*" I close my eyes, and shake my head, needing a clearer sign from my oracle, "Who *they?*"

"The organization that owns and operates it. Lessee," Seth clicks the mouse on the computer, fires up the modem, types a few keys and a Web page shoots onto the screen, "here it is. Grays Harbor Historic Seaport, Aberdeen, Washington. Look, they even got a picture of it." And there she is. Under full sail. Huh.

"Grays Harbor?"

"Yep."

"*Gray?*"

"Oh, you think..."

"I know."

"No, you *think* you know. But you don't *know*."

"What's the difference?"

"Reality."

"Oh, that." I absent-mindedly open the envelope, and fish out the floppy disk. "Reality is what I make it." I toss it over to Seth, indicating him to slip it in the drive. Waiting for it to load, I'm curious -- what of me in this work remains?

"You should get some rest."

The word "MASE" fills the screen, then a box superimposes upon it.

Do you wish to install *SEXTANT* now?

Seth raises his eyebrows, and turns back for confirmation. I nod.

This program – it's was all so familiar, yet cosmetic changes here and there stand out like skin grafts. They cover, but are no substitute for the original. My influence is ingrained into this entire work like marbling in a fine piece of meat. Thad's cutting at corners has only done so much. The only way to remove the rest is to burn it out -- and the whole beyond all recognition.

"I've taken another Vow, you know," I say.

"Vow? Oh, celibacy? When?"

"When I understood doing what I 'should' and ignoring my instincts was putting me on the fast track to prison. Last night."

"How long this time?"

"Until it's over. 'Til Christmas."

"Why 'til Christmas?"

"I don't know. I guess that's when it'll all be over. I don't just make these things up you know."

"Uh-huh. Uh...huh. Well, since the whole world thinks you have a deadly sexually transmitted disease, I don't think breaking that vow is going to be a problem."

"Why do you think I told the cops that in the first place?"

Seth, having seen the original *SEXTANT* program years ago, gently recognizes its functions. He goes from one Web site to another, feeding the

program with samples of his favorite topics, in this case, maritime and history
sites. "So now, I just leave the computer on and it will find sites it thinks I
might like based upon what I've already spent a lot of time on..."

"And randomly flash them up as a screen saver."

"Pretty good."

I turn away, changing CD's to Beethoven. "It's insulting." I cross
carefully back to my chair, to sit upright, staring out the west window at the
Charles. It is only late afternoon and already dark. Whaaa?

Time change. Right.

"The Captain's vessel, Lady Washington, is being run by the Gray's
Harbor Historic Seaport. The boat he rebuilt," I say. "And used to blaze all
sorts of trade routes -- all for the benefit of others -- the boat he was
murdered on, betrayed by his 'friends' -- that boat is owned by an entity
having to do with Gray? And in a year and a half Lady Washington will
return to Boston, 200 years after she left, by their good graces?" I chatter my
teeth and reiterate, "It's a goddamn insult."

"You're really taking this too personally."

I try to set him at ease with a smile. "No, no. Not me. What the hell --
its just a bunch of genes I inherited. But I can understand how the Bostoner
would feel. Make a contribution and your apprentice, Gray, returns home and
claims all the glory –"

"You sure you're talking about Captain Kendrick and not your
computer program?"

"-- In spite of it all," I ignore his interruption, "he still managed to do
pretty well for himself, and when he finally felt he had redeemed himself, and
could return to the real world again -- BOOM, he was killed. And they want
to bring Lady Washington back to Boston."

I kick at Howay's Voyages of the Columbia at the foot of my chair,
"Gray told the lie. Barrell and Bulfinch believed it, and Howay perpetuated it.
Only time has allowed people to forget it. When *Lady Washington* comes back
to Boston, the stories will be learned again by another generation, and I'll tell
you something, Salathiel, if I identified with old Captain K, I'd make damn
sure that the records was set straight, once and for all!"

I erupt into another coughing fit, silenced by another glass of ice water
from Seth. God, I've taken in at least a gallon in the past hour, and have to
let some of it out. How fucking pathetic.

The Professor had to return to Harvard, and upon my leaving the
bathroom I can make out some voices on the stairs. The reporters on the
street below are no longer visible except when somebody tries to leave or

enter the building. A couple pester the Professor for half a block down the hill.

"What's up?" Paulie asks as he lays the afghan over my legs. "I've got just the thing," he crosses into the kitchen and holds up two trophies, "Soup!"

I merely nod gently, "Thanks."

My world comes into clear focus as Paulie boils the soup on the stove. My world, this chair, the bathroom and my bedroom. The bedroom is to be avoided at all costs since all it leads to is sleep and self-indulgence. The bathroom is a damned necessity. My chair is simply my post from which to watch and reflect.

Paulie brings in the soup, "I put in an ice cube to cool it," he explains. The "Simmer" setting never has been of much use to him. A stove has only two settings -- HI and OFF.

Between blows on the surface of the steaming bowl, I try pointing to the terminal. "Check out the computer."

"What is...?" he's curious.

"No, no. Don't look. Just back up to the main screen."

About ten seconds pass before Paulie turns around from the screen, wary-eyed. "Is this *SEXTANT*? It is, isn't it?" he points.

My question has to be framed correctly, or else it might allow for an altogether different reaction. Direct and simple. "Did you know this had been produced?"

"No," he shakes his head. "No, I mean, I'd heard from Thad, and seen him working on it, but I've always tried to stay out of it, so I never asked. How did you find this?" I explain the chance meeting with Thad the week before, and subsequently placing an order from their distributor. Paulie's charity is valiant. "Well, that's good that he told you about it. I mean, he didn't deceive you. He was straight, right?"

"Mm. What choice did he have?"

"So, what're you going to do?"

"About what?"

"Listen," he lays his hand on my shoulder, "I know you feel betrayed. He should've said something to you --"

"This," I indicate the computer, "is nothing. Not right now. If there's one thing I've learned, it's that people suffer by my absence. For the time being I shall withhold that which I hold most precious -- my time." I chuckle painfully, "As it is, they may already feel bad -- everybody thinks I'm on my death bed. For now, as a favor, could you withhold the truth?"

"Sure."

The truth. The truth is I am the most famous sick person without AIDS in Boston -- probably the country for the next couple editions of Headline News. But I am sure it will keep the reporters scared of picking through my garbage. For this same reason, I can't go to a doctor or any hospital since I would be tested as a routine procedure. Inevitably, word would get out that I'm just fine, thank you, save for a bad cold, bad ankle, and bad neck. Crying wolf doesn't help one's reputation. Especially when one is under a mild form of house arrest.

The truth is, based upon my purported declining health, I will not -- cannot -- leave town. The Feds are at ease to decide if a formerly crazy, terminally-ill slacker blew up his boss and a couple of other people for -- for what? Money? Kicks? Revenge? Bad breath?

Not that it matters. My world involves a grand total of 200 square feet of creaky hardwood floors. Surrounded by plenty of research material, I have enough time to become a lay-expert on an obscure subject in history before the rent is due again. This could be my life. All I need is the some sack cloth.

"I've taken a Vow. Not that it matters."

He does not approve, and shakes his head, "Why? Why do you want to do that to yourself? Because of all this?" he indicates the computer.

"No. I wouldn't waste a Vow for such a minor transgression. It's about the case. I gotta solve it. The Vow, it's just a tool... so to speak." There have been other Vows, at different times. All involve celibacy. Never for more than four months. They were prompted more by intuition than a well-reasoned, concrete decision. They started with that last, great period of darkness, when my reality ripped apart. Sex is a powerful release, thus retention of sex is retention of power. In and of itself, the Vow is a demonstration of power. I am denying the world -- the carnal, selfish, inconsiderate world -- myself.

"But it makes you crazy," Paulie protests.

"Too-late," I sing-songed.

Off the Island of Fernando de Noronha, in the South Atlantic
January 15th, 1788

"I'm going crazy! I can't put up with this -- can't you see that we'll be lucky ever to see Boston again!?!" The words had echoed in the Commander's Quarters for the Commander and the Commander alone.

"The Schoolmaster," as the crew had dubbed Jonathan Nutting, the Astronomer, had become unglued just a few weeks out of Cape Verde. 'Twas to be expected after crossing the equator. The sky was different in the southern hemisphere. The man's usual guides were turned upside-down.

The Commander's soft and gentle words appeared to do the trick, though. "Despite the loss of Woodruffe and Doctor Roberts, we shall prevail, and enter Boston Harbor together, my friend." The Commander was a keen navigator himself, to be sure, and had shown an uncanny knowledge of the ways of water and wind.

Any Yankee deckhand who learned his figures in school could determine his position north or south -- latitude -- by way of a using a sextant to measure the sun against the horizon. But the mystery of figuring position east or west -- longitude -- had eluded sailors. It required projecting where certain stars should be in relation to where one's voyage began. Mars was in this point in the sky when we left Boston, but now it's someplace else -- so where am I?

On a journey westward around the globe, knowing precisely how far west one had traveled was essential. "I need you, Jonathan," the Commander told him again. "Without you, one dark night I might just sail right into Brazil."

Nutting spoke Greek, Latin, French, and Spanish, the latter perhaps serving well enough if the Commander chose to set him ashore at the Portuguese fort at Trinidad. After the Astronomer left the room, Mr. Treat (ship's Furrier and Nutting's cabin-mate) observed, "He's frail, you can see that, Captain. Jonathan doesn't trust his abilities south of the equator, and thinks his calculations will bring us all to ruin. He'd... rather not be held responsible."

It was all so much squabble over nothing, thought the Commander. They were well on their way now. The mizzen mast -- the rear of the three on Columbia -- was found to be split recently, but not too late to be fully repaired. Five days lost were acceptable when the alternative was continuing to Cape Horn with only two masts. Better he had been carrying less sail or the strain might have snapped that mast altogether, and then where would they be?

Young Mr. Ingraham, had been working out nicely as First Officer, and Mr. Haswell, though rough, seemed to affect his promotion to

Second Officer as well. Woodruffe was no great loss, then. Perhaps a Ship's Surgeon could be found in China. The medical arts there --

"Man overboard!" came the cry from the foretop.

Kendrick found the quarter-deck flooded with officers. His son, John Jr. commanded this watch, and now directed the crew to lay lines upon the water from all directions, and bring the ship about while signaling to the more maneuverable sloop, Washington. Captain Gray was just on the forward horizon, though, and in the twilight would be of little help.

Every man had come up on deck, and would stay through most of the night in either the ship's boat trawling, or in the rigging, hoping the next sign wasn't another whitecap or albatross. Any other ship of any other nation would not have wasted another minute -- men at sea were expendable, and none could actually be expected to swim. The Commander finally abandoned the search as the fruitless tedium only further impressed the sense of loss upon the men and their officers.

I re-read the letter Treat had sent of his accounts in China to Joseph Barrell. The whole of Jonathan Nutting's epitaph is but a fragment of a sentence:

> ...our Astronomer, who being insane
> threw himself overboard and was lost.

The ice has melted to lukewarm, flat water in my glass, and I shuffle off to the dark kitchen for a refill. Then, by a single light in the living room, I continue my examination, guessing, perhaps, it is ten o'clock.

Somewhere off Paraguay
February 1st, 1788

The man's face was covered in blood. It streamed down from his nose and into the bandanna 'round his neck, turning its pale gray into a collar of dull crimson. Otis Lipscomb held one hand up to cover his nose, the other to ward off any further blows from Mr. Haswell. Mr. Ingraham, taller than either, had them both by the collar as he led them up the stairs to the quarter-deck.

Mr. Haswell cursed under his breath, "Leave it! You're no better than the crew with the bottle. Leave well enough alone, can't you?"

As the companionway door opened, Mr. Ingraham shot a look of scorn and disgust upon Mr. Haswell, "We didn't sign on board a British Man-o-War. Captain! I wish to report a disturbance."

Captain Kendrick was not happy having his meal with Captain Gray and Washington's First Officer, Davis Coolidge, disturbed. Less so by the sight of his bloodied seaman. "Mr. Ingraham, Mr. Haswell," Kendrick nodded as the Second Officer shook off the collaring, and glowered. "Explain."

The issue had been clear enough. The officers of both vessels were sharing the Commander's table for the evening's meal, and the lack of progress of Columbia had been noted again by Captain Gray. More sail, indeed, Kendrick had relented for once, and ordered Haswell to get the men up in the rigging to add canvas. What followed was unclear.

Mr. Haswell claimed the men were laggard from too generous a rum complement to their water. "Lipscomb was insolent. He did not come up from his bunk upon my order, or my repeating yours, Captain. When I tried to pull him from his bunk, he used insubordinate language, so I cut him a blow."

The Commander gave a hard look at Otis Lipscomb, cowed by even setting foot on the quarter-deck -- an action by a crewman that would regularly warrant a flogging -- and by the surrounding of so many officers.

"That's not entirely the truth, Captain," Mr. Ingraham added. "Mr. Haswell did not appear to be allowing Lipscomb the opportunity to get up at all. I found him kneeling foursquare on the man's chest, delivering a devil of a beating."

"Lipscomb, you'll get below now," Kendrick said quietly. The man backed away, wiping his face as he descended to the main deck and into the hold. From the rigging, the rest of the watch were conspicuously tending to their lines or the horizon. "Mr. Haswell," he spoke, "your hands." Mr. Haswell looked down at his hands. They were not only bloody, but bruised from the blows delivered to Lipscomb's face. "They do not become an officer of my command. Go wash them."

Mr. Haswell moved to the door to his quarters, but found it closed by Fourth Officer John Kendrick, Jr. The son had been signaled by the father. "No, do not dishonor our water with your disgrace," the Commander growled. "You shall attend to that duty below, in the hold. Thereafter, you shall attend to Lipscomb, as he seems to not want for your attention."

Mr. Haswell was indignant. "I am an officer, Captain! I was performing my duty --"

"Boy! Get off my quarter-deck!" the Bear charged at Haswell, grasping the youth by the lapels, and holding him high in the air.

Eager not to have such a display of command discord seen by the crew, Captain Gray rushed forward to the Commander, "Sir --"

Seeing an opportunity, Haswell sent a solid kick into Commander's chest, sending them both crashing to the quarter-deck. Equal numbers of the officers grappled to keep the two separated.

"Bloody little prick, don't you dare lay your fuckin' girly hands on one of the men again or I swear I'll cut them off and stuff them up your ass!"

"Captain," Gray was shocked, "there's no call for the men to witness this."

Kendrick turned on Gray, "Let them!" adding, "Mr. Ingraham, Mr. Kendrick, this man is no officer of mine!" To show his contempt, he turned his back on Haswell, and continued with a bellow loud enough for crews on both vessels to hear: "Clear out his quarters, and remove him to the hold! And," he reached over to grasp one of the handspikes not presently attending the end of a line, "let him have the better part of this should he attempt to cross up here again, for if I do find him within my sight, you can be assured I shall blast his brains out!"

With that, the Commander returned to his cabin, to poke furiously at the remnants of his meal.

CHAPTER NINETEEN

Fair American

Thursday, November 2, 1995

These people just push and push and push. Then when I finally lash out, stop them, they are surprised, and act as if *I* am being unreasonable. Which way is it -- let them walk completely over me, or always be a tight ass?

Better to be rid of them.

It is noon. Or one. Have I reset the clock? Can't remember. Does it matter? Not when I'm sick. Not when the world is dying.

So many feelings are resurrected reading the notes, letters and logs surrounding *Columbia* and *Washington*. I can empathize with Captain Kendrick and his problems -- consistent bad luck always destroyed the fruits of his visions and talents. Faint-hearted men kept bailing out on him, but he remained on course, until all that was left was simply himself to count on. By that point, other forces were at work to take advantage of his isolation.

The congestion is building in my head, and while painful and irritating, I take it as a good sign. The water I've taken in is becoming mucous, and has gone to work capturing the toxins in my body. At this rate, they'll flush out of my system slowly over the next week, mostly through my nose. Still, in the mirror, the cuts and bruises have taken on a more permanent, solid look. Like they're meant to be there, and are part of the landscape of my face. Yeck. Another week for them, too.

In the mean time, I can always attack Howay.

Brett's Harbor, West Falkland Island
February 28th, 1788

Cold, desolate and not a tree in sight. The tussock grass here, though, grew on the rocky hillocks, and in the bogs to over the height of most men. The birds were plentiful enough, and an old spring had been found. But with winter coming on, this place was no better to stay than old Cape Cod.

Having arrived near the onset of the southern hemisphere's winter, the Commander had proposed to his officers that the two vessels remain in this kelp-infested harbor before proceeding west 'round Cape Horn. That idea was rejected, despite the dangers of attempting the dangerous passage into the Pacific this late in the season. "Near six months have passed since I saw Boston last," Captain Gray stated, "and for this salary, I daresay I dare not delay *beginning* our voyage another day, sir."

Young men are so eager, the Commander remembered. He himself was in no rush to make mistakes. But if the captain of the little *Washington* was so eager to face Cape Horn's monsters, then God bless him and have mercy on his crew. Still, there remained the matter of the boy.

Haswell stood before him, stiff and barely hiding his contempt. Oh, he was full of fire and independence. One day he might make a fine captain, but he needed a bit of humbling. If not the direct hand of Captain Kendrick, then that of the Almighty. Following their fracas, Kendrick had spoken more kindly during his former Second Officer's standing watch. The "Old Man" had agreed that, should Haswell catch sight of a passing vessel, he was free to transfer to her with no ill feelings.

None such chance had befallen Haswell, the long voyage this far south was to be followed by another of even greater length back north, up the west coast of the Americas. Clearly, the boy had this in mind when he went ashore in search of supplies with Lieutenant Howe and Mr. Treat. Clearly, Haswell hoped to find an English ship at anchor when he ran off from his sleeping companions. An attempt to investigate that anchorage four miles east? Previously, the Commander had made his decision to depart the following day quite clear to all, and this was Haswell's last chance.

Any other ship's master would have bidden good riddance to bad rubbish. For Captain Kendrick, to care less, to be less forgiving of this young man, than any other of those under his care, would be the height of hypocrisy. A watch and signal had been ordered, with search parties sent out. Haswell expected to be flogged after his absence of a day and a night. Instead, he was welcomed back to the warmth of his commander.

"Captain Gray will have you then?"

"Yes, Captain," Haswell replied stiffly.

"As Second Officer of *Washington* I expect you'll not get a moment's rest 'til you're well clear of the Horn. You understand there'll be no shelter -- the seas will pour into that hold. With only twelve to crew, your hands on that bilge pump or on those rat lines will be torn to shreds.

"I am aware of my duties, Captain."

"Yes," the Old Man took the pen from Lieutenant Howe, and searched for the place on the orders to sign, "well, very good then, and Godspeed, *Mr. Haswell.*"

"Thank you Captain." Haswell was eager to proceed, but remained to take one more letter as written by the literate Lieutenant Howe and competent Captain Kendrick.

Upon delivering it to Captain Gray aboard *Washington*, Mr. Haswell saw no reaction in his new commander, save for an even sterner manner thereafter.

I read Captain Kendrick's orders quite plainly. *"... My orders is that you Sail with the Columbia and do all in your power to keep company with her..."*

Seth returned early from work, and is busy popping the top off a ginger beer as I refill on ice. Captain John Kendrick, I have the benefit of hindsight to guess the gist of Gray's private reaction. When Seth asks if I could grab a few ice cubes, I can't help but give voice to the thought: "Yeah, right."

"Beg pardon?"

Catching myself, I hand the tray to him. "Here. Uh, I think I better sit down."

"What is it? You looked a little better."

I have a seat in the kitchen, and take a few deep breaths. "It's moved to my head. I mean, whatever this fever is. Cold -- flu -- gangrene -- I dunno. It's not that -- I'm just -- this whole thing keeps getting so frustrating." I hold up my *National Geographic* map marked with points tracing the route of the ship around Cape Horn. "I mean, I can see where they're going -- does it matter little points of longitude and latitude here and there when I know all along they get to Nootka, switch ships, Gray abandons Kendrick, then comes back, discovers the Columbia River -- and Kendrick continues pretty successfully until the British decide to take him out? It's so fucking predictable -- pure Shakespeare."

"More like Conrad," Seth snorts.

I blink.

"Heart of Darkness? You know -- what they based *Apocalypse Now* on? Mr. Kurtz, or Colonel Kurtz, sent out into the frontier, becomes a rogue

element, operating just for himself and starts taking everybody's game away, so they decide to send someone to 'terminate with extreme prejudice.'"

There it is -- so clearly. Life seemed to be imitating art, because all along art has simply imitated life. There is no original thought -- simply variations on experience. Kurtz. Kendrick. Yeah, right. "But Kendrick wasn't crazy."

"He probably looked that way to other Westerners."

"But he wasn't -- it was just convenient to characterize him that way since he was more successful in his way than they were in theirs."

"You don't know that."

"I know."

The Professor pulls up a chair, and sets his ginger beer aside. "Miles, you don't. You're reading too much into things. You're making assumptions that contradict the historical record to suit your own ends."

"Hey, I was a blank slate here two weeks ago. Sure, family pride is a little factor here, but very little. Look, I'm working mostly from the private logs and letters of people who, almost to a man, had something to gain by denigrating Kendrick. All except Hoskins. No wonder the Bostoner holds him in such high esteem."

"Have you considered that the more you pursue the possibility the Bostoner, rather than someone like Lewis or a western lumber company, did this, the more it looks like you did it?"

"Me?"

"Yes."

"I'm not the Bostoner."

"How is the rest of the world supposed to know that?"

The thought is absurd. I look him straight in the eye and state most directly: "I'm from Cape Cod."

"So was Captain Kendrick."

CHAPTER TWENTY

Iphigenia Nubiana

Friday, November 3, 1995

Maps. Everywhere. I must see everything to understand. Anything. Everything.

Data. I have plenty. It covers the floors. Books. Papers. Photocopies. Every available roadmap of the Northwest, every atlas has been raided and taped to the walls. Colored pencil criss-crosses them. Blue for *Columbia*. Green for *Washington*. Red for... for whom? Vancouver? What about Meares? And the Spanish? And there were some French ships, too, right?

Data. I have it. I just have to process it.

From Howay I know that between 1788 and 1794 there were 39 vessels plying the Pacific fur trade, thirteen American. The *Columbia* and *Washington* entered the Pacific on April Fools Day of 1788. By 1800 almost every competitor was registered out of Boston.

Boston men.

"Why are you doing this?" Paulie asks as he places the fresh glass of Coke next to me. "You've been here all morning."

"I don't know. I guess to help me put some more order to it all."

"Like what?" He *is* trying to understand something he knows nothing about.

"Okay -- it's 200 years ago. Remember what Napoleon said, in a war *men* are nothing, but *a man* is everything? It's that way in this period of history. Today there are so many ships in the Pacific you can probably jump from one coast to another and not get your feet wet. But back then there were just a half dozen vessels in any one season doing the same things in the *same* places -- buying furs on the Coast from the *same* natives, wintering a few weeks in Hawaii with the *same* islanders, selling their furs in Canton or Macao through the *same* corrupt officials, then loading up with the *same* cargoes, and heading for home -- England or Boston. 'Cept, of course, Kendrick never left, so he was able to develop relationships with the locals."

"Uh-huh." I'm losing him.

"You're a captain. A quarter of the earth's surface is YOUR domain -- you and your little 75-foot boat. Nobody else except a couple of other guys just like you. No cops. No laws. And the ultimate superiority over the natives with your cannons."

Dawn breaks. "Aahhh... well, I wouldn't track these ships on a map."

I am astonished. "Why not?"

"Didn't you tell me the other day that Kendrick's First Officer --"

"Ingraham."

"Yeah, I guess -- that he came back the next trip as captain of his own ship?"

I jump back to my notes and find the reference. "Yeah, the *Hope*. That season he was probably the most successful at collecting furs. Why?"

"That happened a lot, right?"

"What -- oh, yeah. Most of the captains of these later voyages ended up being 20 year-olds who had shipped out as junior officers on earlier expeditions. WHY?"

He taps a map, "You're just tracking ships. Ships don't have memories, but men do. There's your treachery."

Treachery. I look down at the map, my notes, the books. I've become so involved in compiling and absorbing I've forgotten what I am looking for and why. "Track the men." I rifle through my briefcase and find Mag's cards. Connections. Conspiracy.

"Wanna take a break?" he grins.

"Yeah, I think I better."

Paulie plugs the television back in, and for a half hour we blissfully sink into channel surfing. Daytime television. Families squabbling over ridiculous things. "I don't care. I don't care about their problems. I don't care enough to watch," I say, handing the remote to Paulie.

Mental fatigue has begun to combine with physical strain, and I drift into one of my now-frequent naps. When I awake, I hear Paulie fiddling in the kitchen with lunch -- baloney and cheese with mayo on wheat bread -- having left the set on the default -- CNN. The talking heads are discussing how the rainforests in the Northwest are caused by the Kuroshiro current from Japan bringing wet, tropical weather and being stopped by the high peaks on the Coast. Instead of rain being caused by high and low pressure systems clashing, the constant rains of the Northwest are due to the irresistible force of the currents meeting the immovable object of the mountains. Lots of rain means lots of growth.

Lots of growth means lots of timber. It also means lots of wildlife. I've been hearing it for years -- environment versus money. Conservation versus utilization.

I try to ignore it, especially the part featuring the protesters. Extremes seem to be the rule in the west. There were radical environmentalists, mostly from cities and suburbs, against the rah-rah-industrialists of the more home-grown brand. I have little sympathy for either.

The environmentalists should head back home and restore the former paradise they come from. The loggers should remember that it was 200 years of fighting by people "from away" that allow them to live near those forests, so they better not think they, alone, own them. God help the country if people near missile silos took this same approach.

But this report says something about Canada. "Crown lands." The Queen owns them. As far as I'm concerned, I own them. So who the fuck cares?

"The non-violent protests took a tragic turn today here on the Island of Vancouver when a lumber truck apparently tried to back over some protesters. One was rushed to hospital here in Tofino, and doctors have placed 34 year-old Juan Kendriqué on the critical list. Reporting live from Tofino, British Columbia, this is --"

In fumbling for the remote I accidentally turn the set off. Paulie emerges from the kitchen to find me kneeling before the television, searching frantically for the ON button. I turn to him, pleading, "Make him come back!"

"Who?" he laughs nervously.

"Juan Kendriqué. John Kendrick, Jr. I've found him! I've found the prodigal son."

Off the San Fernandes Islands
August 3rd, 1788

The rat would come back, Don Blas hoped.

The Governor had been most kind, most hospitable to a non-Papist. Six days, His Excellency Don Blas Gonzalez had allowed *Columbia* to make repairs in Cumberland Bay. After three months at sea, this first stop in the Pacific found the crew in hard shape, and the grasses and berries from the hillsides were as vital to the continuation of the voyage as repairs to the rigging. One man had already been lost to scurvy, and two yardarms to the Horn. Captain Kendrick had requested permission to touch at the island of

Más a Tierra.

Most graciously, His Excellency had allowed another four days to Captain Kendrick in which to wait out a storm. Ten days for repairs off the west coast of South America with no sight of Captain Gray and *Washington*. After a month of beating around the Horn, the winds had shifted from Northwest to south, and while Gray's neat little sloop could easily turn, bulky *Columbia* prepared to "wear ship". First, running off before the wind, then placing the ship sideways in the trough between two waves, only to catch the full impact broadside in the turn.

Columbia's high rails kept many of the men on deck from being swept off by the mercilessly pounding of the waves from the south. When the turn had been completed, however, no *Washington* and no Captain Gray were to be spied from the crowsnest.

Two more months, and finally the San Fernandes were sighted to the northeast. Five hundred miles east would be the coast of Chile. *Columbia* was still below the equator, but with the shelter of a nearby cove, the needed repairs to vessel and crew could be affected.

Orders to Gray were to continue to either the main island, Más Afuera, or this one *Columbia* had stayed at for the better part of a fortnight. Upon inquiry with Don Blas, the answer had been, No, no visit by any other Americans -- you come first.

Mr. Kendrick, Third Officer, had impressed his father and fellow officers with his rudimentary proficiency in Latin. Mr. Nutting, while a capable astronomer, had also been retained to act as translator in the event of encounters with Spanish and Russian authorities on the Coast. After the frail Schoolmaster's demise, the bidding for his personal effects began, allowing John, Jr.'s acquisition of the massive *Book of Languages*. The text concentrated on Latin first, as the key to proficiency in French, Spanish, Italian and Portuguese. Thus, while the crew of *Columbia* began their debilitating descent into scurvy, the Third Officer poured what free time could be had into the dead language of Cicero and the Holy Father of Rome.

It was one thing, Captain Kendrick knew, to be diplomatic, gracious and charming when one was desperate and destitute. Such was the lot of anyone growing up on Cape Cod. But to be so in a foreign language -- that was another.

The Governor commanded a regiment of cavalry to rule these islands, and as horsemen tend towards the same small stature as seamen, the Spanish were overcome by the massive red Bear of the Yankee Captain. A big man was to be respected and feared. But he tempered this mantle with good

humor and respect for the office and uniform of the Governor. Adding to
the compliment, the Commander insisted his own son speak as interpreter,
though with the arrival of a multi-lingual Frenchman from a passing English
vessel a few days later, translation problems ceased.

After presentation of letters of passport signed by the President of the
Congress at Washington praying for safe passage for Captain Kendrick and
vessels under his command in their "voyages of discovery" (not trade, no, no,
not in the Spanish lake of the Pacific, dear me), Don Blas most graciously
provisioned *Columbia* with her needs. What else was there to do at this edge
of the Spanish Empire? The natives were fine and enjoyable, to a degree, and
followed their masters' orders, and the climate was ideal enough. But this
"vacation" for a cavalry contingent simply led to idleness. The occasional
ship -- His Catholic Majesty's galleon from Manila, or a renegade English
trader -- was not only notable, it was *something* happening. This American --
big, hearty, courageous -- here was something new! Something remarkable!
Give him what he wants and send him on his way. As if there were any other
pressing matters of state on these rocks.

But now the chains rubbed his wrist raw, drawing the fleas to the open
flesh. The lice in Don Blas' hair were nearly driving him mad -- if he had but
a bucket of seawater he could at least douse himself and rid the infestation.

There would be no bucket, of course, he knew. There would be, maybe,
a few crusts of bread thrown down by any one of the Inca deckhands. In the
dark below decks, through the shadows and shafts of light, he waited for the
rat. It would come. Earlier yesterday -- today -- which was it? -- something
had run on clawed fleet across his ankle. If Don Blas were patient, he would
soon eat again.

The last crust pulled from his pocket lay in broken crumbs by his right
hand. But when vermin have all the ship to choose from, squeezing through
cracks and nooks in the woodwork, nosing into flour barrels and around
forgotten dinner plates, what attraction could there be in the stalest of biscuit
next to a broken, fetid wretch?

The warrant from the Viceroy of Chile was clear, Don Blas had seen.
"Take measures to secure this vessel and all the people aboard with
discretion, tact, cleverness, and caution." It clearly stated the name "John
Kendrick" as the captain, so there could be no doubt, even if the ship names
Columbia and *Washington* could be others. Both were said to be owned by
General Washington, and out for conquest. Kendrick had been a successful
privateer against the British. Against an indolent and unprepared Spanish
treasure galleon, a Mexican mission or a Chilean village, the two American

vessels could wreak havoc.

So the Viceroy of Peru claimed. He had not met this man, Captain Kendrick. But then, the Viceroy was more concerned with his Inca slaves and building cathedrals, and failed to send the warrant to his governor at San Fernandes until after Don Blas had sent word to Lima of receiving Kendrick in the first place.

Yes, the Viceroy's warrant came. With a company of infantry to deliver another warrant for the Governor's arrest. So Don Blas was supposed to know *without orders* to arrest any vessel not flying the colors of His Catholic Majesty. He had also been blamed for delaying the dispatch of his report to the Viceroy, for it took another week to send a frigate from Peru to hunt for *Columbia*.

God help John Kendrick, his son, and the officers and men under his command. Men like the Viceroy saw a brave man and feared him, though he meant them no harm. They blamed others for their own failures, and cared not for the consequences of their actions. Even so, there was small chance the Viceroy's frigate could catch up to *Columbia*, never mind capture, the Yankee trader. But should Kendrick touch upon the coast, at San Blas, Monterey or San Francisco, that was another matter.

There was a scratching noise near his right ear, and Don Blas raised his eyes to see a small form furtively edge towards the crumbs.

"So," Seth begins, "why are you asking me?"

"I don't know." I don't. I can think up good reasons, like I need him to stay quiet, or I'll need his help if anything happens, but they don't need to be said in the first place.

He taps at the metal of the side cellar door. "Well, at least you're honest."

"I don't like to lie."

He laughs with mock astonishment, "Could've fooled me!" As he leans up against the door, he taps out a jiggedy-jig tune that matches the "Huh-huhs" of his thinking. "Let's, just for the sake of argument, take a look at what you've got. Your sole argument against the theory of a rational person blowing these people up is the letter to Jean-Pierre Hoskins -- that anyone in Boston could've sent. Like you."

"There were other letters from other places, and I haven't been out of this time zone in years," I say.

"Easily overcome. You could've had someone else mail the various letters for you. But let's just grant you the benefit of the doubt for the moment."

"Fine. What about the pattern?"

"What pattern?" Seth demands. "You have an old drunk dead from exposure and a doctor killed by pro-life extremists. Coincidence."

"But their names are the same."

"Coincidence. Can you guess how many Doctor Roberts there are in the U.S.? Some of them *had* to have died in the past few years -- if you hadn't found this guy, you would've found another who died in a fire or car crash -- would they have been killed by your Bostoner, too? How do you know he hasn't killed *all* the Doctor Roberts in the past ten years?"

"Because *I* wouldn't," I shrug. "The point was made. One's enough."

"Apparently not. There keep on being more. The bomb's proof of that."

"Yes! My point exactly. This sort of thing doesn't end or peter out. It keeps on getting worse." I'm able to pace a little bit, despite my hobbled ankle. "First victim, Woodruffe -- simply left to die. Second, Roberts -- stabbed, once. Third, fourth, fifth, sixth and seventh -- Kendrick, Gray, Meares, Bulfinch and Barrell -- all in an explosion. It's getting more violent."

"Wait a minute. You're counting Barrell as a victim?"

"If Bulfinch deserved to die, Barrell did more so. Old Joe was the controlling partner who ordered Gray to command the second mission. Hell, Charles Bulfinch left the whole affair to his father, and walked away so he could design the State House and U.S. Capitol."

"Barrell thought Barrell deserved to die. That's what you're saying." He's trying to get it clear.

"The Bostoner determined it. Or some part of our present-day Barrell. Anyway, it was supposed to all end with his death. It didn't. It hasn't. It won't. So Juan Kendriqué's next."

"How do you figure that?"

"Okay, fine. Let's do it your way --"

"I don't have *a way*," the Professor says. "You just talk."

"Right. Let's say they were killed for the money, the land. If the Juan Kendriqué out in B.C. is the descendant of John Kendrick, Jr., then he's got a pretty good claim on those deeds. Better than me, since he's a direct descendant. And he lives out there and is active in preserving the area. Hey, if I owned a logging company and some *white* guy started waving deeds around, I'd pay a lot more attention than to the natives who said they never sold the land to the government in the first place."

"But why would your Bostoner kill Kendriqué?" Seth asks. "If he's a descendant of 'his' son, then that should put him in the same camp as Hoskins, right? Protected?"

"No, 'cause he tried to kill *me*. I'm the genuine article. Deep down the Bostoner knows he's a fraud. We John Kendricks are a painful reminder that he can never really be us."

"Your pop-psych worries me more than your fundamental grasp of maritime history."

"I *know* hatred."

The Professor frowns. "Let's say you do go out there, and lo and behold Kendriqué dies. Who's to say *you* didn't do it? You'd have been linked to two deaths, then connected by a hypothesis you seem to understand intimately."

I can't answer that. Not anymore. He's making too much sense. Checking my date books back to May 1994, it had been one of those rainy days when my father had dismissed the crew early -- more than enough time to dash up to Lawrence and run through Doctor Roberts. And New Year's Eve 1992 is clear to me since our plans had been ruined by my sudden twenty-four hour flu. Paulie and company had been sent out to First Night in Boston with my best wishes while I stayed home alone. I remember.

What concerns me even more is my complete lack of corroboration about Mags. Not just about that night in Salem, or her job at Peabody-Essex -- but her, herself. I've always told Paulie and Seth about her, but anytime she's stopped by, both were either at work or out of town. My imaginary friend?

"Okay, look Seth," I explain, "I gotta go. I have to do this. It matters. Look at me! I'm almost 30 and I'm barely scraping by doing what it takes to survive. It provides cold comfort to live life on my own terms. I wasn't designed for this world -- or this existence -- maybe just not this time. I don't fit in -- not the way I'm doing now. Hell, I'M TIRED OF LIVING IN OTHER PEOPLE'S HOUSES, DOING OTHER PEOPLE'S WORK!"

I'm red in the face, angry, embarrassed, wired, trembling with the rage that comes from acknowledging one's own wretched situation. Seth stares at me hard, sighs, and opens the cellar door to the rear alleyway. "Wait here."

? -- That's a new direction to go. My curiosity at his sudden and unorthodox departure is quickly sidelined by my rocking back and forth in an attempt to expend the adrenaline bouncing through my veins.

I have to go. He has to understand. This cramped space in this cramped city in the cramped corner of the country is closing in on me. Stuck in the dusty attic of the New World, surrounded by forgotten family mementoes, it's stifling. The Feds might eventually tire of looking for someone else to pin this on, or they'll get wind of the letters to Hoskins. By the time the Bostoner strikes again, I'll be dead.

I'm not going to prison.

It isn't meant as a threat, but a promise. I will not allow myself to be held in a place at the mercy of people who see me only as meat. And then to truly get AIDS. Better to be shot evading the authorities.

I won't be taken alive.

The Bostoner will fare better. He'll eventually be caught. He might go after Meredith again once the heat's off. Or maybe the Queen of England. That'd be an escalation. Hell, the City of Vancouver --

The cellar door opens and a pink-cheeked Seth slams it behind him. "Okay," he nods, "but I need your guarantee."

"What? Where did you go?"

"First, your guarantee -- you'll come right back, or I'll spill the whole thing. That's everything, including your apparent complicity."

"Oh, I'll come back. It's my home. But if I'm wrong, the FBI won't scare me. If I try to set a foot across this door, I want a bullet right though the forehead," I say, tapping the spot. "I want it over. I'm tired and I'm losing my patience. If Kendriqué dies while I'm out there, you have to do that for me."

"Well, let's hope you're right." He starts up the stairs, "When are you leaving?"

"Nope, that's all you get. You're too involved as it is. Say, what was that --" I point out the door, " -- a run around the block to change your mind?"

He turns at the top of first staircase and hands me a note written in stained felt pen. In his handwriting is the number for Barrell, Bulfinch & Gray, with the notation below:

JOS. BARRELL

-- OUT OF THE COUNTRY FOR THE WEEK

-- FAMILY BUSINESS

"You owe me a dime," Seth notes.

"At least."

The rumbling from below is getting louder. It's a wonder the whole hill doesn't just fall in on the Red Line. Slicing beneath Beacon Hill from Park Street, the heaviest subway line of Boston's "T" veers northwest under the

State House, and emerges to cross the Charles River via the Longfellow Bridge. On streets closer to that end, you can feel the heavy four and six car monsters lumber through their tunnels every ten minutes.

This is not the direction I want to be going.

After about five minutes' work with the crowbar to the new plaster, Paulie had found the twin of the hatch on the opposite side of the cellar. Hefting the black leather briefcase under my shoulder, I smiled. He hung back at the steps, not the least assured as I balanced on the sill of the opening. "I feel like I'm never going to see you again." The affection inherent in that statement forced a smile onto my otherwise determined face. "For the love of God," he pleaded, "be careful."

"I will."

"No, I mean it. I know you. You're going to do something stupid."

"That's kinda inevitable."

The third building in this direction had two doors in its laundry room. I was tired with my predictable route this far, and opted for the one I guessed led across the street. It didn't.

Instead, it hooks a hard left, and drops half its height. I am glad I'm wearing my dark dress pants, just in case any slime got on them. With all the spider webs around I wish I had use a flame to burn them out of my way. With my luck, I'd poke it right into a fire alarm.

The duck walk is not pleasant on my still-recovering ankle. It's also slow. I have half an hour -- maybe less -- to get to the Aquarium. And I've got the creeping suspicion I'm working slowly in the opposite direction.

Dead ahead is something that looks like a door. It's metal, at least. With hinges. A utility box, maybe ten years old. There's about six inches on either side to get by. What idiot thought to place this thing right where I have to go?

This will not stop me.

I begin to strip down so as to not tear or smear my suit on the mildewed sheet metal of the box or the slimy brick walls. I wrestle with the overcoat first, and set it on the floor next to me, right beside where I set my briefcase. Both have disappeared. I frantically paw in the dark when my overcoat also drifts out of reach. Flashing my penlight into the darkness reveals nothing. Not even the floor.

I nearly fell down a shaft and didn't even know it. On its sides are newish rubberized rungs, and facing it a number of heavy-duty electrical lines leading to the box behind me. A substation.

Poking my head down, I can see little below. But the roar of a train comes louder. At its most deafening, I catch sight of my briefcase and overcoat in the headlights. The top of the train fills my whole view down, as car after car passes. After, the briefcase is thrown open and the coat gone.

I climb down the shaft and dangle ten feet above the tracks from the roof of the tunnel. How the hell am I supposed to get down? Or up? Not wishing to get pegged by the next train, I drop. The soft wood rails and hard gravel catch me full in the back. I turn to see the ominous "third rail" half a foot from my face. Just one swing sideways in that fall would have placed me across both rails, and ended this escapade with a premature 10,000 volts. In the shadows between the rails, mice dart about. Large mice. I hop over to my briefcase and gather together its contents.

The angle of the tracks reorients me. Down is further into the hill, towards Park Street station. Up is Charles Circle. That last train had headed down, so another won't be due for at least ten minutes. Friday night. 7:15. Yeah, ten minutes.

I'm probably closer to Charles Circle station, but way up above the traffic circle in the open air I'd be conspicuous, especially during the fifty yard hobble out of the tunnel. Anyone on either platform could see. Park Street is underground and expansive. Anonymous. Besides, it's downhill. Quarter mile maybe. No big deal. I move at a quick pace, tripping only twice onto my face, when the lights and noise ahead signal an approaching train on the opposite track. I hadn't thought of that.

Now, I've seen plenty of workers out on the tracks in my years riding the subway. Seeing them loom out of the shadows with their flashlights reminded me of those cheap horror rides at the Barnstable County Fair. More alarming, though, would be seeing a man in a tweed suit hopping along the Beacon Hill subway tunnel. All a driver had to do was call the T Police.

I must say, the mice are pretty quick, and I catch not a single one under me as I throw myself to the corner of the tunnel wall and floor. Stretched out lengthwise, maybe I'll look like a bag. Or nothing at all. As the train passes, I hope my head is covered enough. Not that I fear the train's rear brakeman noticing the back of my head. I just don't want the big mice to find the long, thick hair too compelling a nest. Big mice.

The last clickety-clacks fading up the hill, I leap up and raced at full-hobble. Rounding the corner I see the yellow dinge of Park Street's furthest platforms. The booming behind me can not be acknowledged -- a man *running* out of the tunnel would be noticed by riders on the platform. But a man *walking* along the tunnel and stepping up the ladder to the platform is nothing. The arriving train is more important -- that's what they've been waiting for.

No one cares to invade anyone else's space in subway stations in Boston. Just get out of their way. If anyone notices me, they don't care to do anything about it. At the top of the stairs, on the platform for the Green Line, no one comes out of the ticket box to inquire about me. The trolley to Government Center shuts its doors after me, and I take satisfaction in knowing I've just saved a hot 85 cents subway fare.

Money. That is the problem. Travel is the goal, and the means of travel require money. Cash. Untraceable. Limited.

$197.97. The Connor & Vanzetti paycheck.

The stairs at Government Center station lead down to the Blue Line. Once on this train, it could take me under the harbor to Logan International Airport. Maybe I could slip a hundred bucks to a ticket agent and climb aboard the next flight to Seattle, Portland or Vancouver. Then again, airports are hotbeds of security. Any such offer should be reported, and just like that -- I'd be found sneaking out of town.

I concentrate on the stainless steel bar I cling to as the little blue train hums under the streets of Boston.

I *could* do it.

It would save time. But it'd eat up most or all of my cash. And place me at the mercy of airline personnel, not exactly the most trustworthy people in the world.

The doors slide open at State Street. One middle-aged man in a windbreaker steps in and wanders about for a seat even though most of the train is empty. The Blue Line leads from the back side of Beacon Hill through downtown, then takes a sharp turn northeast, up the North Shore, ending at Wonderland Dog Track. Unless you're going to the airport, nobody heads *out* of the city on the Blue Line early on a Friday night. To the airport. That's what I look like.

The doors open again at the Aquarium stop and I nonchalantly pick up my briefcase and head out. The escalator up spares the ankle and I test it to make the limp appear to be attributed to the weight of the bag.

I believe it to be statutory law that once a year schoolchildren in Massachusetts be crowded into buses and brought to either the Boston Museum of Science or the New England Aquarium. Hence, upon emerging from the Blue Line portal, I find myself in familiar surroundings. It all seems strange now.

Oh, sure, there is the seal pool and the adjacent floating display area for the dolphin and sea lion shows. But as I walk towards the new waterfront

Marriott Hotel, in all its red brick, glass and brass glory, I'm reminded of where I truly am. The Marriott at Long Wharf.

Long Wharf, which 200 years before ran a quarter mile out into the harbor. Boston has grown out to surround all but the wharf's last 50 yards or so. Long Wharf, where *Columbia Rediviva* and *Lady Washington* were fitted October 1, 1787 on a voyage of trade and discovery in the *"Pacific Ocean by J. Barrell, S. Brown, C. Bulfinch, J. Darby, C. Hatch, J.M. Pintard,"* and *"Commanded by J. Kendrick,"* the medal had read.

I see a line of well-dressed people waiting to board the sleek entertainment ship. Preferring not to imitate so many sheep, I wander to the end of the wharf.

This is a powerful place. No doubt the Bostoner has come here to commune. Long Wharf, although highly sanitized and refined for its high-end waterfront condos and office spaces in its old warehouses, still possesses its power. It is the dead center of the waterfront of a city built out of waterfronts. Water shuttles, whale watch ships and party boats use the wider berths afforded at Long Wharf. The economy of the city has changed, but Long Wharf is still working when others have simply devolved into high-priced, semi-private back yards.

The haze of the drizzle obscures the details of the harbor at night. An ominous glow from the ongoing construction of the subterranean sewer tunnel way out on Deer Isle makes it look as if some rock concert is going on far out to the East. Above, the air traffic is apparent by the fading of blinking warning beacons as the planes rise higher and higher. Off to the right, the skeleton of the new federal courthouse emerges from Fan Pier.

In any other American city I would be justifiably wary of the waterfront at night, even in the most civilized of quasi-parks like this found at the end of Long Wharf. But this is Boston. That sort of thing doesn't happen here. It's not allowed.

As I look down at the harbor gently lapping against the massive granite footings of the pier, I notice there is another platform jutting out six feet below, like one low stair. In an earlier age, if a vessel arrived at high tide, then the gangplank would accommodate the street level. When the tide had dropped six feet, the lower step was used. In this age of assumed public stupidity, the steps down to the landing have been chained off. Too bad. It's important for people to be able to touch the water if you want them to care about it, even if it is filthy. Especially if it is.

The boat blasts its horn, and I turn to see the scurry of the finely-heeled lingerers towards the gangplank. Checking my watch and my briefcase, I departed the end of Long Wharf and cross the plaza, wherein is laid a design in the pavement.

I hesitate. At first, the design looks like a star, maybe twenty feet across. But with all my recent readings, it finally registered -- a compass, with all its points of North, Southwest, East-by-Northeast and so forth. I hover but a moment, tracing its perimeter, wondering how big it is.

The horn blasts once more with finality, and I walk the axis from northwest to southeast before heading to the *Delphi*.

"Good evening, sir. Do you have your invitation?"

"Certainly."

She is quite pretty, and that's the point. Political fund-raisers must -- absolutely *must* -- have attractive, bright-eyed young men and women at the check-in booths. Because of the unorthodox location of this event, however, the doorside table has been dispensed with so as to comply with Coast Guard regulations. Instead, a podium is improvised.

I reach inside my tweed jacket and pull out the linen-wrapped invitation. In highly ornate, swooping lettering it reads as a most gracious invitation from His Excellency, the Governor of the Commonwealth, and his sidekick Lieutenant Governor, for a soirée upon the ship *Delphi*, with accommodations at the one stop to be made two hours later. The courtesy of a one thousand dollar contribution is requested. How nice not to ask directly.

"Will you be staying in Provincetown this evening?" she asks as she scans the list in her book, "Mr....?"

"Kimball. No, I'm afraid not. What time do you expect us to arrive back here? I'd like to arrange for a cab."

She has dusky skin and curly, deep rust hair. Indian? Definitely the subcontinent. The black dress hugs tight to what I can see of her behind the platform. She's smiling, perhaps at my long hair among all these J. Crew preppies -- then again, she's paid to smile.

And I remember the Vow.

"I'm sorry, I don't see your name here," she looks up, still quite pleasant. The gangplank bangs off, and the roar of the engines signals getting under way. It's already too late.

I frown quickly at the distraction, then continue absentmindedly, "Oh, yes," I fish through my pockets and produce a card, "the Senator sends her regrets." Imprinted on the front is the gold and blue seal of the Commonwealth of Massachusetts -- an Indian carrying arrows, tips pointed down indicating peace -- along with the name of a state senator I know to be terminally ill and unable to attend. I always keep people's cards since I never listen when they introduce themselves.

She takes the card, raises her eyebrows a hair, and smiles sympathetically, "Of course." I can see her flipping over the invitation to reveal the small tell-tale "C" marked in red felt pen in the corner.

If a Governor wants to be a United States Senator, he must continually cultivate the loyalty of independently-elected politicians. An easy way is to allow them to attend his high-powered fund-raisers *gratis*. They won't be embarrassed by the indication in the card. Why, it is only meant to be... Complimentary.

"I'm told we won't dock in Provincetown until at least 9:30," she says, "so don't expect to be back at the earliest... midnight?"

I turn to say something, catch myself, then grin. "I suppose," I begin as I slowly take in her full brown eyes, "that's a pretty good deal for you -- a boat trip to P-Town, a party, stay over in some nice inn, then, what -- a drive back?"

"I *wish*," she's letting down her guard, but still maintains a wary smile. "I have to take the boat back tonight to prepare for the second trip back there on Sunday. A whale watch, if you can believe it. It's for all the environmental biggies."

"Oh," I nod, "Hm."

"See you on the way back tonight."

I nod, oblivious, "Guess so. Thanks."

"Okay."

And sometimes I don't even need a Vow.

The *Delphi* isn't a ship. She's a floating nightclub and restaurant. Probably a hundred feet of steel and fiberglass formed around two and a half enclosed decks, it is designed to hold tables and couches full of people consuming mixed drinks, shrimp cocktail and prime rib. That means she also had to be quite steady, or else those same people would soon be expelling mixed drinks, shrimp cocktail and prime rib, which, unless I have lost all my political sense, is not the fast track to Washington.

Dodging between the six-person tables of old preppy money and new ethnic money, I dash up the stairs to the top deck where only a few of the hardiest souls hung out. This deck is covered in front, and open to the mist aft. I am heading straight for the rear doors when a red-haired gentleman in a blue blazer beckons, "Ho, there!"

Busted. I turn the handle and try to continue, unhearing.

"Excuse me," he's at my shoulder.

I turn, quite surprised, "Oh, yes? Just needed a breath of air."

He smiles knowingly. My ruffled clothes, grown-in beard and long hair at this occasion matched, in a fashion, his waxed mustache, stained khakis and the yacht club patch on his blazer. "Oh, of course. But you won't want to miss Bill. He'll be on through soon enough. Up on the bridge with his daughters."

I try to be impressed. "Taking command, huh?"

He laughs. Old school, he must think. Only those not threatened by money dress without care. "The Captain is showing them how to pilot out of the harbor. Don't stay too long outside."

Sticking my head out into the spitting fog, I raise my collar, "No danger of that."

Back at the rear of the deck I watch the Boston skyline disappear into the shroud of fog. Below, the foam from the stern continues hypnotically. On the ferries to Nantucket or Martha's Vineyard I've often wanted to dive down into that chaos of water, even though I know the suction would probably drag me back into the propellers. The confusion is enthralling.

From the corner of my eye, a tall strawberry blond man in a light gray suit steps through a hatch into the top deck lounge, flanked by two long-haired versions of himself in dresses. One or two of the lounge lizards creep closer to hear his account of the passage. I step behind a stack of life preservers.

Shit.

I recognized many people on board from my political years following college. The money people. Practically every member of the Republican State Finance Committee, along with various new faces that speak of the same desire to "help, if we can."

My problem had always been the money. I quit that world because I simply couldn't stand the constant pitch for money. The hunt obscured everything else. On issues and strategy, I was right on the mark. At twenty-three, state-wide candidates asked my advice. More importantly, they liked what they heard.

Inside that lounge are mostly people I had seen, but never spoke to. They won't recognize me because they never had to deal with me. There is, however, one man who will. He remembers people. That's why he's so successful in politics. The only man who can blow my cover on this boat is the Governor himself.

The mist has turned my unbound hair into one mop of chill plastered to my skull, and I've tried concentrating on the drips forming at the end of my nose, seeing how they would take form, then fall onto the deck. Cold isn't normally a problem for me, but I can't remain sick, or get any sicker. My thoughts would break down, and I might collapse in public, then where would I be? **"Pathetic Deranged Derelict Found On Governor's Yacht"** the *Herald* would read. Or something like that.

I figure by edging stealthily along the railing, I can make it to the bridge of the ship beyond the lounge, from where I might find another way below. If I can just find a nice warm bathroom to hide out in, I'll be fine for the rest of the passage. At some point the attention of the host and his crowd in the lounge will all be drawn away from back here, and I'll be able to make my way forward.

The deck is too wet to sit on, and I'm too tired to stand, so I hunker down to a squat, trying still to favor my bad ankle. What a way I have come in five years. In the spring of long years ago, at a convention center, I allowed a good man to fail because I would not lie. He was my candidate, my client, and my friend. His opponent at the convention had taken an extreme stance to placate party conservatives -- a position that could not pass the muster of the general electorate of the Commonwealth.

I could have sent those extremists scurrying at that convention by a whispered innuendo that the bright young man *they* supported -- well, he wasn't married, and he didn't appear to have a girlfriend, and in fact was never known to have one, you see. You see? And while Massachusetts then had the only two openly gay Congressmen in the nation, they were also liberal Democrats, and thus not hypocrites, at least not on that issue. One word would have done it. My word.

So we lost. If we had won, I'd be -- probably on this boat right now, too. Clean cut. Well-dressed. Chatting up that pretty greeter. Married. Warm. Dry.

But it's not like I carry any form of resentment with me.

At the following primary, the present Governor and his hand-picked running mate beat the conservatives nominated at the convention, and went on to win the general election in an upset. He's quite popular now, having just won re-election handily. Good for him.

In a way, I feel a kindred spirit. He is quirky, tends to laziness, and possesses a good sense of humor. Must be nice to inherit money. To never worry about how long the corn flakes are going to last, or if the rain this weekend will stop the drought and provide some lawn mowing work. His family made their money early, and simply banked it. A couple hundred years of interest means never bouncing a check. Where did that money originally come from again? Easy.

Shipping. Everyone in Boston was into it a couple hundred years ago. Have a little money to invest -- try the China trade. Returns ran 25-50%, sometimes as high as 300%. Not bad turnaround in a few years. The risks were, well, that maybe the ship wouldn't come back.

I peer around the corner of the life preservers, to the lounge full of Brahmins. Barrell could be here.

I shoot bolt upright. He'd know me. Not like *maybe* the Governor would. The Bostoner would *definitely* know me. But he's out of the country on family business, right?

I certainly hope so.

But with all the old money on board, all inter-related from centuries of marrying the "right people", there are bound to be some descendants of the Owners of *Columbia* and *Washington*. Hatch, Derby, Brown. They believed Gray's lies and distortions about it all being Kendrick's fault. They are all responsible, and they all have to pay.

... So the Bostoner would reason. But he's not here.

Am I sure? *I'm* here.

I crouch back down on deck again. No, I'm not here for that.

I review my plan of escape from Boston. Airport: Out. Train: Out. Bus: Out. In fact, any sort of public transportation: OUT. They all might be watched. The Mazda is definitely out because its absence from where it's sat for the past week would instantly be noticed. Too obvious.

The answer was taped to the refrigerator. One of the invitations I display there as a joke. Wonderful to be on the most exclusive mailing lists after all these years.

I know the tricks of the trade to get on board. I can pass. It's a one-way ticket to somewhere a hell of a lot more familiar than strange, and so it makes sense. Paulie doesn't know. Seth doesn't know. No one. Except me. I know why I am here.

... I think. Seth's suggestions of my own possible involvement reverberate in my head. I can justify too easily. Slowly, I begin to draw my gaze to my attaché. I remember what I put in there. Just what I need to bring out to the Northwest. I think about checking inside, just to make sure nothing else is there. Something deadly. Sinking this boat would be the next logical step in an increasingly violent trend.

No, I know what's in there. My confidence is shaken, and I need a leap of faith. I refuse to open it. Still, to be sure, I could simply throw it into the ocean. That'd prove it, surely. If I can throw it away now, surely...

No, I need these things. I'm not going to throw them away just to satisfy some silly paranoia. I grip the handles tightly and march directly to the lounge.

Amid the hubbub inside, my entrance and passage down the stairs is barely noticed. On the bottom deck, I find a bathroom and immediately set to work squeezing the ocean from my hair. No one comes in, and I use about half a roll of paper towels when I notice there is no urinal in here.

I'm in the Ladies Room. I'm in the Ladies Room, hiding from the host, and afraid I'm going to kill everyone aboard.

I quickly grab up my bag and slip out the door. The pretty greeter practically tips backwards over an empty dessert tray, and I have to lunge to catch her.

At this angle, with me leaning over her with my dripping hair falling all about my shoulders, I must look like a crazy man. Pulling her back upright, I try to apologize with a simple, "Pardonez-moi," but her "Ummm..." stops me.

Ladies Room. I smirk, sheepishly, "Thought there might be a hairdryer in there."

Her name was Prima. She is 25. Graduate of Bates with a degree in Business. Bright. Charming -- the red hair a tip-off -- a cutting wit.

Her story that she's hiding out from some lech on the upper deck is as believable as are my excuses for being in the Ladies Room. Her favorite is the undeniable truth: "I'm stupid."

"Well, I don't think so," she says.

Why the hell do I have to find a nice person *now?*

We remain in this little alcove in the aft section because it is out of view of the rest of the ship. Also, the low hum of the engines below is like a gentle massage pervading everything. When the deckhand moves to throw off the gangplank, he's surprised to see a couple in this horrible part of the ship. Then he starts whistling as he goes to work securing the ship to the Provincetown's Lewis Wharf. Prima almost blushes.

Shit. I have to go.

She has served her purpose, keeping me occupied until we pulled into port. If I was going to do anything violent, I was pretty sure I wouldn't with her around. I know myself well enough to know when faced with either time with a woman or death, martyrdom can always wait. The problem now is contriving a way off the ship. Fine.

"I'm going to call for a cab to pick me up when we get back to Boston,"

I start to head off the ship, conspicuous with my bag.

"No, oh, wait. I've got to make sure these people are all unloaded okay," she indicates. "Can you wait a minute?"

"I'll only be a few seconds. I see the phone booth up at the head of the wharf." I turn down the gangplank, and am washed along by the staggering, boisterous flow of political funding. Ducking between them, I am able to get out of sight of *Delphi* and race up the wharf.

Goddamn Vow!

Thirty-five miles. Nope, make that thirty four. Maybe thirty three and a half. In a car, it might take an hour or less, what with all back roads. But I didn't have an automobile in my briefcase when I stepped off Lewis Wharf, and onto Commercial Street in Provincetown. Nor did I fancy one would appear for my use. Finding this bike was hard enough.

Dodging in and out of people's back yards is not a wise thing to do at night anywhere, but in tightly-built P-Town, it's almost impossible with all the picket fences.

The municipal limits are about 90% National Seashore, confining the remainder of useable land to a small strip along Commercial Street. Long a haven for the sexually liberated, ambiguous or indescribable, P-Town is the very tip of Cape Cod, the fist at the end of this arm bared into the Atlantic. As I searched for a mode of transit quicker than my own weary feet, creeping amongst the Greek Revival storefronts celebrating seashells, leather or art, I adopted the more introverted, down-Cape attitude: Now that I'm here, how do I leave?

I had one thing on my side – it's November. More than any of the other Cape's towns, P-Town celebrates the summer hard. After the three month party come nine months of hangover. The New Yorkers go back to their Greenwich Village Bistros and Fifth Avenue firms, and the remaining mix of old Cape Codders, Portuguese and wash-ashores clean up. About half the town goes on unemployment during the winter. Thus, the shipload of wealthy Boston partiers might give the place a shot in the arm. A little shot. Meanwhile, the natives are still hibernating, and I might just find...

Lots of locked-up bikes.

It's easier getting through the narrow streets of P-Town on a bike than a car. Everything is within walking distance, so why take a car? There isn't any parking, anyway.

Up the hill, past the Provincetown Monument, through the cemetery and back down into town I trudged. Nothing. Half an hour and all I had to show for it was a screaming ankle. At least the cops were cool -- they saw plenty of freaky people about, day or night. I would only be in trouble if I were caught in the act of stealing or murdering. The first I intended. The second...

The horn sounded as the *Delphi* cast off. I looked up as she slid out of Provincetown Harbor. In my need for control, I had used someone, a good person I might otherwise have had a nice time with, and now Prima probably felt like crap. She didn't *have* to be nice to me -- she *wanted* to. Of course, there was always a certain energy about me during a Vow, like a containment field. The power to repress within also attracted from without. It was inevitable. It also sucked.

I needed a bike.

Marching down Commercial Street, I commenced straight out of town.

I didn't care. I had to get out of here before it gets light. One way or another.

The bike was resting within the garage two buildings down. Inside the house, the TV was on. The garage held an old Volvo, but the bike seemed pretty new. Nobby tires. A dozen or so speeds. And light enough to be picked up with one hand and carried out of this garage without even waking the dog.

The tide is low in Cape Cod Bay, and makes for a shorter route. At this point, the Cape arcs from north-south back to the west, and the extra land revealed at low water allows me to cut the corner. Along the shore, I see the rows of tiny white cottages, some still with their lights burning this late in the season. Beyond is the Route 6, Pilgrim Lake and the dunes. Not that I can see the rest in this mist and darkness. But it provides a point of reference.

Fifteen miles an hour. If I can maintain fifteen miles an hour, let's see, that's 45 miles total at that average speed -- three hours. Three hours. Average. That counts going down hills -- maybe twenty-five miles per hour.

Uphill, too. Five.

That averages to -- fifteen. How did I know this already?

South to Truro, cliffs rise up from the beach, not the broad expanse I'm hoping for. Cape Cod is supposed to be broad and flat. That is further south. All I'm finding here is soft sand on my left -- the east -- and a closer shore on my right -- the west, broken up by the occasional rock breakwater lying quite inconveniently across my path.

Water to the west. Land to the east. What an odd concept.

When the Pilgrims landed in November in 1620, it probably wasn't so odd or at least not the first thing on their mind. They took refuge in Provincetown Harbor and landed on these shores searching for fresh water. They desperately raided an Indian burial site of its supply of corn, after spooking a few of the Nauset tribe further down this same shore. Finally, *Mayflower* turned due west, finding Plymouth with a fine harbor and a running brook.

I'm pretty sick of the place myself, and I pull up the first landing I can find. The soft sand led to a steep asphalt road, which then sharply dives down the opposite side. Welcome to North Truro.

Hills and hollows. That's all I remember about Truro. In its own way, it has moors, too. Truro is vast dunes, covered by the rattiest of vegetation, and between which are mostly idyllic little cottages built over a hundred years ago.

Painter Edward Hopper came here with other artists in the 20' and 30's, drawn by the desolation and the light. The light is still here, and the desolation was held onto by the purchase of most of the town by the federal government for the National Seashore.

Streets. Little lanes winding in and out. It's costing me time, but I'm out of Provincetown and can afford a higher profile. The only way out of town is past the new police and fire station.

Highway. This is not fun. Route 6 is mostly four undivided lanes with virtually no life on either side. Slicing through the stands of stunted pitch pine, I find horribly long hills that seem longer going up than down. Eventually a state or local cop should stop and ask why I don't have a light on my bike while riding this dangerous stretch of road. Unless I want to chance the spider-web of back roads that might easily dead-end, Route 6 is it.

The only consolation is the drink I bought at Wellfleet liquors. 11 PM closing time and I got mine! The Coke never even reaches my stomach before my system absorbs it.

Running works the calves. Biking works the quadriceps. Ten years ago I raced bikes -- thin little ten-speeds. Now I am a runner -- riding a bike. The burning in my upper legs is tremendous on these steep hills, but I comfort myself with the notion that *running down* a hill is almost as hard on an ankle as *running up*. Not so, on this bike. I coast into Wellfleet.

Quite taken with the town with the nation's highest number of art galleries per capita, I take time to admire its finer points. Its sandy, wet roads, its dark pine forests, and its utter lack of police -- at least while I am here. But the best part is the little green sign with a white "1" in South Wellfleet. It directs me to the left. I obey.

One hundred beautiful Wellfleetian yards away I enter the fast track, the Jet Stream, the pneumatic tube of biking. I laugh quite joyously upon hitting the Rail Trail.

Back in the sixties this abandoned rail bed was torn up and left for dead until someone at the state had the idea to pave it over. A six-foot width of tarmac graces the flattest length of Cape Cod. It mostly runs dead center from here to the middle of the Cape in South Dennis, where the tracks pick up again. No cops. No traffic. No hills.

No light.

Twenty miles an hour. Easy.

I wish I could remember more of Eastham, save for the rabbit -- dog -- raccoon -- thing. Whatever it was, it was *wrong*. Pure, undeniably WRONG. This is a *bike* trail. Wildlife should know these things, or at least be equipped with running lights when crossing.

All I know is, I hit it. If it died, it didn't do it here because it had enough energy to scream -- or make some noise best forgotten in the dark of night -- and go off to a place not near my crumpled form. Luckily, I hit the semi-soft sandy bank on the side of the trail, and not the semi-destructive trail itself, at what I guess was thirty miles an hour.

Feeling around for the bike and briefcase takes some courage. I don't want to suddenly feel bloody fur or foaming teeth. I find the heavy leather bag next to the frame of the bike, and rearrange my clothes to their same general order. I push the bike pedal. It moves without the slightest resistance. The chain has been knocked off its gears. I only have to push the bike a quarter of a mile to the next cross-street to find a street lamp.

Twenty-five miles to go. Easy.

My youngest sister, Elise, lives around here.

CHAPTER TWENTY-ONE

Nootka

Saturday, November 4, 1995

The Cape, and therefore the Trail, begin to arc west at Orleans. I need to continue south. I jump off near the Purity Supreme supermarket. Food. Food holds all the answers.

The trees in Orleans are different. The tall black locust, with their coarse-grained bark are in Eastham and Wellfleet, too, but in Orleans things finally become lush. This isn't the barren moors -- there is underbrush between the trees. Grass. Houses. Ponds. Life.

And bumps. Bumpy, not hilly. The long, slow hills of Truro are gone. These valleys and dips I now encounter are annoying. Straight-aways are few and far between. After the bottom of the last big hill, I start up another, only to stop myself at the sight.

The Captain John Kendrick House.

Ancestral Lands.

This small Cape house of cedar shingles and yellow trim was built by the later John Kendrick, *my* Captain Kendrick, nephew of the big man himself. The younger who made his fortune in the China trade. Thanks for showing the way, Uncle John.

Edward Kendrick, the original settler, bought this land in 1701 from a Nauset Indian, John Sipson. We *bought* our land. And we sold our land.

The light is off inside. Two hundred and seventy years later, the house was out of the family. I think somebody from Connecticut bought it as a second house. I turn my bike back south, hardly noticing the Orleans police cruiser opposite the South Orleans post office.

Nobody bothers me on my own land.

I knew it was coming, but still the sight of water to the east is grand. The moon is poking through the clouds as I zip down the long hill. Route 28 south from Orleans follows the old Indian path along Pleasant Bay, and there it is -- quiet and gentle. Sprinkled with islands, all protected by the Great Beach. Beyond is the Atlantic.

Home. I'm almost there. Eight miles. The up-and-down, twisty-turny path of the road continues into Harwich, but the trees have gone back to pitch pine and scrub oak. Well, it *is* Harwich. It would be over in a few miles.

The last opening to Pleasant Bay passes by a small beach next to Jackknife Harbor and ascends slowly up the earthworks over Muddy Creek. Halfway up the hill, I know, I am inside the municipal limits of the town where I have voting rights, dental records and a few charge accounts.

Route 28 continues on for about two miles, and finally bangs a right at one of the town's two stop lights. I continue straight, down Shore Road past the million-dollar houses built California-style -- huge and too close together to be worth it.

One stop sign later I enter the old center of town -- Scrabbletown -- now the Old Village. Or Olde Village. Or Ye Olde Villagee. I don't know since I haven't seen the most recent real estate ads. As far as I'm concerned, it's Lower Main Street.

Three o'clock. AM. Wet. Cold on the outside. Burning on the inside. I pedal right behind *Nautilus* to the barn and slide through its doors.

There she is. In the darkness I find a rafter on which to place the bike, then open the rear passenger door and crash in her back seat.

I made it. I can't leave. She needs some care, but she will serve. I love her dearly.

Home.

Scurvy. A deficiency of an essential amino acid. Lacking ascorbic acid from fruits, vegetables and potatoes, the body's connective tissues begin to break down. Capillaries, whose fresh blood is transferred for tired blood to the veins, cease to function. Oxygen and nutrients from the heart can't reach cells, and cells can't purge themselves of carbon dioxide and waste.

Like a broken-down city water and sewer system, the extremities back up first. Hands and feet turn yellow and begin to swell. The accompanying smell is putrid, owing to each cell drowning in its own waste. The gums, most tender and exposed, bleed painfully. Eventually the entire body, suffering from this dietary anemia, simply putrefies to death.

Scurvy. So easily avoided.

Wednesday, September 24th, 1788
Friendly Cove in Nootka Sound

"Son, do try to drink," the voice in the darkness coaxed, "it's foul enough, but we've come too far to lose you here."

Solomon Kendrick, sixteen year-old able-bodied seaman from *Columbia* resisted, for what little good it did. Buried up to his waist in the cool mud of the shore, and hovered over by a man with the power to break him in two, he felt the Bear's grip on the back of his head. His father was a patient man, but tended to anger more quickly with inanimate objects. Solomon ventured a, "Yes, Captain."

The birch beer was just this side of bilge water in taste, but it went down well enough. The accepted treatment for scurvy, generous amounts were brewed whenever supplies allowed. But the only known cure was land itself, and after *Columbia* had arrived yesterday from four months at sea, the sickest were hauled off and placed within the safety of this beach.

Off to his left and right, Tommy Foster and Jim Crawford accepted their medicine with more resistance. But then, they weren't getting the personal attention of the Old Man -- or his direct order. In all the months at sea, Solomon had never received more than scant attention from his father. Perhaps it was because the sons were identical in appearance as well as age, and so when the Old Man saw John, it was as good as seeing the other. But the distance with Solomon was as it should be. Not being a harsh captain, and thus a friend to the crew, meant there was no slackening of the rules for the son in the foc'sle.

Third Officer John Jr., on the other hand, was able to have more personal contact with their father by simple virtue of his rank. More often than not, however, when the Commander took his meals with his officers, the one assigned to the watch on deck was John, Jr.

There were a few months of harsh ribbing about how the Old Man kept his twin boys on ship -- one to watch over, the other as a spy. Maybe so, but there never seemed to be any time for Solomon to see his father, apart from the few holidays when rules were relaxed. After a time, though, the crew came to realize this lowly-placed son of the Captain was one of the best up in the rigging when weather began throwing the sails this way and that. He'd earned their respect, too, by staving off scurvy as long as possible, until *Washington* had been sighted in this, the long-promised land of North-West America.

"Captain Kendrick!" the tenor voice from the water cried out, "Sir, a word!" Captain Gray's boat was being rowed ashore, and he swung his staff about like a torch.

The Commander stood, waved an acknowledgment at Gray, then passed thoughtfully about recovering men. "Son, lo this past year since we left Boston I have persevered not to show you a minute's more attention than was your due as a humble seaman, and I would hope," placing a hand on Foster's head to steady himself, "that no one will take what I am about to do as an act of favoritism. You wouldn't accuse your Commander, of such, would you, Foster?"

The sick, helpless man half-stuck in the mud tried to shake his head in the vise-grip of the Bear paw, "N-no, Captain."

"Fine. Excellent. Then I hereby appoint this company as the Mud Watch, and for its short existence, Mr. Solomon Kendrick here will serve as your officer."

A chuckle spread through the dozen men in their captive state.

"Silence!" the mock cry rang out from the Commander. Coming ashore, Captain Gray reached for his sword hilt, but quickly recognized his commander's high drama.

"This is most serious duty, and I will have no man take it lightly!" The Commander drew his sword and pointed across the cove to the small schooner anchored in front of a ramshackle hut flying the British Union Jack. "There you see the fine mansion of our English *friend*, Captain Meares, and what a fine dwelling it is! Yes, yes -- I daresay old Joe Barrell himself would forsake Bowdoin Square in an instant should he learn of how commodious a house these environs allow."

The Commander moved most lightly amongst the men, although each feared his two hundred and fifty pound bulk might slip and crash onto them at any moment. With his sword, he waved to the surroundings of high, densely-wooded mountains driving up from the sea. "The English Captain claims trading rights to this whole region!" He paused, adding quietly, "... by some *unwritten* agreement with the local chief, Maquinna -- Oh!" he gasped and gaped in mock horror, "but look! Look, they're taking it down."

Sure enough, the gang of Hawaiians, Chinese and European sailors under the command of Captain Douglas, the old Scotsman, were seen pulling apart the beams of the building, salvaging the best parts for removal to their launch. Captain Kendrick squatted down next to Johnny Gilbert, conspiratorially, "They *say* they're finished for fur this season. They *say* it's no good for us Yankee boys to seek out the furs from the natives since there aren't any more left. How sad if true, Gilbert. True?"

Gilbert blushed at the attention, "Captain, no, not true...?"

The Commander jumped back. "No! No?" He searched his thoughts, "Gilbert, you insolent wretch! Impugning the honesty of a fine English Captain, late a lieutenant in His Britannic Majesty's Navy -- or is it Portuguese Navy? Hard to keep them straight -- they keep changing their flags at their convenience." He waved away the thought. "Gilbert, if you're correct, and Captain Meares and Captain Douglas have not exactly been forthright, then we must remain here and see, when they leave, if there are indeed furs to be had, yes?"

Gilbert nodded, "Yes, Captain!"

"Then it is settled. Thank you for your wise counsel, Gilbert. You shall be second to Mr. Kendrick on the Mud Watch. Mr. Kendrick!"

Solomon tried to twist about to face his father, "Yes, Captain!"

"Mr. Kendrick, it is the idea of Mr. Gilbert that the English intend to leave and we should stay. I tend to concur, HOWEVER, do you agree we must remain vigilant?"

"Yes, Captain!"

"Good, sir! Your duty and that of the men and officers under your command shall be to maintain a close eye upon Captain Meares' men across the water. They may see the lot of us here, and decide to gain this fair piece of territory for themselves. If so, you must repel them using all means at your disposal!"

"Captain?"

"Give them hell. Most of you still have your teeth, I gather. Give them a royal bite in the ass for King George himself, if you must --" the men erupted into laughter, causing Meares' company to stop their removal and stare at the strange evocation on the opposite shore. "We've clawed our ways here, and by God, I mean for us not to surrender one square inch!"

The men cheered as the Commander sheathed his sword and strode away in triumph. Down the shore, Captain Gray waited upright and bemused. It was highly inappropriate for a captain to get to chummy with the crew, but in cases of illness there was a degree of latitude. The two continued alone down the shore. After a distance of conversation, Captain Gray stopped. "Stay? And do what?"

"Nothing," the Commander replied, as he glanced across to Meares' camp. "We have plenty of work to keep busy. The ship is in need of repair, and supplies will need to be gathered for the coming winter."

"Winter? Here? Why?" Captain Gray was astonished. "On my way up

from the south, I was able to gather almost enough cargo to bring to China
-- ," he stopped, wanting to add -- *if you hadn't arrived.*

It was amazing. Captain Kendrick was a great laggard once in port, but
at sea... *Washington* had attempted a call at the San Fernandes Islands in late
April. Captain Gray saw nothing of interest and continued north until
hitting the Coast over one hundred miles south of Nootka (in modern day
Oregon) in August. He had cruised up the Coast, trading with the locals
until he arrived in Nootka last week, finding Captain Meares and his ships.

The English had tried to warn away the little American sloop, and had
even lent the services of their blacksmith to repair its broken rudder.
Meares even offered to take letters to Boston, but a day after his departure
to China in his *Felice Adventurer*, Captain Douglas returned them
accompanied with the feeble excuse the English had no idea when they
might have an opportunity to reach Boston. Then *Columbia* arrived.

Captain Kendrick left the San Fernandes June 6 and arrived in Nootka
September 23 -- a week after Captain Gray, even though a month separated
the time of their arrivals at the San Fernandes. It was a testament to Old
Man's ability to navigate in strange waters.

"We winter here to establish good relations with the natives," the
Commander explained. "They are the people who trap these sea otters and
provide us with furs. They are our customers. Would you trust the street
peddler over the shopkeeper? No. Why should this be any different?"

"Captain, you are ascribing an element of civilization to them they do
not possess."

"They are people and they possess the same common sense of you or
me," the Commander grinned, "more or less."

"Then allow me at least to take *Washington* north with more goods to
trade. I hear Captain Douglas is preparing one last cruise north."

"Yes, I know. That schooner they built," he nodded to *Northwest
America*, a double-masted vessel designed especially for this Coast. "They've
asked our help on that cruise, and I shall send Mr. Treat, Lieutenant Howe
and Mr. Ingraham. They should be able to illustrate the nature of the trade
to the north."

"I would take *Washington* out before they leave --"

"No," the Commander glared at him. "You already lost that cabin boy
you picked up in Cape Verde to the natives. There will be no ventures until
we are safe."

Normally, a captain should be able to pick up a new crewman at his
next port of call, but in the wilds of North-west America, seamen left on

the same boat they arrived. Unlike the islanders of Hawaii, the natives here did not seem interested in a life at sea and far-off lands. The scurvy had claimed two men on board *Columbia*. Captain Kendrick did not wish to lose any more to inhospitable natives like Captain Gray encountered to the south -- a place now dubbed Murderer's Harbor. Gray displayed his disgust by folding his arms and turning his back. "A whole season wasted and we wait."

Kendrick pretended not to notice. "We can do nothing until the English leave, and we must do everything in our power to help them along. Offer food, labor or any means it takes. They shall be gone soon enough, and their 'fort' with them, and then we shall have the place to ourselves. I even offered to purchase the roofboards of Mr. Meares structure."

Gray turned, curious, "For what purpose?"

"Oh, it's good, solid cedar. Very hard." Captain Kendrick had been impressed with the Western Red Cedars stretching well over forty feet around -- not like there tiny cousins still surviving in the east. "If we wanted we could even add another mast to *Washington*... would make you less dependent upon just the one in heavy weather --"

"What?! Turn this God-forsaken spot into a shipyard? With what supplies? Those roofboards?"

The Old Man laughed, and began wandering down the shore, cheerful. "No, I've not lost my senses. But I intend to keep the dampness of this place at bay while I can. So, as the months turn ever-so colder, I shall take great pleasure to see this great effort of the English burn to ashes as mere kindling in my pot-bellied Yankee stove."

Cramped. Pain.

Every muscle is coiled and bent in just the wrong direction. Sleeping in the rear seat of a subcompact car is an exercise in persistence for those taller than five and a half feet. My luck is to have been completely exhausted when I first collapsed here. The first five hours were sweet oblivion. Waking is pure pain.

It is chilly, too. The open ocean is less than a quarter of a mile away, and its damp winds pervade the small barn. I consider turning the Hyundai's heater on, but that requires turning the engine on, and that is too much of a danger.

Not that I care about asphyxiation. It would be too charitable to this drafty structure to assume it could hold anything either in or out.

No, I am more worried about a nosy neighbor hearing the car running, assuming the worst and calling the cops. Attempted suicide would simply enhance my reported mental imbalance.

My valiant effort at sleep ends at noon. For some reason, my ankle seems better, but my neck is felt firmly locked straight ahead. It doesn't matter because I'm not going anywhere. Not until dark. Meanwhile, there is plenty to keep me busy.

I had finally given up on this "old reliable" of a car when she stopped being "reliable," and became just plain "old." It was my own fault for allowing needed repairs to go unheeded -- I was getting a new one, so what did it matter? Now I need her again, and it does matter. I draw a spark plug wrench from my briefcase and go to work.

The major problem with the Hyundai is it needs new steering, and I'm not about to perform that several-hundred dollar job myself. So I concentrate on the other major concerns. Flushing the air filter with gasoline. Cleaning spark plugs. Checking oil. Cutting brake lines.

This part requires my changing clothes. Here it is, the beginning of November and I'm in a ramshackle old barn by the ocean, stripping down to nothing. I pray no little kids from the neighborhood use the barn as a hiding place. Carefully folding the tweed jacket and pants and stowing them in the back seat, I put on my old green jeans and gray work shirt. Then I climb under the rear axle.

Sawing through the brake line only took a few minutes with my Swiss army knife, but trying to find the right place to cut takes forever. Having left the car parked with the emergency brake on for three months allowed the line to rust shut. The car just won't move -- front wheel drive versus locked rear brakes produces precious little else, save for small furrows in the dirt floor under the spinning front wheels. Luckily, I still have the front disc brakes.

Reverse is also a problem. The gearbox doesn't like going there half the time, or staying there the rest of the time. A new clutch is needed. Sadly, I forgot to pack one in Boston.

At 2:30 PM I chance a trial start.

Click! Groan! Click, click!

Shit.

Click, click! Groan.

Fuck me.

There is juice, but not enough to start. I look at the dashboard clock, knowing it is the power drain on the battery for all these months. When darkness comes, I will have to push-start the thing. Alone.

The final piece of resurrection is the license plate. Massachusetts requires only one plate on personal vehicles, but two on commercial vehicles. The police won't pull your truck over *just* for carrying only one plate, so Paulie figured he could spare from his Jeep. But if I'm stopped, I'll be found to be driving an unregistered, uninsured, unsafe vehicle with a stolen plate. Bad. Very bad.

It actually looks decent out today, and for once I am happy to know it will be getting dark early. I'm famished and dehydrated. Last week I could've ducked into *Nautilus* for a drink from the faucet -- but with the water drained for the winter, not a drop is left. Not even in the toilets. I think of it, yes.

My only nourishment gives me precious little relief from my need for fluids. On first glance, an onion bagel would seem like a good thing to grab when rushing for some food to pack. But without the spit to swallow, it's a whole other matter.

Bored, tired, hungry and uncomfortable, I lay back in the front seat. The silence is only interrupted by the occasional car passing on Water Street or by the skitter of animals in the rafters. The hum of the clock fills the small moments.

That damn clock. I gotta get rid of that thing. If I don't, I might never get outta here.

I lurch forward, ram my hand behind the dash and yank at some wires. The clock stops. What else have I unplugged?

Great.

At 6:02 I open the barn doors, shift the car into neutral and let the car roll into the deserted side-street. I have to turn the car at the last moment or else slide into the neighbor's picket fence, then shift into first and get out.

The street light just *has* to be on, right over me. Water Street is only wide enough to allow two careful cars to pass without ripping off each other's sideview mirrors. As I run back to shut the barn doors, I hope no local police cruiser will come along and ask why I'm blocking the road with a dead car.

I could con a cop into giving me a jump start, I bet.

The idea amuses me. It would be easier than a push-start. If it wasn't for the extremely good chance I would be instantly recognized, I might actually wait until one of the town's finest came along.

I get behind the car, give a hard shove and then jump in. Only forty feet of Water Street beyond the intersection with Main Street before Street ends in Water. There isn't enough momentum down this slight incline to pop the clutch. So I gracefully slide through the stop sign and turn left onto Main Street.

Failure to stop for a stop sign. Five seconds after becoming a criminal, I am breaking another law. Guess it is easier after the first time.

The street edges downward increasingly past the white-washed picket fences. I want to wait for at least fifteen miles per hour, but see that the speedometer is just sitting still at zero. Wonder what other wires I removed?

The lights aren't working, either -- not enough power. That is until I pop the clutch.

It catches. It fights. It slows.

I push in the clutch. It coasts.

The bottom of the hill is approaching. I wait for more speed. I shift into second this time. And release the clutch.

It catches. It fights. It catches.

The bottom of the hill is ten feet away. After it, a gradual incline. A powerful grating thump comes from the front passenger-side wheel as I pull a hard right and swing around the corner. Down another narrow side-street, towards the ocean. The engine fights and catches the entire way.

Twenty feet from the water, it catches, and holds.

Gunning the engine, I turn on the lights. Before me, the turquoise Atlantic pounds on the meager rip-rap of boulders laid down as a breakwater. I wish I could get out for one last time, but the emergency brake is gone, and I need to keep the car running. Settling for a face full of spray rubbed into my arms, face and hair, I turn the car around and head away from this ocean.

CHAPTER TWENTY-TWO

Princesa

Sunday, November 5, 1995

Patterson, New Jersey

I have no concept of time. The interior lights don't work and I can't read my watch unless I pass under a street lamp. All I know is it's not today anymore. It's tomorrow.

My first stop for gas was at an obscure station on Cape where no one knew me. The second, in Connecticut near the New York border. Sometime around midnight I crossed the George Washington Bridge, from the Bronx into New Jersey. Going west there is no toll -- good, 'cause that's four more bucks I can use. The slice of gluey pizza in Stamford, CT was overpriced at a buck and a half. I'm out of New England, out of my element. I'm in the rest of the country.

Creepy.

The great danger subsided when I hit the Rhode Island border just two hours out. Once free of Massachusetts motor vehicle laws, I'm just another out-of-state car.

The radio doesn't work, either. I'm alone with my thoughts and my singing.

Times like this, urban areas provide a little entertainment. The giant blue locust atop a building outside Providence, the Pirelli building on stilts in New Haven, the cliff walls of the Cross-Bronx Expressway -- they're something to look at besides the yellow lines on either side of the road and the dashed white ones down the middle.

With no speedometer, I waited until the well-lit highways of southern Connecticut. See a mile marker, note the exact second, then wait until the next mile marker. One mile in sixty seconds is 60 miles an hour. Easy.

At the turn onto I-80 West, I catch my second wind. Take this road until Chicago. Only one great hurdle left tonight -- a state that has not been kind to me. Pennsylvania.

Oh, I can bitch about it on its own merits enough. Driving its entire length on this stretch of highway, one gets to see hills. Long, tall hills covered by hardwood forests. They call them mountains here. They're not. They're just big, old wrinkles. I'm glad, in this darkness, I don't have to look at them.

Pennsylvania, alone of the original thirteen colonies, has no coastline. Lake Erie doesn't count. Neither does the Delaware River. People get strange away from salt water. Has any President ever come from this state? Is that a surprise?

Like Massachusetts, it's a Commonwealth. Ben Franklin was born in Boston, and made his name in Pennsylvania. On the surface, a hell of a lot in common. How very deceptive.

I'd gotten beyond her. Beyond all of it. Hadn't I? How did I find myself back here?

Pennsylvania had her one chance, and she failed. She was a young woman in a red bathrobe, standing at her dorm room door, bidding me good-bye with a heavy smile at two in the afternoon. As I walked down the hall with my bag, a few of her friends at this women's college crept out to talk. At the end of the long hall, I turned to catch one last glimpse before leaving, but found she was wrapped up in conversation. I lingered a moment, hoping for one last look. She didn't look back. I left.

Six weeks. It was going to be only six weeks. She had finals and graduation in the interim, and I judged it best not to be a distraction. She eventually, reluctantly agreed. We hadn't gone more than three weeks apart since hooking up on Christmas.

The return to the Cape led to a successful initial negotiation for the *SEXTANT* program, and I was on top of the world. Just three more weeks, and summer would bring her back to my universe. It was all a dream -- never a fight -- a talkable, considerate relationship.

There had been a physical element pervasive throughout, one she admitted not enjoying before meeting me. In the stolen holidays and weekends that winter, emotions balled up into some quick release. I felt powerful and content. It had all been for this.

SEXTANT fell apart a week later, and with it, my entire support system. For once, I *needed* a kind word, a supportive voice. The timing was wrong. She needed *my* support for her own time of trial. Misunderstanding never recovered over the distance of 400 miles. Having done nothing wrong, I never realized that what had begun on Christmas ended on Easter, until Easter had long passed.

At first, she thought to make me go away would only take being consistently unreasonable. It just made me persistently angry -- why was my best friend behaving like this? A psychology major, she came to believe my emotional state hinged on danger. She accused me of lurking around her haunts in *my* home town. I couldn't stand it -- I wouldn't allow it. Professionally and personally, my integrity had been questioned. I had nothing left. The damage done, the lesson learned.

I was thoroughly broken. That was years ago. The dark years.

I took a Vow -- the first. If she was right, there was something wrong with me. I couldn't impose that on another. If she was wrong, the world was wrong, and didn't deserve me. Besides, I needed that power to rebuild.

That was when THE PRIEST took over. With nothing left myself, he convinced me to show how close I could come to the ideal. Already, I was on my way. No drugs, no alcohol, no smoking, ever. No abuse of myself or others. An ability to forbid all carnal pleasure – the Vow. It was a step towards total control.

FOCUS. That was the word. Said aloud, it eliminated the rage and pain whirling around every thought for eighteen months. In that time I had sculpted myself physically, grown my hair and reinvented myself. I saw her a year ago. She accosted me in a local dive while I was with two beautiful female friends. "Remember me?" said she.

Yes, I had wanted to say. Yes, it was her words that caused me to doubt my faith in myself and the entire female gender and the line I had accepted since birth from my sisters that they were kind, understanding and unselfish. And when Pennsylvania left me to discover the pleasures of herself, she forever shattered my world and lowered my opinion of women almost to those of men. But most of all, while it took a summer of self-imposed confinement to work the body, it was that month at Pocasset that re-established control over the mind.

Instead, at the dive I humored her, and spoke casually for twenty minutes. The lack of care was damning. Not hers, but mine. I knew better. Pennsylvania.

I growled at the steering wheel, thumping it hard. Attacks used to hit me when I would simply think of her -- worse, her enjoying what we had shared now with another man -- or other men. Paulie had hinted at things he had heard. Then my seizures would turn into frustration at being so blind and stupid -- it was my fault, not hers. Then I saw her. It was different. The pain had melted away, the frustration with myself gone as the understanding of human beings began to connect.

The cars here have plates that read "YOU'VE GOT A FRIEND IN PENNSYLVANIA." They used to say "KEYSTONE STATE." Both used to be true.

Poor state. Poor Pennsylvania. I tried. It all seemed to be there, but the timing was right only for so long. I don't need you anymore, that's the real tragedy, because I don't need anyone anymore. This was the ideal THE PRIEST had led me to. Casual indifference.

She was the last woman I ever allowed myself to fall in love with.

But I'm not bitter.

Argonaut

Off Santa Cruz de Nutka, Island of San Miguel, Nootka Sound
July 4th, 1789

The American four-pound guns had silenced after the thirteen-round volley. Upon the orders of El Commandante Don Esteban José Martinez, the Spanish fort on shore responded, as did the packet boat *San Carlos*. Between them, a frigate of His Catholic Majesty Carlos III of Spain remained silent, again under orders. Unlike the salute of pure powder fired all about Friendly Cove, her cannon were filled with very real grape and ball shot, and were trained on a very real, very broad target -- the fourth of Meares' vessels, *Argonaut*.

Very stupidly, its master, James Colnett, had entered the Sound without any degree of caution. Very stupidly, upon finding the Spanish firmly established opposite the site of last year's house, Colnett had raised his Portuguese flag of protection. And, oh-so-very stupidly, Colnett had received Don Esteban by announcing that the numerous Chinese artisans and other supplies on board were for the establishment of a fur trading and processing post, adding he was taking possession of the entire area in the name of King George III of England.

Very, very stupid Englishman, Captain Kendrick observed.

Was it any wonder Don Esteban drew his sword on the man? Or vise-versa? Did it matter? Colnett was thrown in chains and his ship seized. At least everyone appeared to set aside their troubles and enjoyed the American's Independence Day banquet aboard *Columbia*.

Meares' ship *Iphigenia Nubiana* and schooner *Northwest America* were here. Their papers from the Portuguese Governor of Macao bordered on a warrant for piracy. Captain Douglas was thankful just to have his 180 furs seized and to sent packing back across the Pacific to China in *Iphigenia*. However, the schooner, renamed *Santa Gertrudis* (for Don Esteban's beloved wife), was due to be sent south to Acapulco as a prize.

After two months of friendly relations since the arrival of the Spanish masters at Friendly Cove, Captain Kendrick had no intention of leaving. While it appeared wise to depart as soon as the authorities allowed, *Columbia's* hold was not yet full of furs. The slow, but steady supply smuggled under the cover of darkness each night from the great chief Maquinna and chief Callicum was not enough, even if El Commandante was turning a blind eye. Illicit trading within this Spanish possession? No, Señor. Only a voyage of discovery.

Barrell's medals became a curse. Intended to entice the natives and be a memorial of the voyage, they had made their way into the hands of Don Esteban. With orders to act as he saw fit should he encounter this particular Captain John Kendrick and his two vessels, the Spaniard perceived these medals as portend to a threat. Perhaps the upstart American Congress and its dictator, General Washington, sought to lay claim to the opposite side of the continent.

He planned to send the medals along to Mexico. But from time to time, he would produce a copper one from his waistcoat to tacitly express the uncertainty in which he held the big *Yanqui* he referred to as "Don Juan Kendriqué." Hence, Don Esteban's request yesterday to Captain Kendrick to train *Columbia's* guns on *Argonaut* and *Princess Royal* as they were seized.

"She's a fine vessel," Captain Kendrick noted from atop the quarter-deck of *Columbia*. "Captain Meares did fine work out here." The vessel they spoke of, the schooner *Santa Gertrudis*, drew only seven or eight feet of water, and was handy in the countless coves and fjords of the Coast. The same was true of *Washington*, though Captain Gray had recently managed to bring her straight onto the rocks of the Queen Charlotte Islands. Gray blamed the continuous fog. Probably couldn't be helped, no matter Mr. Haswell's harping on the incident.

"I intend to sail her," El Commandante declared, "to survey this jagged coast." His English was admirable, little surprise as he was a refined gentleman of learning. John, Jr.'s translation services, though, were helpful, especially among the junior Spanish officers... late at night... when the spirits would flow and tongues loosen. "I hear, Don Juan," Don Esteban added, "the fur of the sea otter is quite valuable in China. You are sailing there soon, yes?"

"Indeed," Kendrick replied, "no later than the end of this month. I would offer you my word, but as you know, your Excellency, the tea markets of Canton have been my sole destination from the start."

"You will grant a favor?" Barrell's medal was out of the waistcoat, placed alone on the rail in plain sight.

"Anything it is within my power to grant, surely."

"Shipment. Not much. Some cargo. The former crew of my schooner -- I have no need of such *desperados*. Capitan Meares sends them here from Macao. I wish to send them back."

"By all means," said Captain Kendrick. *Columbia* needed every man she could get, and these rabble of Meares' would work hard for their delivery. Hadn't they just caught wind of *Argonaut* and *Princess Royal* heading for an indefinite stay in Mexico, crew and all?

"And," Don Esteban continued, "its cargo. You can receive a fair price?"

"I do hope so, your Excellency." One hundred eighty of the luxuriant deep brown furs, most six feet across, could not take up too much space in the hold of *Columbia*. For freedom, it was a price the Commander was willing to bear. "How shall I make payment?"

"Oh, yes...perhaps upon your return to Boston you may forward the amount to the Spanish Consul. These furs are, you understand, as are all furs along this coast, the property of His Catholic Majesty."

"A point of law I am fully aware," Captain Kendrick noted. Strange -- the medal was still out. Don Juan cleared his throat.

El Commandante continued to concentrate his attention upon *Santa Gertrudis*, whose officers were at this moment bidding good-bye to a dory holding *Columbia's* Third Officer. "Your son, Don Juan, is very skilled. He is a fine pilot of these waters, and speaks well the language of the Spanish and natives here."

"You are most gracious, Your Excellency."

"Like his father, he can navigate within unfamiliar areas."

"Indeed."

"He expresses an interest in the Catholic faith, but you know this, true?"

It was true that the friars accompanying any Spanish military mission had captured John, Jr.'s attention. "Something not seen in Protestant New England, Your Excellency."

"Nor is an American in Spanish service." The ice broke. "He has asked of his own free will, to convert and to serve. He will make a fine pilot for *Santa Gertrudis*. But I shall stop, let you address the matter with him. Good night, Don Kendriqué."

Descending the stairs to the main deck, Don Esteban called for his launch. In the twilight John Kendrick considered the gloom and brilliance over the Pacific, and slowly slipped the copper medal into his own waistcoat pocket. Bad luck to separate twins, Huldah said, encouraging him to take both John, Jr. and Solomon along. But nothing he shouldn't have already expected.

CHAPTER TWENTY-THREE

Princess Royal

Sunday, November 5, 1995
Off I-80. Outside Youngstown, Ohio.

The ship's day supposedly began at noon. I read that somewhere in the past two weeks. Makes sense, as it's easier to figure out the middle of the day than the middle of the night -- there's that big yellow thing high in the sky. Most of the time.

My internal clock's been knocked off so bad that noon seems like midnight. That's the middle of my night . When the sun began to lighten the sky behind me, I knew it was time to pull over. Actually, it was time a hell of a long ways back, but I wanted to put Pennsylvania behind me. Miracle of miracles, I have.

Welcome to Ohio. The Square State. Or something like that.

On the other side of the Appalachians I find that "rest of the country" culture. More land than they know what to do with, Americans spread out along vast tentacles of asphalt and sodium vapor lights. Nothing is too good or too bad to displace corn fields and hog farms. I'm sure there is charm off the well-worn path I travel, but I am left to revel in the look-alike franchised restaurants and cut-rate hotel chains.

As I wake and lift the canvas up a crack, I can see the truckers here in Girard, a cross-roads town in northeast Ohio. The big rigs are huddled around the various all-night breakfast spots like piglets on a sow. Last night -- this morning? -- I noticed behind one greasy spoon, a rig that looked as if it had met with the business end of a flame thrower, all broken glass and twisted, charred steel. In the dim streaks of another rainy day, I placed my car just beyond this hulk, double-checked the locks on the doors and attempted to sleep. That is over now.

Food.

There is something anonymous about interstate highway culture. Everything looks the same, only the people change, until they too are one large blur. Stops for gas and food. Islands for wood and water.

Three dollars is my limit for breakfast tonight -- a bargain of protein, cholesterol, fat and complex carbohydrates. The coffee cuts the grease, but the entire dietary intake is intentional. I need food that will plug up my intestines for longer than an overpriced bran muffin. Good health could wait. "Plug," I say out loud after the waitress leaves the plateful, and chuckle, "Mighty fine plug, at that."

A couple miles back, I-80 became a toll road. So much for buying lunch. Or whatever my mid-night meal should be called. Breakfast is supper and supper is breakfast. Through the clear, straight, flat darkness of the highway, the Midwest spreads before me like a frying pan.

Probably the only meaningful piece of legislation to come out the American Congress prior to the adoption of the Constitution was the Northwest Ordinance of 1787. Prior to this act, individual states laid claim to competing sections of what would one day be Ohio, Michigan, Illinois, Indiana, Wisconsin and Minnesota. The states of New York, Connecticut, Massachusetts and Pennsylvania, based upon their original colonial charters granted by various monarchs of England, all ran westward across the continent to the Pacific Ocean. Virginia's claim was simply to everything that wasn't already part of an established state, and that set the original 13 at each other's throats.

Under the Articles of Confederation, any legislation had to pass the single house of the American Congress unanimously. So it was a wonder that they finally agreed on such a controversial piece of work. Later that year the Constitution was written and obliterated this awkward process.

The Ordinance, of course, remained in effect. Still does. It simply said, No, none of that land belongs to any of you -- it belongs to all of you collectively as the federal government. That also meant no one could buy land from the people who had already been living there for generations (i.e., the Cherokee, the Miami, etc.), since the title was held by the government.

Instead, under the guiding hand of George Washington, then President of Congress and a man more of surveying than military talent, the territories were divided up on a grid pattern. The ideal was 640 acres for a lot, 36 lots to a Township, hence each Township 6 miles square. Four lots out of every township were reserved for future government sale, one lot for support of the public schools of the Township, and one seventh of the lots for Revolutionary War veterans.

When a territory reached a population of 5,000, it had the right to elect a legislature. Upon hitting 60,000, it could become a state. All so nice and neat. A grid pattern for orderly development and an orderly process laid out well in advance. It helped that it was relatively flat out here. Settlers appreciated that sort of thing.

Two hundred years later, those broad-shouldered, broad-browed sons of Irish, German, and eventually Italian and African immigrants would take the field in defense of the University of Notre Dame, doing what they had been drilled and bred to do. The legacy of this last gasp of doomed governance. This all began with Notre Dame.

Notre Dame -- my then-wife Justine -- had come back to me for Christmas. Law school break lasted a few weeks. She had mentioned over our dinner out that her concentration in entertainment law would eventually lead her out to California.

"Uh-huh," I had nodded. Politics was going full-bore for me on a campaign then. We had weathered the geographical separation that came with her scholarship. "A lot of couples are bi-coastal."

She shook her head, and slowly mouthed the word: "Divorce."

Too bad. Too bad. But for the best, I guessed. Our relationship had started off with a great deal of physical attraction, then an early marriage. Over the following years, it had completely turned on its head. My friend felt she had to go her way. It was unfair -- and impossible -- to stand in her way. "I understand."

Being in law school she could handle the paperwork with ease, and the cost would be limited to the filing fees. There was no squabble over property since we had none to speak of. We both knew who owned what. It was all so reasonable. She was reasonable. I was reasonable.

I had been built this way by my sisters. Still, Justine had from the first seen me as a project -- a lump of clay with potential. The cavalier, cocky kid got married and was drilled into her ideal of the perfect husband. Kind. Funny. Considerate. Totally faithful. Strong. Dependable. In the service of Notre Dame.

As I grew more "perfect", the electricity waned and eventually ceased altogether. We became close and cozy -- familiar companions. We saw no reason to separate simply because we weren't the traditional husband and wife, or at least not as they should be in their twenties. Fifties, maybe.

The agreement, as she had proposed it years before this dinner, went like this: "Should you ever find anyone you like more than me, someone you believe would suit you better, tell me before you do anything about it. As your best friend, I deserve that consideration, don't I? And YOU BETTER BE SURE about what you're doing because there's no coming back. And in any event, don't ever allow yourself to be put in a situation that would hurt me, even by misinterpretation."

The day before Christmas, I proposed a reasonable request for this interim divorce period: "Until the paperwork goes through, could you just not *do* anything with anybody."

She got upset. "It could take months."

That didn't seem like all that much. Where was the much-vaunted self-control?

She was uncomfortable, unusually so, like a cat trapped in a cage. A hunter caught in her own snare. Where was the problem? Unless...

Her excuse was to spare my feelings. She had thought me weak by her ability to mold me. The fellow student I had never felt a second's jealousy for, the one from outside Hollywood, a reformed street hood, the bad boy, was my own discovery. I wasn't even looking, but my intuition and sense of duty guided me.

Years in the gulag, bound and gagged, *The Rogue* returned, flexing his wings. Where had this road of good intentions led? There was nothing. No friends. No family. A job that only mattered as long as there was someone with which to savor the victory. Her veneer of honesty shattered, my trust washed away, I could love, but no longer be *in love* with her.

She had said no politician could be romantic -- it was innate in the creature -- but that wasn't everything in a man. Tell a man he's crazy long enough, and he will act it. Tell a man he's not romantic, and he won't be. I was pacing back and forth furiously. She sat still in her chair in the corner of the living room, gripping the arms and watching me with round, downcast eyes. "What are you going to do?"

I whipped around, pointing, "Quiet! You don't matter anymore. I will do whatever I decide to do. I don't have to consider you anymore and I don't have to tell you anything. You are irrelevant."

"Please understand, I didn't want to hurt you. You're so sweet and gentle, and I knew the truth would crush you."

"Well done." I shook my head, "*Well* done." What was left for me? Nothing. Revenge.

"John --"

"Shut-up," I demanded of this poorly behaved child. "I'm trying to figure out what I should do with you."

"You can't --"

I was immediately in her face. "I can do anything I want. You've taken it all away. Right now, you've made me the most dangerous thing alive -- a man with nothing to live for."

"You'd kill yourself?" She tried to regain the upper hand with a sneer. "How weak."

"No weaker than a hypocrite and a liar. How does that feel, being called a liar and knowing it to be true?" She'd rather have been called a whore, her claim to fame being her insightful, honest, direct nature. She not only was breaching her own rules, but she had been caught by her own creation -- a golem out of her power.

The pacing began again. I could do anything. Go anywhere. Any flight of fancy was possible. Women? Not the least bit interested. And lack of cash didn't limit me -- if she didn't matter there were always our joint credit cards. What I wanted to do was to go, get off Cape Cod before its winter gloom sent me to the bathtub with razor blades, or the local bar. Survival was short-term victory.

Survival. I had decided upon it. If I were to have ended this, I wouldn't have been the first to go. But that would have upset her family. They had always been nice to me. It would have been inconsiderate.

Victory. That was the word. She shall not be right. I had convinced myself all these years that she had been. I had questioned my own judgments and perceptions, substituting hers. Now she was proven wrong. She was not infallible. Notre Dame would rationalize her conduct if I crumbled without her.

Victory meant winning her back. It would take more of what was being displayed here. It required the subtlety, force, deception and brutality of *The Rogue*. A demonstration of power.

What a ridiculous concept for a civilized human being. And how blessedly effective.

Still, it's not like I let it shatter my faith in my upbringing.

The time changes outside Notre Dame. South Bend Indiana. I have traveled backwards, to where I was last week. The sign reads "Entering Central Time Zone". The hour I lost switching to Eastern Daylight Savings Time has been regained, so there is another hour of darkness in which to drive.

Yi-pee.

The last of my tolls ends at the Wisconsin border.

Columbia Rediviva

*... the voyage will not turn out to the Owners expectation,
all for want of a nimble leader, so I conclude and remain
Your affectionate Friend and ever well wisher...*
-- Robert Gray to Joseph Barrell,
written at Nootka Sound, July 13th, 1789

Clayoquot Sound
July 30th, 1789

"It is agreed, then."

"If you are willing," Captain Gray nodded, "then, yes, I think this wise."

"Then you may inform Mr. Haswell of his reassignment and demotion," the Commander laughed.

Captain Gray breathed a sigh of relief. "He shall be pleased to receive your charity and consideration."

With Mr. Coolidge's temporary service to the Spanish as master of the *Santa Gertrudis*, Mr. Haswell had risen to First Officer of *Washington* -- and had been almost as insolent there as aboard Captain Kendrick's *Columbia*. In their present agreement, Mr. Haswell would return to his former position on the flagship, but with one remarkable change. The masters were trading vessels.

"I shall require Mr. Treat's services," the Old Man added. "His absence will allow Mr. Haswell his old quarters in full. Perhaps he will think better of me when I am gone."

"No doubt."

Suspicion and accusation had been the order of the day, with Captain Gray's insistence that another cruise to the north was necessary to fill the empty hold of *Washington* prior to heading once and for all to China. Upon doing so, he had returned to Nootka with plenty of skins and dreadful repairs needed after colliding with the looming cliffs of the Alaskan shore.

Risk *Columbia* to the same spot? Unwise at this late date, thought the Commander. He had been right all along to leave her at anchor in Nootka. Besides, how could he explain his passing north by Nootka again, this time on their way to the Queen Charlotte Islands, when he had already informed El Commandante two weeks before they were leaving to go directly to China without any stops for forbidden fur trading?

It was better to risk only the much smaller *Washington* by wreck or seizure. In either case, the Old Man obviously had the talent to weather such storms better than his underling. Surprisingly, Captain Gray agreed.

Command was clear, however. Captain Gray's mission was to proceed with *Columbia* by way of Hawaii. He was to seek out the Barrell's designated agents, Messrs. Shaw & Randall at Canton, to sell the furs and purchase a cargo of whatever valuables (tea, silk, porcelain) available from the proceeds.

After his cruise northward on the Coast, Captain Kendrick would proceed with *Washington* to China, and ascertain from Captain Gray the best course of action -- sell his furs in the legal markets of Canton, smuggle them past the Portuguese authorities at Macao, sell *Washington*, or return to the Coast for another season. One thing remained absolutely clear: although Captain Gray now commanded *Columbia*, Captain Kendrick still commanded Gray.

> *Being too much exposed in the Roads, on the third day*
> *after our Arrival we moved our Station to Dirty Butter Bay*
> *where we lay Securely moored -- and very lonesome.*
> -- Captain John Kendrick
> to Captain Robert Gray and Lt. Richard S. Howe,
> written at Macao, February 6th, 1790

Dirty Butter Bay, Macao, China
February 12th, 1790

"She's leaving," Mr. Coolidge called from the quarter-deck. "No doubt, Captain."

John Kendrick emerged from the cramped quarters below that he shared with his First Officer. In his hand he held an octagonal cylinder of oak, which he extended with a snap. As he peered through one end of the telescope, the image of a square-rigged, three-masted vessel came into focus. Running before the wind, every inch of canvas available strung from the rigging, it tore out of the Pearl River delta and past the island of Macao.

The prevailing wind from the southwest had changed to an unfamiliar winter drive from the north. This gale wind had kept up for the past day, denying passage to merchant traffic north from Macao up to the Pearl River to Canton. The Chinese New Year festivities had just begun, and those hanging back from entry to Imperial China's sole port to the outside world knew government offices would be shut down for a good three weeks. It would appear Captain Gray had settled his business with *Columbia* in a most timely fashion.

The Old Man steadied himself against the rudder, tied in place since they had come to anchor here a week ago. Lately, he had contracted some vile fever from the tropical heat. It kept him warm in the stiff breeze as he tracked *Columbia* passing the islands strung south of the great island of Macao -- Taipa, Coloane, and his own, Wong Kum.

"Mr. Coolidge!" The Commander heaved the words from his hot, heavy chest, barely audible above the snapping of the empty rigging. Mr. Treat had come above decks with the balance of the ten-man crew, and he scrambled up to his commander's side. The Commander turned and smiled, "Thank you, Mr. Treat. Would you be so kind to inform Mr. Coolidge of my order to hail *Columbia*?"

In addition to his duties as Furrier, Mr. Treat had assumed those of Second Officer following Mr. Haswell's transfer to *Columbia* last summer. Thirty-one months at sea under Captain Kendrick's guidance gave the young man an opportunity to learn the sea first-hand.

Entering the port at Macao, they had found a number of American vessels already there, but none came from the mysterious Northwest laden with furs. The only other to make that voyage was within sight, but showed no intention of stopping. "Yes, Captain!" punctuated Mr. Treat's leap down to the main deck and wave to Mr. Coolidge to join him at the portside four-pounders.

Washington stood within the lee of the islands, out of the gale. The regular watch of two men, one fore and the other aft, had been doubled to take care that none of the numerous waterborne thieves dare try their luck at the tiny seventy-foot sloop. It was not unusual for even the tremendous East Indiamen, bristling with British armament, to find their mooring cables cut, and anchor spirited away in the night. Every swivel, musket, pistol and cannon was kept at the ready. Captain Kendrick did not have to watch over the removal of the two-foot long cannister of grape shot by Mr. Coolidge and Mr. Treat, and its replacement with a double charge of powder -- so confident was he in his officers' abilities, so impressed was he with their desperate situation.

The two young officers huddled behind the cap rail to strike a light, but the breeze proved too much for the flame. The first letter of instruction Captain Kendrick received upon arrival at Macao had been written by Barrell not long after *Columbia* and *Washington* left Boston in October of 1787. Someone must have led the chief investor to believe that the market for furs in China might not be so "prosperous" as originally thought.

A letter received from Captain Gray, dated November 2, 1789, bespoke the same concern for his Commander. From both above and below, Captain Kendrick received advice to *not* come up to Canton to purchase a Boston-bound cargo, until he smuggled the furs ashore at Macao. Such would avoid the excessive Imperial duties and bribes of at least $2,500 per vessel, regardless of size. The agents, Shaw & Randall, agreed.

Moreover, the Commander was further advised by both Owner and agents to dispose of *Washington* at Macao, for which he might receive $10,000-12,000. Small, well-handling vessels such as she, no doubt, would fetch as much as the cargo within her hold. Captain Gray's letters from Canton consistently urged his commander not to come up, explaining Captain Kendrick would not receive a third of the price of the value of his furs, while Macao held many buyers. *"This, Dear Sir, is the opinion of Captain Douglas and every one that wishes you well."*

As his flagship ran along before his eyes, he remembered his own response to his sub-commander -- a demand for an accounting of the skins. Lt. Howe's duty as Supercargo required this, no less. Perhaps, if the price were so poor, it would be prudent to return with *Washington* straight away to the Coast, rather than wasting time returning with *both* vessels to Boston. The goal was profit. Captain Gray had not even specified if the cargo he had procured for Boston was purchased on behalf of the owners or in return for provisioning for *Columbia*. Although a Portuguese gentleman had it in his mind to purchase *Washington*, how could the Commander do so until the furs on board were sold? Captain Kendrick's final word to Captain Gray was that there would be no movement until the subordinate provided more explicit data.

BAH-DOOM!

The officers had managed to light the charge and the echo filled the bay for a moment, only to be filled by the howling of winds, crashing of seas, and snapping of lines. Ten men waited a full minute.

Mr. Coolidge looked up at the quarter-deck. "Shall we try again, Captain?" Mr. Treat, assisted by midshipman Green, was already manhandling another charge. Captain Kendrick kept his eye on the ship, knowing it would take Captain Gray half a day to bring her about at the rate she was moving. Still, he nodded, for the men's sake.

Holding the glass to his eye again, he searched the decks and rigging of *Columbia* for familiar faces. The slight, dictatorial figure on the main deck could only be Mr. Haswell. Above, on the quarter-deck, Captain Gray stood ramrod straight as a ship's master should beside the crewman at the wheel. The noble Mr. Ingraham, however, was not evident -- strange for a First Officer under such circumstances. Likewise, the yardarms and ratlines betrayed no glimpse of the son remaining aboard, Solomon. It seemed the boy would see home and mother before the Old Man himself. The second discharge rang hollow.

B-DOOOM!

No response as she passed beyond the point. Crestfallen, the men who had signed on at Boston for a voyage 'round the world saw their hope of home riding out in a blaze of glory. The passage from here through the South China Sea and Malacca Straits were rife with Malay pirates, and convoys were the only form of limited protection from attack. Little *Washington* stood little chance alone heading west. Too little chance, in its Commander's judgment. They were stranded -- Crawford, Bowles, Barber, Green, Foster, and Maud -- without even the slightly brighter future an officer might have, being on the opposite corner of the globe.

Worse was their lot than they knew, their Commander thought as he struggled to steady his heavy frame against the hatch. Captain Gray knew *Washington* was destitute of supplies or the means to pay for them -- save for the sale of furs. The only way to pay the men and officers for their long suffering and diligent service, never mind continue to feed them should they wish to remain, was to utilize the property of the Owners.

Without a signal to anyone on deck, the Old Man made his way to the companionway and descended into his cabin. When Messrs. Treat and Coolidge reached the quarter-deck and peered down inside, the sight spurred them immediately below.

Face down and sprawled out at the foot of the steep stairs lay the Old Man, and his two officers searched for footing not covered by his immense bulk. Despite the continuing noise above on deck, they proceeded quietly, lest they alarm the crew. Five minutes passed before they could wrestle the massive Bear into his bunk.

The Old Man reached out his hand, tracing the planking nearly surrounding his tiny berth. His eyes opened slowly, and fully to take in his surroundings. Mr. Treat offered a full measure of rum, the near-last draught from the last keg on board. For once, the Old Man brushed it away. "No, thank you, sir."

In 1789, Messrs. Shaw and Randall had commissioned the building of the massive 820-ton *Massachusetts* for a voyage from of Boston to China, hiring Amasa Delano as Supercargo. But finding the market not suitable for his cargo of New England ginseng, Delano had sold the vessel to the Danes and returned by himself via various European vessels with a 300% profit. Shaw & Randall, as agents for *Washington*, would doubtless counsel the same to his Captain Kendrick. Take your percentage now. Meaning, *so I can too*.

Book passage to Boston. Alone. In comfort. It would be helpful if those crewmen he abandoned here in Macao might never return to collect their pay.

Mr. Treat cleared his throat, and Mr. Coolidge ended his vigil at the Old Man's door. They were about to head back to reassure the men when they heard a groan and a whisper from the direction of the Old Man.

"Captain Douglas."

Mr. Coolidge returned to find his commander's eyes closed. "Captain?"

"Captain Douglas," the Old Man repeated, and chuckled, soon becoming a cough. "Captain Douglas advises that I remain at Macao and not come up to Canton -- as does everyone who wishes me well. Like Captain Gray."

"Captain, please do try to rest. You shall determine better in the morning."

"Yes, yes," the Commander nodded as he ran one hand over the thick red stubble of a beard. "Captain Randall and Major Shaw do not wish me to come up to Canton. They must wish me well. They *all* must wish me well."

"Indeed, Captain," Mr. Treat offered from the door. "Shall we inform Captain. Randall of your course? We could launch the long boat tomorrow, as you say, should the wind change."

"When the wind changes... Yes, the wind shall do so. And we must make ready in preparation. Mr. Coolidge, if at first light the weather is fair and wind from a favorable direction, rig the long boat with a sail."

"The long boat, sir, with a sail...? We make short progress to Macao without one."

"Well, I can't very well risk our entire vessel to the Chinese. It's the only one I have now."

"Yes, sir, but our course?"

"Canton. We shall take the longboat up the Pearl River. I am most curious to find our most considerate Captain Douglas and wish him equally well."

CHAPTER TWENTY-FOUR

Santa Gertrudis

Monday, November 6, 1995
The University of Wisconsin. Eau Claire.

I'm sorry to have missed most of the scenery since it appears in the moonlight to be pretty idyllic. After the flat, flat, flat squares of corn in boundless succession along I-80 from Ohio through Illinois, the rolling hills of Wisconsin are a blessing. There are more trees, it seems, and the red barns with tin roofs are much more welcoming. The horizon ends at the next low hill, rather than somewhere beyond a hundred miles' line of sight.

The cross routes are interesting -- lettered as well as numbered. US Route 14 and State Route M were encountered just across the state border. Then Route T. And V. It's cute. I imagine they lettered their roads first, about maybe 80 years ago, never considering there might be a need for more than 26 cross-state routes. Later I notice a sign for Route TT. Tricky.

The names of certain towns around the state capital belie the origins of their founders. Roxbury, Cambridge, Middleton, Hanover, Stoughton and Arlington. By the middle of the 1800's, their eastern Massachusetts namesakes were over-divided farming communities. Nothing but poor, rocky soil. Third and fourth sons traveled 1,000 miles here, and found their ideal in the wilderness.

Forsaking I-80 south of Chicago last night -- yesterday -- whatever -- I jumped onto I-90 and I-94 West. These interstates piggy-back each other in a great northwest arc through Wisconsin, then I-90 breaks due west through South Dakota. I remained on I-94, on course for the one place I am familiar with in the center of the continent. A college campus.

In my condition, a sprawling Midwestern state university is terrific. Lots of out-of-state license plates, young people and new faces abounding. My spot under a tree in a far corner of the campus allows me a little darkness in which to rest.

I could be spotted here. The thought pervades my being. No, Jane wouldn't recognize me. But why have I parked down by this twisty, turning little river, where I know she might come on a warm, sunny November Day?

I hope.

We had sat by this little river and thought about taking tubes down its length to the Mississippi. Or a boat. Down the Big Muddy, past St. Louis, Memphis, New Orleans. Then along the Gulf Coast, around Florida, up the Intercoastal waterway back home to the Cape. All by water. So easy. So perfect. So idyllic.

It was too damned poetic. Jane was my reward after all those years in the service of Notre Dame. She was the reason I had been molded and broken and rebuilt. She was the One.

A few months after I drove then-wife Justine to Logan Airport, wished her well at law school and taken my only real vacation in months, she returned. Disgusted and disillusioned with her studies, Notre Dame returned to my steady, considerate acceptance.

And then twelve months later Justine was back in the bosom of her family with my encouragement. A financial crisis -- she could help out 'til they were back on their feet. Just a few months in San Antonio, then, who knows? Yes, yes. How can I help?

The subsequent summer of inadvertent moves found me sharing a house with Thad, my acolyte. From my teen years, I had nurtured the creative talents of a boy five years my junior, and now it had come to full flower. His busy circle of friends included one young woman I only later discovered to be his first, and unrequited, love. Maybe his only one. Jane.

I truly didn't mean to fall in love with her. Thad had acted most honorably, staying dutifully out the way, encouraging our outings to the beach, movies, whatever. All in friendship. Innocent. Never allowing for situations that could be misinterpreted.

We talked. We communicated. Long into the night and early morning. She was the image of Life. She saw things only I did. I could talk to her about things Justine never cared for, and that the boys didn't understand. It was too good to let slip away.

Two days before Jane was to return to Eau Claire, I resolved to tell her. Amidst the pounding of the Atlantic against the breakwaters, I steadily and tenderly approached and addressed the subject. She eventually sat beside me. Perhaps we held hands.

The next evening, heart billowing bright, I called Justine, and notified her that I found myself in the same kind of situation she had the previous year at Notre Dame. She accepted it, congratulated me, and told me, "I've found someone else, too."

"O-oh-Great. Good for you." The victory, the triumph, was hollow. THERE IS NO REVENGE, THE PRIEST had said.

Jane had returned to campus a thosand miles away after one final good-bye. I had kissed her once. Gently.

The job I had trained my whole life for awaited me in Seattle a week later. The salary I wanted for producing a radio talk show. There it was -- a clean break with the past. New job. New, long-distance relationship. Stopping over on my way west, my rental car raced from the airport to her dorm to this river.

Summer was over. The endless relationship had changed. Jane loved me -- the hopeless romantic and the tragic soul --, but found, sadly, she wasn't *in* love. A fog had drifted in from the river, enveloping us on the bank. I could have simply dropped into the water and floated off. Instead, I got into my car, returned to my plane, and led the life I was destined to live in Seattle. For three weeks.

Existence was hollow and depressing, but the job didn't help. The show's host turned out to be less well-intentioned than I had thought. I was to write most of her scripts and her pithy, pat answers to callers. Screening the calls gave me more contact with the real world than her, and I found myself more sympathetic to their concerns. Two weeks of it found me finally coping and the host loving my mediocre performance. Another month and that's all I'd've been able to do. On the way back to my sister's apartment in the suburbs I found myself stuck behind a minivan. It was yellow with fake wood paneling. The bumper sticker read:

I'D RATHER BE
COLLECTING STAMPS

I'd rather be collecting dust.

The host understood my sudden family emergency. A lie -- Dad's broken hip would place the family landscaping business in jeopardy. I, the dutiful second son, must return to take command for the winter, whilst father healed. Thank you for your effort, they all said. A position here would always be open.

I'd rather be collecting dust.

Returning to the house of my summer, Thad and I eked out a threadbare existence, pouring our energies into those computer program ideas that came to be known as MASE and *SEXTANT*. With his reference, I took a part-time job at an antiques store. Towards Christmas, I suggested a party be arranged for our little pad, and invited a surprise guest, the summer help from the store --

Pennsylvania, where I began my descent. Jane had been the ideal. Who cared if the next was or not? I was determined to resolve my future once and for all.

Fool. Three broken hearts in a year and a half. No matter how well I behaved. It was quite clear that I was being taught the same lesson again and again. Something was wrong.

But was it with me... or Life?

Tony, a friend from home and one of the creators of the MASE, was starting at Eau Claire back then. I asked him to please look after Jane for me -- there had been a rash of assaults on women there lately. They're married now.

Fool. It hurt to know it was true.

But what was getting angry going to accomplish? Water off a duck's back.

I don't even notice crossing the Mississippi. There is nothing after Eau Claire except the bleak, high plains of Minnesota.

Off the village of Ce-uda'o Inagai, Queen Charlotte Islands
June 16th, 1791

His return, to say the least, was nothing short of incredible. The passage across the Pacific, some 4,000 miles, had been accomplished in less than two months. No need to stop in Hawaii for provisions. Point to point, John Kendrick had set the speed record for one-quarter of the surface of the globe.

To think, Captain Gray had continually fumed at his commander's idleness. When good and ready, a bear can move and nothing will stop him. It was in the preparation that success lay.

The canoes had come off from the village, and the Commander recognized several faces, including the small chief, Coyah -- "Raven". The natives' current attitude gave the sense that they had forgotten the events of *Washington's* last encounter nearly two years previous, but that all seemed so long ago.

The evidence lay all about him. *Washington* possessed more faces strange than familiar in her crew of thirty-six, culled from the docks of Macao. In the intervening months, Mr. Coolidge had been taken aboard as First Officer of Captain Douglas' new brig, *Grace*, and on the Coast last season. Mr. Treat, likewise, became Second Officer.

Of the remainder, all six of the original crewmen joined a mixed bag Chinese, Malay, Filipino, African, French, Portuguese, Spanish, English and Hawaiian crew. More the better, as it was likely a crew member could serve as translator at any of their ports of call -- communication in trade was paramount.

Just in time, the replacement for the Portuguese governor at Macao had proved most sympathetic to this point of view. After initial contact with Captain Douglas in Canton, *Washington* had lay in Dirty Butter Bay for well over a month, its commander wracked with fever. Worse, though, Captain Kendrick was refused entry into the harbor at Macao to sell his furs or resupply by order of the last Governor.

Then, having taken a house ashore in this Mediterranean-style city in the heart of the Orient, Kendrick began to feel the wrath of the influential backers of John Meares. Through the *old* Governor, the Commander's house was broken into, he himself arrested in the street and confined to his home, supplies again refused to the men still aboard *Washington*, and all actions punctuated by the order to depart or be thrown in prison. News of the American complicity with Don Esteban had traveled back here -- thanks to Captain Douglas.

But the old Scotsman had been brought around, as had the *new* Governor. The understanding between former rivals Kendrick and Douglas involved a high degree of cooperation. Captain Douglas smoothed the way for the landing of over 320 furs at Macao. The Yank delivered his two prized officers aboard Douglas' *Grace*. The Scot agreed to sail in the company of *Washington*. The Yank relieved *Grace* of the need of expensive permits to the British East India and South Seas Companies by vouching for its *American* -- not British -- registry. Oh, and Douglas' loan.

Even though 200 furs returned back on board unsold, $10,000 had been realized for the rest, as had another $8,000 for Don Esteban's 137 shipped on behalf of His Catholic Majesty. Financially liquid, Captain Kendrick hauled *Washington* ashore and recreated her as much as economy allowed. Replacing the single central mast with two. The main square-rigged and the mizzen with a triangular sail. Another two small pieces of canvas -- the spr'it sail -- were added to the bow to take advantage of any extra wind. His record performance across the Pacific proved their worth.

During this extensive and prolonged resurrection, Captain Douglas had returned from the Coast, delighted with the performance of *Washington*'s two former officers, and flush with furs and news of what was trading with the natives. Tiring of the scraps of iron dubbed "chisels" by the sailors, the natives of the Coast wanted western clothes and firearms. Captain Kendrick then took advantage of his new partner's bounty by tapping him for a loan of $2,320 to pay for most of his new cargo. Another $3,000 for the same purpose came by way of the agent, Major Shaw, to be credited against the Owners of *Columbia* and *Washington*. Let Barrell lay that bill at the door of Captain Gray.

All had been made ready in March of 1791 to sail with *Grace* when Captain Kendrick struck upon a new market for the 200 furs left aboard *Washington* -- Japan. A country closed to all outsiders, save for the one ship allowed per year by treaty -- a Dutch East Indiaman to Nagasaki. Could one Oriental culture be so different from another that they too would not value these supple furs?

Taking the point, *Washington* had wandered into the waters of the main island of Honshu, while *Grace* held back to await the news. Captain Kendrick's excuse for trespassing was to take shelter from a typhoon. That bought him about a week at the towns of Kashinozaki and Kashinoura. In that time he had learned of the Buddhist Japanese distaste for the concept of wearing the skins of dead animals. However, the locals looked upon the massive Captain himself with fascination -- a giant, red-haired barbarian.

Without any reason to stay, and aware the local authorities had summoned the Samurai from the provincial capital, Captain Kendrick departed from the shores no American had until that date visited. It would be over fifty years before another Yankee would be so bold as flaunt the restriction so flagrantly, and finally succeed in opening Japan to the world.

As an afterthought in this non-productive but historic visit, Captains Kendrick and Douglas together discovered a group of islands they dubbed Water Islands "on account of the natives bringing water off to sell." But that was all done with. *Washington* was stocked with cargo, bristling with weaponry, overmanned and thanks to some finely-concerted confusion by the officers aboard *Grace*, earliest to the fur trading paradise of the Queen Charlotte Islands.

Goodness, but Coyah had brought a great number of his people out from shore. They swarmed over the rails and appeared quite eager to trade. The Haida people of these islands had no use for iron as the Commander recalled, preferring sheets of copper or clothing. Perhaps providing the males some trousers would allow them to break from their dominating women. One female that Coyah had brought aboard was a proper Amazon. It didn't help that these otherwise beautiful, though most aggressive, women smeared black mud of their faces and wore a labret of wood in their lower lip that extended up to their nose when raised. Frightful shame in the eyes of any sailor who had not set eyes upon a European woman in ages.

Such was not the case aboard *Washington*, however. Below decks, the Old Man had brought along a means of insuring a successful voyage. Having lost the services of his tailor and cabin boy aboard *Columbia*, he realized how valuable a pair of hands skilled with needle and thread could be in a region where clothes were the medium of exchange. The average seaman, true, was no slouch here, but his duties with the rigging were the priority.

The chiefs of the Coast, like their people, tended to be of slight stature, broad-shouldered and often bow-legged -- not a size easily available in the few factories of Macao. But the chiefs would most greatly appreciate custom-tailored suits and jackets. Good relations meant good trade.

Last time, well, Coyah simply had mistaken *Washington* for an English vessel on its last appearance here. Following their cruise northward in *Northwest America* in the fall of 1788, Lt. Howe, Mr. Ingraham and Mr. Treat had related horror stories of the English methods. *"Their mode of trading with the natives was, On arrival at a village to plunder the natives of all their fish and oil they could find and give them perhaps a small piece of copper."* In other words, the Brits took by force what they came for and paid what they wanted.

Hence, Captain Kendrick's orders to Captain Gray prior to trading along the Coast: *"I would have you treet the Natives with Respect where Ever you go Cultivate frindship with them as much as possibel and take Nothing from them But what you pay them for according to a fair agreement and not Suffer your peopel to affront them or treet them Ill..."* It was simple -- the Americans did not have the British navy or economy to back them up, so they would have to cultivate the good will of their customers.

But a man can only be pushed so far.

Upon *Washington*'s prior cruise here in the fall of 1789, the Commander had sent his linen ashore for laundering. Evidently Mr. Coolidge and his crew had forgotten that what hung drying on their lines was worth its weight (or more) in otter furs, and the lot had been immediately pilfered by the natives.

Word reached *Washington*. The Commander, for all his efforts to be fair, lost his temper. When the Chiefs Coyah and Schulkinanse simply shook their heads in ignorance of the theft, the Bear dragged both to the main deck, dismounted a cannon from its carriage, thrust their legs into the wells, and locked the clamps in place. Damning them for their lying and deceit, the Commander threatened to kill them if the laundry wasn't returned.

Even this extreme measure worked only so well. Some of the linen found its way by canoe to *Washington*, and of the rest Captain Kendrick demanded payment in furs. At this point, faced with soured relations, but in need of further trade, the Commander took an extra step and demanded the remainder of the tribe's furs be brought, payment to be at the same rate as before the whole incident occurred. Enforced fairness.

Captain Kendrick, upon this return a year and a half later, preferred to believe Coyah had accepted this as his due. Crawford, the gunner, wasn't nearly as confident, with fifty natives on board and another hundred in the surrounding canoes. He wound his way through the mass of flesh to the quarter-deck, and seized his commander by the sleeve. "What the devil are you doing, Captain? They've as good as taken us, letting so many aboard!"

John Kendrick had been indulgent of the natives and expected kind rewards. When this was not appreciated, he felt no remorse striking back at one who knew better. The same followed for his crew. Maritime tradition commanded any non-officer found on the quarter-deck to be flogged ten strokes. Crawford should count himself lucky. The back of the Commander's hand sent the man flying to the rail.

Coyah, standing next to the Commander, needed no more prompting. Having spied the keys to the nearby arms chest, they were in the Chief's hands in an instant. He signaled to his people to join him atop them. A horrid scream went up as those in the water about the vessel swarmed on board. More canoes set off from shore.

The Commander whipped about to see his unarmed crew scrambling into the scant refuge provided above in the rigging. Others pushed and shoved at their captors who fought for their colorful kerchiefs and hats. Behind him, bow-legged Coyah laughed and yelled, demanding the Commander's attention. Pointing to his legs and then to the gun carriages on the main deck, the sense of the Chief's taunts was clear: *"Now try to lock me up in there!"*

Quickly, the Commander grabbed up a six-foot pry bar and swung it in all directions to keep the natives from the companionway leading below to his cabin. "Mr. Barber! Mr. Bowles! Fetch my linen, if you please!"

Washington's new First and Second Officers fought to free themselves. On orders of Coyah, they were thrown down the steep, narrow stairs of the companionway. On the main deck, the Amazon was exhorting her people to do the same with the rest of the crew -- go quietly into the main hatch to the hold... or a dagger was shown being drawn across the scalp.

"Into the hold, the lot of you! Don't give a quarrel!" The Commander edged closer to the companionway on the quarter-deck, as another native approached brandishing a marlinspike tied to the end of a club. A flail of the pry bar kept the menacing weapon at a distance, as well as a few more aggressors with drawn daggers.

Greed was getting the better of the marauders on deck. Disregarding the crewmen skulking down into the hold, the natives let loose in their candy store grabbed at everything not nailed down.

With the crates of firearms nailed shut in the hold, it would take time to unpack and load to do any good. But the arms lockers lay up here on the quarter-deck, directly below Coyah's feet.

Catching the Commander's glance down to his quarters, Coyah realized the two officers in the little room below were easy prey weaponless. The Chief leapt atop the companionway, swinging his dagger in Captain Kendrick's face. Perhaps he had understood the reference to the linen, as well, and decided to make them yet again his prize. The Commander veered back. Coyah jumped down the companionway with a shriek.

Seizing the opportunity, the Commander burst down after him. The Bear crashed onto the Raven, but his small wiry frame served the chief well. Grappling on the floor of the cabin, the Haida dagger found its way to the Commander's waistcoat and across his stomach.

Rising, the Commander ripped Coyah from his chest and flung him at the stairs like a rag doll. The native chief stopped himself, and saw the Commander catch a musket as Mr. Barber and Mr. Bowles drew pistols and cutlasses from their bunks. "Nothing you want here, little savage," Mr. Barber breathed.

Scrambling back up the companionway gave Coyah but a moment to sound the alarm. On his heels, Captain John Kendrick emerged, bellowing, "You better run! Get off my vessel, you bloody savages!"

The natives surged at the Commander. He swung the butt of the musket to knock one over the cap rail, then drew down in steady aim on the other charging with the marlinspike.

The crack and puff of the musket echoed across the deck and the harbor as the corner of the man's face blew apart from the impact of the giant lead shot. Another blast from Mr. Bowles' pistol caught Schulkinanse in the cheek as he charged the Commander. Mr. Barber cleared the way to the arms chest by shooting one of its guards and cleaving the other neatly across the chest.

Coyah sprawled down onto the main deck, amidst his people now caught unawares. They surged back like a retreating wave. But halfway up in the rigging, the Amazon taunted and berated them, directing the wave of over fifty Haida to return to crash upon the three white men on the quarter-deck.

Rolling over, Coyah brought himself up onto all fours. He barely had time to draw a breath before another blast from behind at the main hatch shot him below the left shoulder. Then Crawford and the men of *Washington* came pouring out of the hold, swinging the iron bars they had brought in trade. In a matter of seconds, the main deck raged in hand-to-hand combat.

The Commander roared out: "Mr. Bowles, have you got that damned chest open yet!?!" as he drew his sword and cut another Haida out of the rigging.

The First Officer's reply was the eruption of a pistol round into the chest of another woman ascending the quarter-deck. "Captain, quickly -- they were never locked!"

Captain Kendrick glanced at the chest of powder and shot, wide open before his excited First Officer. Throwing his musket over to be loaded, the Commander jumped to main deck, yelling, "Well, for Chrissakes man, move your ass!"

The swivels at the rear of the *Washington* rained down a fiery death upon the surrounding canoes, and whatever survived quickly fled from the brigantine. The muskets began to pick off the stragglers in the rigging one by one as the crewmen ran to the quarter-deck for a fresh weapon -- protocol be damned.

The natives on board, finding their numbers rapidly diminishing and their reinforcements driven off, ignored the demands of the Amazon and jumped into the water. They, too, were hit by the flying nails and scrap of the swivels.

The Amazon herself finally landed on the main deck, putting up quite a struggle. Mr. Barber brought his cutlass down upon her left shoulder, sending her arm to the deckboards. Even so, she managed to throw herself over the rail and swim toward the village. Under the hail of fire, it was unlikely she made it ashore.

In but a few minutes *Washington* was retaken. Blood drenched her decks, the acrid smell of powder hung in the air. Then a groan was heard from next to the gun carriage. The Raven himself. "Mr. Bowles," the Commander spoke, towering over the bleeding and beaten Chief, "our host lives on. Bring him to the main mast and prepare him for a lesson in shipboard courtesy."

"Aye, Captain."

Ascending the companionway stairs, John Kendrick was brought up short by the small figure that met him below. "Oh," he began, with a grave look towards deck, "you don't want to see this."

"Don't trouble yourself. Looking for this, I believe?" the small voice replied coldly.

He took the felt-wrapped handle from which long strands of rope dangled. On worse vessels, the "Cat" frequently needed to be kept clean of the blood of its recipients. On *Washington*, there was barely a stain. "No doubt you were the party responsible for delivering a musket into Crawford's hands?" the Commander asked.

"*You* kept it away from him. He appeared to understand what he was doing."

"Mind your tongue. I'll suffer it in the privacy of my own quarters, but not on deck from any person."

"Not that I suppose you shall let me out of my prison as it is."

The Commander turning to leave, stopped to emphasize, "For your safety. These natives have not yet laid eyes upon the likes of you, and I daresay they'd have control of this vessel if they but knew you were aboard." He leaned closer, "And take care -- the hold is no place to be venturing, either -- even if it did save us all."

At that, the Commander rose up the stairs and swung the hatch closed. Below, the large, round eyes returned to the bunk installed below the round center table, to focus on the needle and thread. They dropped again, and the shawl rose up to her ears in an attempt to block the snap of the rope and anguished screams that followed from elsewhere, above decks.

Rocking back and forth, humming a tune her grandmother had sung at her spinning wheel, Florence McCarthy, still not twenty years, for the first time since she left Macao, had no desire to investigate events topside.

CHAPTER TWENTY-FIVE

Princess Real

Tuesday, November 7, 1995
Stark County, North Dakota

"WHY NOT MINOT?" the bumper sticker on the brown Ford Fairmont ahead me reads.

Time changed again just outside of Bismarck. I've driven six hours since I left Eau Claire and now what was half-past midnight becomes thirty minutes before the end of today.

Mountain Time.

There are no mountains here. There are no trees here. Only low rolling hills of short green grass. That started just halfway across the state. From the Minnesota border west, all is flat. Not the homey, comfortable flat of knowing there's some Great Lake nearby, or some friendly mountain. It is dead-center of the continent, endless horizon, pool table-flat. Driving across the plowed-under fields speckled with frost, I feel as if a giant eight-ball is going to come rolling out of the north, crush my car and plow a lane of destruction clear to Texas. I am so exposed. Fifteen hundred miles in any direction to the nearest salt water. Out of my element.

On a road like this, flat and straight, truckers tend to fly by. A sports car or two test the upper limits of their engines. Confined to this aging box of plastic and tin, I can only go as fast as I always have -- a mile a minute. No mechanical problems -- not even a drop of oil missing -- have plagued this crossing, save the original defects. The vehicle would not die.

The first few flakes drift across my windshield when the time zones change. Only November, but this is the center of a land mass, and temperatures change more quickly. With no trees or shrubs to catch the blowing snow, the drifts form quickly across the road.

I can drive in snow with little problem, especially in a vehicle with such a compact center of gravity. However, the tires deteriorated through the previous spring and summer, and now grip the road about as well as my fingers. As for the steering, the constant tugging back and forth between me and the drifts is aggravated by my inability to remember where "straight" is. The alignment is so out of whack to begin with, I have to hold the steering wheel at about 60° to the left to keep from veering to the right. The snow sends me every which way and I lose my guides for maintaining course.

By the Stark County line, the worst of it passes, but the flecks flying at me like errant stars are rounder, fuller with moisture. The baby powder snow left behind on the plains is replaced by soap powder.

The landscape of gently rolling hills become accentuated by the complete lack of matching elevation to the highway. I proceed on a direct course amongst the waves of land about me. At one point, I turn my lights off and allow the partial moonlight to reflect off the snow. It possesses an eerie familiarity, one that recalls postcards and photographs of Cape Cod a hundred years ago. A lone house accompanied by a tree, maybe two, nestled in the nooks of barren bumps.

The snow eats up most of my gained hour from the time change. Back at the Mississippi I decided not to stop until I'm out of the Plains and into the West -- wherever that is. The boundary of the West lies beyond the entrance to Mountain Time, I know. It lies beyond the civilized state capital of Bismarck, and the crossing of the Missouri River. Perhaps the snow is a sign -- slow down -- go no further -- don't push it. On the other hand, I've got plenty of time to drive, and I don't feel like spending a snowy night in open country.

The Fairmont is my lead from Dickinson, ND, forward. The license plate is of a red sky. White horizon and blue land are a contrast to the otherwise dull car. I read out the bumper sticker as I approach.

"Why not Minot?"

"Why not *My* knot?"

"Why *not*, my Nut?"

With no radio, this sort of entertainment fills my otherwise uneventful night. I sing out:

Why-not
Mi-not?
The town where pigs and goats trot!
Why-not
Mi-not?
The place to let your brain rot!
I say -- Why-not
Mi-not?

You're bound to get a blood clot!
They're singin' -- Why-not
Mi-not?
The burg where I won't get caught!

This continues for a good twenty minutes. I remember that Minot is a town in the north central part of the most north central state in the country. Minot is noted for its state fairgrounds and Strategic Air Command Base. And now its bumper stickers. My sister Elise's boyfriend had been stationed there.

Why-not
Mi-not
It's more than just a big dot!

Reaching into the back seat, I fish out my plastic jug of orange juice and take a hefty swig. It was my one healthy indulgence at the supermarket back in Fargo, and is greatly appreciated. The vitamins were long ago absorbed into the plastic, but it feels better than taking in copious amounts of Coke.

For the millionth time, I shift in my seat. A bundle of crushed newspaper is able to add only so much to the cushioning. The pain in my lower back will pass, but in the mean time the spasm takes almost all my attention.

Wriggling back into position, I find the Fairmont has surged ahead, or, rather, I have fallen back. It's been like this between verses. Squirm uncomfortably and let the Fairmont gain some ground, only to be reclaimed for the few minutes of non-discomfort. I decide to put me out of their misery, and move to pass. It takes a little more speed than I'm comfortable with, but I hate this stupid cat-and-mouse game. I'm also tired of the song. Too many words rhyme with "not."

The Belfield exit is #42. I entered the state at something like #350. In the northeast, exits on interstates are pretty much written in stone since no one can imagine the need for more than already exist. Accommodating these damn roads to towns that have been there for hundreds of years was tough enough without adding more. Settlement is pretty much already established. But the rest of the country follows the scheme of numbering by distance, from where the highway enters the state to where it leaves. Never know when you might need to install another exit in between.

I've been clicking off the miles by exits. 42 miles to Montana. I could stop, though. I know someone near here. Lisa won't turn me away. It might've been smart to call ahead, but I'm not about to reveal my whereabouts to anyone, especially by using a calling card. Using coins would be murder -- or the price of my breakfast, to be more accurate.

The sign for the next exit says something about "Painted Canyon."

The coil of muscle up my neck begins to send feelers out to link with my lower back. I've been scratching my greasy tangle of unwashed hair for the past day. My skin isn't much better, despite the constant washing at the truck stops. These clothes must smell like one big old gym sock.

The roll of hills gain a little in height and then simply stop. A bend in the road reveals... something. In the dark and falling flakes, I can't see too well, but the slopes nearest the highway rise sharply. That the grass is gone is apparent, replaced by... rocks? Focusing on exit #27, I pull onto it, following it to a single paved road cut through the hillside -- no, cliffside.

Lisa once mentioned the ranch is "just beyond the entrance to the park", but "just beyond" is deceptively far. Eventually the road turns to gravel, then dirt. Three miles further, a high wooden fence masks the entrance. There is no sign for Sully Creek Ranch. It's not something they want to advertise.

The main house is a rambling white-washed thing with all sorts of new dormers here and there. The driveway is probably lined with flowers in the warmer months -- it has the marks of attentive landscaping. The house is dark. No surprise at 2:00 AM. The garage doors are closed, so I can't see if any vehicles are about.

God, I must be a sight, emerging from my little hulk. Conscious that I am still hunched over, I attempt to stretch myself into a less grotesque posture. The few steps in the darkness up to the front door are the only sound I can hear in the whole canyon.

It seems a shame to break the spell with a knock.

Nothing.

I have nothing.

Driving back up the road, the snow seems so pointless. I can easily go the 40 mph at which I came down this road. Instead I find myself creeping away at just over 20.

Stupid idiot. Me.

She's not home. The placed is locked up tighter than a drum and I've wasted the better part of an hour getting my hopes up. No shower. No hot food. No kind face. Just a continuation of the same pointless schedule I've been at for... ever, it seems.

Tired of this travel. Tired of moving. It feels as if the world is moving all about me, and my own efforts are unnecessary. Boston and Cape Cod are just a memory now. The Coast is nothing -- a forgotten dream. The only reality is where I am at the moment. I shift out of gear and roll to a stop.

I've got to stop this all.

I've come so far, but where has it brought me? Three nights of buffeting to be left alone, surrounded by all this land. Suddenly claustrophobic, I turn off the ignition and jump out of the car. I wander about it for a moment, approaching the car, then backing away again.

This car is my home. She is all I possess. She gives me movement. She shelters me. Beaten and tired, still she continues. She's the only thing I know. My own *Lady Washington.*

The front left corner of the car is practically touching the gravel of the road. I bend down to make sure I see this right. The tire iss flat.

Yes, of course.

I cross to the trunk and open it. The light inside actually works, and I carefully remove the various bottles of windshield fluid, antifreeze and decrepit flashlights, to get to the spare and the jack.

The spare tire rests in half an inch of rusty water, probably from a leak in the trunk. The jack, though not soaking, is encrusted and corroded. Squatting down before the flat, I set the jack up in an attempt to get it to work. The threads simply grind off.

I've got a half-empty, near-bald replacement for this flat tire, and I still can't put it on because the fucking jack is a rusted piece of crap!

Leaning back, I sit down with a thump. That's it. Twenty miles back to any civilization, probably. No way to move except by foot. At two in the morning.

I'm tired. It's not *that* cold, and I begin to appreciate the silence. My coating of sweat and odors, added to the flush of frustration, seems stave off any chill. I lie down on my back and watch the snow fall.

For the first time in four nights, I am able to stretch out. The pure, hard flatness is incredible, allowing every bunched-up muscle group to relax.

After a moment, I struggle to bring my knees to my chest. Holding it, the cables running along my back stretch slowly as I feel the distance between my knees and chin decrease. 200. That was the count. I used to hold it for that long, I remember.

200. I release and feel larger snowflakes, some big enough to obscure my whole eye, to cover my face. Turning on my side, I pillow my head with my hands and close my eyes. Like this I could fall asleep and freeze to death.

Why not?

The dream ends in a glare of lights and the cutting of an engine. The cautious, tentative steps across the gravel stop pretty close by. A flashlight reflects off the rim of the flat tire. The feet aren't going to go away, I know, no matter how much I want to be left alone. People aren't like that here.

I pull myself up to one knee, facing away from the light, then slowly turn toward it, looking more than a little sheepish. "Evenin'."

"You okay?" she asks.

I chuckle as I get to my feet, "Uh, no." I shake my head and wave at the front of my car. "Flat tire. Soft spare. Useless jack. Out in the middle of nowhere and my friend I was going to visit ain't where she's s'posed to be." The light draws upon my face, and I try to appear innocent. "I know I'm a sight, but I've been traveling out straight for the past few days. I usually don't appear so scary."

"You say you got a friend around here?"

"Oh, you mean -- hey, could you shut that off or point it somewheres else? Thanks. I was just down at Sully Creek. My friend's, I guess, the head resident."

"Who would that be?"

"Lisa Ormand."

"Uh-huh, and who are you?"

Ew. Identity. From her bearing and the nature of her vehicle, I take her to be a cop or maybe a park ranger. It's smart to keep the headlights on and stand to the side so I can't make her out well. All I can guess is she is shorter than me. But most women without a thyroid problem are.

"I'm a friend of hers from back east. You wouldn't happen to know if she'll be back soon, would you? I was just passing through and she'd be pretty pissed if I didn't say hey."

"Wa-el, I don't know. I was just going down to check on the place myself. It's closed for the week since they've gone for a week down to the show in Oklahoma. Funny she didn't mention it to you."

Cop. I can feel the handcuffs on me already.

"I didn't even know I'd be coming this way, so it's a surprise."

"Uh-huh. What did you say your name was?" She's moving away, towards the cab of her truck."

"Miles."

"Huh?"

"My name is Miles."

There's a pause, then a heavy clunk inside the cab. "Oh -- did you say *Miles*?"

"Yeah. Can I go now?"

The headlights dim and a young woman in a red hunting jacket comes into view. "Jeez, I'm sorry. Miles, huh? You're Miles? Well, I don't suppose you're going anywhere tonight in that. There's a jack in the truck," she checks out the spare leaning against the car, "but you can't drive very far on this anyway. Why don't you wait 'til a garage is open in Belfield and I can bring the rim to get fitted with a new one?"

"Thanks, but if Lisa's not around I gotta get going."

"Oh. Okay." She sounds disappointed. "If that's what you want. But, listen -- like I said, I'm heading down to the ranch. You look like you could use some coffee."

Nice people. Nice lady. I can't refuse.

She is a funny little thing, a bundle of energy driving that enormous 4x4, talking a mile a minute, and asking all sorts of questions of a man she just found lying by the side of the road. I can't see much of her in the dark of the cab except her profile. There's a certain tight, ruggedness not usually found in women's features.

Before I can absorb the changes from just minutes ago, I find myself seated at a long wooden table, chandelier overhead. She is in the adjacent kitchen, with her head in the refrigerator. "Whaddya want?"

"Whaddya got?"

"Have you eaten? You know, I'm pretty hungry."

"I could stand something -- anything." I'm being catered to. It's delightful.

"Wa-el, there's this carrot cake I made but no one got to eat 'cause they left too soon, and I don't think is going to last 'til they come back..."

"I think I can help you out there, BUT..."

She perks her head up, frozen. Her eyes enormous, taking in everything. "Hm!?"

"There is something I need more than anything else. Can you help me?"

She is wary, but not too afraid. "It depends..."

"Something I haven't had in a long time and for which *you* should be most grateful."

Her eyebrows raise and she cocks her head, "Really. And what is that?"

I open my eyes fully and appeal most sincerely: "The shower. Where is it? I can barely stand myself."

The guard falls again, and she launches herself up the stairs, "C'mon, c'mon!"

Drenching, pounding hot water. Oh, there is simply no substitute. I let it open every pore, then rinse through the skin. The soap is some sort of creamy body bar, but with all the rinsing doesn't do too bad a job. The adhered layer of grime disappears. I had forgotten my skin can be soft. My hair takes several washings before the lather works in. The conditioner is first rate, but I nearly take out half my scalp combing it through. Upon emerging from the shower, I find my clothes have disappeared, in their place a dark green velour bathrobe.

She's been in here. She wasn't afraid.

Wiping the steam off the mirror, I proceed to check out my post-shower skin. Not too bad. Beard could use a trim, though. Inside the medicine cabinet is a razor and some shaving cream. A man's razor. The hair in it is a thick, dirty blond. Curious.

Lisa told me of her engagement, but the evidence still surprises me. That he should visit here is even more incongruous. I feel more than a little uncomfortable.

The Sully Creek Ranch was just one of many options Lisa told me about last year. After her internship and masters in psychology, she took the summer off, and returned to the Cape -- but not Pocasset. No responsibilities, just a mindless waitressing job 'til Life came calling in September.

We had hit it off, now outside of the institution, in a funny way -- first cautious, then heartfelt, interspersed with a form of sarcastic tennis, piling idiocy upon each other's idiocy in a conversation no one could follow:

"Where are you going?"

"The beach. Thought I'd try for some fish."

"Yeah, bring me a whale."

"Sorry, babe -- they're outta season."

"You could jump on its back and ride it."

"True, but it's pretty slow. Anyway, you gotta find another to go back once you get where you're going. I prefer flying saucers."

"Me, too. I met Elvis in one."

"Him again? Jeez, I'd wish he'd go back to hangin' out in the produce aisle at Stop & Shop."

"He does -- just weekends now."

"Good, 'cause I need to pick up some plums for the beach. Wanna come?"

"Wouldn't miss it."

She also disapproved of my Vow that summer. "Why would you do that to yourself? Try to have some fun." It was her summer to do so. It was mine to prove I could rise above it all. If she hadn't had that boyfriend...

Maybe that's why she disapproved.

My resolution to ideal behavior was strengthened by that boyfriend back in Denver. Put in the same position, I would appreciate knowing there was one guy hanging around my girlfriend that wouldn't be a dog. If it hadn't been for him...

Too late now.

And this is the thanks I get. Lisa took the job at Sully Creek, head resident at this facility for kids with a history of parental abuse and neglect. Boyfriend has a job that gives him every fourth week off and enough money to visit every other month.

Then, the one time I come to visit, Lisa's off with her gang, out of reach. As I lather up the perimeter of my beard, careful not to reveal the old scar, I find myself unable to wear my glasses in the fog of the tiny bathroom. I take them off and lean close to the glass to see. Better to be rid of the prosthesis for a while – they've left two little dents on either side of my nose.

I'd tie my hair back for the first time in a while -- a little control -- but the only thing useable are big poofy girlie ties, and that would give my host the wrong impression. Instead, I pour on the goo Lisa adds to her hair to keep it from frizzing out. Her hair so much like mine, she could be my sister. For all intents and purposes, she is.

Facial hair neatened up, I thoroughly dry myself and clean up the bathroom. The tiny, round scar is still on the inside of my left thigh, near the knee. In a teasing mood one evening at the local dive, Lisa on the bar stool next to me, held her lit cigarette perilously close to my leg.

I moved my leg away. She noticed, and moved her ash closer. I moved a fraction more. She came closer. I gave her a serious look. She practically stuck her tongue out at me. I moved my thigh straight into her cigarette.

She immediately drew away with a gasp. "Why did you do that?!"

The sting wasn't that bad. "To get it over with."

I come down the stairs, self-conscious in the deep green bathrobe and wet mane of curling hair, like some ancient king after taking the waters at Babylon. The sight on the table holds my attention as it mingles with the smell of the various spices. She's rushing around between kitchen and table, setting places and various pans of something or other.

The loose sweatshirt and sweatpants give her an even more frantic appearance, but it's all well under control. Her long, wavy brown hair never once falls in her face as she jumps around. Despite the layers of masking, it's apparent only a wiry frame can keep up with all these sudden, mechanical movements.

A wok full of stir-fry placed on the table between the candles and rice, she flings out her hands, "Ta-daa!"

It's all I want.

Why not?

"Shell?"

"Or Shelly. Short for 'Shelisa'." She piles my plate full of foods from different pots -- wild rice, vegetable stir-fry, beef tips. "I can't go by 'Lisa', since we already got one here."

"And she's the boss."

"That's right," she agrees with a firm nod, "damn straight. Should be called whatever she wants. Call her Queen of the Zulus if she wants."

"Unless you become Boss Lady."

"Naw. I'm just here for the winter, helping out. Then I'll move on. I don't see how Lisa could stay much longer than her two year contract."

The food is, without question, delicious. Better, it's good for me. I can feel every cell in my body breathing a sigh of relief at absorbing nutrients from food that hasn't been cooked in the grease of a thousand burgers. Crunchy pea pods, peppers, mushrooms with a hint of olive oil and pepper. The rice is fluffy and light, and the beef incredibly tender and mild. As the aromas and tastes swirl around my head and fill my stomach, I understand the reason for her hospitality.

"You're the cook."

"Yeah," she digs into her plate as greedily as I have been, "and I do some work with the horses and more or less keep the kids out of trouble. It's cool," she shrugs.

Shelly is from Florida, at last count, although originally from New Hampshire. You know Daniel Webster? Like *The Devil and Dan'l Webster*? I'm kinda related."

"Which one -- the Devil or Daniel Webster?"

Having taken a mouthful of rice, a laugh and a cough send a few more grains back onto her plate. She smacks my shoulder hard and takes a swig from her water. "Don't do that! It's not nice."

"I'm sorry. You're right. It's not nice... but it is funny."

"No, it's not."

"You laughed."

She picks up the empty plates and moves towards the kitchen. "You know, I shoulda left you layin' in the road!"

"Yes, I know."

"I didn't have to cook all this stuff."

"No."

"Or set a nice table."

"Or wash my laundry while I'm in the shower."

"That's right -- oh."

"That is where my clothes are -- being washed?"

Dropping the plates on the counter, she dashes over to a closet, and flings the doors open to reveal a washer, "You see...?" Reaching inside, she pulls out my pants and underwear, "Oh. I guess they've been done a while."

"Better dry them. Low heat please."

"Yeah." They are all quickly thrown into the dryer.

The carrot cake sliced and served with coffee, she returns to the corner of the table next to me. "You're really aggravating, you know that?"

"Everybody needs a hobby."

"Well, find a new one! Jeez!" She digs into her carrot cake and throws me a faux-glowering look with those round hazel eyes.

It's as if I'm looking into a mirror. Fascinated, I lock my eyes onto hers. She says nothing as she chews, and takes another sip of her coffee. A breath for courage, then asks, "So, uh, what brings you here? I mean, nobody's 'just passing by', ever, here."

I draw back, holding her eyes but lessening the intensity. "I was on my way back from Vancouver. Out there doing some kayaking and mountain climbing."

Shelly is interested. Lisa has thrown up a couple of Paulie's photos on her bedroom walls, but it's always my postcards and notes that she will point to on the fridge. Lisa doesn't have much of a family, and it must impress Shelly that I'm part of her boss's small world. I get the feeling she is experiencing with me the male version of the sort of play normally coming from Lisa. There is something clandestine about her nature -- a sort of "Let's not tell the grownups" look.

The sleeves of her sweatshirt are rolled up to reveal the little cables of sinew that constitute her arms. There are no extras wasted on her, nothing to impede her way in whatever she shoots herself at. Cook. Wash. Clean. Do it all now. Sit down. Eat. Talk. Get up. Wash the dishes. Coffee. Dessert. Eat. Drink. Talk. We're talking. She is intent on this conversation. I never take my eyes off hers.

When she speaks, I open mine wider to more easily absorb every word.

Her voice eventually loses its edge, and becomes softer and quieter. At one point, after describing her next possible direction from Sully Creek, she stops. I look down only so I can only look up at her directly again. Then I pick up our dishes. "Sit," I order.

She pensively remains in her chair as I rinse the plates and hunt for their place in the washer. "Down -- no -- to the left -- ", she calls out, and finally jumps over to lend a hand. From deep inside the machine, I swing my head up and crash my forehead into her temple.

Luckily, I don't drop the plate. The coil in my neck locks.

"Ooo! Oh! Hurt!" she yells out, holding a hand to her head. "Why you *do* dat?"

Blinking hard once, I reply, "Ow -- I wasn't really trying -- Ow." I can't move my head.

We move away from the scene of our collision, back towards the table. The stiffness of my movements catch her attention. "You sure you're okay?"

I smile bravely. "Yuh. Just pulled a muscle in my skull. The long drive didn't help."

She traces a line up the back of her head, "You mean this one, right?"

"Yes!" Ow. She understands. "Exactly."

Turning, she flips her hair away from her neck. "I get it right here if I turn my neck too quickly. It's a nerve pinched between the vertebrae."

I reach out to where her fingers run along the back of her neck. Just below the hairline. "Right... here. Yeah."

She draws her hand away, and breathes a sigh of painful recognition. With my left hand I turn her around with her back to me, and ease her head forward. My right hand stops tracing the line and begins to exert a circular pressure at the base of her skull. I can feel her exhale, "Ee-ah... yup. You got it."

Both my hands begin massaging her neck, reaching slowly up into her hair, then out into her shoulders. I apply a surge of pressure, and she falls forward, catching herself on the edge of the table. "Oh... you know what you're doing."

"Things my sisters taught me." With her arched back before me, I am able to continue the neck massage with one hand while bringing down the other, and give a firm dig into the middle of her back.

Her arms unlock and she falls forward. Catching them, I stop her downward momentum and bring her around to face me. Her huge hazel eyes grow even bigger as she gives a little bite to her lower lip. I can take this further.

Why?

The question freezes in my mind. It is followed by: To what end?

I have no answer. Here is a woman, as engaging and attractive as any I've encountered. She likes to cook and is good at it, to boot. We connect in a quirky way, in a way I haven't in a long time. She's a bundle of hyperactivity that is truly endearing. Moreover, here lies her form, before me, easily in the power of my hands. I have but lean an inch lower --

Why?

A wild spirit, she can not be contained. I am here for a single night. She knows this. Odds are, that is part of my attraction -- to indulge and leave. Is that what I have become after all, but a man in the service of women? Is that what I was created for? Here is a demonstration of that power.

Why?

The best, and only, answer I can think of is: Why not?

The telephone rings.

Jumping back, I dodge behind the counter as she moves to answer the phone, shaking off the spell. "Yeah? Oh, hi -- Nope. Well, yeah. Tomorrow."

Chilled by the abrupt dislocation -- her sudden attention to the phone -- I realize the dryer has stopped running. I reach inside, find the load done, and ball the warm clothes up into my arms. My retreat upstairs proceeds while she is still hopelessly connected to the phone.

Clean underwear. Clean socks. Unwrinkled pants and shirt. I am a new man. My hair has even dried, and I brush out the curls and tangles. A few grains of rice fall into the sink -- I hope they aren't the legacy of my wit. The toothbrush in my jacket pocket used and followed by a good soak of caustic mouthwash puts the meal behind me.

My watch reads 4:30. Is that good or bad?

Downstairs, Shelly instantly recognizes the symbolism of my clothing, and pulls off a good performance of nonchalance. My attempt at sleeping on the couch is spurned. "That road was probably more comfortable," and I am led past a host of rooms stripped bare of their linen. Up the stairs and above the garage lies a simple, broad futon.

"Are you sure?" I ask.

"Yeah. Go. Lie down."

A bed. I'm not going to argue. Shelly leaves, turning off the lights and I curl up to enjoy. Five minutes later I am aware of a body next to me, smelling of toothpaste.

"Hey," I say. "Turn on the light."

"Oh." A tiny bedside lamp went on. "I'm sorry. Are you comfortable?"

"It's not that. It's very nice. I just wanted to say thanks." She leans on one elbow, and tries to turn her head away, "Aw, it's nuthin'," but I catch her and bring my hand up under her chin.

"No, it's not." My eyes lock with hers in the dim light.

She finally speaks. "Oh God... your eyes."

"What?"

"Sometimes, like just now, when you look at me, it looks like you want to..."

Eat you.

"... hurt me...," she pauses, searching.

I continue to take her huge eyes in.

"And I guess, 'cause you're not saying anything, I'm right." Her breathing becomes heavier, and she bites her lip again, as if to convey that maybe this isn't such a bad idea.

I pick up her hand and look at her. "Do you know, I once read that the French custom of kissing the hand meant something -- something very important." Her hand held palm down, I tap the back. "To kiss the back was to show respect." I turn the palm up. "But to kiss the palm was to show passion." Bringing her hand to me, I turn it over, and kiss the back. As I settle into my pillow, the light goes out, and I find her snuggling into my chest.

From somewhere below my chin come the soft, gentle words, "Thank you."

Florinda

September 20th, 1791
Fort Washington, Clayoquot Sound

The smell of the blueberry muffins wafted throughout the cabin. The tea was hot. The eggs fresh and perfect. The ham perfectly seasoned. The Old Man followed the nubile form as it bustled back into the kitchen to clean up. "She is a treasure," he marveled.

Across the table a wide-eyed young man of nineteen tore his gaze from the cornucopia before him, to the present occupant of the kitchen, Florence McCarthy, and then slowly to Captain Kendrick with admiration. John Box Hoskins was impressed. "You continue to surprise and confound the world, my friend," he leaned forward with a whisper "a man of your age..."

The supreme gloat of the fifty-one year old Commander, red hair and beard still thick and luxuriant, indicated negative with a slow shake of the head. "Yes, Miss McCarthy has proved a blessing here on this wild romantic coast. More than she ever bargained for, to be sure."

A head poked back around the corner, with a flash of green eyes at John, then disappeared as quickly followed by the sound of the back door swinging shut. Both men waited a moment to be sure they were alone and unheard. John grabbed the Commander's arm. "How?"

She was the best kept secret on the Coast. When *Columbia* had reunited with the errant *Washington* here three weeks prior, Captain Gray and his officers had come for dinner and breakfast. Their surprise at Kendrick's spread almost overwhelmed the fact that he was both alive and trading on the Coast.

"I found her in Macao. She had come out to marry a young agent of the British East India Company -- or so she was led to believe -- in Canton. Upon arriving in Macao, she learned of the complete restriction by the Chinese upon western women at Canton."

"Good lord -- you mean it's a city of men? What a dreadful thought!" John recoiled. He knew it could take several months for *Columbia* to trade its cargo of skins for a shipment of tea, silk, and porcelain. As Supercargo, Barrell's personal business agent, John's duty was to account for all transactions during this second 'round the world voyage of the *Columbia*. He was accountable only to Barrell, but required to work hand-in-glove with Captain Gray. The idea of being sentenced to several months in a crowded corner of China, surrounded by countless Captain Gray duplicates sent a chill up his spine.

"Fear not," the Commander reassured him with a touch of lasciviousness, "the prohibition is only against white women -- the Mandarins don't want any foreign power to start a colony there by importing families. Other beauties await in those flower laden boats of the Pearl River, or Macao -- take care my boy, or you may find yourself returning to Boston with more than you left."

"Like poor Cassacan," John added sadly. In June, Captain Gray had found few skins in Clayoquot and so had brought the *Columbia* south for a short cruise. In the strait of Juan De Fuca, off the village of Nitinat, they had met the chief Cassacan and his wife, showing obvious signs of syphilis and smallpox. The chief had sold a slave girl to a passing trader for a few sheets of copper, and before leaving the Coast, the captain had returned her ashore. Availing himself of his returned property, Cassacan contracted the disease and thus passed it to his wife.

In his journal Hoskins had written:

Infamous Europeans, a scandal to the Christian name: is it you, who bring and leave in a country with people you deem savages the most loathesome diseases? Oh, miserable inhabitants! You, by being in a state of nature, are considered savages; but from your intercourse with men who dare call themselves civilized have you not become more wretched than the beasts of the forest? Where is your native happiness? You so long uninterruptedly enjoyed. Is it not gone? Never, nevermore to return.

"Better to busy yourself with the natives here and on Hawaii," the Commander advised. The opportunity had already presented itself to John in the Queen Charlottes, despite Captain Gray's orders that no one aboard ship abide the amorous, aggressive females.

Captain Kendrick, upon meeting *Columbia* last month here, told of his altogether different reception from Coyah and his females. *Columbia* had encountered the Raven soon afterward and he told a tale of woe, displaying the scars on his back and a shaved head, by Captain Kendrick's own hand. Debased to the status of "ahliko," or the lowest caste of society, Coyah offered no explanation for Kendrick's conduct, only adding that the trader had killed his wife and taken all the skins in the village. The defoliated Raven had added that following the attack, Captain Kendrick had threatened the village with cannon fire if he was not compensated for what was taken from his vessel during the takeover.

"But you keep your own Lady on board," John attempted again, in obvious reference to Miss McCarthy's duties.

"*Mister* Hoskins, I'm a married man," the Commander began, "a native girl is one thing, but this Irish lass could come a-calling one day in Wareham, a familiar-looking lad in tow, and what would Huldah say?"

"What *does* Huldah say?"

"The same – SEND MONEY," the Old Man lamented, "which I am presently trying my best to accomplish, or, to my dear wife's grief, return home myself. While in Macao, after finally getting permission from the new governor to enter and refit *Washington*, I encountered this young lady waiting in an anteroom of the Governor's offices. Her fiancé had died, quite inconveniently, leaving her destitute, abandoned, and at the mercy of too many willing 'friends' at the British East India Company. She had hoped to secure passage back to Portugal so as to return home to Ireland, and I dread to think what she must have done even to secure an appointment with the

Governor, never matter his eventual price. If I hadn't offered to pay her passage back to England myself in return for a season's service as cook, seamstress and housekeeper I am quite sure you'd have run into her in the darkest corners of Macao, no better off than dear Cassacan."

"A noble effort, sir," John agreed, "shrewd, too. But I hear you are having more success with the natives, trading in armaments rather than clothing."

The Commander indicated the stack of parchment bound in ribbons behind him. "My *coup de grâce*, as our French friends would say. You've seen their ship? A wondrous thing."

Mr. Hoskins nodded, grimly, recalling the 300-ton *La Solide* sighted off Barkley Sound, near to the south here, just last week. "Everyone seems to be on the Coast."

"*My* Coast," the Commander pronounced, "*our* Coast, if the Owners understand the opportunity. I have five deeds here, for each of the four best fur trading harbors on this island. As double proof, I sunk a bottle in the ground with a copy of the paper for this one soon as Wickananish signed it over. My boy," Captain Kendrick smiled triumphantly, "*we* have won."

John picked up the deeds and read through them again, to confirm what seemed fantastic. Four of the five covered various points in Nootka Sound, all in circles of either 18 or 9 miles across. Recalling his geometry and sums, the clerk figured, "Not counting any overlap, it amounts to over 2,500 square miles in Nootka..."

"2,500 square miles *is* Nootka," the Commander explained.

"... and just over one thousand square miles here at Clayoquot. Captain, granted that your deeds represent a sum total, approximately to, say, the East Coast of Massachusetts, what good can such remote lands be?"

"I am sure our Pilgrim fathers were asked the same question," the Old Man mused, but waved the airy thought away, "but read -- they are granted with all the lands, mines, minerals, rivers, bays, harbors, sounds, creeks and all islands, *with all the produce of both land and sea.*"

John frowned at the handwriting of Mr. Stoddard, the Commander's clerk and author of the deeds. Recognition spread across his face, and he fell back in his chair, "Sea otters."

"Sea otters," the Commander repeated, "Sea otter furs. Whales. Salmon. Timber. Gold...?" He smiled as John leaned forward again, "all for twenty muskets, seventy pounds of gunpowder, three sails and an American flag -- silk -- Miss McCarthy's handiwork."

"I see," John began munching on a blueberry muffin. Perhaps Miss McCarthy might find the streets of Boston more to her liking than those of

Ireland. "If a chief in Nootka starts flying *our* flag... but why are these deeds into you personally? Mr. Barrell empowered you to purchase lands, and it would appear, although I do not doubt your motives, my friend, dear me, no, but it could be contrived that you've used the Owners' property for your own enrichment."

"The term, dear Mr. Hoskins," the Commander said, attacking his own salmon steak, "is *barratry*. I would take care to use that word within cannon shot of Captain Gray."

So, it had been said, at long last. When *Columbia* had arrived in Clayoquot the afternoon of August 29, 1791, she found the Old Man settled into his latest Fort Washington and *Washington* fit and re-rigged as a brig, just off this little island. Captain Gray had invited Captain Kendrick aboard and ordered three cheers all around. But what else could Gray do?

In return, Captain Kendrick was gracious to the subordinate who abandoned him at death's door eighteen month's prior. Barrell's letter, empowering Captain Gray to seize *Washington* should he encounter her, was apparently held in little regard by either vessels' masters. Captain Gray was not anxious for Captain Kendrick's return to Boston, and besides, it was the Old Man's harbor now, flashing the deeds.

John Hoskins, but a boy clerk in Barrell's counting house when Captain Kendrick sailed *Columbia* out of Boston Harbor, rejoiced at finding his ally and old friend. A young man could learn a thing or two from this old sea dog about navigation, women and the world in general. The stories Captain Gray had reported back in Boston of Captain Kendrick's lethargic deliberateness fit the character of the man, but *cheating* the Owners? The Old Man may have been unduly slow, but he was honest as the day was long. Captain Gray's conduct, on the other hand, subsequently gave lie to Mr. Hoskins' suspicions, and, he supposed, Barrell's as well.

Two of the original investors for the original voyage of *Columbia* had dropped out when most of the low-grade tea Captain Gray brought back from Canton was found to be water-damaged, fetching a trifle remittance for the venture. Worse, Mr. Randall had shipped cargo aboard, in exchange for provisioning *Columbia* -- cargo sent directly to Mr. Barrell's competitor in Boston. Not exactly what the controlling partner had in mind.

Nevertheless, a second venture was outfitted at the urging of Captain Gray. He claimed it was all for lack of a nimble leader, and if he were in command everything would be different. Only six weeks passed in Boston's shipyards before *Columbia* was ready for another circumnavigation of the globe. Was Captain Gray afraid his old commander might return to Boston too soon and expose the truth? In any event, of the original crew, only Mr. Haswell and Nancy the Goat would be returning with Captain Gray. Of the three, John held the most faith in the goat -- at least she produced milk.

Not a week out of Boston, John Hoskins had barely cracked open his accounting books when Captain Gray gave him an assessment of his duties and presence: "Damn Joseph Barrell! He doesn't know how to keep books or anything else, except his damn mean ways, of setting his clerks to overlook people!" The saving grace was that Captain Gray and the rest of the rest of the officers, were, for the most part, illiterate, and needed John to write and read letters from home.

Thus, John was allowed to go about his business as best he could. Mr. Haswell wasn't much better. When he wasn't bemoaning his Captain's seamanship (they'd twice run through fog into rocky shores), the First Officer was drunkenly announcing he'd take $10,000 of the cargo and retire to his native England. On top of it all, Nancy the Goat died off Chile.

Upon arriving in Clayoquot first in April, Captain Gray boasted of beating Captain Kendrick's time from Boston to the Coast by *four months*, due mostly to not stopping to prevent the scurvy. The reckless abandon and high-handedness towards the crew extended to the natives as well. In June, Attoo, a Hawaiian prince Captain Gray had made his cabin boy on the previous voyage, fled to the safety of the shore. What transpired aboard ships at sea, John Hoskins had heard, but it was worse than imagined, and he possessed little anxiety for the boy alone with the natives.

Captain Gray saw it differently, and took the local chief's elder brother, Tootiscosettle, hostage aboard *Columbia*. The demand to the natives was an instant return of "his boy". So Attoo was, and for insolence, he suffered the Cat. Quickly, Captain Gray had set a poor tone for further trading at Clayoquot.

Yet here was Captain Kendrick, laden with furs. Captain Gray, true to his word, brought *Columbia* cruising to gather furs, as Captain Kendrick had not. The new captain had been on the Coast since April and gathered near 500 furs. The Old Man had been here for half that and possessed over 1,000. Last voyage, Gray's 800 furs had sold in Canton for $21,000, Kendrick's mere 350 in Macao for $18,000. Captain Gray returned to Boston with nothing but poor tea and may well do so again for all this blasted cruising. Captain Kendrick, by learning the language, adopting the customs and being fair, not only had arranged for the natives to gather the furs for him, but bought something for the Owner's that couldn't sink, depreciate or be stolen -- the source of the wealth, itself -- the land.

Taking a measure of the man across from him -- the gentle brute taking care not to sport too much of his eggs in his beard, the most denigrated person in Boston short of the Republican Secretary of State Thomas Jefferson, and the visionary with the potential power to corner the entire Pacific fur trade -- John Hoskins chuckled to himself. Funny. As Commander of *Columbia*, in charge of a simple mercantile voyage, Captain John Kendrick proved not up to the task. *"But a better man might have done worse,"* he would write years later.

The Commander, stuffed, considered the pewter plate in front of him. "In Nootka," he announced, "the Spanish eat on nothing but solid silver plates."

"They have abandoned their fort, again, for the winter," John replied.

"As I shall here before the close of this month," the Commander sighed. "Probably should check on Boyd. Dropped my carpenter and two others on Kauai to collect sandalwood two years ago. Chinese can't get enough of the stuff from India, so perhaps the Hawaiian stock might do. I suppose Miss McCarthy will, no doubt, be crowned Queen of the Islands, and may never want to return to her own dank little isle. That is, if Boyd hasn't cut the place down to bare rock."

"And from China, where?" John searched for tact, "I ask as a friend, not as agent of the Owners."

"That is up to you, as agent of the Owners." The Commander became serious, taking one last sip of tea, "Mr. Hoskins, consider this offer: take this vessel *Washington* -- improved as it is --, the cargo, to sell in China, pay these poor men's wages and the vessel's debt of $4,000 in Macao."

"And...?" John ventured.

"And nothing more. That is all. I will take it to China, and from there it is yours to dispose of as you please. Most of my pay was advanced to me prior to departing Boston. But grant me the satisfaction to hand the deeds to old Joe Barrell myself?"

John was cautious. "What is this debt?" He didn't want to run into something that might entangle *Columbia*, too. "I'd heard you'd made a sale of the vessel to yourself."

"A sham," the Commander dismissed, "to allow me to get credit. Money is more forthcoming to a captain in his own vessel than an Owner on the opposite corner of the globe. Captain Douglas lent me a sum at twelve percent. It's grown. God rest his soul, Mr. Coolidge took command when the old man died on board last season -- in the middle of the Pacific, on the way to the markets of Canton. Lord knows *Grace* could use the money. The price of furs here on the Coast doubles every year."

"And falls by the same in China, no doubt," John added. He bit his lip. "I-I can't accept the offer -- not that I do not want to. No, no. But Mr. Barrell gave me precious little power aboard *Columbia*. If I could, I'd put Gray ashore this instant, and cut the Owner's losses. As it is, we're to proceed to a cove nearby, and build a sloop over the winter. Another Christmas with the savages."

"They're fine people here. Don't underestimate them."

"I was referring to *Columbia*," John laughed. "I can't say no to your offer. I cannot even say I don't know. You shall have to deal with the owners directly. I am sorry."

The Old Man got up and patted the boy heartily on the shoulder. "No matter. Mr. Barrell sent his best man, but he tied your hands. His fault, not yours. Care for some shooting? I see some geese over on the flats."

"Certainly." John bucked up, revived by the Old Man's good humor. "I'm surprised you have any firearms left. The Spanish claim you've provided 200 guns along the Coast."

"If I had there would be no Spanish -- or so I informed the new Commandante. I keep a few guns for defense and trading. They fetch a good price for land."

"You've bought the best of this island already," John gestured to the five deeds. "You don't mean to head north to the Queen Charlottes for real estate? Coyah would not be amused, no matter how *ahliko* he is."

"The Haida people are through with me," the Old Man sighed as he stepped out the front door and gazed to the horizon. First to the north, then slowly following it to the other. "No, south is a better direction. The furs won't last forever, and these mountains are too foreboding, jumping out of the sea like this. You've seen the region below the strait of Juan De Fuca?"

John had on their way up the Coast in April. "On the whole, less treacherous from what little I was allowed."

"Maybe. One more purchase with what little I have left. There are some fine harbors and rivers." The Commander put his arm around John's shoulders, "But do me one favor, won't you, boy?"

"Anything."

The Old Man leaned in close and whispered, "Don't tell Captain Gray."

The Badlands

I wake up alone. It's nothing different, but the room is strange. Unfamiliar. It isn't my home. It isn't the interior of my car -- variations on subdued synthetic blue.

Eight hours of uninterrupted horizontal sleep leave me alert but stiff.

Days of exertion have left their mark on my back and neck. It could be weeks, months maybe, before I will *jump* out of bed.

Early afternoon is awfully quiet. It's too incongruous to the brightness seeping in from every window. Instead of hiding from it, I face it head on. Emerging from the front door, I find myself in the shelter of canyon walls, with winding crevasses creeping off in every direction. Behind the house is a barn and a paddock. The road dead-end into this circular driveway. Nice setup to keep track of kids. Or to keep off unwelcome visitors.

It is definitely dry here. My clean skin can feel it, independent of any cold. In the shelter of stratified red, yellow and beige cliffs, the air hangs still, and the sun creates a heat sink. The reverse will hold true in early morning, no doubt.

This is the same area a young Teddy Roosevelt retreated to following the death of his wife, Alice, in childbirth, and then his mother a few days later. Resigning his seat in the New York legislature, he sought out the rugged, lonesome life of the cowboy, to rebuild himself. Here in a place called "Hell with the fires put out."

My car is parked in front of the garage. I notice that right away. Circling around it, I find the tire replaced by the filled spare. The former flat is sitting in the trunk, solid with air. The keys are in the ignition -- did I leave them there? The driver's seat is shifted forward, to accommodate legs far shorter than my own. On the dash a note reads:

Miles –

Your car stinks! What the heck have you been doing in here?!

I know someone who is a mechanic and he fixed the flat for nothing. I changed the other one and if it's still holding air when you're up then it's probably O.K.

Back around 5:00 (?). Gone riding up north. Help yourself to goodies in the fridge.

- Shelly ☺

She did it all.
I can't last another night.

Outside Billings, Montana

The exits on I-94 West began at #248 after leaving North Dakota, so I figured Montana would be a breeze. Then reality sank in -- it's a much bigger state that than just 248 miles across. Sure enough, a sign indicates the link-up again with I-90. The exit numbers from here on will descend from #455. Oh my. Montana.

This is old land geologically. The Badlands just across the border in North Dakota are the remnants of an ancient mountain range. Montana is the basin of a former inland sea. Dinosaur hunters have been picking up bones here for a century. Big sky country. It feels ancient.

The Missouri River, which separates from the Mississippi at St. Louis, meandering north across the Plains, runs the length of Montana. It served as the fast lane for the better part of the Lewis and Clark expedition sent out in 1805 by President Thomas Jefferson to investigate the new Louisiana Purchase. Above the Badlands, a tributary forks off from the Missouri, heading southwest. The highway parallels this water across half the state before the Yellowstone River reaches up into the headlands of the national park. Forking off before this is another tributary, the Bighorn. I don't pay much attention until I see where the branch veers south -- the exit for Custer. As the Bighorn passes under I-90, it sends another feeder through the Crow Indian Reservation. No one could give this big creek a better name than the Little Bighorn.

I forgot what it's like to drive in daylight, but by my second rest stop it's dark again and I feel less conspicuous. From mileage calculations, if I drive straight through the night to dawn, I'll be just crossing the Washington State border. It will leave me with only a five hour drive to Seattle, and I guess, two more to Aberdeen on the coast. The time lost in the Badlands will be made up and I'll get to my Thursday morning appointment no problem.

A deadline. That's what I need. A tight one. A race. Possible, but impressive. My own timetable. It feels right.

Pangs of guilt and regret begin to well up as I approach the mountains outside Bozeman. Now *these* are mountains -- high and snow-capped, rising up sharply, presenting a firm, distinct line. Cross or go back.

I'm angry. Dammit. I had a good time just talking to Shelly. She is funny, attractive... and willing...? I need those things. Hunger. Passion.

Gripping the wheel, a short growl comes out. Frustrated. But how long would she provide what I need? Damn. Too bad.

But I won't let these female contradictions bother me.

CHAPTER TWENTY-SIX

Mercury

Wednesday, November 8, 1995

Crossing the continental divide, I curse again, not having someone else to drive, not being able to see anything but inky darkness. The sign indicates the elevation to be 5,767 feet and there doesn't appear to be land on either side of the road sometimes. Maybe on the way back. If I come back.

Once on the other side, the lights of the small city of Butte lie at the bottom of a flat valley in a little grid pattern. Something is lit up in the mountain side, and when I pull off for gas and cranberry juice, I see it is white and pretty big. Inside the station, I find a postcard depicting "Our Lady of the Rockies."

Perhaps it could serve as the subject of a B-grade horror flick: *Attack of the Fifty-Foot Mary*. I can make jokes like that. I'm old-line Yankee Protestant. We don't believe in heaven. Hell, maybe. Heaven, no. This is as good as it gets.

Our Lady -- in French, Notre Dame. Standing on the cliffs from whence I came, she looks down on me, arms down, palms turned up. Behind her, I can slide all the way back to Boston. Past her, I will be drawn towards a city and a land I had been accepted into, thrived in, but failed to hold my interest.

Perhaps I hadn't gone far enough. Or I hadn't been equipped then as I am now. Four years ago, I had been in the middle of the process, half-done. If I had stayed, I wouldn't be me.

Falling into the trees and the mountains and suburbs of the Northwest, I would have ended up married (again), with a house, kids, a new car, and money in the bank. The poetic pain would never have taken hold, nor the frustration, nor, finally, the indifference.

I start to close the door, then stop, and look up at the glowing white lady, trying to connect. There is no common ground. No anger. No emotion. No passion. Nothing.

"I don't care," I tell the statue. Strapping myself in, I shake my head, "What a waste. God, what a waste that is."

The Continental Divide, as one might imagine, is not the center of the continent. That's I-35, from Duluth, Minnesota to Laredo, Texas. Instead, it's a line connecting various mountain peaks from just north of the Bering Strait to Panama -- where, I guess, it becomes the Continental Divide for South America. It's not necessarily a line of the highest peaks, per se, but a demarcation of which way water flows. East of here, rivers drain into the Atlantic. West, the Pacific. About a dozen miles separate two streams on the Idaho-Montana border. The divide determines their different destinies. It's all downhill from here.

In the final moments, after my last gas stop at Missoula, I await the lowering exit numbers. Alberton -- #75. Superior -- #47. St. Regis -- #34. De Borgia -- #18 -- Where *did* they get these names? At last, Lookout Pass, elevation 4,725 feet, Exit #5. Six miles later, Idaho!

Not that Idaho offers much, other than a mere 71 miles of interstate to cross. It's the Delaware of the West. Pass through and good-bye. If they weren't so reactionary here, they'd institute a $1.00 toll -- at least to out-of-state drivers.

A little more than an hour from rest, I rejoice at another fruit of my labor. Pacific Time Zone. The last. 3:00 AM, not 4:00. While my body isn't happy knowing another hour of driving lies ahead, I can't help reveling in my victory. I'm almost there. It's so close.

Out of the Rocky Mountains soon.

Why is it so dark out?

Avenger

Off the Philippines, South China Sea
September 10, 1792

Laid on her beam ends, *Lady Washington* took the full force of the typhoon across the bottom of her hull. The tips of the masts lay in the churning sea, her sails tearing to rags.

Out of the inky darkness, the typhoon struck without warning. Rain fell horizontally, wind blew straight down, and the ocean, whipped into frenzy, attacked the brigantine with waves from all sides. Just five days out of Macao and finally bound for a winter on the Coast, Captain Kendrick found himself at the mercy of the elements hundreds of miles from shore.

There was no turning, no trimming of sail or other tricks of seamanship possible, for that would presume a degree of sense in the course of the tempest. There was none.

The hand pumps kept the cargo hold mostly free from water, but buoyancy was not a problem with this cork of a vessel. Rather, as a monstrous wave loomed directly to port, high as a mountain, the Commander hoped the cargo of firearms, tools and clothing would remain fixed in the hold. Otherwise --

The two men up in the rigging, sent to lash the sails to the yardarm, simply disappeared as the sheets of salt water sent the vessel sideways. With the deck at a 90° angle, the masts and the starboard rail provided the only footing to move about.

Lashed to the rudder, Captain Kendrick heard an ominous crack, and turned to see the aft section of the rail and gunwale behind him cave in with the sudden impact of a smaller vessel. Dodging again, he cursed the tender he had purchased and refit during his longer-than-intended stay in Macao. Five thousand dollars of Asian cedar still in tow now menaced its Captain. The wind and waves would catch its aft section and send it on an arc, by its tether, into *Washington* like the closing of a giant lobster claw. If the *Washington* didn't right herself soon, *Avenger* would drive the masts lower into the water while tearing up the main deck.

One final surge sent the tender plowing directly at the Commander as he struggled to free himself from the rudder. A giant arm reached up, grasping the remnant of the rail above, and Captain Kendrick pulled himself up as *Avenger* drove hard into the quarter-deck, snapping the rudder like a match.

With a massive shove, he kicked the tender away with both feet, and dropped onto the opposite rail, submerged in two feet of water, now free of his tether. "Mr. Green!" came the bellow from the quarter-deck. In the howling gale, no reply came. "Mr. Wood!" Nothing.

Making his way forward along the rail, the Commander could see his First Officer, John Green, clinging to the main mast, inching his way towards deck slowly amidst the crashing seas. At the stairs was his Second Officer David Wood, arms wrapped around the rail, fighting for a foothold. The Old Man reached down into the water, and hauled Mr. Wood up by his belt. "Get to the hold, man! Bring the axes!"

As the man scrambled and tripped his way forward, in the shelter of the main deck, *Avenger* swung in for another incursion. The sea behind tipped her sideways, sending her rigging directly into those of *Washington*. Quickly listing, the weight began to turn the angle of the brigantine's deck downward.

Three men crawled out of the hold -- chastised and berated by the caustic Mr. Wood. His old crew and officers from *Washington* had left upon returning to Macao, bad blood following an incident the previous year in Nootka Sound involving the departed Miss McCarthy. The population aboard now were all new to him, remnants of Meares' and some Salem competitors, but they had heard stories. On *Washington*, an officer wasn't much better than a crewman, and the Old Man was no better than a savage. But the pace was leisurely, and he knew how to get out of tight spots, no matter the cost.

At the main mast, the Commander heaved Mr. Wood up and handed him the tree saw. "When you meet Mr. Green," pointing to the First Officer nearly halfway down the mast, "start cutting!" The Second Officer nodded and inched his way up the mast with the saw.

Grabbing an axe from the frightened Macanese crewman, the Bear set to work on the mizzen mast. Furious swings sent the blade driving into the pine he had so carefully set in a year prior. Every other swing, he cast over his shoulder as the swamped *Avenger* sunk lower, bending the masts of *Washington*.

A crack like a rifle shot echoed through the storm as the main mast began to give way under the officers' relentless cutting. Waves dashing over their heads, the Commander hoped they could hold on to finish the job.

With one final effort, his axe found its way to the core of the mast, splintering the wood. Under the weight of *Avenger*, the bottom of the mizzen mast sprung up and away from the deck of *Washington*. Ahead, Mr. Green atop the dismembered main mast, grabbed at Mr. Wood's hand, missed, and went riding the rigging up, then down into the sea.

"MAN OVERBOARD!" could be heard from three dozen voices, and lines thrown to the First Officer finally found their mark. The Commander insisted his men know how to swim.

Slowly, slowly, as the crew worked in the hold to shift the ballast and pump out the bilge, the center of gravity forced *Washington* upright. And as the winds withdrew and the seas calmed, Captain Kendrick assessed the situation.

All but one cannon lost overboard. *Avenger* and her cargo lost. Masts, sails, rigging -- all gone. With the hold completely drenched, the muskets and clothing were retrievable, but the powder was lost. Out of a crew of thirty two, only three men gone.

The fruits of one season's labor destroyed in a matter of minutes, and lay at the bottom of the South China Sea. Another season would be lost, he saw, as he made preparations to jerry-rig a sail from what remained and limp back to Macao. Six months prior, his letter to Joseph Barrell attempted to portray the circumstances and hardships *Washington* had labored under, and that fortunes looked bright for this year's voyage.

Next morning, two hundred miles off the Chinese coast, the first of dozens of swamped Chinese fishing boats were encountered, their occupants clinging to the flotsam desperately. If he couldn't be successful, Captain Kendrick thought, at least he could do something right.

"Mr. Green! Lay lines! Pull those people aboard!"

Westbound lanes, I-90, Coeur D'Alene, Idaho.

Dawn has crept up my back. It's not raining, for which I am forever grateful. Cars still have their headlights on, which is a good thing. The Spokane River Valley opens up before me, and there are plenty of shadows, still. I can see the cars. They can see me.

Walking.

Up, the high collar of my wool coat keeps the chill off, but I didn't bring my gloves. One hand in my pocket. The other, carrying my black leather briefcase, freezes in the raw morning air. All in subdued gray-green with business accessory. I must look like a lost military courier.

It was the alternator.

High on the new section of interstate, on the hills above Coeur D'Alene, I lost her. The headlights began fading out at 3:00 AM and I drove the breadth of the Idaho panhandle in the dark. The lights had been running on nothing but stored juice in the battery. The alternator, which transfers energy from the engine into the spark plugs and charges the battery, must have ceased functioning an hour earlier at 3:00 AM -- Mountain Time.

The last incline did it. From there it would've been all downhill across the Washington State border. Instead, the car died. No power.

The problem then wasn't as much my next mode of transport, but the prior. A thousand pounds of evidence to be disposed of before a helpful highway patrolman came by and offered to call AAA, which I couldn't risk using. Or maybe he'd notice the expired registration decals. Not his state, but police are trained to notice everything.

Lake Coeur D'Alene is said to be bottomless. The water that gathers here before emptying into the Spokane River was at one time crystal clear and pure. Continued recreation and shorefront development have changed that, so I don't feel so bad about having sent the car careening down a residential street, to the shore, into the depths. This last section of I-90 defied construction because of these steep lakefront cliffs. A few dump trucks fell down there, into the lake. The state left them there since they couldn't figure out how to retrieve them from such a precarious depth. Another little Hyundai on top won't hurt.

An hour later finds my five mile-an-hour pace ten miles from the Washington border. I could have stopped in Coeur D'Alene, a city of 25,000.

But I don't want to. I'm not stopping. I don't want to be in this state. If I had been able to make it up that last summit, I'd be well beyond Spokane, parked all warm and snug into some farmer's forgotten back forty. I could have check out buses in Coeur D'Alene, or the train. That would take time.

I'm already wasting time. That same train could be leaving from Spokane. Spokane, *WASHINGTON*, and I'm going to get to that state, at least, under my own power. I can do it. By God, I *will* do it -- *ON MY OWN*.

The Bus Terminal. Spokane

"There's a bus leaving in five minutes, sir. It gets into Seattle at 4:15 tonight. You can check with the driver to see if there's a seat."

I glance out at the dingy covered busway, and see the detritus of the country filing onto a tired silver tube on wheels. "Is there connecting service to Aberdeen?"

"Aberdeen,... Aberdeen, Washington?" the ticket clerk ask.

No, Aberdeen, Scotland. I guess he wouldn't understand the reference, though. Might as well say Aberdeen, Zimbabwe. "Yes."

"No. But you can change for the Olympia bus. There's one from Seattle at five o'clock. It gets into Olympia at 7:00 PM. There appears to be another carrier from there to Aberdeen."

A carrier. What a perfect name for a cross-country bus. "When's the next bus?"

"2:15 AM. The 11:15 broke down."

"2:15 AM. In the morning. When does that get in?"

"7:35 AM into Seattle. You can connect to Olympia at 8:05 and arrive at 9:50 AM."

"Into Olympia?"

"Yes."

"And how long is the ride to Aberdeen -- you don't know."

"No," he shakes his head, "Sir, the bus is boarding."

Stay in Spokane all day and most of the night to catch a bus at 2:15. Where the hell would I stay in the meantime -- the library? 'Til 2:00 AM? A bar? With what money? I catch sight of the map of Washington on the wall. The local road from Olympia, at the head of Puget Sound, to Aberdeen, on the coast, looks to be a good thirty miles. Even walking at top speed, I wouldn't make my appointment tomorrow. Better to get there sooner rather than later.

"Sir --"

"Fine. How much?"

"Twenty-eight dollars, one way."

Ouch.

As I turn away with my ticket, a tall guy, 25 at most, with long scraggly hair, hiking boots, worn jeans and flannel shirts, followed me out the door. "Uh, sir, excuse me. Are you going to Seattle?"

Sir? I stop. Grunge. I used to dress like this in high school. That was twelve years ago, when it wasn't cool, and therefore was. Now it is, so it can't be. "Yes, why?"

He shuffles and asks uncomfortably, "Well, you see, I've got to catch that bus back to get to work in the morning, but I just had to serve a night in the county jail here on an outstanding moving violation. My folks aren't at home now, and I live right in Seattle. Do you think you could lend me the money for the ticket? I'd pay you back as soon as my dad came to pick me up. It'd only be half an hour."

I look at him, straight in the eye. How did I appear to him? Long hair, glasses, freaky military clothes and briefcase. Cool but artsy? Tired but wealthy and eccentric? An easy mark?

I could say I don't have the money to spare. I could say I don't have the time to spare in Seattle. I could say I feel uncomfortable lending money to strangers. All this information could easily be used against me, vulnerable, at a bus station in Seattle, crossroads of the Northwest. "I'm sorry. No."

"Aw, c'mon, man, have a heart," he starts that familiar sideways

shuffle guys do with other guys. "I'll lose my job if I don't get on this bus."
He smiles, "C'mon."

"No." I'm Yankee-indignant. Get into trouble, it's your own fault, pal.
But people are more casual out here. It's repulsive.

"Hey, don't get a stick up your ass. I's just lookin' for a hand." He
places his hand on left my arm holding the briefcase.

I glare at it, at him as he does not remove it, and I breathe through
clenched teeth, "*GO-AWAY.*"

His eyes narrow with a grin, and he starts to draw his eyes down my
left arm to the case –

With my right hand, I grab his throat and shove him up against the
concrete wall of the busway. "I don't care – d'y'understand?" I say. "*I-
DON'T-CARE.*" He removes his hand from my arm, saying something I
can't hear. I turn my back and head to the bus. In my periphery, I see him
amble back into the bus station. As I hand my ticket to the driver and
board, I catch Grunge Kid inside, talking to someone else.

The bus is half-empty. I take the last seat with no occupant next to it.
Room to stretch out. Then a few more people board. A woman takes the
seat next to me. Grunge Kid and his friend get on and sit at the opposite
end. *That* was quick.

Bus travel is for people who can't afford a plane or train, or don't own
a car -- since driving is always cheaper in the U.S. The desperate. The tired.
And, on this bus that originated in Chicago two days ago, the cranky.

Sleep? Yeah, right! Besides being crammed into one little bus seat with
my briefcase held dearly in my lap, there is a child screaming half the time
in front of me. And one behind me. Amber. I'll never forget her name.
Seems everyone else on the bus has learned it, too, and they all take turns
trying to calm Amber, to little avail. Out of this six hour ride, I hope I can
sleep two.

The door seals shut on me and what appears to be the cast of some
post-apocalyptic movie. Nothing but public transit from here on. A couple
hours prior, on the outskirts of the city, I had forsaken the conspicuous
highway for the riverwalk. The serenity of the river as it flowed past the
backyards of prefabricated housing was comforting, and it felt like I was
moving faster not having cars and semis whizzing by.

The springer spaniel bounded out of the underbrush, happy, wet, and
covered in burrs. Her mistress came running along the riverwalk a minute
later, apologizing first, then stopping short at the strange sight I presented.
Must have been the briefcase. Or the asking where the closest city bus was.

She was helpful. She was pretty. I wished I had something for her — save for my single-minded determination.

With her help, I caught the bus from the valley into the queer little city of Spokane. It's the biggest thing between Seattle and Minneapolis. Mountains to the north and east. Rolling hills and prairie to the south and west. A river and waterfalls in the middle. A compact, charming downtown that looks like it was built between 1900 and 1930. Best of all, no people.

There are more people on this bus than I saw walking through the streets of the downtown. West Coast mentality, I guess.

My wallet is already in my briefcase, so there's nothing to worry about. I can fall asleep if I want to, without fear. Lord knows, I'm tired enough. Between screaming fits of Amber and other talk, I begin to drift.

Grunge Kid seems to have struck up a friendship with the people aboard already. How? We're not even out of the city yet, and they're talking about ex-husbands and serving time in jail.

I turn my head against the window, feeling the hum of the engines, reverberating through the glass. People are strange here. They're nice, but they're not considerate. They demand respect before earning it. If I stay here too long, I'll end up killing them.

Oh, that's right. I forgot why I've come in the first place.

Argus

I endeavored to reconcile myself to my narrow prison
hoping the variety of objects which usually occur on such voyages
would tend to make it pass away lightly
-- thus deceiving myself in the best manner left for me to practice.
-- Joseph Ingraham, *Log of the Hope*

Port Independence, Island of Hong Kong
January 1, 1793

Silence covered the decks of *Washington*. The minister removed himself from the makeshift pulpit at the head of the stairs to the quarter-deck. Behind, the somber, well-dressed expatriates of Boston shifted uncomfortably, waiting for the Commander, who, head down, frowning, spoke not a word.

Crossing to take his familiar place of command at the rail, he took in the view before him. The skeleton crew attending to the brigantine was augmented by former shipmates from other vessels. Hanging their heads, the Hawaiians, Chinese, Africans and Malays understood the gravity of the scene before them just as well as their Americans, English, Welsh, Irish, French and Portuguese comrades. It rested in the two unmistakable six-foot wooden boxes at the edge of the main deck.

"Thank you, Reverend Howel," the Old Man began, and stopped again, considering. "To depart this life far from home is said to be a pity. Away from the warm affections of loved ones, a man is assumed to be alone, and left to join the soil of some foreign nation, perhaps to convey a permanent break from whence he came, and that which made him the man he was."

Beyond, in the wild slopes of Hong Kong, with sampans and Chinese pirate junks plying the waters like seaborne fans, the setting was indeed a far cry from the wharves of Boston or farms of New England. In an effort to evade the increasingly curious Portuguese customs authority in Macao, the Commander had removed his vessel to this dubious refuge. Across the channel of Macao Roads, on the unsettled island of Hong Kong, a shelter had presented itself. With the usual humor, in honor of his newfound freedom, the Old Man dubbed it Port Independence.

But removal from the sins of the Portuguese colony had come too late for the Second Officer and the Commander's Clerk. The venereal had caught up with David Wood and Jonathan Stoddard just past Christmas. Even the best doctors from across the Roads were unable to assist with their liniments and herbs. The debts the two men had taken in the flower boats of the Pearl River came due in a painful week of increasing decrepitude.

"You who sail for Boston soon shall return with memories of these fine gentlemen, and what you convey to their families and loved ones will be used to construct a lasting portrait. Perhaps, in breaks from their duties, they lived too fast for these climes, and such is their lesson to us all. But in remembering, let charity guide and indulge your fondest memories of their deeds, for without them and men like them -- men like you -- our nation would simply be begging at Europe's doors for scraps. Let there be no doubt about these men's legacy of courage, skill and duty, to their shipmates, to their Captain, and to their country." The Commander nodded to his First Officer, "Mr. Green, you may perform the duty."

The Commander stood motionless as the board slid away from the end of the coffins. The bodies, weighted with cannon and chain, wrapped in white sheets, sank to the depths. The salute fired, the group up on the quarter-deck retired to the Commander's crowded cabin.

A dour air hung over the half-dozen gentlemen -- partly for the lost men and partly at the idea these survivors hadn't lived so slow around these climes themselves. John Hoskins desperately yearned to check his trousers one more time. The Old Man, climbing down last, drew the companionway hatch closed behind him, and leaned back against the stairs. "My friends," he announced with resignation, "good, trained seaman are our most priceless commodity in the Pacific, and I've lost the last of my Boston men. My years are approaching an end, and so, to your great collective relief, no doubt, I shall return to Boston at the conclusion of my next trading voyage."

At last. Captain John Kendrick would bring *Washington* home to Boston. For each man in the cramped quarters, it held different implications, the Commander knew. Of the five, three were his rivals as masters of competing vessels. Of the three, two had served under him, and learned, to varying degrees of success, his ways of navigation. Only one was not a mariner at all, but Reverend John Howel had already been drawn in by the Navigator and his actions.

Captain Gray saw his own day of reckoning fast approaching, after returning *Columbia* into the hands of Barrell. John Hoskins, incorruptible for the most part, had discovered from Shaw & Randall the extra $5,000 of income not recorded in *Columbia*'s books on the first voyage. Such discrepancies had allowed Captain Gray to buy into the partnership of the second voyage, at the cost of over $3,500. How else, at his pay of $400 for the last voyage? With the Old Man back in Boston, supported by the young Mr. Hoskins, to refute all sort of slander Robert Gray had spread, it was hardly possible for him to command another voyage to the Coast, China or elsewhere. Gray would have to find his money outside New England.

It wouldn't lead to Canton, John Hoskins knew. It was no plainer than the downcast face of Captain Joseph Ingraham of *Hope*. A better man might have done worse than Captain Kendrick, indeed. Ingraham, former First Officer of *Columbia*, had gathered *Hope*'s cargo of 1,700 furs in forty-nine days, only to find a complete embargo in Canton last winter. The Chinese, at war with the Russians, had prohibited the importation of sea otter, believing that since the Russians had started the whole trade, they must be benefiting from the entire commerce.

Captain Ingraham's second voyage to the Coast this past season was marked by an utter inability to provide articles of trade in the quantity desired by the natives. Writing in his journal, he described both inflation of furs and growing influence of his former commander with the natives:

> *Every one of them enquired particularly after Captain Kendrick, saying they had plenty of skins for him and they would not sell them to anyone else... they all seemed very fond of Captain Kendrick, for he ever treated them with great kindness. But I believe their principal view for wishing to see him at present was to dispose of their skins at an exorbitant price which none but Captain Kendrick will give.*

Captain Ingraham would leave for Boston soon, with *Hope* $40,000 in debt to various Chinese creditors. But, to be fair, how much of that in rum went down its master's own throat?

For Captain James Magee of *Margaret*, it meant at least another season competing with the only man older than him on the Coast. Upon entering Clayoquot Sound in 1792, for the first time, Captain Magee saw first-hand the effect Captain Kendrick was having on the English. Three vessels from London, the ship *Butterworth*, schooner *Jackal* and sloop *Prince Lee Boo*, had arrived on the Coast and immediately attempted to trade with the chief Wickananish. The chief refused, saying all furs were reserved for Captain Kendrick.

Gone were the days a simple "chisel" would buy a dozen furs. With Wickananish, Captain Kendrick had developed a sophisticated system of arriving at Clayoquot, advancing payment equal to 50 to 100 furs, then cruising the rest of the Coast for the season while the chief gathered his stock from neighboring peoples. Yankee efficiency -- allow people to perform the task to which they are best suited.

Enraged, Captain Brown of the *Butterworth* ordered his crew to cut the furs off the natives backs, as in the old practice. The English killed four of Wickananish's people before finding their victims also possessed firearms, and fled back to *Butterworth* in their long boat, with one of their own dead, two wounded.

Encountering the natives in their massive canoes hot on the heels of the English long boat, Captain Magee put an end to the chase by firing between the parties. This changed environment was reported back when Mr. Lipscomb of *Margaret* was sent to Wickananish.

"Wuktahook pool!" -- *We are not afraid of guns*, they had replied, brandishing their own. True to form, Captain Brown reported the incident as an unprovoked attack by the savages.

John Hoskins, youngest of the group, simply hoped the Old Man would come back with enough to see himself through his old age. A profit from this last voyage? Perhaps, despite the total loss from the typhoon. But politics had begun to rear its ugly, unpredictable head again, first in here in China, then in Nootka.

If the behavior of the "Butterworth Squadron" (as the three vessels were known) towards the natives hadn't been bad enough, its men had begun taunting the Americans at Nootka, claiming a squadron of the British Royal Navy would be arriving to cast the lot of foreigners out. First came the store ship *Daedalus* direct from England via Cape Horn. Then the ship-of-war *Discovery*, bristling with ten cannon and numerous smaller guns, and its attendant, *Chatham*, from their voyages of exploration throughout the Pacific. Yet, their commander, Captain Vancouver, followed no such course as suggested by the English merchantmen.

Instead, there was a disagreement over what, specifically, the British envoy was to receive back in the name of Captain Meares. Captain Vancouver claimed it was the entirety of Nootka Sound, and by the Convention, the Spaniards must remove to their northernmost settlement. In the precise observation of the British commander, this would have meant all the way to the Presidio in San Francisco. Don Quadra, the benevolent and most gracious new Commandante of Nootka, said his only instructions were to hand over the half-acre plot upon which Meares' hut stood.

With impeccable timing, Captain Vancouver's flagship, *Discovery*, chose not to follow the directions of the pilot provided by the Spanish, Juan Kendriqué, Jr., for entrance to Nootka Sound. Subsequently, the mighty British warship lay upon the rocks at low tide, much to the delight of the Americans. Likewise, Captain Vancouver declared if he could not have the whole of the place, he would take nothing and await further instructions.

But Reverend Howel had witnessed these events most intimately, John recalled. In fact, the "Historian", having taken passage from Boston in the interest of writing an account of the voyage of *Margaret*, had even drafted Chief Maquinna's deed of gift for Nootka to Don Quadra. This legal instrument, of course, excepted Captain Kendrick's purchase a year prior.

Here was an intriguing gentleman with an most unusual background, this Howel, whom the sailors called "Padre". Always arising at the right moment. *Columbia* first learned of him when it sailed into Clayoquot soon after Captain Magee's encounter with *Butterworth*. Captain Gray had found Wickananish aboard *Margaret*.

His elder brother having been held hostage by Captain Gray,

Wickananish was wary of personal invitations to trade on these sailing vessels. The Padre, then, offered to be sent on shore as a hostage. Brave man.

Later, Captain Magee took sick and accepted El Commandante's offer of a house at Nootka – and the Padre began service as official translator for Don Quadra at Nootka,. Arriving in China last week, he resumed his old vocation as Episcopal minister for this morning's services. "Captain Kendrick was fortunate to find a man such as yourself available, Mr. Howel," John added after the meeting below decks had fallen to rum and talk.

"Indeed, I find my services again called upon by this vessel's master," the Padre replied.

"A history of the brigantine *Washington*, perhaps? It would do better than that dry account by Captain Cook or the pure fabrication of Captain Meares."

"No doubt, sir, but no," said the Padre. "For the benefit of passage, I shall accompany and serve as humble Captain's Clerk for a season on the far, murky Coast, and then return to work for God, to educate and enlighten the natives of the Sandwich Islands."

"A missionary? How noble," John thought of the precious girls of Hawaii, sporting only a maro, cool from the waters, who for a two-penny nail, would launder his bed linens (it was a blessing to have one's own cabin!). On the other hand, the Padre, he mused, apparently felt Wickananish and the inhabitants of "the murky coast" were already children of God. "Perhaps we can take up a fund from your friends in Boston?"

"Charity from Boston," the Padre sighed, "one might as well say 'charity from London', for I know not but poor copies from either."

"Uh, yes, to be sure," John stammered, "excuse me, sir. I do need a breath of air."

The minister-historian-translator-clerk smiled, indulgent of this youngest of their crowd. As John climbed up the companionway, he felt a cold chill run up his back.

On the quarter-deck, Captain Ingraham was grappling with the tiller, making all manner of BOOMs and SLOOSHes, swaying this way and that. He grinned devilishly at being spotted by his youthful peer. "Ho, there, young John Hoskins, scourge of ship *Columbia* and nettle in the side of old Rob Gray. Good name, eh -- *Rob* -- for him, don't you --"

Mr. Hoskins' hand found its way to the drunken man's mouth. "He's below, for God's sakes, Joseph! I do wish to make it home in one piece!" came the whisper, then a laugh. "What *are* you doing?"

Joseph Ingraham played with the tiller, flipping it from one hand to the other. "Just remembering... that first time 'round the Horn with the Old Man. It'd be black as pitch, blowing a hurricane, and he'd come up with a double measure of hot rum and ram it down my throat -- I think more to take the fear out of me than the chill."

John sniffed at the mug nearby, drained of its "flip", a potent mixture of rum and beer. Once leaving Boston on *Hope*, Captain Ingraham had made drink his only friend.

Ingraham straightened a little more as he saw John examine the evidence. "He's not coming back, you know."

John whipped around, shocked at the rapid lucidity. "Whatever do you mean?"

"As I said. He can't. We'll all return to Boston, and for our labors and sins, we'll be relegated to rowing the ferry across to Charlestown. In China, we're scoundrels. In Hawaii, we're gods. On the Coast, we're... Boston Men. The Old Man opened this ocean to us, trained us, and now we wander it like bastard sons. And like bastard sons, we've come to his knee when he's called one last time."

"Don't be bitter."

"Bitter! Bitter? Far, *far* from it. I love that Old Man as much as my own father -- more. He gave me the skills and taught me the rules, set me loose, then whipped me fair and square. I jumped in on my own. But, see this, Mr. Hoskins, we're all leaving him -- you, me, Haswell, Coolidge, hell, even Gray, just as his own sons have -- just as *Columbia* left him here on his own..."

Here the pain was evident on the fine young captain's face. On that blustery day so many years back, off Macao, Mr. Haswell, knowing the First Officer's weakness for the bottle, had provided a bounty of plum wine. *Columbia's* escape beyond Captain Kendrick's power had been accomplished at the price of an incoherent First Officer Joseph Ingraham.

"... But instead of the Portuguese in Macao," he continued, "the Old Man's got the British in Nootka. Maquinna himself told Don Quadra he never sold any land to Meares or anyone else, except our Captain. They don't like us there -- what do you know about *Butterworth*?"

"Well, for one thing," John observed," they haven't yet collected enough furs to come sell here."

"They're not even supposed to be doing that. They're at Nootka and Clayoquot for whales," he hissed.

"Oh," John recoiled, "whalemen." In the maritime trade, these filthy ships were considered one peg above slave ships. "But they couldn't have had much luck."

"No, of course not. Our dear Captain Meares spread all the news around London of the whales at Nootka. What he forgot to mention was that they were these paltry little gray ones, not the Spermaceti or Right whales. Not even worth the effort. And with the inflated price of furs on the Coast, far above what these English were told *and* Captain Vancouver not throwing the Spaniards out post-haste, it's only a matter of time before they...," he stopped suddenly and shook his head, "... nothing. Too much drink -- too much think. A piece of advice from one Yankee lad to another," he shook his finger, "don't listen to Russians."

"Russians? What on earth...? Not *Torkler!*" John laughed, trying to dismiss the ridiculous idea, "No, you think the Russians are going to sweep down from Alaska, with their captive Inuit, and take *Washington* by storm, I suppose."

"Never you mind," Joseph put a hand onto the rigging and began to climb. A hand at his ankle stopped him. "Go 'way. I want to see my *Hope*. I want to see my narrow little prison. Leggo."

"Captain -- Joseph, please." John eased his tall friend down.

The master of *Hope* shook his head, "It's no use. Go home -- be ruined. Stay here and be destroyed. It's that Russian, remember?"

John remembered. For all their claims, and starting the whole Pacific fur trade, he had seen but one. The previous August, the immense 600-ton French ship *La Flavie* burst out of the fog north of the Queen Charlottes. Mr. Hoskins had been sent along with the tender *Columbia* had built over the winter, *Adventure*, commanded by *Captain* Haswell on this solitary cruise.

The first thing they found was *La Flavie*, a shipload of Frenchmen, drunk and stuck on a sandbar. Captain Haswell had gone aboard and discovered the Supercargo to be the Russian Agent for the settlement at Unalaska, Peter Torkler. In exchange for piloting *La Flavie* across the bar, the French paid in wine and cognac -- the sole nature of their trading cargo.

Then, for a reason Captain Haswell never imparted to Mr. Hoskins, *Adventure* continued around the north of this island for *three weeks*. No trading at all. Eventually they took shelter in Henslung Cove, on Tadents Island -- a tiny rock across from the north island of the Queen Charlottes archipelago. Coolidge's *Grace* arrived from Macao. Then Ingraham's *Hope* from Nootka, shadowed by the *Butterworth's* consort, *Jackal*. And finally the brig *Fenis & St. Joseph*, commanded by the old master of Meares' *Felice Adventurer*, Captain Duffin, arrived the next day. In the evening, Captain Haswell left Mr. Hoskins in command of the tiny *Adventure* -- a lonely vigil in the constant fog -- to venture for entertainment.

At first, it looked as if the launch had taken Captain Haswell to *Hope*, but through the fog, a break opened, and no boat lay tethered thereabouts. When Captain Haswell returned early the following morning, smelling more of wine and cheese than rum and biscuit, John knew *La Flavie* must have played host to some party, complete with labretted native girls. But he wouldn't give Haswell the satisfaction of his envy.

Captain Ingraham had attended, too, no doubt. It was a wonder he possessed any recollection of the Russian Agent, the French ship, or most of the voyage to the Coast at all. But the element that had continued to unsettle John was the prevalence of the English.

"What did that Russian tell you?" John demanded, but not truly wanting to know.

"Conspiracy. Seems to be that nation's past-time. Spotting them. Creating them. They're all the same. Brought some ships to the Baltic when I was a kid, and met *plenty*. Never trust anyone. Pretty good rule, if you ask me."

"*What* conspiracy?"

"Oh." Joseph was surprised to find anyone interested in his stories. "Well, it's like this... uh,... Right." He tried to remember, "First, the *Fenis*, owned by Meares, was carrying Captain Vancouver's courier, Lieutenant Mudge, back to London, asking for further instructions how to proceed at Nootka with the Spanish."

"Yes, yes," John urged impatiently.

"It happens to meet up with the *Jackal*, one of three ships financed by the Lord Mayor of London, himself."

"I see," John nodded. British commercial interests working hand-in-glove with the government. "There's nothing new about that."

"But that isn't the entire plot. When Haswell and I came aboard *La Flavie*, that Mudge fellow threw a perfect fit, crying '*No damned Americans!*', as if the French would listen. Torkler told me later the Brits had tried to recruit his government in a scheme to close the Coast to us. Then the big three could divide it -- Spain down the south, Russians up north --"

"And the British in the middle. I take it the French weren't too impressed?"

"To say the least. That ship of theirs could have taken out any damn thing floating, Vancouver included, but they were too interested in chasing native girls. I hope they don't spoil the Hawaiians."

"I wouldn't worry. There're plenty to go around." Poor Joseph. Drink and debt had the better of him. Setting him down against the rail, he fell asleep against the tiller. Rising, John stepped over the man, then stopped

short. Crouching down quickly, he slapped Joseph's face lightly. "Joseph --
Captain, wake up!"

Captain Ingraham frowned, opened his eyes and smiled. "You're not
Mama. You must be my wife. Give us a kiss, Sweet."

"Serious, man." Mr. Hoskins grabbed the slumping shoulders, "How
did you know the Lord Mayor of London owns the *Jackal*?" It was not
common practice for any captain to announce who *his* boss was.

Joseph leaned against the rail again, closing his eyes. "The Padre told
me. Claimed to have voted for the gentlemen. Howel's a Tory from London,
you know." And then he promptly fell asleep.

US Route 12, Grays Harbor County, Washington

I feel... dirty.

It's not the bus ride. Seattle was, again, underwhelming. Of course, I
was confined for five short minutes to its bus station -- never the garden spot
of any metropolis. But the city is strange. Not in the way other cities along
the way have been. Those were all inland, river cities. This one's on Puget
Sound, salt water. I should have felt rejuvenated. But I'm not. I think it's the
port.

From the highway I had gotten a view from the harbor. It was pretty
tight, but there were plenty of big cargo ships pulled right up to the docks --
the same would have grounded out in Boston Harbor. Recalling from my
first impression years back of the place, the more I saw of Seattle, the more
parts of it reminded me of other cities I've been through. Is it Boston with a
better harbor? Kinda. San Diego with a colder climate? Mobile with
mountains? Well... *I got it*. Seattle is the Portland, Maine of the West Coast!
Except Portland doesn't have Boeing and Microsoft (or any modern
economic base). "*And that*", as Robert Frost said in *The Road Less Traveled*,
"*has made all the difference.*"

I hadn't had a shower in 24 hours. I smelled like a cross-country bus.
Thank God for the toothbrush I brought -- the interim in the bus station
bathroom was just long enough to use the darn thing. And watch as Grunge
Kid disappeared into a waiting Ford Taurus. Safe again.

As we had pulled into the city, a woman noted: "There are two kinds of
weather in Seattle -- warm rain and cold rain."

Cold rain. How appropriate.

Mountains. Mountains and ocean don't mix. From my New England
point of view, mountains must be far from the coast, maybe a day's drive.

You have to *earn* your mountains.

The stopover in Olympia wasn't that bad. I sprang for the blue plate special at a nearby coffee shop after I asked the ticket clerk when the next bus was and how much.

"Another hour and a half," she says, "You can pay the driver when you board."

"But how much is it to Aberdeen?"

"It's a dollar."

"I beg your pardon, did you say the fare for an hour and a half bus ride was *one dollar*?"

"Mm-hmm."

I nearly kissed her.

The mashed potato and meat loaf sit in my stomach like a lead sinker now. Gray's Harbor Transport, run by the county of the same handle, operates a fleet of mildly clean yellow and brown buses. It is a transit bus, not a motorcoach. Like a subway, some seats face sideways. I don't care. It was a buck.

But I feel dirty. It's not the grungy teenagers in the other seats. It's not the bus. It's not the pervasive fog and the dim yellow interior lighting of the bus. It's Gray. I am in Grays Harbor County. Going to Grays Harbor Historic Seaport. On Gray's Harbor. I want to scream.

From what I read, after Captain Gray brought *Columbia* into this harbor, the crew named the place after him. The crew. How humble. Well, he had named practically everything else after Joseph Barrell, George Washington, John Hancock, John Adams and even his ship -- it was only a week later he entered the mouth of the great river to the south.

A Kendrick in Grays Harbor. Enemy territory. But she's here. That's all that's important. My journey is almost over.

Through the darkness, I finally see the lights of some civilization. A supermarket. A McDonalds. A fruit stand. Up over a tiny bridge lies a careful pattern of one-way streets leading through Aberdeen. The bus pulls alongside a little brown bunker and everyone gets off. Here.

Where?

It is dark. Spitting rain in the mist. Aberdeen, Washington has the highest rainfall of anywhere in the country. 140 of 365 days of the year here have rain. The rest are probably fog. I can't see anything except closed-up storefronts and streetlights. The sign on the wall of the bus stop points me to the Seaport. Just back over the little bridge, on the harbor. Of course.

Dodging the cars racing down the streets, I find the bridge. It is too dark to see much, and the lights from the McDonalds behind me don't help. Fifty yards beyond and I am back at the farm stand. Behind it, a box of a building, log-like, stood at the head of a circular drive. Next to it, a sign points to another door: GIFT SHOP. Dark, save for the safety lighting. 10:20 PM. Nobody home. I'm here early. Twelve and a half hours. What the hell am I going to do with the rest of my time, here on enemy territory?

After an hour in the supermarket, I've bought a few bagels, cranberry juice, a few slices of baloney and a cucumber. Wandering along the waterfront walk behind the stores and seaport, I can see the Weyerhaeuser plant on the opposite side, churning pulp into the water. The light is faint and I nearly trip on a circular walk at a bend in the river. A large, boxy warehouse stands before me. The security lights are on, and I can hear music coming from the other side.

The plank pier leads around the corner, and I inch along with my briefcase in one hand, plastic grocery bag in the other. Poking my head around the building, I see her. Light cast out from the aft cabin, and music flows out liltingly from the hold. The gangplank is down and the sails furled. Every inch of her looks shipshape and Bristol fashion. Two masts, both square-rigged, as a brig. Swivel guns on the caprails, and ports below for cannon.

Lady Washington.

But she is untouchable until morning. People are obviously living onboard. Unable to restrain myself, I walk the full length of the pier, searching the shadows for details. When a voice signals the emergence of someone from the hold, I head down the pier, to a gangplank, out of the spotlights.

A man and a woman, dressed rather frumpily, emerge onto the main deck. And hang around. I'm going to be here a while. In fact, I realize, I have nowhere else to go.

Backing down a ramp at the far end of the pier, I find myself under a canopy, under which are two broad, stout boats. One has a cover.

It isn't that cold out, but it is damp. *Damp* – hell, I teethed on damp. The front of the boat has a little cubby, and after I climb in I cover myself with the lifejackets and windbreakers stowed there. The boat rocks, but barely. The feast consumed, I rock slowly to sleep in the shelter of the ketch *Spitfire.*

CHAPTER TWENTY-SEVEN

Lady Washington

Thursday, November 9, 1995

"Give a pull – there!"

There is tar on the line to help me catch a grip. Even so, gloves would help. I refuse a pair, and pay for it. The line wants to slip and tear through all seven layers of epidermis to the raw flesh. The calluses and muscles from five thousand hours behind a lawn mower catch, hold and pull. The yardarm rises up the mizzen mast. Slowly.

I've already been up in the rigging unfurling the main sail ("mains'le", they say). In a few hours *Lady Washington* will sail south for a couple of weeks of exhibitions and charter cruises first along the Columbia River, then onto San Diego. Appropriate.

If I hadn't arrived here first thing this morning, I would have missed her, and could've ended up chasing her all the way down the Coast. Not really, from the shape my wallet is in – I'm down to my last fifty-dollar bill and change after downing two cold cans of soup for breakfast earlier.

The surrounding environment above-boards is odd. For the first time in the Northwest, I see deciduous trees -- leafy hardwood, rather than the pervasive, coniferous, needle-bearing giants. The fog and drizzle obscure the peaks at either side of this broad river valley at which Aberdeen and Grays Harbor sit. Yet, closer, I see the pulp-clogged estuary on one side, and the steep hillsides of new trees on the other.

There could be two explanations for these trees -- moisture and man. Leafy trees generally need more moisture than needle trees. That's why the mountains of the dry American West are covered with conifers. Leafy trees also point to civilization of a hundred years ago -- the tall, straight needle-bearing cedars and firs had already taken for lumber then. On the moist, civilized East Coast, the hardwood forests are returning, for the most part due to a change in agriculture. In this little pocket of the West, the conifers were probably the first taken down 150 years ago since they were close to this great natural harbor – the one discovered by Gray 200 years ago. With the lumber mills on the other side of the river and the birch and maple on this, Gray's legacy is a little patch of Maine in the Northwest.

There is a pavilion down beyond the supermarket, by the river, commemorating the history of Gray's Harbor County. Different huge murals by various grade schools depicting various periods. The first, with *Columbia* entering the harbor under Robert Gray hit me so hard I had to take a good run away. I wanted to explode.

The Seaport Office didn't open until nine. The man who saw me poking around the front door was walking across the driveway with a bag filled with produce from the farm stand. I recognized him as the same man who had emerged from *Lady Washington*'s hatch the night before. Short, wiry, bespectacled, sporting a bristle mustache. Layered, durable clothing. He identified himself as Billy, the First Mate.

Upon learning who I was and why I was there, he took me aboard the vessel I had crossed a continent to find, and gave me the full tour. All was being made ready for the voyage, Billy's bag of grapefruit and oranges the last of the provisions. Four people on deck, dressed in varying degrees of post-Colonial period attire, were all pleasant to me. Men, women, teenagers, Americans, Canadians, Australians. Below, in the hold, the kitchen served up a vegetarian stew that smelled heavenly. On the walls hung various awards from boat shows all along the Coast: Best Decorated Sailboat, Opening Day 1993, Seattle Yacht Club, or Tall Ship Society of San Diego County, 1994. The public was impressed with this little brig of 72 feet. I tried not to snicker at the label "Washington State's Tall Ship," having learned first-hand how tall a "tall ship" can be.

The display of "chisels" and a beaver fur caught my attention. A sea otter fur would have been pretty hard to find since their hunting was outlawed by international treaty in 1913. There were also some things I took to be rocks -- a little smaller than my palm. Ship's biscuit. This and some gravy were the staple of a seaman's diet for the long months at sea. It had the consistency of particle board, and probably the same nutritional value. A couple centuries prior, I wouldn't have blamed the crew if they slit Mr. Billy's throat to get at his oranges.

Back on the main deck, I was struck by the amount of rope on such a small vessel. *Constitution* had one long deck, six-foot high rails and three masts that justified all the rigging. But on *Lady Washington*, one-twelfth the tonnage and a third the length, I feel as if I am under a naked circus tent.

After the demonstration of how to raise the yard, turn its sail to catch a more favorable wind, and so forth, I still can't help but think that one big triangular sail is a much better idea. No wonder Captain Kendrick spent so much for refitting in Macao -- a mile of rope is strung over my head.

The cannon are another thing. Two four-pounders. On the rails sit the swivel guns -- two feet long, with a cork stuck in one end, and shrink-wrapped in plastic at the rear. A foot-long handle at the end imitate an old carved dueling pistol-grip. I pull the cork off one and look down the black, cast-iron barrel. With a rod, I could stuff a sack of cannister down it and deal some death at close range.

Up on the quarter-deck I find a long tiller, rather than the stereotypical ship's wheel. Opposite is the binnacle cab, covering the compass... and the electronic depth finder. The compartment is beautifully lacquered wood.

The whole vessel is in impeccable shape. The paint on the rail isn't chipped. The decks are clean. Every inch of exposed wood buffed to a polish. Even the ship's bell, engraved with "*Lady Washington*", betrays not a fingerprint.

Behind me, I hear, "You're welcome to come down." Turning, I see the hatch, and down the companionway. The steps down are steep, meant more for ascending, so I catch hold of the rails and swing down into the Commander's Quarters.

"It was here. His place -- where it all happened," Billy says, seated at the round table in front of the curving window. "He'd've set his charts out on a table like this, write his letters -- or, really, his Clerk -- the First Mate would've kept the log here." A round booth, like the best corner table in a good pub. Cozy, dry, warm, with a great view. Off to the left and right, Billy points out the two sleeping quarters -- about big enough to fit a body, and that was it. An economy of space.

"Electric light," I observe, switching the small lamp on above the Commander's bunk.

"All part of Coast Guard Regulations. What you've seen above -- the radar, the depth finder, the life preservers, the running lights. It's pretty difficult to reconcile the layout of a vessel like this with the new requirements. But I guess you wouldn't have us using whale oil," he laughs.

"Naw. I'm just here to see what is here, not pass judgment. Still, there isn't much room in here -- where's the generator?"

Billy grins and nods. "You're standing on it."

A two-foot square board under my feet had a small half-inch hole drilled in it. I pull the camera out of my briefcase. "May I take a picture?"

"Better than that," replies Mr. Billy.

The foot-wide catwalk runs along the keel, just above a long metal rod about three inches in diameter. The clearance is just an inch above my head as I duckwalk along.

So this is how she did it. Crawling through here, Florence McCarthy must have passed the word to the crew, perhaps along with a powder horn, to await the Commander's signal following the takeover by Coyah's tribe. Below decks, the hold beyond the quarter-deck would have been wide-open space, with the men finding what little shelter they could amongst the cargo. So it had simply been a matter of getting there quickly -- and the Old Man would have had no time with Coyah under his feet --

-- I suppose. The only record of Florence McCarthy aboard *Washington* are her signatures as witness to Kendrick's deeds. She really could have been anybody. But for the sake of understanding the Bostoner, I've made her a carbon copy of Shelly. Timing, I guess.

There is another light hanging ahead of me, lit, and I duck by, coming into a compartment tall enough to stand up in. Metal paneling everywhere adorned with dials and gauges. I nearly fall onto the huge Volvo engine. The rod avoided on the catwalk I now discover is the drive shaft for the propeller. A series of rungs lead to another hatch.

As I climb up, I see Billy's face accompanied by another's on deck. The man stands the same stature -- just under six feet and wiry --, forties, balding with a traditional seaman's beard -- no moustache. "Hello," I greet the man, adding to Billy, "A power plant, huh? I was surprised."

"Coast Guard Regs. Anything this big either has to have its own source of propulsion or have a motor tender to push it around. An engine's cheaper." He turns to the other man, introducing him as the Captain and Director of the Seaport.

"This is Paul Kimball from Massachusetts. He's come to do -- what did you call it -- a photo essay?"

Lifting myself fully out of the hatch, and dropping lightly on deck, I assume the part. "Yes, I'm doing a little story on connections between New England and the Northwest, and just wanted to snap a few shots before you sailed. Guess my timing was pretty good, huh?"

"Sure is," the Director chuckles. "You want to sign on? We have room and the need."

I hadn't thought of that.

"There's more of a connection than you think," the Director explains as we continue along the riverwalk, "Right down the road here we've got some cranberry growers for Ocean Spray."

We talk trees. Funny connection to Maine, huh? We talk shellfishing. What might you find around here if you dug in the mud? We talk cranberries. Southeastern Massachusetts had finally found something to do with its sand and swamps. I explain how my pictures will be shown at the Paulo Kimball Gallery in Boston, pulling out a business card. Maybe I should've given a couple to Paulie after I printed them out on the computer.

"Perhaps we can set up something to coincide with *Lady Washington's* visit for *Constitution's* birthday in 1997."

The Director sighs and nods, discouraged. "That's a nice thought, but not likely. We're a public entity, privately funded. Most of our crew is unpaid -- for the experience and the meals -- and we draw the few paid crew from them and them alone. Some money comes from charters and sea education programs, but you can see every dime goes back into her."

"A fine job, too. But no one wants to pay to be on board all the way to Boston, huh?"

"Not enough," he points to the riverwalk rotunda, "here's what I mean."

Little did I realize we're standing in the middle of a compass laid into the concrete. All sixteen points, and only slightly smaller than the one I left at Long Wharf a week ago.

A week ago. When was that?

Each point measures ten feet in length from the center. Circumference equals Pi times double the radius. "62.8 feet around," I mumble absentmindedly, "approximately."

The Director shrugs a surprise, "So, can you tell me how many bricks there are that make up the points? We're selling them, you know."

Of the sixteen different points, the main North, South, East and West axes are laid in blue bricks. The opposite, Northwest, southeast and so on, are in a dark red brick, and the minor degrees like West-by-Southwest are a lighter red. The whole is surrounded by concentric rings of blue and red bricks.

What catches my attention immediately is the center. The words "Grays Harbor Historic Seaport Established 1986" surround a three-foot across replica of the face of the Columbia Medal. A three-masted ship followed by her sloop consort. *Columbia* and *Washington*. It's the biggest coin I've ever seen.

Most of the bricks have inscriptions in them -- "TWO GREAT KIDS

ALEX AND FOREST," "THE GOLDBERG FAMILY," or "PHILIP MORRIS COMPANY". Most of the arms pointing north and east have already been filled, but not too many to the west.

"We sell a brick for a forty dollar contribution," the Director explains. "People want the ones pointing to their homes, mostly. The ones up top went first."

At the very northern point, a foot-wide symbol of the Boy Scout of America sits in the concrete. Interesting. As is the name inscribed in the top brick. FREDERIC W. HOWAY.

I kick at the brick, the carved letter has begun to dull with age. "Guess it figures. The great maritime historian."

"You know, then. Good. A lot of people have no idea. He lived just across the Canadian border in New Westminster. Did all the grunt work of sifting through papers to track down every ship's movements. You've seen his work, *Voyages of the Columbia*?"

"Mm. A little judgmental, though. But he was a judge way back, right?"

"On top of President of the Canadian Royal Society. Still, a lot of questions remain."

"Like...?" I ask.

"Like Meares' report to Parliament that the Commander of *Washington* was the first to prove Vancouver island was just that -- an island. That would have been in 1789, when Gray was in command. But when Vancouver -- the man -- met up with Gray in 1792, Gray denied the claim to fame."

"And thus the right to claim Vancouver Island and the area around it for the U.S. by right of discovery," I begin to understand. "Vancouver then sailed north to do just that, right?"

"Right. And Gray headed south to enter the Columbia River. Each establishing their respective nation's claims. But, if Gray didn't sail *Washington* around Vancouver Island, maybe John Kendrick did after trading vessels with Gray."

"Any proof?" I'm following each of line of bricks to its end.

"No one's found anything to support it. It's only conjecture."

The brick at the tip of North-by-northeast reads: SIMEON WOODRUFFE. Dropping to my knees, I examine the lines. "What's this -- the name of the crew?" The Northeast brick reads: DR SAMUEL ROBERTS.

"It would appear that way."

I look from him back to the East-by-northeast brick: JOSEPH BARRELL. It looks newer. As does the East brick: JOHN MEARES, the

East-by-southeast, ROBERT GRAY, and Southeast, CHARLES BULFINCH.

The bricks set just in from the tips of each of these appear to have carvings that are older, beginning to fill with grunge and grime. But the other tips read like a Who's Who of John Kendrick's life: R. DAVIS COOLIDGE. JOSEPH INGRAHAM. JOHN HOWEL. JOHN HASWELL. WILLIAM DOUGLAS. COYAH. GEORGE VANCOUVER. ROBERT GORDON. WILLIAM BROWN.

When I come to West-by-southwest, I find the brick empty. Fifteen of the sixteen points taken. I sit down on the granite boundary and ponder, obviously amusing the Director. "Something wrong?"

"Who bought these? I mean, did you -- the Seaport -- reserve these points for all the big players with John Kendrick?"

He looks down, and reads the names. "Oh, I see. You know, I never noticed myself, with all the other names beside them." He shakes his head, "No, each of these was bought and paid for in advance."

"You got an empty one down here," I indicate the blank West-by-southwest brick.

"No one lives out in the Pacific. Why," he smiles, the fund-raiser in him rising, "would you like to buy it?"

Money. Forty dollars. More than half of what I possess in this world. But I need to know why these bricks are here, why these specific names have found their way to the tips. And, most disturbingly, why the four names of the ancestors in the bomb blast seem so new.

"Carved in stone..." I run my fingers along the letters for Charles Bullfinch. Lotta. Gray is right above. Meredith. Like tombstones.

All these men, in some way or another, betrayed Captain John Kendrick. The Owners. His officers. A Haida chief. And finally, the British. There are no names of friends -- John Box Hoskins, Maquinna, Wickananish, James Magee or Don Blas Gonzalez. This isn't a memorial to history, here in the heart of Robert Gray's legend. It's flaunting. It says, "*Look, look what I can do!*"

Eight of these men met untimely, sometimes violent deaths. The others, well, save for chance, Barrell and Meredith should have died, and Woodruffe, Roberts, Meares and Lotta did. Howay? I don't know.

But the name John Kendrick -- my name -- is conspicuously absent. That one blank brick troubles me. "Yeah," I say finally. "Yeah, I think I'd better take it. Can you print the name 'Alfred John Kendrick' on it?"

"Alfred?" the Director asks, "Wasn't that one of his sons?"

"Maybe, but it's also my dad. That arm points to the Philippines, where he served in World War II. And," I add, "I need something else for my forty bucks."

"Just ask."

"Is it possible," I stand up and launch into an easy smile, "to find out the names of the people who bought these other bricks?"

"No problem," he shrugs, "that's public information."

Your tax dollars at work.

It hadn't been *Lady Washington* at all that brought me here. Beautiful and faithful as she is, she's not the same. The engine in her belly convinces me of that. She belongs to Gray and his legacy. The Bostoner would have come here, reveled in the experience, and tried to draw power from this place. It wouldn't have worked. And so, unable to draw upon it, he had decided to poison the well.

From the compass I have found my direction. Or, rather, the compass is my destination. All it took was simply coming here -- the doing of the thing.

While the Office Administrator, an attractive woman in her forties, searches the records, I bid good-bye to the Director, Mr. Billy and *Lady Washington* in the Captain's Quarters.

"Sure you don't want to come? We could always use someone who knows the water and a bit of history," Billy tries.

"Naw, I've got to get back. Tight schedule."

"Did you get enough pictures?"

"I really, *really* think I got what I came for. Yes, I got the picture all right. Hey," I call out as I grab the rail to the hatch, "that table -- was that where they shot the Old Man -- sorry, where the shot hit?"

"Right through here," Billy waves at the panes of glass, "while he ate his breakfast."

"Well, call me paranoid, but I wouldn't take my morning coffee there. I mean, maybe it wasn't an accident."

"*Maybe?*" the Director asks. "Of course it wasn't. Do you know how big a round of shot and grape is for a four-pound cannon? Over two feet long. Any gunner aboard the *Jackal* wouldn't mistake that for an empty charge. No, they killed the Old Man, all right. Too many people benefited from his death."

Maybe I'm not in enemy territory.

The block of tea smells terrific. This is what it was all about. Pressed into a solid brick one inch thick, one foot long and eight inches wide, it would last a family of four up to a year. The original Barrell would've made a mint with the box of the stuff at my feet.

Wrapped in brown paper and embossed with Chinese characters, the latest addition to the gift shop receives my rapt attention. If I had just another $25, it would make a nice present for the Professor when I get back.

Seth, yeah. How the hell had he come by that handgun? Out of us three, he was left pretty unscathed. We'll have a good talk when --

How am I getting back?

That is a bridge I will have to cross soon. About an hours' worth of sifting through the files turns up a nice paper trail. All fifteen bricks have been bought by the same entity. "Barrell, Bulfinch & Gray, P.C." the Administrator announces. "In fact, I remember since last check came in for four at once last month -- $160."

Very nice. A pattern. "What about the others?" I ask, "Simeon Woodruffe and Doctor Roberts -- I'm especially interested in."

She pokes through her folders. "Woodruffe. Woodruffe -- yes, here it is. That was December of 1992. And Roberts was April 1994."

Yes. Excellent. Perfect. This is why I came. My purpose. Forget visiting Juan Kendriqué up on Vancouver Island. Each of the murders was preceded by the placement of a brick. It was a warning. And proof. A display of power.

"And what about the others? Howay, Ingraham and the rest?" I ask. It doesn't matter too much now. I see the route charted.

She pours down the lists, "Here," she points. "They come as a group. All within a few days of each other. Beginning in September of 1992. The last was Howay on October 11, 1992."

"All from Barrell?"

"Yes, in fact, I remember him now. Big man, very... intense." There is a twinkle in her eye. Of course she remembers. He is a powerful presence.

"He was *here*? When? Soon? Lately?"

"Oh no," she reassures me. That the Brahmin might walk through the door at any moment sets every reflex and sense on high alert. Not yet! Just not yet!

"No, he chartered *Lady Washington* for a party in Seattle. We remember that sort of thing. Lots of lawyers. I remember arranging the catering -- Sam Adams, Heineken, caviar, foie gras, Dungeness crab, smoked salmon, the best -- but understated. Not like these hi-tech yuppies. After a few drinks, he even offered to buy the ship itself."

Oh yes, that was him all right. He couldn't stay away from *Lady*

Washington. He possessed her for a night, like Captain Kendrick of old, but he wasn't her master. It must have torn him up inside. There must have been the urge even then to turn one of the swivels loose on the crew, seize the vessel and sail her to Hawaii. "When was that?"

"The same time -- September of '94."

That's what did it -- he couldn't stand not having her, and it sent him over the edge. He made a list of all the enemies he -- the Bostoner Kendrick -- had in life, and saw that Life itself had dealt with half of them quite swiftly. Their names were set down in the bricks first. Then, one-by-one, the others -- by way of their heirs -- fell, each more violently than the rest. That last blank one still troubles me, though, and I remember to carefully fill out the inscription box of the application. **ALFRED JOHN KENDRICK.**

Handing her the cash, she bites her lip. "Only a fifty? I think we have change in the store. It's closed, but I can open it -- sure you don't want to buy anything else? Some tea?"

"Not quite yet." Then I lie, to hurry this along, "But maybe something might catch my eye in the store."

The store next to office is cool and damp, but then again, most every place without heat in Aberdeen is. There are all sorts of things you might expect in a museum shop. T-shirts, postcards, coloring books, posters, pirate hats. "Eye patches?" I ask, holding up a piece of black felt on a black elastic headband. "How much?"

"Three dollars. Don't laugh, at least they're accurate."

"How so?"

"Captain Gray wore one, but you never see any pictures of him wearing it. Makes him look too much like a pirate."

"I dunno," I tease, "pirates are a hotter commodity than heroes, especially..."

She pokes her head up from the cash drawer, "Hm?"

...Especially when it's true, I want to say. Instead, I wander about the store, browsing. The different period-style pins are pretty neat. And the supplies for embroidery. The buttons --

Buttons!

A packet of brass buttons sit in a bag on the display. Holding them close, I can easily see them to be little replicas of the Columbia medal. Just as I had seen on the mystery coat in the Captain John Kendrick House in Wareham two weeks before.

"Excuse me," I hold the little bag up, "but do you sell any coats here with these buttons on them?"

She glances at the buttons and shakes her head. "No. We've been playing with the idea of period clothing, but it's too expensive to do on such a small scale. T-shirts and sweats are our speed right now. But these buttons are pretty, aren't they? Would you like a pack?"

"Yes," I decide. Evidence. It can connect Barrell to the murders decisively, along with the buttons... on... my dashboard.

Oh shit.

The best piece of evidence in the world, and it's sitting in my car -- in plain sight -- on Beacon Hill in Boston.

Oh -- *FUCK ME!*

IDIOT.

I fight to smile. "Uh -- yes -- and the eye patch, too, please."

The bus won't arrive for another half hour, so upon the suggestion of the Administrator, I cross over the river to have lunch at the Breakwater Seafood Market. Clam chowder. Not my favorite, along with most seafood, but it's cheap and sticks to my ribs. Plug, liquid-version. While the Muzak theme to *L.A. Law* plays, I study the harpoons and oars hanging on the walls.

This morning, I had no clue. I had fully lost track of why I've journeyed all this way. Out of touch with time and space, I truly am in a different reality. Nothing is familiar -- and yet everything works like magic.

These people are nice. They've offered me a way out -- a job that pays meals for a quiet existence. No payment means no taxes that means no tracking. I can simply drop off the face of the earth. While it lasts, it's tempting.

Then reality -- a new reality – has come along and literally showed me the answers, giving me what I've forgotten I'm looking for. All my suspicions are confirmed. I am right.

Barrell did it. I have my evidence cast in stone, with dates corresponding to the murders. And except for the buttons in the Mazda in Boston, I'm off the hook.

Oh yeah, and leaving town -- leaving this state -- this time zone. That too. And dumping my unregistered car in the lake. As if it being *unregistered* makes it any worse.

"Paul?"

I can go home. All I have to do is call Paulie, have him reserve a train ticket at Seattle and that'll be it. In three days I'll be home. With a little reward money coming, too. And then I can deal with Seth.

"Paul? Mr. Kimball?" A hand touches my shoulder. A woman's voice

accompanies it. I turn to see the face the Administrator, and smile. Right --
I'm Paul Kimball, photographer. "I'm sorry -- daydreaming. What's up?"

"You have a call at the office."

"Me?" What -- who -- nobody knows me. Apparently, I don't even
know me.

"Hello, this is Paul Kimball."

"Paul!" It really is the Director. Oh, thank God. The cellular phone
connection is terrific, even ten miles out at sea. Salt water does wonders.
"Yeah, I remembered something. Didn't know if you'd be interested, but
you'd have to promise to keep it quiet. I mean, it's just for your own private
knowledge of history."

"I promise -- what?"

"They've found Fort Washington."

Brittania

It therefore becomes necessary
to point out the motives of this discussion
which I intend should convey to you
the embarrassment I have labourd under
in the whole of my transactions at Nootka
not only in respect to the cession of that territory
but likewise had such cession been made agreeable
to what I had conceived honorable and just:

I was still left totally in the dark what measures to pursue.

-- Captain George Vancouver to Under Secretary of State Evan Nepean

Friday, March 14, 1794
Keawanui Bay, Niihua

"You are following me, sir."

"I might say the same of you, sir."

"Yes, yes," Captain Kendrick chuckled, "I must be facing the wrong
way."

Captain George Vancouver of His Britannic Majesty's Royal Navy
managed a weak smile that the third gentlemen at the table knew to be a

horrific attempt to control a passionate outburst. But, to his credit, Archibald Menzies, nearly 30, still laughed easily.

Since leaving the shores of England three years prior, the corpulent little commander of the ship-of-war *Discovery* and its armed tender *Chatham* had passed in and out of his particular illness -- swelling of the joints, yellowing eyes and unpredictable fits of temper -- forcing his continued reliance upon the Ship's Surgeon. But Doctor Cranstoun had perished in the dysentery epidemic not soon after entering the Pacific. Thus, whether Captain Vancouver wished the emissary of Joseph Banks' Royal Society to act as surgeon or not, he was left with little choice. Doctor Menzies would indeed serve two masters.

And what a frightful master the illness created out of an otherwise generous little man. Nearing forty, Captain Vancouver was as shrill as any of the elderly dons of St. Andrew's, Doctor Menzies had found. Protocol and severity were the order of the day. Short tempered and severe, he followed every detail to its exact limit. Mapping the endless inlets and fjords of the Northwest and Alaska, the southern coast of Australia, or here in Hawaii found the ship's boats of *Discovery* and *Chatham* out for days -- weeks -- but when it came for shore leave in Tahiti or other Pacific islands, the most stringent prohibition extended to the crew.

It certainly hadn't helped matters any that upon their first leave, in the Canary Islands, the midshipmen, led by the Honorable Thomas Pitt, had brawled with the local Spanish soldiers, ending with their commander being thrown into the bay.

Mockingly, here sat this massive Yankee Captain at his well-provisioned breakfast table, entertaining his guests, emissaries of the British Crown. Captain Vancouver had intended to quit Niihua, this tiniest and most far-flung of the Hawaiian chain of islands, this afternoon. Yet another season of surveying the dreary Northwest Coast, having completed 1,700 miles of work from the Queen Charlotte Islands in the north down to just below San Diego. And yet another season of negotiating with the Spanish at Nootka for the return of... whatever the Secretary of State Baron Grenville might "further instruct" Captain Vancouver to receive.

No wonder, Doctor Menzies realized as he nibbled on the roasted hind leg of island dog (delectable as any hog, but a touch more potent), his commander was constantly on edge. Dual demands of exploration and diplomacy pulled at Vancouver from without as did illness from within. Upon first traveling up the Coast from California to Nootka, where his Spanish counterpart, Don Juan Francisco de Bodega y Quadra waited daily to settle matters of international gravity, *Discovery* and *Chatham* entered the Strait of Juan de Fuca. Exploring the great sound to its south, they aptly named it for the commander of *Chatham*, Lieutenant Peter Puget. Four months of this work consumed the British expedition before arriving to receive the whole of Nootka from Don Quadra.

And in that time, Francisco José Viana, former master of Meares' *Iphigenia Nubiana* and the American Captains, Gray and Ingraham, gave first-hand accounts of the seizures to Don Quadra. The lands and buildings at Nootka claimed by Meares amounted to a hut on the shore. The hut had been dismantled and burnt to ashes for the comfort of *Columbia*'s commander. Captain Vancouver, when he finally arrived in Nootka to receive the lands, was graciously offered a fine one-quarter acre of beach.

It was not to be, and from the way Captain Vancouver picked at the boiled yams on the plate, this diplomatic errand had begun to consume him. This would be the third season on the Coast, the third attempt to resolve the matter with the Spanish.

The last vestiges of morale were ebbing. The lowly Able Bodied Seamen provided by the press gangs of London were no better than fishermen's sons and blue water sailors. The Midshipmen, just above, were the teenage sons and nephews of the Whig government of William Pitt. Of the officers, half from his service on *Europa*, the others foisted upon him by the Earl of Chatham, John Pitt, First Lord of the Admiralty, none escaped Captain Vancouver's temper. Puget's *Chatham* sailed too slow (yet out of the company of Vancouver's *Discovery* always outsailed the larger ship). The men were insolent (no matter their years at sea without leave). The native chiefs of Hawaii were treacherous (despite their continued friendship).

But what finally brought the British Commander to sit at this table of a brigantine half the size of his smallest vessel, yet sporting more armament then his ship-of-war, was the fact he had grown disgusted at cleaning up after the irresponsible messes created by her master, John Kendrick. "Mr. Kendrick, I asked King Kamehameha to deliver to me the *renagadoes* that have come to occupy these islands. The influence of these handful of Europeans upon the native chiefs had provoked a constant state of warfare, both between the islands, as well as within them," Captain Vancouver announced from his seat, sweeping his arm broadly before the window, the relatively flat horizon of Niihua just beyond.

Received aboard His Britannic Majesty's ships, the Captain of *Washington* had been addressed as "Mister" He was a merchantman of a rebellious province since cast away, and deserved no better title. And yet

Kamehameha was addressed as King, and shown all the respect due his position by Captain Vancouver. Protocol, to be sure. But on his own vessel, Captain Kendrick was in command. "George," he mumbled loudly while slurping coffee to wash down the pineapple, "half of those *renagadoes* are men I left here myself. If you propose to return them to me, why did you not do so last week when we met at Kauai?"

Or three days before that on the opposite corner of that island, Doctor Menzies thought. Or six weeks ago when the two commanders first met in Kealakakua Bay on the west coast of the big island, Hawaii itself? Of the nine major islands of the chain, only the big island was controlled by the great King Kamehameha. Oahu and Kauai were under the sway of a regent, Kahekili, and his relatives. Between, four islands were in contention by these factions.

The easy answer was that Kamehameha did not have all these *renegadoes* -- Captain Vancouver's term for shore-bound sailors who had ingratiated themselves with local chiefs for their knowledge of English and, more importantly, firearms. The real answer was that Kamehameha found some of these men quite helpful in negotiations, although he never attempted, unlike other chiefs, to actually seize any wintering trading vessels. There were only eleven of these men scattered about, and if the two he employed should die, there was a scarce supply from which to find replacements.

"These islands are not your private playground, sir!" Captain Vancouver shouted, pounding the table. "I have seen what you have done in Kauai. Shameful, sir! Shameful, indeed. Instigating a minor chief on Kauai to declare his independence from old Kahekili on Oahu. Then serving as mercenary when the old man's emissaries came to investigate the incident. He was distraught, as he enjoyed quite popular support across the Kauai channel."

"As did George III claim in my own nation, young man." Captain Kendrick, surpassing his tablemate by a dozen years and a whole foot, burped and lit his pipe. "And indeed he did by not quite a third of the population at the beginning. But, with the help of greater powers, such as the King of France (God rest his soul), we realized our independence."

"Even King Louis did not receive payment for his services," Captain Vancouver sneered, "although the latest word from Paris purports he may yet have, by way of the guillotine."

"Take care, sir," Captain Kendrick warned, "when you speak of the bloody downfall of tyrants. Your reputation for severity of punishment precedes you. *Really*, a dozen lashes for the most minor offenses. Your incompetence as a navigator, I think, surpasses only your wholesale lack of qualities as a leader of men." The words of Captain Kendrick drew the little man into a scarlet fit. "But your actions with the young Mr. Pitt, the nephew of the Prime Minister and First Lord of Admiralty. Good God, man, can you even see where you're going?"

Doctor Menzies chose to intercede rather than allow his commander to explode. "Mr. Pitt, was insolent, sir, no matter the... severity of his punishments. It was better that he be set ashore at Hawaii last month and return to England by way of New South Wales in *Daedalus* rather than continue his service under Captain Vancouver."

"Indeed..." the Commander of *Washington* nodded. Then, sighting a rogue yam still on his plate, popped it into his mouth, and began again with a shrug. "I fail to grasp your agitation towards myself, Captain Vancouver. It is certainly no more than your own countrymen have done, here or on the Coast. Why, look at Captain Brown --"

"Yes, let us examine his conduct, sir, and compare it to your own," said Captain Vancouver. "Do you know that after your disgraceful conduct attacking Kahekili's emissaries, Captain Brown felt obliged to bring that dear old man over from Oahu in the *Butterworth* to negotiate a peace?"

"Hm," a laugh began to well up inside Old Captain Kendrick. "*How* kind," he gasped through the laughter. "Out of the goodness of his heart -- Captain Brown!"

It took a moment for the Old Man to expel his mirth, and Doctor Menzies cast about the small cabin for any object of interest except his own commander's furious, yellowed eyes. There was, hanging from a hook near the barometer, the great helmet presented to Captain Kendrick that had so enraged the junior officers of *Chatham* -- it being markedly superior to that presented to their commander, Lieutenant Puget. And folded above hung the luxuriant cloak of red feathers. At nine feet by twenty-four feet, it was the largest ever created in the islands. Kamehameha had traded this prize for two small cannon off *Washington*, and dwarfed the same presented as a gift to be presented by Captain Vancouver to King George. It was quite obvious to the British that the natives of these islands regarded men not by their rank as by their level of commerce with them.

"Sir!" Captain Vancouver finally demanded of the Old Man.

Captain Kendrick, recovered, sighed, and continued, red-faced, "Oh my, you do amuse me, Captain. Yes, indeed. The idea of charitable Captain Brown playing the peacemaker tickles me to no end. Why, did I not show you his letter in which he claimed your 'Old Kahekili' ceded the whole of

Oahu to him in exchange for 'valuable presents'. Do you know what those 'valuable presents' were?"

"That letter has no force --"

"Muskets, sir. Cannon, sir. And the hands to use them. Captain Brown traded his services as protector of Oahu in exchange for it. Is it any wonder he offered to act as diplomat and bring the old chief to Kauai to negotiate? He was simply protecting his investment."

"So your forces on Kauai are set against Captain Brown's," Captain Vancouver spat.

"Hardly, sir. A peace has been agreed. My men are on my vessel, and I was able to procure what I needed at Kauai -- the sandalwood, the pearls, --"

"The ambergris," Doctor Menzies blurted out absently.

The Old Man grinned smugly. At their last meeting a week before in Kauai, Doctor Menzies laid eyes upon a king's ransom wrapped in canvas in *Washington*'s hold. Eighty pounds of what Captain Vancouver ignorantly called "beeswax", but which the Naturalist knew better. Ambergris, the waxy substance created in the belly of Spermaceti whales to hold indigestible matter, vomited, and found its way to these shores. The natives of Kauai had been sent searching for even the tiniest amounts, for its quality of holding smell made it the single most valuable ingredient in perfume, and thus, the single most valuable commodity in the world. Only a few months back, the French East India Company had sold 225 pounds of the stuff for a whopping $52,000. Captain Kendrick had some 80 pounds and growing last week. He expected to receive more upon his return from the Coast this autumn. Then, so he said, he could finally return to Boston.

It was this final note that stuck in Captain Vancouver's craw. "Damn you, man, you can't leave these people here to despoil this paradise like human rubbish!"

"Human rubbish? Is that what they are? Of no use, but to ruin this place?"

"Yes, sir! Undoubtedly!"

"Oh, I beg to differ, dear George, I do. Last I spoke with James Coleman on Oahu, he said you threatened to impress him into service despite his service to Kahekili."

"*Because* of his service to poor old Kahekili." Upon first arriving in the islands in 1792, Captain Vancouver found a different paradise from the one he had left aboard *Resolution* in 1779. Then they had been treated as gods --

save for the murder of Captain Cook. Supplies of hogs, yams, fruits and water were theirs for the asking. The women used to be demure and modest. All had been as it should. But now the deck of any visiting vessel was assaulted not only by canoes demanding payment *in firearms* no less, but by hordes of nude women under the pretext of offering laundry services. Within minutes the decks would resemble a scene from Sodom and Gomorra. Disgusting, Captain Vancouver declared. Not on his vessels, to be sure.

And the reason? Simple -- men like James Coleman. Left by Captain Kendrick at the last minute here on Niihua in 1789, the man had reached a horrendous state in three years. He did not wish to be rescued from this heaven on earth. Left with no clothes by the Old Man other than those on his back, he appeared before Captain Vancouver in a maro worn rather more loosely than the natives themselves. He also claimed to be the emissary of King Kahekili.

When the British Commander demanded to know what happened to his clothes, Coleman responded that they were hanging up in his hut for the admiration of the natives. Vancouver suspected the man, despite his protestations of being an American born at New York, to be a British subject, and thus able to be seized for service upon His Majesty's ship. But kidnapping the King of Oahu's emissary would not bode well for British relations in these islands. Coleman remained, even if he had inspired decadence in these people.

"*Poor Old Kahekili?*" Captain Kendrick gasped. "Why, if such is the case, why did Captain Brown appoint Mr. Coleman his agent in charge of Oahu? To be quite sincere, sir, you appear to only like my *renagadoes* when they work to your advantage, and I must say they are doing a world of good."

In the immediate past, Doctor Menzies recalled, the Yankee captain was correct. John Williams and Isaac Davis had been promoted by Kamehameha to near-chief status in return for their services to him. And William Boyd, former Carpenter's Mate left by Kendrick to collect sandalwood, had eventually turned his attentions to building a thirty-six foot schooner for the king of Hawaii. His fortunes were lacking for want of proper tools and assistants, and Captain Vancouver had seized this opportunity during their six weeks there last month.

Kamehameha claimed the vessel would be used for greeting visiting Europeans in their own fashion, but all on the island knew it would be a ship of war against Kahekili's dominions. Offering the help of his shipwrights, Captain Vancouver allowed the schooner to near completion by the time of *Discovery*'s departure. And just a day before, Captain Vancouver and his officers sat down with a council of Kamehameha's chiefs and negotiated the ceding of Hawaii to His Britannic Majesty King George III. The chiefs demanded protection from their neighbors, perhaps a vessel left here? Out of the question, Captain Vancouver announced, unless... Boyd's handiwork would be ample protection. Quite. In commemoration of the cession, the vessel received the name *Brittania*.

And then there was the Padre. Mr. Howel. Reverend Howel. Editor Howel -- that was the one item that surprised Doctor Menzies as he and Lieutenant Baker had ascended Mauna Loa with the Padre. Having conquered Hawaii's great western peak of Hualalai, three weeks earlier, the ascent up the volcanic cone of Mauna Loa's 13,679 feet led to some startling revelations. The only two university-educated men in the Pacific had met briefly at Nootka in 1792, during the Padre's service as Don Quadra's official translator.

But that strange occurrence the following year! The Alder Squadron -- the brig *Three Brothers* and schooner *Prince William Henry* -- merchantmen under Lieutenant William Alder of His Majesty's Navy – arrived from London. And quickly Mr. Howel took the chance to take a cruise to the north on the *Jackal*. His absence stalled the diplomatic process between Captain Vancouver and the latest Commandante of Nootka, Brigadier General Jose Manuel de Alava, (although, still without any guidance from London, there was little to discuss).

There is nothing like travel to remote and exotic locales with a man to loosen his tongue and allow him to forget himself. Thus was the case of the climb up Mauna Loa. Perhaps, too, the thin air helped. Whichever the case, upon Doctor Menzies' innocuous query, the Padre explained that he had 'Despised the *Three Brothers* from the instant I set foot on its putrid decks.' 'Upon what occasion had you ever before?' 'Oh, upon passage to Boston, by the (snicker!) good grace of Joseph.' 'Banks?' 'Oh yes, as blessed a patron Saint as a flatulent catamite could be. And then the newspaper in that pathetic little village on a mudflat. I had my moments, to be sure, especially when I chose to change the name from *Herald of Freedom* to *Argus*. Wouldn't Captain Colnett appreciate the situation?' 'Colnett? You know the man?' 'Only by reputation.' 'Oh,... yes, of course, we served together years out here on the *Prince of Wales*, along with your Lieutenants Hanson and Johnstone.' 'I am glad to see the young man received his promotion.' 'Lieutenant Johnstone, oh yes, quite, though I must say he was passed over by Captain Vancouver upon the next occasion of promotion, preferring to pass command of *Chatham* to Lieutenant Puget...'

Not a half-hour later their troupe reached the snow line, and the Padre had become even more effusive, perhaps in part because their native guides, extremely apprehensive about crossing into the snowy unknown, had remained behind. Talk turned to Captain Kendrick, his method of adopting native custom and tongue, and, most assuredly, his deeds to the lands on the Coast. In March of last year, the Captain had asked his then-clerk Howel to forward the deeds on to Secretary of State Thomas Jefferson, along with an explanation of the present situation. The United States should consider these purchases by Captain Kendrick to be in the name of the great republic. Investigate post-haste. Especially the land around the Columbia River...

But then the Padre had stopped himself, perhaps realizing Doctor Menzies had ceased to remark upon his words. For his part, the Naturalist found the Historian most intriguing, his cryptic words giving so much food for thought. It wasn't until the peak was achieved at atop the great crater of Mauna Loa, and the entire island paradise, was surveyed, did Doctor Menzies make the connection...

Argonaut.

He directed his attention to the breakfast table.

"Captain Kendrick," the Commander of the largest British force in the Pacific, attempting to be respectful, failed in tone, if not in word, "your presence is unwelcome in these quarters. You shall consider Hawaii the realm of His Majesty King George, and therefore refrain from all traffic with that island. Likewise, should King Kamehameha bring peace to the other islands, I should expect you to find an equally poor reception."

A broad, blustery statement such as this could have easily been met by any number of insightful responses, Doctor Menzies thought. Shouldn't Captain Brown decide about Oahu, considering he was a British subject and apparently now owned the island of Oahu? And in the cession accord, Kamehameha certainly had the right to decide with whom he wished to trade, not some passing British warship. Really, wasn't this an overreaction considering the Old Man would be leaving the hemisphere soon, and at his age, unlikely to return? But Captain Kendrick said none of this.

He barely made a sound. At first.

Then the growl began. Vancouver's glassy little eyes narrowed. Suddenly, the Bear sprang to his feet, dumping the table and its contents of scraps and tea onto the Brits. Doctor Menzies dove out of the way, rolled up against the cabin wall, and turned to find his commander pinned to his seat by this far-from-toothless Yankee Captain.

"Don't you ever cross me again, you worthless little sonofabitch! I trade *where* I please, in *what* I please, and *I DON'T GIVE A DAMN* if that upsets the plans of your Britannic Majesty, His Britannic Navy or His Britannic Merchantmen!"

To his credit, despite the unusual circumstance of being the *recipient* of a violent temper, Captain Vancouver was struggling, but quite futilely. The grab for his sword was arrested by a single giant paw that ripped the scabbard off with a violent jerk, and sent the whole implement crashing through the window and out into the sparkling waters off Niihua. Then the other paw placed the round, bewigged body upon the fourth step of the companionway. Hint taken, George Vancouver deliberately made his way to the hatch.

"And take care, Doctor, of your patient here, that he try not to behave so rashly within MY LANDS in the Northwest, for I might have a mind to cause my Indian allies there to rise up and throw the lot of you, Spanish and English, into the sea!"

Such a humiliation of a British Naval Officer -- being stripped so handily of his sword by an elderly America trader -- would never be entered in either the ship's official log nor Doctor Menzies' personal diary. It was an unofficial visit at that, a great breach of protocol to attend to a lessor rather than receiving him aboard *Discovery*. Captain Vancouver had thought to be charitable to the Old Man, to provide a warning. But as the launch ferried the two back across the bay to the discipline of their warships, a great cool had descended like a fog upon the two gentlemen, each absorbed in his own thoughts.

George Vancouver simply wanted instructions to arrive on how to proceed at Nootka. All that came were dreadfully vague dispatches first in *Daedalus*, then in letters carried by Captain Brown and Lieutenant Alder from London. Archibald Menzies, on the other hand, recalled his Greek mythology. Jason and the Argonauts chasing the golden fleece. The Argonauts being the sailors aboard his ship *Argus*. James Colnett in the *Argonaut* captured by the Spanish in search of an otter's fleece worth its weight in gold. That much had been bandied about the parlors of London when the whole issue came to a head.

But Howel's entertainment at renaming his paper in Boston from *Herald of Freedom* to *Argus* -- the name of a monster sent by the queen of the gods Hera to guard Io from the lustful king of the gods, Zeus. Argus had a thousand eyes, and thus could allow all but one to close and sleep, and to remain ever-watchful. Menzies imagined the Padre perched atop Mauna Loa, keeping watch on all Hawaii, its neighboring islands, and the traders stopping at this nexus of the Pacific for supplies. But what sovereign or deity had sent him and why?

The Border, Canadian Customs

"And your reason for visiting Canada?"

I don't know. I really don't.

Everything's done. It's all wrapped up neat. I can go home now. The Vow will be over. I can clear my name definitively. I'll be a hero. I'll have money, respect. I can send a ticket to Sully Creek, fly Shelly out to Boston and finish what I started.

Okay, at least begin something. Maybe.

I will have kept my silent promise to Meredith. Everything will, finally, be all right.

But I don't want to. I've come so far, passed so far beyond where I began, it all seems so hollow. Instead, I have a higher purpose. Clayoquot.

Hell, I didn't even know how to pronounce the damn word 'til I heard the Director say it: "Kla-kwit." Even so, I have to go -- there are too many selfish reasons not to.

Fort Washington has been discovered. Not the one where Gray and Kendrick wintered over in Nootka. That was theirs, both, and eventually became part of the general abandonment. Rather, the Fort Washington I seek is the one Kendrick bought, with the rest of Clayoquot Sound, from Wickananish. The Old Man was there many times -- it was his base.

And I recall there is a man named Juan Kendriqué lying in a hospital bed in Port Alberni, in the middle of Vancouver Island. He had been trying to defend Clayoquot Sound from destruction when he was injured. I need to tell him that there's more at stake than he knows. 'Cause it's *his* Clayoquot Sound.

The Customs Officer, dressed in a royal blue jumpsuit, seem so harmless. On the other side of the highway, her American counterparts wear Navy blue and carry .45's. They also rarely check anyone. But I'm coming in by bus, have long hair, and Paulie's fake I.D. is just a little blurry... "I'm visiting family."

"Where?"

"Vancouver."

"And for how long?"

"Just a day or two." The round-trip bus ticket and my small briefcase with only one change of clothing are proof of that. The I-lost-my-wallet-story sends the flags up, though.

"What do you do?"

"I'm a photographer."

"Where?"

"Boston."

"How'd you get out here?"

"I flew into Seattle."

"Do you have your plane ticket?"

"Not anymore. It was in my wallet. I'm having another one issued."

She digs down into the foul-smelling briefcase. I know she'll find nothing terribly unusual. A camera. An orange. Couple cans of soup. Some papers and toiletries. The buttons. An eyepatch. She pulls it out, curious. "Do you have any alcoholic beverages?"

"As appealing at your invitation is," I begin as she quickly drops the eyepatch back into the bag, and zips the whole thing shut, "I have to say, no -- no alcohol."

I'm lucky they don't haul me into a back room, then call in the sausage-fingered guard for a strip search.

"New Westminster."

After the border, there was nothing but low, flat, wet farmland. Nice, after the trek up I-5 in Washington with mountains on one side of the highway and Puget Sound on the other. The darkness and drizzle has dulled my senses, so I don't say anything until the door shuts at our first stop after the border.

"Wait!" I jump up, waving. The bus lurches to a halt after six feet of movement. Annoyed eyes reflect in the rearview mirror. "I'm sorry, did you say New Westminster? This is New Westminster?" I can hardly say it myself without spitting.

The driver looks up at me, takes my ticket, and asks, "Have any luggage below?"

"No, sir."

"You're ticketed to Vancouver. Are you sure you want to get out here?"

"Yes."

The door slides open. "Okay. Have a good night, sir. Stay dry."

There is nothing lonelier than an empty bus station on a cool, rainy night. The directions I get inside the place bring me to the river. Half a mile later, the steam on my glasses makes it almost impossible to see. That doesn't matter, though. I have no idea where I'm going.

Frederic W. Howay was a judge here back in the first half of the century. That's all I know. There is no doubt in my mind he's been dead for decades. But his name is at the top of the compass in Grays Harbor, like hitting twelve on a clock. But is that noon or midnight?

Was he the last to die by Life's avenging hand -- or did the Bostoner kill one of his heirs back in October of 1992 to initiate this most recent round of revenge?

The rain doesn't bother me when I'm thinking. Nothing really does, unless it's knocking me around. Searching through my brain for a way to construct this puzzle, the body is put on automatic pilot. What do I know about Howay?

He lived here. He was a judge. In the 20's and 30's, I think. And he judged men of history by his contemporary standards. By far, Captain Kendrick was lacking.

The river is actually quite pretty. The Fraser runs out of the Canadian Rockies and meets the Straits of Georgia below the City of Vancouver. To the south, the Fraser River Valley is one verdant plain, apparently well-settled, as evidenced by the lights on the opposite shore. New Westminster is a different story. It's a hill.

Not a bunch of bumps and rocks. The whole of this grid-pattern, compact little city is built on the sloping riverbank. About fifty yards -- no, *meters*, since everything metric here -- separates the bottom of the hill from the riverbank.

The whole of the place was laid out by a regiment of engineers from the British Army in 1860. In searching for a capital for the Crown Colony of British Columbia, this hill was considered ideal for defense in case of invasion -- the hill faces south. The invasion was assumed to naturally come from across that river valley, the 49th parallel and the U.S.

New Westminster now is just a little corner of redevelopment tucked behind Vancouver. In 1866, B.C. was combined with the Island of Vancouver to form one colony with its capital at Victoria, on the island. The city of Vancouver, on the mainland, was founded the same year with that name, either for spite or confusion.

Above my head, the Sky Train glides along on its elevated concrete ribbon. Tomorrow, I plan, it would take me into downtown Vancouver where I can find a way to the ferry across the Straits of Georgia to Vancouver Island.

I have no cash at all, except for a little change in my pocket. What does it matter? It's different money here -- but at least my nickels and dimes are worth 33% more than theirs. Tomorrow I could find out what I need here in New Westminster. Find out why I'm here to begin with -- that it is too easy to pass up.

I'm cold. I'm wet. I'm in a strange city. There's no car to sleep in. There's no boat to shelter in. I cannot be caught doing anything illegal. I just have to make it until morning.

There is no sleep.

There is no refuge.

There is only me. And my thoughts.

Why am I here?

Aranzazú

September 10, 1794
Friendly Cove, Nootka Sound

"Lee Boo?" Captain Juan Kendriqué laughed, "They actually say 'Prince LEE BOO'? Oh, that *is* funny!" The young captain of His Catholic Majesty's supply ship *Aranzazú* rocked back and forth, trying to contain his mirth within his cabin. His father caught the fever, with help of the Madeira wine, and they soon had a good laugh at their competitor's expense.

This farewell dinner between father and son was the second in five years. The first, after Don Esteban's request on behalf of John, Jr. to join the service of Spain, was a punctuated by tearful goodbye from the Old Man in front of all hands from *Columbia* and *Washington*. Upon their reunion last month here at Nootka, Captain Kendrick found his namesake son a proper California Don, master of his own ship, and conversant in Spanish, Russian, the various Nootkan dialects, and, to the point now, French.

"Lee BOO!" The father bellowed, in imitation of Captain Gordon's cockney accent. The hilarity to the two men was at the English affectation to love everything French, except the French themselves. *Lee Boo* was the tortured attempt at pronouncing "Le Beau", thus making a French name sound positively Oriental. But what was to be expected from men who contrived "Canton" from "Guangzhou"?

"Oh, but too bad they leave tomorrow," John Jr. reflected, sighing, "and me as well."

The Old Man smiled, a tear in his eye, and patted his son's hand warmly. There was a marked difference, he had seen, between the twins now, but in appearance only. Solomon, aboard *Jefferson*, had come back to the Pacific promptly following Captain Gray's first return of *Columbia* to Boston. Wintering over in the Marquesas Islands in the west central Pacific, *Jefferson*'s crew had built a schooner of similar dimensions to *Washington*, and entrusted it to Third and Second Officers, Gollard Burling and Solomon Kendrick. Small though she was, *Resolution* could easily sail circles around the lumbering *Aranzazú*. While Mr. Solomon Kendrick dashed up and about the Pacific, from one exotic isle to the next in search of furs, Don Juan Kendriqué delivered cattle and flour to Nootka from the Governor at Monterrey.

John Jr. felt the loss at having missed his brother during his wintering over at Clayoquot this past year. He had hoped to bring Solomon riding on the few fine horses kept at his house at Tepic, in the hills above San Blas. But the news brought by both his father, and the English Captain Anderson of *Jenny* of late, did not provide encouragement.

It was his duty, perhaps for one last time, to cheer up the Old Man. "So I must go back to my horses and beautiful senoritas in Mexico, and leave you to the gentle comforts of your dear friend, Captain Vancouver. I hear he is to arrive any day from his surveys in Alaska."

"Please, son, he is not to my tastes, though he may, in that little powdered wig of his, resemble your mother, under the right light. Regardless, he won't be the least bit of fun unless he gets more explicit instructions from his masters." The Commander shrugged, "Too bad the Spanish never saw the wisdom of stocking this mission with women. Indian laborers from Peru, silver plates, over a dozen finely constructed dwellings, but not one, mind you, *one* female have I ever seen aboard your supply ships."

It was intentional. The Spanish feared the extent to which the natives might be driven should they be tempted by even the lowliest of scullery maids. Good relations with Maquinna aside, the Europeans, once on land, were vastly outnumbered by the natives.

Hence that problem with Florence McCarthy a few years back. Refused to land by El Commandante (protocol demanded her own quarters, and there were none to be had), the poor seamstress remained aboard *Washington* the entirety of her stay at Nootka. Worse, the crew had, upon the occasion of one their commander's frequent evenings ashore with Maquinna, invited some lesser chiefs aboard to view this most unique of commodities. The bidding on Miss McCarthy started almost immediately, and could have filled the last corners of the hold of *Washington*, despite the protestations of the more loyal seamen.

The unexpected return of the Commander for a forgotten gift of a flag to his host occasioned a predictable and, in the light of the circumstances, restrained response. The guilty, at least, still had their lives, if not their clothes -- cold comfort during their week of isolation on that desolate little islet in Tahsis Inlet. Only the warmth of the Cat awaited them on board.

"I hear Captain Moore need not concern himself with such matters," John, Jr. observed. "I know the trouble a woman aboard can cause, but I wonder if his wife is aware the *Phoenix* is equipped with its own prostitute from Calcutta?"

"That *is* the trouble with a woman aboard. But, his advantage, being under the auspices of the British East India Company. Supplies come cheaper there," the Old Man laughed.

"Or here..." John, Jr. frowned. With the inflation of the otter price, traders had cast about for new article of trade. Chisels and copper sheets were near-worthless, and the natives were well-attired in clothing. The baubles and beads brought aboard by the cask in *Columbia* were now barely accepted as gifts, and the Commander chuckled when he recalled the sight of this past July in Sitka, Alaska -- the natives, awash in trinkets, adorning their dogs with earrings.

Now, there seemed to have developed two profitable means of trade. The first, which disgusted these two Yankees, was in flesh. Slavery was commonplace throughout the native villages of the Coast. Following a successful war, a Haida chief in the Queen Charlottes might have more slaves than he could support. A Nootkan chief may need more in order to hunt sea otter or whale. It was simply a matter of the transport along the Coast for some merchant captains.

The second medium had been discovered a couple years back. Captain Kendrick, upon his own entry into the Columbia River, had traded whatever *Washington* had left, pursuing his successful strategy of engendering good relations with the native chiefs. Unlike the craggy, isolated coast of the north, the surrounding valley was relatively open and fertile. No sea otters about, but land furs, like beaver and deer. More so, a trade item much in demand in the north -- clamons -- dressed elk hides of such strength to be used as armor. It had been on a mission to resupply *Jefferson* with such hides that Solomon's *Resolution* had been sent south.

That was in May. In August, *Jefferson* had met *Jenny* off the Queen Charlottes and heard of the capture of vessel matching *Resolution*'s description. *Jefferson*'s First Officer, Bernard Magee (brother of Captain James Magee of *Margaret*), took the news to Captain Kendrick at Nootka, although word certainly would have passed quickly on the Coast. Still, it wasn't unexpected.

John, Jr. saw his father now, worn and tired from his adventures on the ocean sea, ready at last to return his *Lady Washington* to Boston, with payment to the Owners and profit for himself. Then, the Old Man had said, he could die. But his discovery in Cumshewa's Inlet in the Queen Charlottes was a blow the Old Man could barely take. By his own estimation, the floating hulk had burnt down to its waterline, and possessed not a shred of a soul on board. From its charred timbers of pandanus palm, the Commander guessed it must have been constructed in the East Indies, unlike the oak of a Europe, the pine of the Eastern United States, or the cedar of the Coast. He had never called at the Marquesas, but imagined the steep hills covered with these towering palms. The hulk could only be the remains of Solomon's *Resolution*.

Two sons lost to the Pacific. There was no getting beyond the loss for the Commander. It was too immediate, too violent. Men lost sons to the sea just as trees lost their leaves in autumn. But the Old Man had opened this entire ocean to other men's sons, and many had perished in these few short years. It was only fair, upon his leaving, he should lose one of his own.

Clearing his throat, Captain John Kendrick of the American brigantine *Lady Washington* attempted to collect himself. A deep breath helped, as did the arm of his son as he rose. "Thank you, boy. I can still call you that, you know, even on your own ship. Father's privilege. Make sure you give a proper federal salute on your way out tomorrow."

"Thirteen guns, yessir," the commander of the *Aranzazú* nodded bravely. "Give Mama my best."

"Give it yourself! You know your way around the Horn. Get to it, or by God, I'll pull a dory into the Wareham River and get you myself!" he laughed.

A hug. A salute. A handshake. A wave.

The Old Man was finished.

CHAPTER TWENTY-EIGHT

Nancy

Friday, November 10, 1995

> He was a judge of such exceptional learning
> and judicial balance that I and other
> members of the Bar who had the privilege of
> practising before him, always had the
> satisfaction of knowing that, whether we
> won or lost our cases, we had been heard by
> an honest, impartial and fairminded judge, in
> whose learning and discretion we had
> absolute confidence.

I read these words of Judge David Whiteside, spoken in the fifth
year of the Second World War, given in eulogy. The photocopy blows in
my hands, the paper wrinkling with moisture and occasional drops.
Judge Frederic W. Howay is now dead in my mind -- the New
Westminster Historical Society provided the clippings.

Pallbearers included Roy Howay and Gordon Howay, and survivors
included two sisters and a brother, his wife and daughter predeceasing.
There is plenty about the man, frequently shown with a crown of hair,
either black, gray or white depending upon whether he was receiving a
medal, retiring from the bench, or simply expiring. However, I focus not
on the obituary of this man, but of his daughter.

Her hair was cut to flapper fashion, round and short about the
head. Beautiful, large eyes. The French government had awarded her a
scholarship of 10,000 francs, so who could blame young Undine Howay
for running off to the Sorbonne? Paris at 21. Hemingway, Fitzgerald,
Pound and Picasso were there, at the zenith of the Roaring Twenties.
Poor, beautiful, talented young woman, dead of Infantile Paralysis. Her
father would travel to return the body personally. Poor man. Her

mother, his wife, would die within two years.

No children. No heirs, save nieces and nephews. The photocopy of the old photo show the house located at the corner of Dickenson and Elliott Streets. Searching around, I can't find it. Or is it at Carnarvon and Elliott? Not there either. It's distinctive on the corner -- can't miss it.

? -- I am here to question this judge, this boy who arrived in this frontier town at age seven and became its most prominent citizen. Chairman of the Canadian Historical Sites Board, where are you? President of the Northwest Fellowship for the Arts, where did you live? President of the Canadian Historical Association, Honorary Member of the American Antiquarian, Oregon, Hawaiian, Massachusetts, and California Historical Societies, I have come to confront you, your conclusions, and your turn-of-the-century judgment.

Instead, I find a man who had lost all that mattered in the space of two years. Even the house is gone, replaced by a faceless, modern apartment building.

> ... he was fairminded and most capable, and never did anything of which he or the members of the Bar, or the members of the Bench, need be ashamed.

I take issue with Henry L. Edwards, but what else could be said upon burying a fellow Knight of Columbus?

These words echo in my head as I review the report at the New Westminster police station. The fire in October 1992 was of suspicious origin, as the house was slated for removal. The land below had become a dozen times more valuable than the little 80 year-old house.

"*My first desire to destroy the messenger proven pointless not three years ago, I recognize for its want of determinatn...*" the letter to Jean-Pierre Hoskins had read.

The Bostoner had been in the area and began with Howay. Judge the judge. So the first act hadn't been freezing old Woodruffe -- it was destroying the memory of the man who sullied the reputation of Captain John Kendrick.

No one was home at the time, no one injured. It started in the wee hours of the morning, when the glowing flames would have called out the neighbors to witness this display of power. All that fine gingerbread moulding up in smoke, along with the bungalow-style porch and the lace curtains at the windows. I can barely make them out in the photocopy. But I know these curtains remained there to the day of the fire. They would have been drawn by a small bead, such as the one that occupies a small paper bag on the dashboard of my car in Boston. Buttons. Trophies.

As I trip and slip down the hill towards the Sky Train, I understand why I've come here, what pulled me off the bus. Perhaps the spirit of Judge Howay called to me, or beautiful, young Undine. Or maybe Captain Kendrick reached out, across the centuries and asked me to stop this impostor, the Bostoner, who pretends to greatness and vengeance. Charity, kindness and indulgence were his ways, not calculating baseness. Most importantly, I have answered the question plaguing me for the past two weeks.

On October 12, 1992, at 5:00 AM PDT -- 8:00 AM EDT -- I was planting a tree with my father. I remember. It was his birthday. I bought him breakfast. Like any parent, he appreciated the gesture more than the gift itself.

I have not killed anyone. I don't fit the pattern. I am not the Bostoner.

The Sky Train is my quickest, easiest way downtown. The system relies on purchasing a ticket for a certain zone prior to boarding, then showing the ticket to an inspector one meets on board, just like a normal train.

But this is urban transit. To send a collector through a four-car train after every stop, with all the crowding and jostling, would create a workforce drain on the budget equal to the construction of this transit system. A whole half hour passes on the high-speed trip, and no one asks me for a ticket.

The public transit system is a touchstone for any city. Boston has the heavy Red line, the medium rail of Blue and Orange, the trolleys of the Green line, trolley buses, and commuter bus, ferry and rail, legacies of the oldest subway system in North America. The Sky Train is high off the ground. The cars are small, clean, quiet, colorful, and, most of all, white.

I've hit an entirely different society. There are no black or Hispanic faces. But why should there be? Latin Americans are absorbed by Canada's behemoth to the south. Canada saw slavery abolished with the rest of the British Empire in 1833. What blacks there were, remained for the most part in the settled East.

White people are here. They are different, however. The skin is pure white, porcelain, which could be due to the high moisture and low sunlight. But, still, these white people are more uniform than I'm used to. There's little ruddiness to their skin -- no Irish blood. The British sent over Scots and English to settle the place in the last half of the nineteenth century. Also Scandinavians from the Canadian plains. Lots of tall women with blue eyes and blonde hair. I'm not sure where the big noses came in, though.

No Italians. No Polish. No mixing. I'd almost say I was in an Aryan paradise if there wasn't another legacy of the British Commonwealth in evidence -- Asians.

One third of the people I saw are either Chinese or South Asian. The Chinese have been pouring in from Hong Kong, wealthy and middle class families not waiting to weather the return of their British Crown Colony to mainland China in June of 1997. The money they bring is displayed in the fantastic amount of new construction everywhere. These economic refugees from an urban island believe every square inch of land must be built to its fullest, so huge houses are erected on tiny lots to accommodate their extended families. These are the kind of immigrants every country dreams of -- professional, stable, with cash in hand, ready to pay top dollar for what they consider cheap real estate.

The other immigrants are the reverse of this coin -- the ones you need, but don't want to admit to. Pakistanis, Indians, and Sikhs work the jobs the Canadians won't deign to. As I exit the waterfront terminus of the Sky Train, and survey Burrard Street in cosmopolitan downtown Vancouver, I am struck by the stratification of the place. The Chinese are wealthy. The Canadians are middle class. The South Asians are lower class. Only the British could have set in motion such a situation.

Clean, quiet, new, wealthy and safe. The downtown is compact, with life and style. This is not Seattle, forever reminiscent of a house the Sunday morning after a party. To the north, between the buildings, I spy Burrard Inlet, with North Vancouver on the opposite shore. The land beyond -- it's not beyond -- it's above. Simply, a wall of green rises 5,000 feet to snow-capped peaks. Supertankers ply the harbor, along with the cruise ships to Alaska.

It's too nice. At the intersection of Pender and Broughton Streets, I see the sailboats, all lined up so cute within a nook of Stanley Park, and it hits me. I got into this country under false pretenses. I rode the subway for free. There are so few murders here because of tight gun control laws. Violent crime is non-existent by American standards. I am an animal – a predator - out of my element, roaming the streets in my wool coat, long hair and increasingly ripe aroma. In this ideal city, I can run amok. A Bostoner in the Northwest.

Located at the tip of downtown Vancouver, Stanley Park is the largest and most impressive urban park in North America. The massive cedar trees dwarf anything I've ever seen, and I dodge between them to the point high above the inlet near Lion's Gate bridge. The overpass presents a beautiful view of the suspension bridge guarded by two magnificent stone lions. I will have to cross Lions Gate to get to the north side and the ferry. The last one out of Horseshoe Bay leaves at 9:00 PM, and that's ten miles in six hours.

I can't do it without food. I have less than one American dollar. The snack shop a dozen yards away from the overpass had Canadian prices, and I guess I've got enough for coffee. Places like this are frequented by tourists, so my American cash will be accepted.

Blessedly allowed to drop my briefcase, I wait in line at the counter. Ahead of me, a woman confers with the child at her knee on the choice of ice cream, her back to me. The Chinese girl at the counter shoots me a look as she takes the woman's order, reflecting my apparent state of dishevelment. Taking this as a cue, my eyes scan for the men's room -- opposite corner. Good.

My beard doesn't look that bad, but my skin -- awful! Pale, greasy. A quick rinse does nothing, but it's warm, at least. Better? No, but not worse. My hair, down still, is layered and flattened, but needs nothing less than a heavy wash. It will come soon.

Stepping out the door of the men's room, I see the boy, maybe four, below the counter. His mother pays the Chinese girl for the cone as it's handed over, but he's not paying attention. That's the first thing that struck me -- boy does not want ice cream?

The second is his short, tightly-curled black hair and deep brown skin. He is the first black person I've found in the city. But, from the back, I can tell his mother is blond-ish, probably Caucasian. It's his mother, too, because I hear his words: "Justa minute, please, Mama."

But then I see what captures his attention -- my briefcase. Mama can't see below the counter to this curious boy's stare into the bag, open from the jumble of clothes and whatnot. It looks like he's pulled out a soup can. A soup can without a label. I'm not angry at the intrusion. I was the same way at his age.

But that's not a soup can.

It has no label. It has no soup inside, I know. It's Arthur's cannister.

I told Seth it was in my father's toolshed because I wanted to test if he's with the FBI. There had been too many coincidences. But I forgot I left the damn thing in my bag all this time... didn't I?

And that isn't just his "Mama". It's my sister, Nancy.

I haven't seen her in years. Not since she moved here from Seattle, months after I left the radio job after three weeks. The job she pulled a lot of strings for me to get in the first place.

That must be her son, Will. I remember his adoption, that's all. That was around the same time as well. My father had mentioned, so long ago, it seems -- Nancy likes to take Will on walks below the bridge in the afternoon and have an ice cream up here.

It is thirty feet across the snack shop's black and white floor, and I cover its length at full speed. She is just turning around to hand him the cone, when she stops to realize Will has pulled a prize from this strange luggage. But the tin cylinder us ripped out of his tiny hand, and the force of the removal of the bag nearby trips him up. The ice cream cone drops on the floor as she snatches up her child from me, this anonymous, charging menace. But by then I am already out the fire exit, his cries decreasing in my ears.

Around the snack shop. Down the cliff. Mud. I slide and tumble my way to the bottom, to the path to the lions.

Churning my legs across the bridge, I wind up and throw the cannister with all my might into the water. Then every content of the bag. Camera. Paulie's license plate. Tweed jacket. Socks. Toothbrush. Then the bag itself.

Halfway across the bridge, collapse. Good, no one saw me. I am still anonymous. My victory was almost ruined by a boy cast in my own image.

"The boy," I gasp as I strain to stumble on, "the boy.... Why am I still here?"

PART THREE

bard

*We must come down from our heights, and leave our straight paths,
for the byways and low places of life, if we would learn truths by strong contrasts;
and in lands, in forecastles, and among our own outcasts in foreign lands,
see what had been wrought upon our fellow creatures by accident, hardship, or vice.*
-- Richard Henry Dana

Chapter Twenty-Nine

Halcyon

Saturday, November 11, 1995

The heavily scuffed floors led past a desk with a computer screen, a telephone and an elderly woman in a pink shawl. "I'm sorry," she said, "but visiting ended hours ago, sir."

"Please?"

She smiled. "Well, I suppose I can check at least, can't I? But you can't see anyone until tomorrow at eleven."

"Thank you."

"What's your brother's name?"

"Juan Kendriqué."

"Oh --"

"Hm?"

"Um, well," she pulled herself away from the computer, "I won't have to check, dear." Her expression betrayed sincere guilt. "I'm sorry, but he passed away a few days ago. You said you were family -- a brother? Oh, I'm very sorry.... why didn't anyone let you know?"

"I've been traveling," he said. "Can you tell me who else was here? I'd like to know where to contact anyone -- his wife or friends? I really don't have anywhere else to go."

"Oh, you poor dear. I'm sorry, we don't show anything on his records except his address for his insurance coverage back in California. Oh dear, dear, dear... Perhaps you can spend a night on the couch in the waiting room. It's not much..."

The round gold eyes glimmered in the shadows. "Thank you."

The janitor found the men's room door locked, which was unusual at such an early hour of the morning. Patients had their own lavs, and all the nurses were female. Perhaps a doctor had run out of surgery and found the others in use. The sound of the running water from within stopped when he jiggled the handle again. "Sorry!" he said, "I'll come back later."

The door swung open. "Are any of those clean? May I?" asked the occupant.

"Uh, well, I don't see why not, sir. Sure, but just one."

A hand reached out, grabbing a white towel with PORT ALBERNI HOSPITAL stamped on one end. "Thank you, sir," said the voice from the bathroom.

The faded mustard '78 Chevy pickup pulled over, the brake lights signaling a hesitancy in their flashing. The driver rolled down the passenger window. "Hey," the older gentleman in the heavy denim jacket and baseball cap called out, "need a lift?"

"Thanks."

"Where you headed?"

"Clayoquot."

"The village or the general area of the Sound? I'm going all the way to Tofino, and believe me, that's pretty much all there is out there, 'cept for the native villages."

"That's fine. Thank you, sir."

The driver's words were clipped short in the traditional Canadian fashion. "So, what brings ya out here in November? Not too many visitors this time of year."

"I'm doing some historical research."

"Are ya, now? Huh," said the driver. "What, on the native peoples?"

"The fur traders two hundred years ago. I was told somebody discovered the sight of an early American fort on an island in the Sound."

"Oh, sure. Yeah, that'd be Captain Gray's wintering place, where they built the sloop *Adventure*. Fort Defiance, he called it. It was discovered in 1966."

"No, this is another one. Same era, but it was Captain Kendrick's fort. I was told some remains were discovered, but they've never gotten the money to do a proper excavation."

"Fort Washington, uh-huh."

"You know the story?"

"Oh yeah, but most people tend to pay more attention to Captain Gray since he discovered the Columbia River... and because Captain Kendrick was supposed to have cheated the owners and stolen the *Lady Washington* from them," said the driver. "Say, who told you about the fort?"

"The Director of the Grays Harbor Historic Seaport."

"Oh, yeah. I was down there a couple of years back for the whole bicentennial celebrations they were doing for Oregon, Washington and such. A number of people went up to Nootka Sound to check things out, but nobody ever came to Clayoquot. I would have been happy to show them."

"Show them what?"

"The island. I figured the fort's on one of them."

"You're an archaeologist?"

"No," the man chuckled, "least not intentionally. I'm a marine contractor."

A winding path of asphalt traverses the spine of a partially-submerged mountain range dubbed Vancouver Island by the British. At its height, the road is only about twenty feet wide and rises at 18% grade. Any hint of valleys are inundated by either fresh water flowing down in streams of white water, or saltwater up from the ocean.

Scars of varying degrees cross the mountainsides, showing the clear-cut lines where the trees have been demolished, and debris left behind. The mere threat of taking trees from North America's only sea level temperate rain forest had sent waves of protesters to Clayoquot in 1994. A partial solution to the cutting had been reached between white environmental groups, the native peoples and the provincial government of British Columbia. Unlike other logging areas just south of the border, the people around Clayoquot were not screaming about job loss -- no two local people could be found employed as loggers.

The Sound, especially the district of Tofino at the end of a fingery peninsula, drew most of its economy from fishing and tourism. With the decline of the fin fishery, the local boats had been turned to whale watching just inside the Sound, and other aspects of ecotourism. The attention drawn to the area by celebrities like Oliver Stone and the Kennedys in the 1994 protests brought a second, more devastating and permanent impact. Real estate.

"It's a long walk into town," said the driver. "You sure?"

"I'm okay. Thanks."

The door closed and the truck pulled out of the tiny dirt parking spaces under the shade of the trees. The path to the beach led by a small stream. It was low tide, and the broad, sandy flats at Cox Bay lay exposed several hundred feet out, punctuated here and there by massive, moldering logs. A few rocky promontories covered with trees formed a barrier to the open ocean, behind which a cross-rip formed, with waves hitting each other at 60° angles against the sand.

Kneeling at that apex, the water rippling in past his buckskin loafers,

John Miles Kendrick took up a handful of fresh Pacific Ocean and splashed it on his clean-shaven face. He did so with his bare arms, chest and shoulders. Facing west into an open ocean, with the rising sun on his back, he breathed in the salt air and licked the water from his freshly-naked lips. The cool water tightened his pores and sent a bolt of energy up his back.

On either side of him, and behind, mountains stood within easy reach of this flat. He gathered up his shirt and long coat and began the trek past the new million-dollar California houses into Tofino.

The one road connecting the Esowista Peninsula to the rest of Vancouver Island is dotted with businesses advertising whale watch excursions and motels featuring breakfasts. At the northernmost tip of the bumpy, tree-infested finger sat the uncrowded village of Tofino. A circle of islands dance around its head, and across Clayoquot Sound lies the village of Opitsat.

For a full hour, Miles stared at the Sound, its various islands and especially the double-humped mountain rising above Opitsat. The constancy of the three native Water Taxis were like the tides -- or the rains. The sky would cloud up. It would rain inoffensively. It would stop. It would brighten. Then it would either rain again or clear. All within a matter of an hour.

The young man in the sweatshirt, his straight jet black hair covered by a baseball cap, nodded as Miles passed by on the gangplank. The older man, a native clad in similar fashion, barely acknowledged the tall stranger beside his boat. "Hey," the old man said at last.

"H'lo." Silence as the old man fiddled with the ropes. Miles stood by patiently. Then he mentioned the name of the marine contractor. "D'ya think you could run me over?"

"They expecting you?"

"No."

"Shame, that guy dying."

"Yeah."

"Okay," said the old man. "I have to head back soon."

"Thank you."

The island was a quarter-mile long by half that wide, but rose to a height of over seventy feet. Between it and the various other islets, large and small, currents of three knots or more ran through the natural channels of 80 feet in depth. Sea birds flocking to the broad, open mud flats stood on the only level ground.

The nose of the aluminum boat was able to come within a foot of the shore. The drop-off from exposed rock down through the water to the bottom was a good six feet, and the old man held off the forward momentum of his craft by throwing the engine into reverse. Miles landed on the slippery, mussel-encrusted rock and waved as the boat made way to Opitsat.

On such short notice in November, the Marine Contractor couldn't provide a boat or spare the time to show Miles ashore. He mentioned that the island had a couple houses on it, the whole place being owned by some rich Californian. If Miles could stick around a few days, the Marine Contractor would be back from his rhododendron show in Seattle, and they could look over the island together.

Standing at the foot of a small circular beach cut into the black rock, Miles could see a house just within the trees. Approaching it carefully, he saw that a couple windows had boards on them, indicating a closure for the winter. Behind it, the land rose sharply, mostly slick, moss-covered rock underfoot and a sixty foot-high solid wall of pure vegetation. Apparently, there was just a small beach, the house, six feet to move on either side, and high, sloping rocks.

Miles faced south and examined the beach. Black mussels the size of shoes covered the rocks, along with huge brown kelp. The mud was black silt. Holding his arms out before him, as if to place something on the beach, he frowned and shook his head. "Nope. Too small."

East of the house, a small foot path rose up to hug the shore as best the cliffs and trees would allow. Within the rain forest, the moss draped over the limbs of monstrous cedars three feet across and seventy feet high. This canopy filtered out all direct sunlight, but allowed for an incessant dripping of moisture. This land had never known drought. Any soil was a product of a decay of the rock from the relentless assault of moisture and moss.

The drop of the path in places was sometimes treacherous, with the slickness of everything, and so lacked any firm hold. When in doubt, he simply leapt down to the next level, onto the spongy earth. Another cove presented itself, this one much deeper and protected. At its head, a number of old stumps stood around a newer style house. It, too, was sealed up tight for the season.

Miles examined the old stumps. Of all the places on this island, only around this house was there even a sense of being clear and level. The stumps were well decayed, and he was easily able to poke his finger into the softened wood. The cove here was littered with kelp and small-to-medium sized stones. At the head of the cove, he could hardly make out the house through the surrounding leafy trees. The whole of this notch of an inlet was well hidden, but still stood next to the deep, swift channel. Holding his arms apart, again, as if to touch either side of the cove, he rocked from side to side, from one foot to the other. "Hmm. Maybe."

Further southeast, the path again sprung up into the woods along the shore. Overheating, Miles stopped, slinging his wool coat over his shoulder. Off the path, high above the water, a small wooden bench surveyed the whole of Clayoquot to the south. He plopped himself upon it, and drew his finger along the horizon, from the tip of Tofino, then back down the peninsula to the flats near the mainland. "The North End, Beacon Hill," he said as he drew southeast, "the South End filling either side of Washington Street... then the whole Back Bay. That means I'm in... Charlestown with Bunker Hill behind me."

Pleased, he stood and continued along the path. The last cove held a broader, deeper beach with a 30 foot high outcropping on the southeast corner. Below was a small opening in the rock where a gangplank led down to a dock. Above, a house almost entirely of windows commanded the straits to the south and the east -- the entrance to Lemmens Inlet and the path to Fort Defiance at Adventure Cove on Meares Island. Atop the house was a strange S-curved antenna, but no black parabolic dish to indicate a television in the middle of this rainforest.

The sound of footsteps echoed through the cove as a figure emerged from the house and descended to the dock. There was a shiny foot-long tin in his one hand. Over his other shoulder he carried a double-ended paddle.

Miles on the edge of the opposite cliff, stopped, climbed into nearby branches, and watched the "They" the old man had asked him about. This man on the dock was in his mid-twenties, tall -- taller than Miles --, and athletically built. He wore a white Oxford shirt, jeans and a blue windbreaker with some insignia on the chest. As he slid into the two-person kayak, his movements were slow and stiff, often repetitive, as if forcing himself to concentrate, and angry when he couldn't get even the simplest things right. Placing the tin in the aft seat, he paddled slowly and quietly into the channel.

The murky clouds to the west had created a false horizon higher than actual, and the sun shot beams of silver and gold across the quiet waters of the Sound. The Kayaker paused by the head of the straits, just opposite the house, and reached for the tin. Leaning over it silently, he held his stature while the current drew him along, closer to Miles' vantage point. With one last heave of breath, the Kayaker opened the tin, gently dropping a line of the gray powdery contents as the current caught it.

He finished after a minute, rinsed the tin, then dipped it gently below the surface of water. Withdrawing his hand, empty of the tin, he sat in the kayak for a moment, hung his head, recovered, and took up the paddle to return to the dock. Then he carried the paddle back up to the house, and slid the door closed.

The whole of the ceremony contained less than a quarter-hour.

From inside, the sounds of choral music could be heard. Not loud, it drifted across the cove to Miles. Still in the branches, he leaned against the trunk of the tree and closed his eyes. Sleep came quickly.

Jackal

December 12, 1794
Honolulu Harbor, Oahu

The Gunner's Mate was weary, through and through. His service under Captains Brown and Gordon had put him into the thick of actions in the past week. With the death of old King Kahekili a few months prior, his brother Kaeokulani, chief of Kauai, and eldest son, Kalanikapule, chief of Oahu, had been at each other's throats for control of Oahu. The island's sworn protector, Captain William Brown might have wished he hadn't sent his flagship *Butterworth* home the previous season, orders from Lord Mayor Curtis be damned. Cynically, Captain Brown could have waited for the invasion forces of the elder chief to prevail, then taken sides at the last moment to curry favor with the new king. Instead, the victor was chosen by the guns of the *Jackal.*

Peace on the island once more meant an extended shore leave for the Gunner, in the female company of grateful islanders. A few weeks of that, then once again to China, and home to England. Thank Christ! There was trouble in Europe. Wars with the mob controlling France, so he heard, and no doubt he'd be mustered in for service aboard some warship for the duration. But better the Devil he knew at home than these savages, delightful as their paradise islands were. Three years among the corrupt Mandarins in China, thieving Indians on the Coast, and these murderous Islanders had made him so increasingly fearful, it was a wonder a nights' sleep was possible. And the reason for this dawn-rise? That bloody Yankee, of all people! What in the hell was this business of a salute all about?

"Oh, my man, you do appear so tired -- allow me," a hand at his shoulder surprising him.

"Huh? Oh, beg you pardon, Reverend Howel, sir. No that's quite a'right. I can manage."

"Nonsense," the Padre replied, ignoring the Gunner's warding away, and proceeded to open the powder chest. "Thirteen guns, is it?"

"Y-yes, sir," the Gunner split his attention from the starboard guns to the entirely too-helpful Padre. The decks were clear at this hour, save for the morning watch, as the sun's rays rose beyond the cliffs at Waikiki. Not a soul had been ordered to help him. Even more unusual was the manner of the request. Captain Gordon broke in at mess, marched the Gunner up to the quarter-deck and explained the honor.

Captain Kendrick, sensing his fortunes in Kauai were much improved by the death of its great chief, sought to acknowledge the work of *Jackal* and *Prince Lee Boo* by firing a federal salute -- thirteen guns, one for every state in the Union -- which of course would be returned in kind by both English vessels. The Gunner must make the guns ready at dawn's first light tomorrow, before any Islander attempted to come aboard and learn too intimately the craft of heavy artillery.

Strange request, but so be it. The Gunner could load these four-pounders eyes closed in the blackest pitch of night. The task became doubly easy by its being a simple salute -- nothing but a charge of black powder down the barrel. "Please, sir," he called out to the Padre examining the cannon, "are you quite sure you know --"

"Oh, most assuredly. My old friend, Captain Kendrick, required such knowledge of all who served aboard his vessel *Washington*. My...," he stopped to admire the American brigantine at anchor a stone's throw away, "she does look so peaceful there. I had forgotten how easy it is to rock oneself to sleep aboard a sailing ship, what after all these months under the protection of King Kamehameha."

"Beg pardon, sir, but I fancy a footing underneath to rest easy. At least about here," said the Gunner. "Say, I don't suppose you might be willing to get that Bible of yours and read to me as I finish my work here?"

"I see. Oh, yes, quite, my dear fellow. Good thought, upon one's rising early. I shall not delay. I do believe I left it in the Captain's quarters last night."

Thank you God, and I promise I will listen to this man's words when he returns. For the moment, with the Padre absent, the Gunner hastened to finish the priming of the guns. Of the eight on board, three of the four on the starboard would fire three times, and allow the smaller *Lee Boo* to carry out the remaining four. It meant keeping two charges of powder ready at each gun for the second and third primings.

"Here you are," the Padre announced, returning with his Bible open. "Perhaps a Psalm to assist your labors. Oh dear --" he was brought up short by the Gunner raising his hands, ashamed.

"Couldn't help m'self, Padre. But if you wish, you are certainly more than welcome to accompany me to the mess and bestow your guidance upon the whole of the crew." Oh, they'll curse me, for sure, he thought, but those buggers didn't have to rise an hour early for this foolishness.

"A fine idea, but, sadly, one I cannot accept, for this morning I must perform the same service back aboard the vessel that delivered me unto your good graces, and her master."

The Gunner's mate stared blankly. It was too early in the morning for this flowery speech. "Cap'n Kendrick wants a breakfast prayer, eh?"

"Precisely."

Kalanikapule would be watching, Captain Brown knew. The old Yankee, Kendrick, had no part in last week's military victories, to be sure. Yet there need be no indication of infighting amongst merchant vessels. Reverend Howel had the right idea, as agreed the previous evening's dinner after Captain Kendrick retired to *Washington*.

Strange how much the two rival commanders, Brown and Kendrick, had in common. Service in the late war in America. Commanding whaleships off Greenland. Competing interests in Kauai and Oahu. Still, Captain Kendrick had cornered the market for otter skins, with his close relations with the chiefs there. And those deeds he flashed around, well, to be sure, it *had* inspired Captain Brown in his acquiring Oahu.

Both commanders claimed to be leaving. Captain Brown had only half-lied to his men -- they would be given the choice of remaining on board for another indefinite period in the Pacific or be discharged at New South Wales where men were needed to watch over the penal colony. His employer, the Lord Mayor, had strange notions of fairness (no doubt owed to his friendship with the King), but at least Captain Brown could return home to London to register his personal claim to the most attractive of the Hawaiian Islands.

Upon his last visit here, he had managed to navigate a small channel, discovering a tremendous natural harbor adjacent to the one in which he was now anchored. Old King Kahekili's cession of the island was perceived merely as proprietary use of this new harbor by all other European vessels -- with resident James Coleman to collect a port fee for all who arrived. Such were the rewards, but only if the commander of the *Jackal* could return to collect.

Likewise Captain Kendrick. Why would he leave, never to return, when he had all he needed on the Coast? Last season at Kauai, he had even found the sugar mill Captain Brown had built and proceeded to make 50 gallons of molasses to trade for furs at Clayoquot and down the Columbia River. If Kendrick didn't return himself, no doubt his son, the Spaniards' pilot, would. Enhanced by both his father's reputation, deeds of title, and power of His Catholic Majesty, Juan Kendriqué would effectively own the place so designated by its namesakes, Vancouver and Quadra's Island.

Short work had been made of the other son, Solomon, aboard *Resolution*. Captain Brown's tip to Chief Cumshewa that a small, lightly armed trader would attempt to steal his furs, as the father had done to Coyah in years past, was all it took. The description of the vessel was important -- two masts, triangle sails, First Officer named Kendrick.

Coming to trust Howel's judgment over the years had not been easy. It was to be expected that Captain Brown, like any English vessel, might carry dispatches from Baron Grenville to Captain Vancouver, or from Joseph Banks of the Royal Society to Doctor Menzies. But along with these came a single letter by way of the Lord Mayor himself, complete with Royal Seal, to be given to a man who would identify himself by a single name: *Argus*.

The Padre was most adept, to be sure, at keeping the various English captains on their toes once they delivered his mail. *Butterworth* had carried his lengthy treatise home to the Lord Mayor. The Padre insinuated himself into the most ripe situations, especially by frustrating Captain Vancouver's attempts at settlement of the Nootka question, when time, most assuredly, would be on the side of the British. Howel had heard that in January last, the Convention for the Mutual Abandonment of Nootka would require Great Britain and Spain to *"mutually aid each other... against any other nation which may attempt to establish there any sovereignty or dominion."*

Having waited for a month at Nootka this past autumn, Captain Vancouver left, disgusted at having still not received this or any other precise instructions on how to proceed, and the Spaniards still in possession. The Padre described the agreement to Captains Brown and Gordon: both nations would abandon Nootka, with the Coast to be open to their respective trading vessels, but at no time would permanent settlements be allowed at Nootka. It was the section on mutual aid against *"any other nation"* that the Padre had quoted like scripture again and again last night.

And now there Howel was, on *Washington*'s quarter-deck, raising the mizzen-sail to catch the crosswind, then raising the Stars and Stripes from the halyard, much to the amusement of the lazy watch of Pacific islanders on deck. Finally racing down to the main deck and lighting the powder to each of its cannon and swivels.

The tide had been running opposite the wind this morning, Captain Kendrick knew, but that in no way explained the view from above his plate of pork and poi. From the broad (and recently patched) window, he could see *Jackal* and *Prince Lee Boo* swing into view. There was no reason for vessels anchored so close to each other to point in opposite directions. Neither Captain Gordon's nor Captain Brown's crafts had a single stitch of canvas raised.

That meant one of his own must be.

Things to be expected when his First Officer, Jim Rowan, spent a night ashore in the arms of the Island lovelies. Nodding to the Malay servant boy named after a younger son, the Old Man murmured something like, "Poke your head topside, Alfred. Ask Mr. Howel when he plans to finish his breakfast. And see if any of the sails are unfurled."

His answer came in the combustion of the cannon.

BA-DOOM! BA-DOOM!

Tearing his napkin from his collar, the Commander's bellow nearly threw poor Alfred up the companionway. "WHAT THE DEVIL IS GOING ON UP THERE!?!"

Not quite thirteen years, Alfred, as he now prided himself, had learned the ways of this vessel over this past year since being taken on at Hong Kong. In the split second his head was above the hatch, Alfred knew this was not the manner in which a sailing ship should operate. The order to make sail should have been heard from the First Officer. The Commander certainly should be on deck for any discharge of the guns. And Mr. Howel should not be diving into the sea.

"Eleven-twelve-thirteen..." The Gunner's Mate counted off. He had seen the signal, the raising of the flag, and now heard the complete salute behind the high rails of *Jackal*. For confirmation, he shot a look up to the quarter-deck. Captain Brown and his officers stood as one.

"Return the salute!"

Gun Number One lit.

B-DOOM!

Captain Kendrick whipped around in his cabin. That last explosion did not come from topsides One more rang out, and he saw the white smoke pouring from the gun ports of the *Jackal.*

Gun Number Three's fuse was lit. Nothing. "Blast it!" the Gunner yelled, and tried again.

"What's the problem down there!?"

"Sorry, sir. The fuse is gone. And I see this gun's not been primed."

"Damn you, man!" Captain Brown cursed from the quarter-deck, "I'll flog the skin off your hide! Did you understand your orders, or did you choose to sleep another hour?"

"N-no, Captain," the Gunner, shaken by the all-too real threat, hurried to prime Number Three again.

"STOP WASTING TIME, MAN!" The Captain yelled again, "You're making us all look like fools! For God's sake -- try Number Four!"

"Number Four," The Gunner said out loud, acting as an automaton under the Captain's threat. "Right."

A fuse set already set. Primed. All set to go. Just touch the flame to the fuse --

KA-POW!

Screaming, tearing through the air, there was no other sound like it. John Kendrick had heard it near twenty years ago, in action seizing His Britannic Majesty's merchant ships off the English Channel. But in all these years in the Pacific, with all the warfare encountered, he had not, until this point, been reminded of the sound of incoming cannon fire.

As the gun on the *Jackal* rolled away from the port, he could make out the confused face of a gunner within, beginning to realize something had gone horribly wrong, the vessels were so close. And that was all.

The patched-up window exploded, frame and all, into the cabin. On the quarter-deck above, Alfred and the Cape Verdean lad at the tiller were ripped to pieces by the flying grape shot and splintering rail. The only other man on watch, a recent recruit from Kauai, had enough time to dive in the water, like Mr. Howel.

Only one man would emerge.

The rain hadn't been hard, but it was enough to drip down upon Miles' forehead and wake him. Darkness surrounded, the only light being the hint of a moon in the mists, and the kitchen of the house. When its fluorescence flashed out, only the flicker of a video screen was apparent. The music sounded more like classical strings or bagpipes.

Dropping down from the branch, Miles picked his way down to the shore. In the darkness, he could only make out the glistening of the kelp on the rising tide. There had been plenty of holes in the mud of the previous two coves. Siphon holes for clams.

Using two fingers like a claw, he dug down into the hard silt. Four inches down, bits of shell dug under his fingernails. "Ow." He sucked on the fingers, feeling the sting of mud mixing with the blood. A few more inches down he felt something solid. Carefully, he worked the tip of his fingers, exerting just enough pressure, to gain a hold, but not so much as to break the soft shell. One last effort and the thin calcium carbonate worked free, and Miles pulled out a two inch-round clam. A rinse in the water and a slight tap on a rock, and the raw guts of the animal slid into his mouth. Nearly gagging, he swallowed without chewing. Back on his haunches, he returned to his hole and sunk two fingers in again.

Pounding bass erupted from the dark house. Miles looked up, his arm still half in the mud.

Eric Clapton and *Cream* penetrated the cove. Miles stood and cocked his head to one side. The volume continued unabated. The flicker of the video monitor screen reflected off the ceiling of the house above. He rinsed his hands and began the slow walk to the base of the cliff below the house.

> *I've been waiting so long*
> *to be where I'm going,*
> *in the sunshine of your love.*

Feet working their way along the cliff edge as the cove edged out into the water, Miles was able to catch hold of the gangplank and hoist himself up. His feet leapt over the steps, and he rolled with a crash, flat on his face. The music overpowered everything.

The gangplank led by a small shack and to a set of steps to the circular front deck. With the only source of light coming from inside, Miles approached the picture windows and sliding glass doors, totally enveloped in darkness.

Inside, the Kayaker was hunched over a computer display. Line after line of code flew across as the man typed away. An empty dinner plate and glass were cast on the dinner table next to the desk. As the last pounding notes rang out, the man hit a few keys with finality and swiveled around in his chair. He was facing out in the direction of Miles, but saw nothing in the dark.

The next song rang out:

> *I went down to the crossroads, fell down on my knees*
> *I went down to the crossroads, fell down on my knees*
> *Ask the lord up above for mercy, take me if you please.*

Miles backed up on the deck, his back to the water, and came into a crouch in the corner. Inside, the Kayaker was in a fury of activity. Picking up a piece of paper emitting from the printer and stuffing it in an envelope. Taking two suitcases out and placing them next to the door. Going to another room, emerging with a bottle of Scotch, and sitting down on the couch facing the deck.

Staring out, the Kayaker placed a tumbler before him on the coffee table, filled it, swigged back the whole double shot at once and coughed. Then he filled the glass, determined. From his pocket he pulled a large pill bottle and spilled the entire contents on the coffee table.

> *In the white room, with black curtains –*

The next song began before he grabbed a remote control and flicked off the music. Another piece began. Mozart's *Requiem*. One last sigh, he reached for a handful of the pills.

The golden eyes at the plate glass window caused him to freeze, and shake with a start. A lanky man with long brown hair and smooth round face looked back, then to the Scotch, the pills, the computer, the pills, then back to their owner, bewildered and a little shaken.

The exchange ended after a minute. A wave of embarrassment, followed by resignation flashed the Kayaker's face. He approached the glass, gave Miles one silent frown, and slid open the door. He cleared his throat and shuffled around a, "Uh, hi. Uh,... so,... What can I do for you?"

Miles' gentle smile, blink of his round eyes, and lift of his eyebrows was followed by, "May I have a glass of water?"

CHAPTER THIRTY

Prince Lee Boo

Sunday, November 12, 1995

Phip.

"When I was born, my sister couldn't pronounce Philip, so she called me that. It stuck."

"What's the whole thing?"

"Philip Greenfield."

"Middle name?"

"Joseph."

"Philip Joseph Greenfield," Miles said to the room. "PJ Greenfield. Anybody call you that -- PJ?"

"At business school."

"Where'd you go?"

"Stanford."

"Not bad."

"Well... yeah."

"No, I mean 'not bad' as 'I'm impressed.'"

"Oh, thanks."

"You don't live *here*," Miles nodded to the computer, "though I guess you could, huh?"

"Our home office is in San Jose, and once a week we'll go into Vancouver to conference. We'd just moved here in September."

"Nice place. The whole island yours?"

"Naw. It belongs to the corporation, but as that consists of the chairman, me and --," he shook his head, "well, just the chairman and me now, I guess, and a bunch of stockholders, then, yeah, I guess it's mine. We've set it up as a corporate retreat. A programmer can get pretty burned out and this is kind of our decompression chamber."

"Looks like you broke the rules."

He reached over and emptied the plastic envelope of the letter and the disk. "I was just putting our latest program to bed. But I'm not the codemaster. I'm more organization and marketing."

"What is it?"

"The next generation in browsing the World Wide Web. We'll start testing next week."

The outside held the logo -- WebWolf 3.0. Wolfe Integrated Technology Systems (a/k/a "WolfWorks") was a company out of Silicon Valley that, with a handful of other companies were vying for a piece of the technology market related to the Internet and its associated graphical counterpart of interlinked files, the World Wide Web. The company started as a spin-off of a doctoral thesis at Stanford, and had grown out of all expected proportion in the past couple years. The initial stock offering earlier this year made Roland Wolfe a multi-millionaire at 26.

"May I -- if it's okay -- may I see?"

The version of the software was quite a piece of work, carefully crafted and easy to use. Phip's pride in explaining its features and advantages of the competitors grew until he stumbled on the name 'Juan' for the tenth time. "Fuck," he mumbled and turned away from the machine. "I'm sorry. I -- fuck. Listen, I'm going through a lot right now. I don't even know you, and I don't --," he stopped.

Miles was quietly looking at him. Calm. Non-judgmental. He took a sip from his glass of water. The digital clock next to it read 1:45 AM. "Juan Kendriqué," he said at last.

Phip ambled around the living room, playing with whatever his hands could find -- books, cards, a bowl of marbles. "Yeah! Yeah. I figured that's why you're here. He got a lot of flowers and cards of support at the hospital, but he never woke up to see them all. It's funny, y'know? He wasn't even one of these earthy-crunchy environmentalists. He was just out for a run, and stopped to talk to some people protesting at the entrance to a clear-cut. When a truck full of logs tried to leave, he figured he'd better get out of there, but the thing jerked backwards... the driver was just going to turn the rig around... and next thing, a log shifts in the load, and they all came --"

He slammed the chimney with his fist, "FUCK! OOOOH, Goddammit!" Burying his face in his arm, a minute of silence and sniffing passed. "Anyway, thanks for coming." He smiled bravely from pink, puffy, glassed eyes. "I guess I have you to thank for more than that, huh?"

Miles reached across and offered his hand. "I'm Miles. Nice to meet you."

Phip shook the hand with a firm grip. "You, too."

"Phip?"

"Yeah?"

"I think I know why I came here."

"Say that again?"

"I know why I came here. And I'm not an environmentalist."

"Why are you here?"

"Because I know pain. Because I know loss." Miles lifted his chin and traced the line of whitened scar exposed from the lack of facial hair across his throat.

They had met at Stanford. Phip was just ending another long, bad, confusing relationship with a girl. Juan was giving a talk on the Internet and its possibilities. It was a technology conference, and only a few of the business school types in attendance. The two had got to talking, and so right after graduation, Phip found himself Number One in the marketing and applications arm of a startup hi-tech company.

Coming from Vancouver, he had stressed the benefits of headquartering their marketing arm in the Canadian city. Drawing on all this educated, professional country had to offer, they could keep pace with their neighbors south of the border, and pitch more easily to Asian markets who held Vancouver in a more favorable light than its more violent, less cosmopolitan neighbors, San Francisco and Seattle.

Juan had taken Phip under his wing, recognizing the young man's talent for reconciling the demands of both the business and development staffs. Phip was a programmer's executive and an executive's programmer. He was a diplomat and a charismatic initiator. Bright, funny, good looking, athletic and outgoing. The All-American Boy -- except that he was Canadian.

Miles never asked about the relationship, and as Phip unloaded, he skirted about it in his grief. He wanted to say a great deal, but held back. "I'm just concerned. All these people are counting on me, and I can't go off on an extended vacation. This program's done, but that's just a week of nothing to do, stuck here --"

"With your memories."

Phip jumped up, pointing at Miles, "Exactly!"

"And your family in Vancouver?"

A cough and a fumbling for words betrayed Phip. "Well... they're not exactly... I just --"

"They're not supportive."

"Yeah." Phip's eyes focused on the fireplace. The immediate sadness was replaced by a wistful, melancholy longing.

"Your parent's still married?"

"You bet. Happily. Thirty years."

"How many kids?"

"Three boys and a girl. I'm the oldest boy."

Miles put down his glass and grinned slowly, knowingly. "Boys. Men. Males."

"Yeah," Phip asked. "So?"

"A person can understand themselves and everything around them better by looking at the opposite side of the coin," Miles said, leaning forward. "Let me tell you a story. I grew up on the other side of the continent. Old family. I'm the youngest of four -- three girls in front, and a boy on the end. Ten years separates me from my oldest sister. My parents divorced when I was four, and I remained to be raised by my mother and three sisters. I possess no concept, as you understand it, of a male authority figure."

Phip raised his eyebrows. "Do you *know* where your father is?"

"I work for him. Done so for the past four years. Caretaking cemeteries and peoples' estates."

"You're a landscaper?"

"I'm a lawn mower."

"Oh. That's cool."

"No it's not. I was raised by my mother to aspire to something more. I was raised in a totally female environment in the 70's. Emphasis was placed on humor, not physical achievement. Intelligence, creativity and consideration were valued -- not excelling at anything remotely male -- sports, that sort of thing. But after three good tries, I felt I'd been sorely misled. I ended up rewarded with no past, no present and no future."

"I returned home to Cape Cod to live with a friend, Thad, and to take a little nothing job. Several months of depression heading into winter in a bleak corner of New England. Not a good thing. Anyway, I lost a wife, a job I no longer wanted, and a woman who by her own admission should have fallen *madly* in love with me. I had played by the rules I'd been taught -- be considerate, be open and honest and you'll succeed. Have you ever felt a gnawing in your gut because you've been told all your life you're going to succeed -- I mean *big* -- and you just hadn't yet and you had to question your guiding principles?"

"Yeah," Phip nodded," in school. I wasn't sure about applying to B-school. But I guess I figured I should. And, by chance, I met Juan and... well, it all worked out like a dream from there. Except with the family. It woulda been so perfect if he..." He cleared his throat and looked out into the murk of the night.

"...Weren't a *he*," Miles finished the thought.

"Yeah."

"I had perfection once," said Miles. "Or the delusion of it. A couple weeks into it, Thad asked me to help with a project. If it worked out, it meant financial independence and prestige."

"Didn't happen," Phip shook his head "I know how that can be."

"No. It *did*." Miles walked over to the computer, and forsaking the mouse, absently punched a couple of keys until logged onto the Internet. "Thad was... five years younger than me. When I first met him, he was kind of a pain. Pimply faced, no muscle-or-skin-tone nerdy eleven year-old. Hanging around the second-hand shop I worked in one summer. When personal computers were just getting coming on the scene. Anyway, he didn't really fit in at his small-town school, even less than I had at his age, so I'd put up with him for a while. To get him out of my hair, I recommended a computer -- a used one. His mother bought it for his birthday."

"Two weeks later I go over to his house and he's showing me all the games he has and wants me to get one, too, so we can talk to each other on-screen. I tell him, 'Thad, we got a phone. A local call costs nothing. That's not why computers were invented.'"

"'But it'd be so cool,' he says. 'So what?' I ask him, 'You got a powerful tool here -- ten years ago it was unheard of, like owning one of the first cars at the turn of the century, or a sextant a hundred and fifty years before that. It's only cool if you can actually do something with it you couldn't do before.'"

"He was little hurt, I think. He was trying to show off to me -- a guy he respected -- and I just wouldn't go along."

"Just like an older brother," Phip observed.

"Except I wasn't. We weren't related by any stretch of imagination. He'd come for summer at first from Philadelphia. Then his folks retired to the Cape, and he became part of the scenery. He really got into that computer, though, first writing simple games and other programming. Lost weight, gained height. Skin cleared up. I think it had something to do with his friendship with Paulie -- another acolyte of mine -- or Jane."

"Girlfriend. That'll do it."

"Naw. She wouldn't go out with him. So they became best friends, to no good end. Kept at arm's length, it was torture for him, year after year, with her going out inexplicably with one jock after another. He always hated every guy she dated. And, that awful fall I moved in with him, I caught a little of his venom myself because, you see, she was the woman I left my wife for. But when it fell apart after only a week, I could see his great relief."

"You left your wife for a woman who left you a week later?" Phip asked. "What happened?"

"I don't know. I thought I did." Miles found the Web page he was looking for, and a screen flashed up, entitled THE MASE. Against the gray background, hi-tech color graphics ads from various computer warehouse stores grabbed the eye. In a small white box in the center he typed in: "Lady AND Washington", and pressed the SEARCH button. "So there I was with a perfect romantic relationship and living with him, and him happy because it meant I wasn't still mooning over the only woman *he* really loved. And he hears about the founding of the World Wide Web in Switzerland that year and decides to apply a concept of a program to it."

Phip walked over to the terminal as it flashed up the results of the search. A listing of ten possible documents containing both the words "Lady" and "Washington", all having to do with the First Lady in Washington, D.C. Miles frowned, mumbled something like, "Se-eth...," and returned to the search box, adding "AND Kendrick", and tried again.

"It wasn't his idea at all. He thought of everything as a new program -- stuck in line at the supermarket -- how about setting up an electric eye to scan the bar code rather than having to key in the price at the register? Already done. Or toll booth with laser scanners of your credit card? Done. Map routing of trips? Done. Computer animation? Done. It was always something someone else already thought of, and was putting together with better equipment. Even so, he was a genius, a real aptitude for programming."

The results flashed on the screen again. The top entry was listed as a file on a computer in Washington State about sailing. The Grays Harbor Historic Seaport was shown among other linked files. Miles clicked the mouse on the highlighted text and the screen blanked as it jumped to this new file.

"Where'd he go to school?" Phip asked, leaning into see Miles' search.

"Didn't. Self-taught. Couldn't bear instruction, formalized at least.

Never liked being told what to do. I think he also was afraid of leaving his familiar environment. Woulda been adolescence all over again. So when all his friends went off to college, all he had left was me, and so he made do. I think that's why he came up with the Web project. To involve all his old friends so they wouldn't lose touch -- here it is."

The Seaport's home page flashed up, with the graphics of *Lady Washington* under full sail. Phip's finger reached toward it, hovering an inch or two from the screen. His mouth opened, a breath drew in, followed by a pause, and awe, "Now... now that's something..."

Down at the bottom, a line for comments directed the reader to a highlighted e-mail address. Miles clicked on it and a form came up in which to write his message. A simple "Thanks again for your help. Found my answer at Clayoquot. – Paulie Kimball" was zipped along the wires of a dozen computers to eventually reside in a file until retrieved by the people in Aberdeen.

"Who's Paulie Kimball?" Phip asked.

"Me. Well, actually, a friend whose credentials I used to look at this boat."

"Ye-ah," Phip laughed, "right, ... So, what was your Web project? Designing Web pages for this place?" Phip tapped the screen, then slowly turned quizzical. "But, no, you said that was four years ago. Nobody was on the Web. It was just starting."

"Right. Thad asked me to help out. A friend of his, Tony, gave him the idea, so Thad ran with it. Created a basic program for the old Internet. Before '92, if you find anything on, say, Abraham Lincoln, it was the electronic equivalent of going into a specific library to look at their card catalog. If they didn't have exactly what you were looking for, you'd hit another library and another."

"But," Phip countered, "you could make a search engine to find certain words in files on the Internet. Like what you did here with this Seaport. Sure, it didn't look as pretty as this --"

"Yeah," Miles added, "but even if I found the right book on Abraham Lincoln, what about certain topics of interest mentioned in it? Like the Gettysburg address, or slavery, or assassination? The Web meant I could click on any of these words and jump to a file on the other side of the globe dealing specifically with that topic -- maybe the Gettysburg Address Home Page or whatever."

"The beauty of the Web. Easy information," Phip shrugged.

"Yeah, but sometimes too much crap to sift through. Thad was working on a search engine for the Web. Tony foresaw this need. The only problem was money. Thad couldn't figure out, beyond the adoration and acclaim of the users, how a person cashed in on a search engine. User charge? No one would use it, not when on-line services had already contracted with a few MIT PhD's to create free search services."

Miles backed up to the MASE search form again, and stared. He grabbed the mouse and began tracing figure-eights around the empty white box. "Anyway, he came to me in January, asking for help. Find a way to make money -- if nothing else, sell it to a service for a flat fee. Be the business manager, the organizer, the PR guy. Maybe help with the graphical layout. He'd do most of the programming, and farm the rest out to his buddies. We'd have it done for a debut in April for a Computer Expo in Boston. I accepted. An hour later, after a walk on the beach, I figured it out." Miles pointed to the SEARCH box. "People spend more time searching for things and most of the time end up with dead ends. They surf --"

"But that's why the Web's so fun."

"Wasting time is fun? I guess it could be if you have nothing better to do. But after a while you find out that depending upon others can lead to unreliable information. So I figured, why not come up with a separate program that could integrate into this search engine? It would watch where you go, pay attention to the subjects of your searches, then, when you're away from the computer, it would independently scan for related topics and flash them up as a screen saver. Since new pages come on-line every minute -- at the time, I figured it would only be daily -- it could keep you up to date without you having to look yourself. An electronic detective."

Phip was incredulous. "You came up with the idea, and that's it? Hey, I hate to tell you, but a lot of guys are doing this sort of thing."

"Not then. Those in the know -- and there were very few then -- really got off on the idea when we demonstrated it. That was my strategy -- go to someone's office and show them the concept before it was 100% complete -- to see if it was really worth doing. I can't tell you how many thousands of miles I put on my car, driving Thad around for demonstrations... poor little thing."

"Sounds like you were this guy's mom."

"I put up with it to get the job done. That was my sole motivating factor. That and the fact my determination and drive appealed to my girlfriend. But it all got gummed up as summer drew near. I had just negotiated a deal with a software company for buying the search engine. I knew that anyone using the it would eventually want to buy our add-on program, *SEXTANT*."

"Why?" Phip asked. "Why give it to someone else. The Web is a perfect place for people to display things on their own -- it costs almost nothing."

"Sure -- *now*," Miles replied. "Back then it was expensive even to get on-line. The Web was just a project then, no commercial service was connected to it, only universities and research centers. We were rolling pennies for food -- Thad had quit his job in February and I supported us pretty much on my part-time job at book store. We needed to be able to get this thing going and we needed money. To eat. To live. Phip, man, I mean the kind of poverty where you're eating corn flakes for a week 'cause you got *nothing* else. Anyway, it was just a licensing deal, pretty generous for the other side, but only for the first year. All that needed to be done was... getting it done."

"Did it? I guess not," Phip said.

Miles waved the pointer about the MASE logo. "Whaddya mean? Of course it did. Do *you* know what MASE stands for?"

"No. I thought it was just a variation upon 'maze', like a lot of names on the Web."

"No. MASE is 'Mighty Awesome Search Engine.' Tony came up with it. That and the concept."

"You guys created this search engine?!? No fuckin' way! Jesus, I use it all the time! Hey, that's great!" Phip stopped. "No it's not. What are you doing here if you own a piece of this?"

"We had a... run-in. A clash of wills. Thad was futzing around, spending his time hanging out, going to movies, while he should have been working. I kept after him about figuring out who would get how much of the pie and contracts to seal it, but he didn't want to talk about it. It meant conflict, negotiation, compromise, consideration. Didn't want to hear it. Finally, we worked out a deal – see, our landlord required us to paint our house before we moved out in May. I'd do that entire job -- all the shit work -- to free up Thad so he could get his programming done by my birthday a couple weeks after that."

"And...?"

"He blew it. Forgot all about it. Even that it was my birthday, too. By the time our friend, Paulie, came back from France in July, it was too late. I said I wouldn't sign any contract if it went on like this, and Thad said he didn't need me, didn't trust me. Paulie negotiated a meeting between me and them. Then they asked to postpone it. I agreed. They said they'd call."

Miles moved the arrow down to the bottom of the page. The highlighted name read:

Created by Thad Dirksen & Company

"As soon as the conflict started, I turned to the woman I loved for support. She was involved in senior projects and exams. Went off to her friend's for a week. Friend's boyfriend was a mechanic. Lived with a buddy who was also a mechanic. A skilled trade. Women like that. Independence. You know, I think, despite the propaganda, women have a weakness for a man who works with hands. But men appreciate men who work with their heads. You think?"

Phip reflected, looked about the house, and nodded.

"Yeah. Anyway, it was all over," said Miles. "My whole support system gone."

"What about your family? Didn't they care?"

"They didn't know, not much at least. None of their business. All they'd do is ask how it was going, I'd've told 'em, and they'd echo what I should be doing."

A stiff shake to Miles' head lasted a fraction of a second before the gentle smile returned. "That summer I had to live in my mother's basement – a fucking *cave*. And I'd already quit my job at the antique store to both spend time promoting *SEXTANT* and because I had thought it best if two romantically involved people weren't working together. As it turned out, there was no danger of that. I ended up working for my father, cutting grass. No friends. No future. All gone."

Shaking his head with arched eyebrows, Phip grabbed the glasses and refilled them in the kitchen. "So, you've come to see me on business?"

"In a fashion."

"About *SEXTANT*?"

"No. It is irrelevant."

"Then what?"

"At first, I thought I came to save Juan."

"Are you a doctor, too?"

"No --," Miles paused abruptly, "no."

"Uh-huh."

"I thought someone might kill him."

"That -- that's not funny. So, what are you, a psychic?"

"N-no-o... Anyway, I was too late. I found myself brought out to this island with no place else to go. So I simply went to the end."

"The end?"

"Here."

"Why?"

"I don't know. Or didn't."

"You do now?"

"Yes."

"Well?"

"To save you."

Phip drew himself back, inhaled and smiled. "Yeah, right. Nice story. Listen, in the morning I'll call the water taxi and you can be on your way. The sun'll be up in an hour. You can play all the games you want on that computer, Mr. Whatever-your-name-is."

Miles looked at Phip placidly, and offered his seat at the terminal. When Phip took it, Miles grabbed the mouse and clicked on the search box.

"Hey, wait a --" Phip protested.

Miles typed a line of code in the box and hit three keys at once. The screen went blank.

"What did you do?" Phip demanded. "Fuck--"

On the black screen, white lettering flew up.

June 21, 1992

Hello.

My name is John Miles Kendrick. I am partially responsible for your use of this search engine. It was originally the idea of Tony Ryder, and was created mostly by Thad Dirksen. But I brought this product SEXTANT before you.

Thad has the rights. Tony has Jane. And, if you are reading this, I am dead. Ask them why.

Phip read the screen twice before looking up. "This file is encrypted within the program."

"I wrote it and stuck it in an hour after that meeting. Thad always left his computer hooked up to his modem. It was a contingency. Every program is set to scan news services for a suicide that never took place, then release this message to every user."

"But I thought Thad was the programmer, not you."

"I never said that. You're a rugged, wealthy and attractive guy -- why aren't you married to some little preppy girl?"

"Because, uh, I-"

"'Cause you don't *want* to. Same thing. Just because you *can* do something well, does that mean you *want* to?"

"But if you could do this all, you should --"

"DON'T--!" Miles yelled, then collected himself as he walked to the window. "Sorry. Please, don't say that."

"What?"

"'You should.' I was raised on 'YOU SHOULD.' It's my family's prefix to anything."

Phip backed away from the computer. "You're John Kendrick? No... the crazy guy from Boston?"

"I am John Miles Kendrick. That," he pointed to the message on the screen, "*was* me. Three years ago. I got through it. On my own. *Badly*. But it brought me here, in time to save you, if not Juan. I thought," Miles turned from the window to face Phip, "the same person who tried to kill me would go after him. I think Juan was my cousin."

"Kendriqué -- Kendrick. Distant cousins."

Miles held out his hand. "Welcome to the family."

CHAPTER THIRTY-ONE

Experiment

Monday, November 13, 1995

"Jeez, you slept right through Remembrance Day weekend!"

Two gold eyes looked up from the black rain coat, squatting over the mud and kelp, at the tall young man on the deck above. Phip, in his yellow rain poncho looked like a preacher in his pulpit, or maybe an angel descending upon a rock. "What's that?"

"You guys in the States call it Veteran's Day."

"Oh. No, we call it Memorial Day and it's at the end of May and marks the beginning of the tourist season."

Walking down the rain-slicked gangplank to the dock, Phip carried the worn and matted buckskin loafers Miles had retired before his twenty-four hour nap in the guest room. "These are in pretty poor shape. Want me to try some saddle soap on them?"

"How 'bout gasoline? I'd say throw 'em in the channel, but I don't want to be responsible for destroying a unique marine habitat for the whales here."

Phip laughed stiffly, stopped, then chuckled a little more. "So what are you wearing? I know we had some rubber boots in the hallway --"

He stopped as Miles pulled back the hem of the black coat, revealing his tan bare feet resting on the brown kelp. Nearby were several clams of nominal size. His right hand held a garden weeder, and his left was smeared with black mud. Miles smiled and shook his head. "Too small. I hope you like these things," he gestured to the clams. "I can't stand 'em myself."

Phip craned his neck forward, as if an inch would make that much difference across the water and mud of ten yards. Then he smiled. "Hang on."

"We usually just buy whatever we can and keep the fridge stocked here. Or charter a fishing boat and try for salmon. But there aren't too many of those left," Phip shrugged, and dug the garden rake with great difficulty into the mud.

"How 'bout the mussels covering all the rocks around here?"

"I dunno. We never wanted to eat a bad one and get sick and die."

"Chances are, if one's bad, they all are. Some are inedible, but I didn't want to find out on an empty stomach."

"So if you don't eat these, why are you digging them?"

After a long pause, the hunched black digger returned to work, answering, "I'm not."

"Coulda fooled me."

"They're incidental. Want 'em?"

"I don't wanna get sick and die."

Miles stood up, gathered together the two dozen little clams into the yellow bucket Phip had provided, and rinsed them in the water across from the dock. Satisfied, he picked his way across the kelp back to Phip and handed over the bucket, with a smile. "Good. Then you won't." Then he added, "Ever been to Boston?"

"Yeah, a lot. Conferences at the Boston Computer Society and MIT. Hi-tech firms around Route 128. Lot of recruiting. Why?"

Miles had assumed another squat, this time in an area more towards the center of the tide-drained inlet. "I can't get over how much this place looks like Boston..." a look at Phip revealed raised eyebrows, "... I mean, before it was built up. It's like a mirror-image, facing west not east. Nice harbor, excellent resources -- timber, whales right on the harbor, mild climate. Hell, 200 years ago, it would have looked even better than the original. Just fill in these flats, and cut down all the trees and you're ready for a million of people to move in."

"Nice idea. Where do you get all this? Here we are, in the middle of an unspoiled paradise and you want to ruin it all," said Phip. "Glad I own this island."

"More'n that."

"Huh?"

Producing a finger-length cylinder of rusted corrosion from the bucket, Miles considered it for moment, then chucked it back in with the clams. "Can I use your phone?"

"What was that?" Phip reached for the prize, but Miles pulled it away.

"Phone?"

"Sure." Phip reached into his back pocket and flipped a small black box at Miles who caught it one-handed after dropping the garden weeder. He stared at it. Then found the release on the bottom.

"I've never used one of these before," he mused. "Wait a minute. Does this mean there's a cellular provider across the sound in Tofino? I'm impressed."

Phip grinned and pointed to the S-curved antenna on the roof. "Not quite. Had it installed before we moved here. More reliable than the underwater cable that pumps in our electricity."

"You guys are your own cellular phone provider? No -- those towers are about sixty feet tall, at least."

"Naw," Phip grinned, proud, "microwave. Relays back to our Vancouver office. Scrambles everything since we never know when a competitor might be listening in. Great for our internet connection, but local calls kill us. Not that it matters. Where you calling?"

"I'd throw a rock with a note if I thought I could make it..."

"Oh, sure," said the old man. "I remember when they were building one of those houses years ago. Really upset some people in Opitsat when they found some old bones when the were digging up the basements. Didn't like their ancestors graves being dug up."

Phip was immediately ashamed. "God... uh, jeez. I don't know. I wasn't here. I mean, I know I only saw the place two years ago. The house's gotta be at least fifteen years old."

The old man kept his hand on the wheel of the boat, and nodded. "Yeah, it was a while ago." The baseball cap and sweatshirt were the same, but the jeans were a slightly different vintage. The water taxi was still spotless, save for the mist being swept off the windshield by the single wiper.

Phip held this old man in great respect, evident an inability to keep from observing the other's every movement at the wheel. Miles stopped fiddling with the metal detector borrowed from the Marine Contractor, and watched the young Anglo-Saxon Canadian watch the old native of Clayoquot Sound. "That's typical. Used to happen a lot on the Cape. You bury people in flat open spaces, and eventually, say a couple hundred years later, someone decides that flat open space is the best place to build a house."

"Yeah. Well, there aren't too many flat open places 'round here," said the old man.

"Not for long."

"Yeah."

Back at the cove, Phip asked, "Do you think you want to let me in on what searching for this fort has to do with you coming here?"

"I think we'll find out at the same time," said Miles.

"This doesn't have anything to do with the bombing in Boston, does it?"

"Yup."

"You're not on the run are you? No, they cleared you. I heard that. But if you know something... why aren't you working with the investigation?"

"Who says I'm not?"

"Well, pal, you're pretty poorly equipped."

"I already have everything I need."

"Oh... hey, you know who'd really get into this?"

"Uh... Juan?"

Phip, having insisted on wearing the contraption complete with headphones, shook his head, then agreed, "Yeah, well, I guess him, too... No, I mean Wolfe. Roland, my CEO. He's a nut about archaeology."

"Well, I'm half there," Miles replied, distracted. Before the advancing tide creeping up the cove, and beyond, along the horizon, even darker clouds. "Listen -- you just keep waving that thing around -- be real methodical now. Can you hear me okay?"

Phip had already turned the unit on, and flashed an "O.K." sign. Beginning at the water's edge, the young man strapped into two generation-old technology became lost in his world of search-and-listen, as the long-haired, lanky figure followed behind with a rake, weeder and shovel. Every minute that passed, the mist crept incessantly downward, the tide steadily higher and the darkness pervasively thicker. And still only three in the afternoon.

After only five minutes, Phip stopped short. "Got it -- yeah!"

The old ship's clock struck four as Miles carried the mesh bag through the living room into the kitchen, only a hint of a track of mud from between his toes. Phip laid the metal detector inside the door and raced to the sink to turn on the hot water. A couple minutes worth of scrubbing with a Brillo pad revealed: "Nails," Miles announced, unimpressed, staring at the three-inch corroded shafts of rust. A crumbled bit of green metal he decided, "Sheet of copper,..." and gesturing to the door way, where a four-foot by one-inch flat bar stood, "pry bar. I think we're lucky to have found this stuff. Usually, as soon as any trader left their place for the winter, the natives would pick it clean."

"You really think that's what it was?" Phip was incredulous, picking up the crumbled copper. "I mean, look, other than being banged up, this doesn't look 200 years old."

"You ever find a rusty penny? Know why? Copper doesn't rust -- it just turns green."

"Yeah, okay. So how do you know this is the place, and not the other coves? What's this ship anyway?"

"Brigantine -- God, now I sound like the Professor," said Miles. "Uh, look, I know I haven't told you much, other than I heard there might have been the remains of an old fort around here, and it would have to be on this island because it's at choke point of the channel, and has three distinct little coves. Sand is rare around here, and they'd've wanted a place big enough to haul the thing out and work on it over the winter -- scrape off barnacles and repair holes -- that sort of stuff. I told you -- we find what I'm looking for, I'll explain everything and you can keep it."

"Jeez, thanks. I mean, it is my house," said Phip. "Wait, you're not trying again tonight, are you? A storm's coming through."

"Yeah, yeah..." Miles waved away the concern, "... and the tide's almost filled the cove. Listen, I realized we've been doing this all wrong. I'm from a place where erosion is eating everything away. Houses falling into the sea for years, the beach constantly moving, all because of *sea level rise*. What I'm looking for would be at the water's edge -- or what was the water's edge 200 years ago."

Phip stopped trying to bend the copper back into shape, and caught Miles' sense. "*Under*water?"

"Not much!" came the voice from behind the spotlight on the dock.

"This is so fucking stupid!" Phip yelled from the front seat of the kayak, the headphones covered by the tightly-wrapped poncho and both hands on the shaft of the metal detector as its probe dipped into the water. "Even if we find anything, how the hell are we going to dig it up? Hey, are you sure this equipment is waterproof?"

"Would a *marine* contractor have anything less?" Miles yelled back through strengthening wind. "Just a couple passes across the mouth of the cove. Got your phone? I want to call him to see how far out we should check."

"How the hell am I supposed to reach my phone from here? It's in my back pocket."

"Never mind." The beam of the searchlight shone out from the foot of the dock as the wet slap of bare footsteps raced up the gangway. The sliding of the glass door silenced most of Phip's protestations and cursing.

Five minutes later, Phip was pulling the kayak out of the water, having managed to not drop the detector equipment into the cove or adjacent channel, when the spot light rose again. "Forget it," Miles said. We're looking in the wrong place."

"Tell me about it," said Phip. "I got nothing out there. I'm lucky I didn't get picked up by a killer whale. They're night feeders, you know."

"Why do you think *I* didn't go out? Anyway, they'd be scared off by the storm activity. You won't have to worry about drowning this next spot. I forgot how different this place is from home," Miles said. "Seems the sea level isn't rising here."

"What?!" Phip cried above the gusts off the Sound. "You had me out there for nothing?"

"Oh, hush. Listen, on the other side of the continent, where I'm from, the ocean is sloshed up on one side. Here, it sloshes *away* from the land. You know -- rotation of the earth?"

"That's nuts! All that means is there's more pressure on your side than mine. If the glaciers are melting, all sea level is rising." Phip stormed up the gangplank with the kayak, Miles chasing after him with the metal detector.

"But don't forget -- THE LAND HERE IS RISING!"

Phip, at the head of the gangway, halted.

The rain came down in sheets, the wind driving the seas deep into the head of the cove. Already the tide had turned, but hardly mattered from the force of the northwest wind whipping the salt spray into the clearing amidst the otherwise impermeable forest. Within, the two men searched with spotlight and metal detector.

"Fuck!" Phip slipped over the moss-covered trunk of a massive cedar. "Way up here?"

"Plate-tectonics," Miles said evenly, with a innocent smile, and pointed the spotlight down at the uneven ground at his feet. "This is some of the newest land on earth. The Pacific plate is riding up under the North American plate, and boom! -- instant mountains. That's why Mount St. Helens exploded."

Phip grabbed the spotlight and pointed its beam up at the living giants surrounding them, their canopy above obscuring everything save an occasional bat. "But how could these trees be here if the water level was so high? They couldn't have lived in salt water."

Miles, in the black slicker, his long hair drenched, leaned against one of the trees, and glanced about. "Believe it or not, these are *little trees* for this place. I'll bet these islands were the first one logged a couple hundred years ago -- they were the most accessible from the water. Look, no one had been cutting them *ever*, except maybe the natives for a canoe every once in a while. And even then, this was their burial place..." He stopped, the permeation of a thought apparent in his eyes.

Phip moved away, still in the beam, to another of the infrequent level spots, waving the probe of the detector. At the beam's greatest extent, he called over his shoulder, "C'mon. Let's get this over with."

The beam didn't follow. The big Canadian turned around, cursed the darkness, the wind, the rain and the man who had managed to somehow get him to do all these things. Phip retraced his steps back and found him seated cross-legged still at the foot of the tree. Miles was looking disapprovingly from the ground about him to the tree-tops. If he barely acknowledged Phip, it was a struggle to tear his attention away. A frown began to develop.

"What?"

"Stupid man I am," Miles shook his head, and laughed as he got to his feet. "C'mon. No use looking up here. I'm hungry." The tug on his black rain slicker whipped him back around to face the furious, rain-soaked face of his host. No words came out of Phip's half-open, hard-breathing mouth. It was met by the round eyes, the gentle voice and the hand on the shoulder. "Phip, the natives here didn't bury their dead," and gestured up into the void above, "They put them in boxes and stuck them up in the trees."

The face within the yellow poncho had already begun to lose its hardness, and now rapidly so, first with understanding, then added appreciation for the culture, and finally a question. "So who's buried in my basement?

Outside the clifftop house, boards had been nailed across the plate-glass windows to keep out the hurricane-force gusts blowing across the peninsula from the Pacific. Inside, the empty dishes and dirty pots and pans lay forlornly about the kitchen. Below, and underneath, two men dug skulked about the dirt cellar floor, one more apprehensively, the other practically diving at the floor with a shovel upon the first's signal.

"I don't want to be upsetting anyone's grave," said Phip. "The guy on the boat --"

"Okay, I'll admit, not *all* the natives were put in boxes."

Phip pulled off the headphones and set down the detector, "That's it! I'm not gonna help you dig this place up, if that's what you've come for --"

Miles, on his knees in the dirt, set the shovel aside. "Wait a minute. All I know for sure is that the upper and maybe middle classes were put up in branches. Burial was reserved for slaves and the like. Get it -- the higher up in the social strata, the higher up they left your body? But I am quite sure the man who would have built the fort I'm looking for would have shown proper respect for their holy places."

"Whaddya mean! He was a trader -- I heard one of them burned down their whole village!"

A sinister smile flashed across the wild face for a moment, then, followed by a breath, was banished by a more peaceful countenance. "Captain Gray... yeah, well, they tried to take his ship after he kidnapped the chief's brother -- bad scene. Tit for tat. Anyway, that's not the guy we're concerned with here. This one was a... competitor of Gray's. Got along very well with the locals."

"We've been looking for an hour and only come up with a few roofing nails and a Stanley screwdriver. I'm taking a break."

"Yeah, a couple more hours of this and we can open up a hardware store... Your pretty tall aren't you?"

Phip laughed at the inappropriateness of this last question. "Yeah, six foot-four. But you're about the same."

"An inch less. Makes a difference in this low ceiling, but I still have to duck." Miles stood as high as could be allowed, and dusted the dirt from his knees and hands. "Would you say it's only six feet high down here?"

"Yeah. Hey, you givin' up too?"

"So, in other words, we're six feet under."

The shoulders of the larger man dropped as he swung his head left, then right, in despair. "Fuck... oh, jeez,... they dug the whole thing up!" He looked to Miles for confirmation -- a grim nod -- and continued, "Whatever evidence we've been looking for was totally dug out of here fifteen years ago."

The trudge up the stairs, one-by-one, to the sink of dirty dishes was the image of defeat. The kitchen task was accomplished by the pair in silence. An awkward moment hung in the air. Miles allowed Phip, shuffling his feet, to break it. "Hey, well, thanks anyway. I mean, this has really done a lot to take my mind off things, even if we didn't find anything. I, uh,... I gotta check in with the office now," pointing to the computer. "They'll probably want me back soon, but, look, I've been thinking. How 'bout hanging around here for the winter? You know, keep an eye on the island and the house. I mean we got everything here -- stereo, VCR, computer -- you'd be all set for... whatever you want to do. But you couldn't go digging up the whole place -- I don't want to piss those people off and come back to find my house burned down," he joked.

Miles chuckled. "Thanks. I-I'd hate to say no immediately. How 'bout if I sleep on it?"

"Take your time," Phip pointed to the guest room. "But, uh, tell me something?"

"I'll try."

"If the FBI isn't after you, but they aren't helping you, how are you helping them?"

"Well, this might sound a little paranoid," Miles let an uncomfortable grin escape, "but I think they've been keeping tabs on me."

"So you're saying that despite their public pronouncement they're *not* after you, they still *are*? Yeah, I'd say paranoid is a good word, but then again... they took the trouble to deny it," Phip reasoned and downed the last of the orange juice. "What makes you think they are?"

"My room-mate, Seth. First, he was never questioned by the Feds when they grilled my other roommate, Paulie, for half the night. Then Seth waved around a nice piece of artillery when our landlord tried to assault me. And then I began to realize he's never been around either time the Feds questioned me -- why? Afraid they couldn't pull the charade off? I've pretty much spilled the beans on my Bostoner theory to him, and he has a background to be able to interpret like a true analyst. Hell, he's studied overseas, and had to get security clearances twice. Once for a marine research vessel cruising north of the arctic circle and the other for meeting the Queen of England. If they've been following me -- and DAMN! I've been careful -- they would've got what they needed by checking with the New Westminster police station on what files I requested. He's a smart guy -- smarter than me. I'm just a bird dog. But I came *here* for me, I think. I just couldn't go home, yet."

"Why not?"

"I don't know. Maybe you just gave me the answer," said Miles. "A little reward."

His walk was slow and deliberate down the paneled hall to the room with the high iron-framed bed that had held him so blessedly within its blankets the day and night before. It was only until he had closed the door and laid down, arms outstretched, and eyes cast at the ceiling, did he let the thought take voice. "A cloister for my reward? Is that it?"

CHAPTER THIRTY-TWO

Chatham

Tuesday, November 14, 1995

The curled body on the bed moved slowly to remove itself from the sheets. Light poured in through the windows to the south and west. A patch of blue within the whiter, puffier clouds, held Miles' attention as he stood and arched his shoulders. Then the stretching routine, gingerly, stiffly, commenced, after so many weeks' hiatus.

The house itself was empty. In the kitchen sink, a single glass held the remnants of orange juice. The slide of the glass door, and the first cautious steps into the cold morning were followed by the exhilaration at seeing the Sound recovering from a night of sea-wrought tempest. Cleaner. More at peace.

There was no sign of the host from the three directions the house deck surveyed. At the rear door, overlooking the hillside approach from the woods, Miles stuck his head out. "I think you've spent too much time around me."

With the headphones still on, Phip could barely hear the call from the house, but turned at last, and nodded at the dug-up soil next to shovel. "Found something."

As Miles raced down the dirt and grass slope, Phip concentrated on his new source of beeps. The shovel retrieved, he dug into the heavy, black, moisture-laden earth twenty feet down the slope from his first excavation. "Thought about it a lot last night when I was lying in bed. Roland said not to worry about things -- testing's going great and my people in Vancouver are all prepped for the release. I told him what we'd been up to, and he said he'd be out here in a minute if he could break away 'cause he figured most the stuff dug up for the basement was used as fill for this hill. Used to be nothing but a cliff here according to an old photo he saw when he first checked the place out."

Up the hill, Miles was silently wiping off the previous find as Phip pulled a small, round tin from about a foot below the surface. With the utmost care, he carried it up the hill. "He said the only other sea captain who built a fort around here was named John Kendrick."

"I am John Kendrick," said Miles, the bottle consuming his interest.

"Yeah, I know," Phip approached the squatting creature with long hair and two-days beard growth whose glaring gold eyes absolutely devoured the old brown glass. Inside, something clinked within the mess of what looked to be long yellow leaves. "Whaddya think is inside there?"

"Truth." Miles exchanged the bottle for the tin. The top came off with a little coaxing to reveal several rusty needles, pins, two pearl buttons and a hand-carved spool of the most ancient thread. The color went out of Miles face, then returned with a flush and several slow tears. A shudder wracked his body, and he had to stand up in order not to tumble down the slope. "And Love," was all he could manage.

Phip took the tin back as Miles covered his face with his hands. Examining the contents, the younger man looked up at the distraught elder one. "What is it? Whose was this?"

"She --" Miles tried, stopped, then grasped Phip by the shoulders, and tried again, "-- I know whose bones those were they found. C'mon," he headed back to the back door, "I'm tired of playing."

Phip was left on the pock-marked hillside, watching the agonizing ascent of the man, silently. The only other sound, above the incessant dripping from the trees behind him, were the words hoarsely whispered from just inside the back door, "I was wrong."

John Kendrick had failed to return Florence McCarthy from the Northwest.

"Would you like your linguini in clam sauce or marinara?" the waitress with bobbed light brown hair and huge blue eyes asked.

"Where do you get your clams? I mean, are they from around here?" asked Miles.

Across the table Phip tried to suppress a laugh.

"N-no, I believe ours come in cans."

"O-ew," Miles worked the disgust out through his shoulders, "marinara, please. Uh, does that come from a can, too?"

She winked as she left, "No, that's homemade."

"I can't leave you here for the winter!" Phip whispered loudly amidst the din of the lunch customers in Tofino restaurant. "You're gonna be flirting with every woman within a hundred miles – luring them to your own private island!"

"I'm just asking about lunch. You're the one who gave me these clothes." Miles picked at the first change of wardrobe in well over a week -- brown jeans, sandals, pale blue tab collared shirt and embroidered vest.

"I'm sorry I did. You know, you look just like the kind of artsy Hollywood type who'd own a place here, too."

Through the window, the Marine Contractor's pickup slowed as it pulled out the parking lot. Both men seated inside the restaurant waved. "Don't you want to keep the metal detector for one more day?" Phip asked.

"Naw. You'll have enough problems when you turn that bottle over to the federal government -- you still have one up here, don't you?"

"Yeah. Glad I keep my assets in U.S. currency. Our dollar took a pounding from the Quebec referendum. So, should I just turn this stuff over to the University of British Columbia?"

"Well, that depends..."

"On...?"

"You could take it to the Registry of Deeds in Victoria."

"What would they do with it?"

"Burn it, probably."

"That little old sewing kit? Why?"

Miles shook his head, somberly, "No. Not that. Take care of that. I meant the bottle."

"Why, is that coin in there worth a lot? Yeah, I guess it would be after two hundred years -- if that's when it's from. I can't wait to see them open it up."

Swigging the last of his cranberry juice and ginger ale, Miles flipped the bottle of malt vinegar on the table into his empty glass. When it was a third full, he placed it in the center of the table, and paused. "Vile stuff. Can't see what the attraction is around here to it." The coin slipped easily out of the vest pocket, and was held between two fingers. The copper was tarnished, but it was otherwise clean. Dropped into the glass, in about a half a minute, the Columbia Medal began to gleam, revealing the picture of *Columbia* and *Washington* a-sail.

Phip stared at it, reading the inscription, then held up the glass to read the bottom. "John Kendrick. Huh. Guess you were right. This *is* worth a lot."

"Not compared to what's still in that bottle. I took a hell of a chance jiggling that thing out of there."

"I thought that's all there was besides a bunch of leaves."

"This," Miles held up the medal, "is nothing. Tell me, and I don't mean to sound morbid, but did Juan name you as sole beneficiary of his will?"

"No," Phip took a deep breath and shook his head again, "I'm Executor. We took care of it last year. He didn't really have a family except for his mother, and we split the bulk of it. But anything found on the island would be the property of the Trust, controlled by Roland and the corporation."

"Deeds don't work that way. That's what those 'bunch of leaves' left in the bottle are. The remnants of the original legal instrument transferring the whole Clayoquot Sound and its environs from Wickananish, the chief at Opitsat, to Captain John Kendrick of the brigantine *Washington*."

Phip wanted to laugh, and almost did, but instead he stared at the shiny copper medal in the glass, and the words **COLUMBIA AND WASHINGTON COMMANDED BY J. KENDRICK**. Kicking back, he gave Miles a resigned look: "How long is this story?"

"How comfortable's your chair?"

"More coffee?" the anxious and harried waitress returned to the two men sitting in the dim corner, late afternoon passing into evening.

The taller, clean-cut one, who barely picked at his plate, simply pointed to his Bohemian companion with the ravenous appetite. This one smiled, looking into her eyes. "Maybe just one more, thank you. And the check, please."

Phip waited until she had left the slip with two little mints on top. "I'm getting that."

"You better, or they'll be getting their clams fresh for a week. I ain't got a penny to my name," Miles nodded to the medal Phip had since wiped off, allowing it to go back to its original tarnish, "unless you count that."

"You wish," Phip pulled it back, and stuck it in his pocket. "I'm checking Juan's connection to your Captain Kendrick --"

"He's not *mine*."

"-- and then the University can have any artifacts, and I, for what it's worth, am giving the Sound back to the people of Opitsat."

"WHAT! Why? They don't own it! They sold it two hundred years ago."

"For nearly nothing, you said."

"Yeah," Miles was becoming animated, "so what? Hell, back on the Cape land wasn't going for much more when Europeans first came! Supply and demand."

"What're you getting so worked up about? You said yourself, the chief probably thought he was just granting use of the place, that's all."

"My point is, you've got a better claim than the Canadian government. And you're a citizen here. Press it in court! You'll have an entire region to do with what you like."

"I'll have my island," Phip sighed. "You decide about caretaking for it?"

Miles fiddled with the embroidering running down the front of the vest. "No. Thank you. No."

"What? But why? You told me about this whole Bostoner bit. Even if you don't get killed, you can't work out there anymore."

"Because this place is not mine."

"But you could stay as long as you want."

"I know. But Phip, try to understand. I was driven out of my home -- the land from which I sprang, the country that made me. And here I am, and I *must* leave because it is not my own -- any more than Cape Cod belongs to those people in Opitsat . I don't know where to go next -- I've run out of land."

"You said there was reward money, right?"

"I haven't earned it."

"But if you're right, and the FBI was using you to pick up a trail, they'll have to credit you -- I mean, wouldn't your roommate do that for you?"

"Yeah..." Miles' fingers slipped the buttons into the holes running down the vest. He frowned at the amount of tightness around his waist, "... musta gained weight? Nah... Oh, uh, no, Seth would go to bat for me, that's for sure. He has a strong sense of right and wrong. If I deserved it, and asked for it, he'd spare no effort."

Phip pointed to the vest. "Juan had that tailored. It's a little more fitted around the waist than most. That's why there's so much play in the chest for you."

There was a billowiness to the top, Miles found. "I never claimed to be the perfect V-shaped man. He must've been in pretty good shape."

There was a pause from the opposite side of the table, perhaps from the weight of the food, the oncoming darkness, and the length of time inside combined with the whirlwind of activity. The smooth-faced man smiled quickly, turned away to see if anyone was about, and cleared his throat. "Y-yeah. He was a great guy... Oh god, I really, really miss him. And

I just mean 'cause we really connected and that's so *gone* now."

Together, they waited in silence until the waitress returned the receipt from the credit card, thanked them, wished them to come again (unconvincingly), and left. Another sniffle was corrected by Phip blowing his nose. "I think I gotta get back to work."

"No." Miles' word was firm.

"Hey, it's been great, and really taken a lot off my mind doin' all this with you, but I gotta get on with my life."

"Right. Got your phone?"

Phip instinctively reached for the phone, then stopped himself. "Why?"

The healer looked him earnestly in the eye. "Do this. Trust me. I know. I know so well."

The phone was laid down on the table next to the receipt.

"Paul! God, thought you dropped off the face of the earth!"

"Where's the Lady now?" Miles asked.

"Well...," Billy's voice crackled off and on, "I'd say we're twenty miles up the Columbia. We hope to hit St. Helens by dinner. Oh, here we go --"

The voice of the Director came on. "Mr. Kimball! Good to talk to you. I called your number in Boston, but only got an answering machine. Are you back there already?"

"Nope. Not yet. Listen, is that offer of volunteering still open?"

Phip sat up straight.

"Oh yeah! We'd love to have you aboard! When do you want to start? You can pick us up in Portland the day after tomorrow if that's convenient."

"Not me." Miles handed the phone over to an entertained young business executive, and whispered, "Sabbatical."

The one-sided conversation started off stiffly on Phip's end, but eventually warmed considerably, what with the specs received on the vessel, its itinerary, its history and requirements. Miles, satisfied with his accomplishment, excused himself and took a chance to step outside. His attention drifted across the view of the Sound outside, from Mount Colnett on Meares Island to Opitsat, and the scattering of islets. From the pocket of his wool coat, he pulled the ancient tin, and took one last peak at its precious sewing implements before putting it back. Before he returned it, for no apparent reason, he unbuttoned the vest again.

Phip was finishing up. "Great! You think you can? Excellent! Can't wait to see you tomorrow. Yeah, here he is --" and handed the phone back to Miles as he took his seat.

"So you got a crewman! Does that mean I get a refund on my brick?" Miles asked.

"Oh, you've made an old fund-raiser very happy, sir," the Director's voice was crowing above the static. "And funny you should mention that brick. That was why I was trying to call you. We got another request the day after you left -- my office called your number in Boston to see if you'd being willing to take another since Mr. Barrell has been such a patron. But this friend of yours may now give you more consideration. I'll tell you tomorrow night. Philip will fill you in. They need me at the helm to turn this around."

"Huh?" Miles shot a curious glance at a beaming Phip. "O-kay...? Wait! Hold on!" He gripped the phone as if it, too would disappear like the voice several hundred miles to the south in a second, "What name was requested?"

The waitress came back one more time, and the tall Canadian reassured her by standing up and brushing Miles' arm proddingly.

"Yeah. Thanks. Okay." Miles clicked the phone shut and handed it back to its owner as they exited the building. It was a half mile down to the wharf, and with the sunset on the far side of the peninsula, only the tops of the mountains to the east received a sense of the brilliant show. Miles paid no attention to it.

"Did he tell you?" Phip finally asked as they rounded the corner.

"Huh?" The long-haired man pulled off his overcoat. "Oh, sure. Good show, man," Miles acknowledged the feat with a respectful grin. "Bet they never had a charter like this before!" Then he pulled off the vest and glared at the hemming in the front.

"What is with you and that vest?" Phip demanded. "You been picking at it for the past hour."

"Something's wrong with it. It was bothering me and now I've figured it out. Halfway down there's an extra button, so I never buttoned it straight."

"Oh, right. Juan said there were too many buttons so he had half them removed and the holes sewn up." Phip took a look as Miles absently handed the vest over. "Uh, do you want this anymore?"

A hard edge had come over the man in long hair walking down to the water. His normally open eyes were narrowing, his cheekbones tightening, his hands every so often coming up to his face as if in prayer, then back down again as he spun slowly around down at the edge of the wharf.

His clothes-laden companion hailed the old man guiding the water taxi in. Another half minute and they'd be on their way back to the island. Miles spun around in a pounce. "I need the medal."

"Wait a minute. I'm giving it --"

The eyes were dancing and intense. "I need to borrow it. I'll give it back. I promise. Please -- before you leave – please -- it's important."

"What's happened to you all of a sudden?"

Miles flung himself around, holding his fists to his head. "I've been so stupid! I followed this line to its logical conclusion. If there *is* a Bostoner, then he *must* think like this. So I filled my mind up with what the Bostoner would think, and it produced clues. These clues validated the hypothesis, so I carried it further, delving deeper and deeper into my own last remnants of anger and madness, and by God, it showed me a path to follow. But what I didn't realize was that all this time I was feeding a part of me that I thought was dead. Phip, I was connecting again with the Magic of Life. What it meant to be something more than a cog, more than collecting dust!"

He buried his face in his hands, and drew them slowly down his face. "I was thinking in ways the world *should* work, what made the most sense. John Kendrick was killed by a conspiracy of the English because they had the most to benefit and were around. And it had to be Howel since it was too much of a coincidence him being around at all the tight moments. And Florence McCarthy returned to Macao because... oh, I don't know -- because I wanted her to! But *that*," pointing to the pocket of the overcoat Phip was holding, "was her sewing kit and why would she leave it behind? No, it was left on purpose because she was left behind on purpose because she *died* here!"

Phip, at a loss, and shot a look at the water taxi's young assistant fixing the lines to the wharf. "Hey, you're getting all worked up over nothing. So what if you're wrong about her?"

Grabbing Phip's lapels, Miles breathed the words into his face, "Because, if there's one thing I've learned, it's that if I'm wrong in one of my results, then I have to look at the calculations again. The whole theorem. The brick. The vest. My roommate...." He released his grip and sunk down against a piling. "I gotta go back to Boston."

"Why? What's going on? You're giving up on everything at the drop of a hat!"

Miles shook his head quickly, violently. "I gotta go. I gotta spend a few days cleaning up my mess, setting things right. Do you know I made myself so nuts..." He shot an accusing look up at the tall man, "... I think I tried to kill my sister Nancy back in Vancouver. I *may* have back in Wellfleet -- my sister Elise. And anybody else I felt has lied to me or betrayed me, and help craft me so hopelessly wrong for this world. God, I hope they *are* tracking me... Was *that* the real motivation behind this trip -- and the search for clues just an excuse to my conscious self?"

"Shit." Miles stopped, took a deep breath and whispered hoarsely, "That cannister – I think I *meant* to bring it with me. *Stupid* Rogue." He nodded a minute, then incongruously refreshed, jumped up and cheerfully grabbed the coat and vest from Phip. "Well, let's go!"

There was not a word spoken by either, except in response to the much more animated old man as he brought the aluminum craft across the Sound. Small talk, really. But it was strange in its congeniality. He waved and laughed a good-bye as his two customers disembarked. They stood on the dock for a moment as he disappeared around the corner of the island. Phip cleared his throat. A signal.

"I need the medal," Miles repeated.

"I can't," Phip shook his head and raised his eyebrows. "Sorry."

"I *know* who's next," Miles offered. "It's ridiculous, terribly unsound in fact, but I do know. And following that line of reasoning, I can figure out everything that's been going on. All from that one little call to *Lady Washington*." He see-sawed back and forth, around the dock and back again.

"The name on the brick," said Phip. "The one you said you bought." Darkness was beginning to envelope the cove again for another evening, and in it, Phip's yellow raincoat was the only contrast. "But you put your father's name on it, right?"

"They got another request," said Miles. "By mail. With a check from Barrell, Bulfinch & Gray, just like the rest. And a request for an inscription. *One* name," Miles had turned his back to the dock and, facing the water, held up a finger. "*One* word," he laughed.

"What? What's so funny?"

"It just happens to be the name of my home town."

"Boston?"

Miles spun slowly around on heel. Beyond, the last wisps of light were streaking off the peninsula, with the twinkle of lights from Tofino turning on, one by one. He shook his head confidently. "Chatham."

CHAPTER THIRTY-THREE

Adventure

Wednesday, November 15, 1995

"H'lo?"

"Hi, Dad?"

"Yuh?"

"It's John."

"Yuh."

"How's everything there?'

"Oh... okay, I guess. Not too busy, except maybe raking Griscom's lawn. Kinda tired this morning – maybe a cold. But okay, I guess."

"Has anyone been by looking for me lately? Not reporters... well, okay, maybe, but I think maybe the police or someone wanting to search the place?"

"No."

"Oh. Good."

"Where are you now? Still in Boston?"

"Nope. I'm visiting Nancy in Vancouver. I was just wonderin' if something happened while I was away. I mean, I *am* out of the country."

"Yuh. No, no one's come by or called, 'cept the same old people. I did what you said and just let the machine answer it. But we did have a little excitement in town this afternoon. I was down the Town Offices and all of a sudden *REEEE*, here comes the fire trucks, and they come and evacuate everybody. I thought it was a gas leak, or maybe a small fire in the elevator shaft -- you know they had problems when you worked there years ago. But this morning Ben said he was talking to one of the firefighters in line at the bakery and she said it was a bomb scare."

"Oh. Uh-huh. Did they find one?"

"No. Wa-el, I don't know. Uh, do you think maybe when you come back you can program the VCR clock again? We had a thunderstorm and it reset -- so it just flashes twelve o'clock all the time."

"Shurh! But, uh, I think I'll be here for a while."

"Uh, is Nancy there? I mean, is she available?"

"Nope. I'm calling from a friend's. Nancy and David took Will down to Seattle for the rest of the week. Anyway, thanks. Just don't let anyone know where I am – until after tomorrow -- I want to get settled in."

"Okey-doke."

"You think you better shave?" called down Phip.

"Why do you always speak to me in questions?"

The broad-shouldered Canadian pulled the duffel up over the rail, and laughed at the American in the aluminum boat as it rocked in the open seas off of Clayoquot. "Because you always come up with the most off the wall answers."

"Oh," Miles scruffy face held in the brig's spotlight considered. "I guess I do ask for it. Well, then, no. I've already shaved once. I don't need to do it again for few months. Not good to remain too exposed."

"At least it'll cover that scar," Phip drew a finger along his throat, and then puzzled. "What a way to go. You really must've been upset."

"Oh this?" Miles indicated the white line below his jaw. "Rope burn. Got it when I was sixteen -- ran my bike under a clothesline. Showin' off for a girl. Guess I shoulda learned early."

Shock, anger and appreciation at the deception was summed up in Phip's three words: "Oh, you bastard!" He shook his head. "I thought you had tried to kill yourself."

Miles placed his hand up against the wooden planking of *Lady Washington's* sides, patted it once, and then gave a little salute to the crew. Billy and the Director came down from the quarter-deck, offering to take the bag below. A man like Phip who forks over the cash to charter a tall ship to come pick him up after a day and half a night of sailing is someone special, even if he is going to serve a month or two as a lowly volunteer crewman. But from Miles' severe angle, it was obvious the big man was gratefully refusing their help.

"Stay as long as you want," said Phip. "You know where the key is."

"And more!" Miles called out, then signaled the old man he was clear to pull away from this precarious midnight drop-off. Soon the wind-driven mist had swallowed up the silhouette, and the two in the water taxi were left to ponder the hum of the engine.

"Okay, this should be close enough," Miles said, and pulled the cell phone from his back pocket, its buttons glowing in the darkness. The boat slowed to a quiet drift in the channel. "What time you got?"

The old man flipped on the dashboard light, harsh and only effective enough for him to read his watch. His passenger, holding the phone to his ear, listening for the dial tone, waited for the answer. "About five minutes to twelve."

"Hello?"

"Hi, Nancy?"

"Yes?"

"It's John. Sorry if I woke you, but I need a big favor. I'm here in Vancouver, and I'm staying with a friend tonight, but tomorrow..."

CHAPTER THIRTY-FOUR

Herald

Thursday, November 16, 1995

"Good morning, sir!"

"Kendrick? Holy... what's going on?" asked the Professor. "It's three in the blessed AM! Where are you?"

"All in good time, sir. By the way, you can call the medical examiner in Port Alberni, British Columbia and he will tell you that Juan Kendriqué died *on the night I left Boston* from complications due to his accident. There's no way I could've been involved. So now you don't have to kill me."

"You can't imagine how disappointed I am," the snide little voice, bitter with sleep, commented. "Did you find what you were looking for?"

"In spades. Is Paulie there?"

"Yeah, but I'm pret-ty sure he's sacked out."

"Uh-huh."

"You want me to wake him, is that it?"

"Please."

"Hel-*lo*!"

"Pau-lie... so... what's up?"

Laughter. "Well! Well, well, well. So, you're alive! Jesus, you had us going there for a while. Where are you? Are you okay? What time is it out there? God, what time is it here?"

"I *know*."

A quickly cleared throat. "Uh, what was that?"

"I know."

"What do you know?"

Playful. "I know something you don't know."

"What do you think I don't know?"

"That I *know*."

Silence. A long, deep breath in through the nose. An exhale through the mouth. "You mean who did it? I thought you thought it was this fucker Barrell."

"Na-na-na-no. I know... about you. And I just want you to know, I understand --"

"Johnny, look --"

"-- I don't appreciate it, but I understand. No doubt, this call is being traced, and you know where I am. The FBI can't operate outside the U.S. unless specifically authorized by the President. I wasn't stopped at the border, and maybe I didn't elude everyone as well as I thought, so I'm *guessing* I was allowed to come here. You thought I was really onto something, and so I was given a really long leash. I do appreciate everyone's confidence in me. Bomb scare in Chatham, huh? Not a day after the Director of the Gray's Harbor calls your answering machine and leaves a message that you take to mean that the next victim is Chatham."

"Okay, but I want you to know I'm not one of them. I don't want to get into this on the phone --"

"Try."

Paulie sighed. "I mean, uh... I'm not inside. I never really was. It was in Spain. And France, when I was going to school over there. I was doing a lot of traveling from Burgundy to San Sebastian. They had a lot of activity there with the Basque separatists, and I got scoped out by somebody on campus. Maybe carry something with me. A small package. I got an American passport, but I could pass for either French or Spanish."

"Uh-huh."

He cleared his throat again. "Yeah, so I don't want to get into major trouble, so I report it to the local American consulate, and next thing I know I get called into the Dean's office and this guy from the State Department gives me a choice of cooperating with French and Spanish intelligence."

"A choice usually involves another option."

"Yeah, it was '*Don't come back*'. They'd've refused to grant me a student visa, I mean *indefinitely*. I'd've kissed my entire course of study there goodbye. Instead, when... uh, when it was all over, I didn't have any financial aid problems from then on. Remember that full scholarship I got?"

"Blood money?"

"Listen, I didn't do anything to anyone. And it would have been someone else, if not me. I didn't want maybe some bomb going off and killing innocent people if I could help it."

"Likewise," Miles observed. "And now they own you. If word ever got out, you'd be a marked man." He thought for a moment. "I guess this means Bill Connor and Frankie Vanzetti were in on this, too, huh? My own lawyers. God, talk about not having confidence in me -- or maybe you guys really did, huh? You know, it almost went too far."

"Anyway, why don't you tell me where you are and I'll come get you myself. I don't care if it's fuckin' Timbuktu!"

Huh. So they had lost track. The snack shop -- that must've been it. Thank God he had thrown the cannister of the bridge. Had there been some sort of device Paulie had stuck on his license plate? Had Grunge Kid really been just a tail – albeit clumsy? Hmmm. "I'll come back when I'm ready. Pardon me if I'm a little pissed at my own country right now. I thought maybe I could trust it."

"Are you still in Vancouver? Listen, these guys are starting to get a little anxious. They don't know what 'Chatham' means. Like, where in the town? Or is it Chatham, New Jersey? Jesus, do you know how many Chathams there are in this country?"

"Or this one. Or England. Your guys have enough to go on. Why don't you pick Seth's brain? Leave me alone for a while, okay? I've been on the streets of Vancouver for the past week, or so I have to assume. I really can't remember what I've done, and I'm not in great shape. Next time, if I'm gonna go crazy, let me do it for my own sake."

A heavy, heavy sigh. "Come back, okay?"

"Not yet."

CHAPTER THIRTY-FIVE

Eliza

Friday, November 17, 1995

"Hi. We're all playing with the our cat toys and watching cartoons, if you haven't hung up by the end of this, please leave message and one of us will get back to you."

BEEP!

"Hello, Elise, this is little bro-bro. I'm in Vancouver --"

"Hello... John?"

"Oh, hi. Screening your calls again?"

"No, just giving Jody a bath. What a pretty girl she's is! Much better than a dog. Where are you? Vancouver? You should go see Nancy."

"Yeah, I was visiting a friend out here and now I'm staying with Nancy. Had to take a little vacation."

"Oh. That sounds nice. Wish I could go off to somewhere that's not New England. I'll have to get blown up, too, though there's not much chance of that in the gallery."

"Probably not. Uh, so everyone's okay there? I was just worried since I'd kinda dropped out of sight for a coupla weeks."

"No, nope, everyone's fine. Mom called me and told me about getting a new toilet for the boat -- like I'm really interested in hearing about what they found clogging up the old one! God... nothing... Oh, but Blackie came in the other morning covered with blood and fur. Some big old opossum got hit on the Rail Trail behind the house here. On a bike path -- can you believe that?"

"Uh-huh."

CHAPTER THIRTY-SIX

Jane

Saturday, November 18, 1995

"English Department."

"Jane Ryder, please."

"One moment."

The beating of his heart began, despite himself, to hasten.

"This is Jane."

The OFF button had his finger ready to depress. It almost did. "Hello, One."

Pause.

"Johnny...?"

A warm smile breezed across his face. "Yeah. Just wanted to make sure you're still alive," he laughed.

"Well, thanks. Oh, boy, I should say the same for you --," then angry, "What the hell have you been doing?!"

"Just walking through life. I was in your neighborhood and I wasn't sure if I might have... seen you. Listen, take care. I gotta catch a -- train. Bye."

"Hello, I'm picking up a ticket being held for me by my employer, WolfWorks. I reserved it last night -- I hope. My name is Philip Greenfield."

"Yes, Mr. Greenfield. I'll just need some picture identification."

"I'm sorry, I was just down in Seattle and my pocket was picked. But I do have my business card."

"Ooh... our policy requires us to ask for something with a picture."

A frown. A smile. "I really have to catch that plane or I'm gonna lose a very important account. Now, I can see the U.S. Customs officer from here across the lobby. If he lets me through without picture ID, you're off the hook, right? Please?"

"Go for it."

"Ticket." The middle-aged man wore a huge handgun on his belt. "Do you have a form of I.D.?"

"Work I.D. -- it's an old picture." Miles fished around in the briefcase. "Maybe I stuck it in with my ticket here..."

The customs officer couldn't be bothered. "Where were you born?"

"Chatham, Massachusetts."

"Go ahead."

CHAPTER THIRTY-SEVEN

Jenny

Sunday, November 19, 1995

"Hey, Buddy."

"Oh, fuck!" The door nearly slammed shut, but Miles inserted the pipe quickly to stop its progress.

Up West Fourth Street, a large black Buick opened its passenger door, and a buxom, long red-haired young woman jumped out to remove the trash can holding the space. When the pale gorilla got out the driver's side and started helping her with the grocery bags from the trunk, she touched his arm, and pointed to the stoop where Buddy hid halfway behind the door, and a long-haired man outside.

As they all proceeded slowly inside, each passed, in silence, the embroidered wall hanging featuring an Irish coat of arms emblazoned with the name "MAGEE."

Jennifer just threw up her arms in frustration and hugged Miles. "I was so worried about you! When my brothers told me what happened I - I - " she buried her face in his shoulder.

"Brothers," Miles repeated, and looked from Buddy to the gorilla. Then he remembered, and held up his hands. "Hey, I'm clean." Buddy was still wary. But the gorilla whom Miles had only seen once before -- in the uniform of a federal bailiff as he pulled Miles out of a smoke-consumed room-- simply exhaled his relief.

"How long have you worked at the courthouse?" asked Miles.

Jimmy shrugged his broad, round shoulders. "I dunno. Five years? Yeah, right outta the Marines."

"And you say Barrell told you about an opening at One Post Office Square, so you told Bernie," pointing at the until-now-Buddy, "and he was hired right on the spot?"

"Lucky for me, too, like that," Bernie offered. "I wanted to take night classes at UMass-Boston on the GI bill, but ones I wanted were in the middle of the afternoon, so it really fucked up my work schedule. Then, this thing just drops in my lap. I found out later I got a good word from the old man's office."

"So when you heard Barrell was after me," Miles stopped, " -- wait, who heard this?"

"They both did," Jennifer was leaning against the hall doorway, next to the large sofa holding her two large brothers. "Our father's a retired cop. It's in the blood, I guess. They mentioned it at dinner that night, and Jimmy said it wasn't like you were in any mood to leave that room when he hauled you out, and I said when you left the office you didn't even know if you were supposed to go over or not. Anyway, I made Bernie call you from the police station payphone, since everybody knew your phones were tapped."

"Everybody?" His laughter snuck in and erupted like wave hitting the beach, washing the tension away. Miles, stopped pacing, walked over to Jennifer, put his hands on her shoulders and looked deep into her eyes. "Thank you. Thank you so very much. You helped out more than you can imagine." He walked over to Jimmy, the offer of a handshake accepted in a meaty paw. And finally, he laid a hand on Bernie's shoulder. "Friend, we have to talk."

Bernie's round eyes turned up to meet his. "'Bout what?"

"I need to look at a photo."

"Yeah, so?"

"On the 25th floor of One Post Office Square."

Bernie's reaction of refusal was immediate, as was the ensuing crush of family from either side of the sofa.

CHAPTER THIRTY-EIGHT

Bounty

Monday, November 20, 1995

"It's the rarest of American medals. We count five silver in existence, five pewter and three copper. One of each, of course, are right here in front of you," the Librarian explained.

The dark mahogany of the paneling, the six-foot high eighteenth-century portraits of famous New Englanders and marble columns gave the Massachusetts Historic Society as much a feeling of either a bank or a private club, which in a way, it was both. And on the heavy oak table before him, nestled in deep red velvet, sat three versions of the same medal in near flawless condition. The gloves the librarian had provided kept the copper and silver from tarnishing. The pewter, rough hewn and scratched, but clean, wouldn't have that problem.

"About how much would you say this is worth, then?" asked Miles.

She puzzled for a moment. "I'd say, well, it's hard to say. Since there are so few in existence, and they were never in wide distribution even when they first came out, they're more like a novelty than an investment. But I think I remember the copper selling for $1,600 at an auction back in the eighties."

"Okay, so this copper one I'm holding is one of three known in the world. Who has the other two?"

"There's one in a private collection in Arizona and another in a private collection in Japan."

"And you don't keep these on display?"

"Rarely. They're usually kept in a safety deposit box until such time someone like yourself requests an examination. Otherwise, we have to insure them when they're out and then we usually carry $100,000 insurance on each piece. It is expensive just to display them."

"So, correct me if I'm wrong, but if more of these were in circulation, they'd all appreciate more? Like, it makes no sense to wish to have all the money in the world --"

"-- Since no one else would know its value," she agreed. "Right."

CHAPTER THIRTY-NINE

Union

Tuesday, November 21, 1995

"Good morning, sir!"

"Who are you?"

"Benjie," the attendant in the baby blue sweater leaned down over the elderly man with pink, feathery folds in his face and light white hair wringing his head like a halo, "this is Mr. Greenfield. He's a nephew of Mr. Woodruffe's. You remember Mr. Woodruffe, don't you?"

The Chelsea Soldiers and Sailors Home held many men like this, who, having served their time long ago, and no family often because of it, came here to reflect upon a different life than most, and otherwise wait for it to come to an end.

"Simon? Damned fool!" he cried out, then frowned. "Damn shame. Healthy as a puppy. Coulda gone on twenty more years, for sure, but I don't know what fun that woulda been 'round here. Where you from, son?"

"Cape Cod. I'm doing some genealogy research. Checking out the family tree and wanted to find out what I could on him. A birthday present for my mom."

"Oh, that's nice. But, uh, hey, you said you were his nephew? I ask because he never said anything about family. Most of us don't here."

"Not exactly a direct nephew. I'm his cousin's son. They knew each other only as kids."

"Ohhhh," the frail face accepted, not needing much more. "So, what do you want to know? I can't tell much, but we were good friends since we both served in the Navy in World War II *and* Korea."

"Oh everything. Whatever you can recall. How about Barrell?"

"Who? What was that?" Benjie asked.

"Uh, I said 'Barrell'?"

"Barrell? Oh, yes. That's right. You mean Barrell's Island, right?"

"Yessir."

"Massachusetts Medical Association."

"Hello, I'm doing a research paper on physicians as victims of political violence and I was wondering if anyone there might be able to help me.

"Okay..."

"I've taken an example of a case of a doctor murdered in Lawrence, and it was alleged it may have had something to do with his practice at Planned Parenthood. I'd like to include a profile on this man, so how can I find out what kind of medicine and where he was practicing throughout his career?"

"Let me transfer you to records. Hold on."

Deep within the confines of a large, dark hall, on a forgotten windowsill, Miles' hands carefully turned the pages of a yearbook. Photos of old hairstyles, resembling most of those worn by the students here at the most elite Phillips Exeter Academy. Eyes fixed upon one page, absorbed, then turned to another, and understood. Then his hands moved to his face, covering them in shame.

Bounding up the stairs came a boy of about fifteen, and wearing a tie and blazer -- a funny anachronism, something he'd wear, more or less, until he died. Sandy hair, gawky, but his pace gave lie to a playful, independent spirit. As he passed, only the fastest glance out of the corner of his eye showed he was at all curious of the scholar in the window.

"Excuse me," said Miles.

There was hesitation, then a stop, and a turn. The eyebrows went up. "Yes sir?"

"Would you happen to know where the alumni office is?"

CHAPTER FORTY

Margaret

Wednesday, November 22, 1995

The books were more bulky than heavy, and Margaret Skinner tested her weight on the ladder before reaching over the next shelf. Once she had the old volume in her hand, her center of gravity changed and she quickly felt the back wheels of the structure lift off the ground.

Then they stopped and became firm again. Sudden stability – strange. She whipped around to find its source.

"John! Omigod, what's been going on with you?"

"Mags, did your date go well?"

"Date? Oh, that guy? Bad, bad scene. Just a little too possessive. Calling here all the time, even when I told him I wouldn't be here -- and after only two dates. Why do you want to know?"

"Just checking. I gotta go."

"John, wait! You have to stay and tell me if your research came out okay."

Striding over, and grasping her two hands, he said, "I have a date."

CHAPTER FORTY-ONE

Phoenix

Thursday, November 23, 1995

"I was named after him. Ten generations back -- on my mother's side. From a prominent Catholic family, which was difficult in England in those days, what with the Reformation and all, I'm sure," Miles explained as the waves buffeted the sleek fiberglass hull. "But he was fraudulently deprived of his inheritance, and so sought his fortune working as a mercenary in the Low Countries. I guess the job offered by the settlers on the *Mayflower* offered him a hope, more than he was finding in Europe. You know, that first winter, when practically everyone else in Plymouth got sick, only he and Governor Bradford remained well, and ended up nursing the rest. After that, he earned a place as one of their own. But since half of them had died -- even his wife -- they kinda only had each other."

These waters were tricky, what with Buzzards Bay flowing into Vineyard Sound through the tiniest of straits off a point of land dubbed Woods Hole. Water was churning and boiling against itself, trying to figure out which tidal flow to obey. The rocks on either shore weren't so treacherous, but they kept the pilot on his toes as he watched the depth finder and the cruiser's forward progress. His sole passenger seated in the darkness of the plush cabin, sniffed at his beer and continued:

"In charge of defense there, he had to turn the saints into soldiers, and made them build a stockade around the town. Four years later they sent him back to London to negotiate for the colony, since they were supposed to have settled in New York. And don't believe what Longfellow wrote -- pure fiction, truth be told. He was already remarried by 1624, and in 1631 he and John Alden founded Duxbury. Now would you go start a whole new town with a guy who stole your woman away from you?"

After a moment, the pilot forced himself to answer. "Depends upon the guy. And the woman. But you people forget about how he also led the massacre of the Pequots -- a tribe that hadn't bothered anybody -- when the Wampanoags began to realize you people weren't going to leave."

"Hey, that was the Puritans' idea!" the passenger answered. "Must be something in the water up in Boston whereby they get the Cape Codders to help with their dirty work. But, after the chief Massasoit died, his son -- nice how the Pilgrims named him after Spain's King Philip -- took a very different view of the new settlers. As I recall, his people killed a few women and children, too, before it was over."

There was little light to guide that night, and remembering the worst of the underwater obstructions were towards the cove at the northeast head of the island, the cruiser's pilot had turned the wheel southwest. A sandy beach might provide a better spot on the north side of the island.

"Arthur *Pompey* Lewis," the passenger had risen to survey the approaching, low looming darkness that could only be land.

The pilot had turned, shocked. "You been checking up on me, huh?"

"Pompey's an old Mashpee name. How much Wampanoag blood you got in you, Arthur?"

"Hardly any. Better to be a Pequot these days, what with that casino and all they got in Connecticut."

"Yeah, you got it rough all right, what with this little canoe to paddle around in."

The rest of the voyage continued in silence until approaching the rip-rap upon which waves broke twenty feet off the beach. Miles, standing on the bow, pulled a set of keys out of his pocket and threw them to Arthur. "You know what fascinated me when I first learned the stories about Myles Standish? His brutality, Arthur. He learned how to fight dirty wars in Europe, and he did the same thing here. Forget all that piety of our Pilgrim fathers. When he finished that war with the Indians, he stuck King Phillip's head on the wall of the stockade, and left it there 'til it rotted off. It was a lesson not to step out of line."

Arthur caught the keys mid-air without barely moving. In the dim running lights, he expressed not a single degree of emotion. Not since the phone call. Not since picking up his tenant at the Wareham dock. And not now with the payment. He could have gotten a locksmith to get into his new building, but this was symbolic. For him, this would mean it was over.

As the boat drifted away from the rocks, Arthur simply stood at the hatch, watching the tall man get a firm footing amongst the wave-splashed rocks. Miles turned to face him, stood, and called out with a laugh: "Enough with the stone face, man! The first Kendrick on the Cape married a Nauset Indian. Welcome," he spread his arms wide, "to America!"

Far, far from the shore now, Arthur popped open another beer and listened to the marine weather reports for Vineyard. With luck, he'd be able to make Oak Bluffs before the last restaurant closed. His wife had been thrilled at the chance to get away from tomorrow's all day of cooking and had taken a plane over ahead of him, booking a room at a bed and breakfast. But he was taking the boat? In November?

Grabbing Miles' bottle, he saw that hardly a drop had been drunk. Well, Oak Bluffs was a dry town. Might as well retire this one, too, while he had the chance.

Recalling the viewpoint of Chief Massasoit and the Wampanoag people in Southeastern Massachusetts took towards the smaller tribes of the barely habitable outer edges of the long, sandy peninsula to the east, Arthur put a little more distance between himself and his former passenger. "Nauset... Jeez, they were fuckin' nuts!"

An island frozen in time. The roads were simply cart paths, two ruts lined with gravel and a strip of grass running down the center. Not a single tire track graced the twelve square miles of this privately-held outpost. Occasionally in the meandering landscape, a stray boulder popped a nose above ground, but was otherwise ignored by the vegetation gripped in the heavy mixture of clay, sand and loam. The trees ranged from huge oaks in the forest to the occasional modest cedar amongst the golden, matted hay and bull briars, to an ancient apple tree gnarled and top heavy, waiting to outlive its own physical structure.

A breeze swirled in the air, salt-laden, carried from west to east across the island. The chill was as much caused by the moisture and the wind, as the temperature. Sounds carried far through the quiet, dark land. The cloud-filled sky portended neither rain or snow, but simply hung there to remind all that no moon, no stars, would grace the ceiling of this world tonight.

The carriage, drawn by a single butternut mare, emerged from the down-island road, and crossed the open field littered with the droppings of the sheep. Through the gate on the far side, the vehicle was able to continue past the red farmhouse where the year-round hired help -- a cook, a carpenter, and farm, boat and stable hands -- were boarded. Before the fork, the driver gave a slight pull on the reins. The horse, familiar with old path even in the dark, ignored the curving, rolling way that eventually led to the massive stone and shingled house on top the hill, lit in all its glory. Instead, the mare continued at a slow, steady gait down towards the cove, along the path lined on one side by a chest-high stone wall, and on the other, the stables.

Not bothering to alert the stable hand, the driver unhitched the horse, led it to its stall, and wheeled the carriage inside, next to others of varying degrees of antiquity and usefulness. From there, the walk down the hill, slowly and carefully between the ruts, gave a view of the island's original mansion, begun in 1785, off to one side of the pasture and atop the hill, and dark. At the foot of the hill and head of the cove, a dock stood with a large two-story shingled boathouse and an adjacent canopy sheltering a small launch and a partially-restored teak speedboat.

The sliding of the first floor door open, then closed after entering, echoed throughout a little cove, filled with a horde of empty moorings sprinkled with a few catboats and Boston Whalers. Inside, the driver's hands rubbed themselves as the newly-lit fire in the Franklin potbelly stove determinedly caught the breeze from the flue, and sprung to life. From within the sail loft, the driver laid a section of canvas upon her lap, and in the light of the lamp, the meticulous stitching began again, with a sigh. Upon the left hand, small gems inset a simple band caught the light.

"Gray," said a voice.

She looked up. The voice had filled the room, but softly. Her sandy blond hair obscuring half her shocked face.

"You abandoned me, Gray."

Anger, anxiety and fear began to mix in her expression.

"You betrayed me to Barrell and the others, Gray."

Her head searched the depths of the darkness, but the body never moved, save to put down the needle and line.

"You denied me, Gray."

The light of the lamp flickered, and danced across her face. As she turned the faint, dusky eyepatch was obvious over her left eye. *'I'M NOT*

GRAY!" she shouted at the darkness. "Not anymore."

From out of the shadows, above, a single disk of copper rolled down the stairs, across the short space of floor, struck her foot and dropped on the floor. Her hand reached down to pick it up, hold it, trace its edges. Disconnected, her face gasped and tried to pull away.

A high black boot descended from the stairs, followed by another. The hem of a long blue coat trimmed in bright brass buttons emerged. His chin was covered with a closely-cut beard, the hair pulled back in a ponytail. But it was the scabbard and sword hilt so prominently displayed on his waist that drew her awful attention.

"Meredith," John Kendrick looked her directly in the eye. "Oh," his hand easily lifted her left hand to signify the ring, "look at you. What have you gone and done? Please, please don't tell me you've up and married -- not to whom I think you have." He knelt down and took both her hands, "Dear God, woman, don't tell me I have to address you as 'My Lady.'"

She shuddered, first it seemed in fear, but the breaking of the faintest of smiles and the closing of eyes, indicated an altogether different reaction. She nodded, breathless, "Yes."

He opened his mouth to speak. Her eyes darted left. He began to turn as the sound of a hand on the outside of the door emerged --

A bright spot of white filled the world for an instant.

Darkness.

"My lord, he's awake!"

The sound of a door closing.

OPEN YOUR EYES. The slumped figure in the chair instantly shot bolt upright, eyes open. Pain overwhelmed his skull, blocking out all vision and sound. Dizziness and nausea followed, then slowly retreated to reveal a rather dashing young man wearing wire-rim glasses and red cashmere sweater over a starched white shirt. His blond hair was beginning to thin prematurely, but a bang kept falling forward into his eyes as he shined a penlight into Miles' left pupil. "Hold it just minute, there, friend. Just look straight ahead..." The accent was odd.

There was no movement seated in this big old leather wingchair. Not daring to move his head again, Miles managed to glance down at his wrists, and saw the nylon line securely tied in place. He guessed the same was true for his feet as they felt firmly held slightly under the chair.

The examiner was becoming a little impatient. "Look, you're not making this any better for yourself. I just need to see if you have a concussion. Now look straight ahead, right?"

English accent. The south country.

Miles' head locked forward, his eyes directly into nowhere. His words were slow, distinct, and deep. "YOU ARE IN DANGER."

The chuckle was stifled, barely. "What, from you? Maybe before, when you were running loose on this island, but that's all over, my friend. The old man said your name is John. Can I call you that?"

"YOU DO NOT UNDERSTAND WHAT IS HAPPENING."

The light went off, and returned to the examiner's shirt pocket. He sighed. "John, I'm a doctor. A medical doctor. You took a pretty stiff blow to the head, so I'm going to have to ask you to relax. This," he indicated the ropes, "is for your own protection —"

STOP HIM. Miles began tightening the pressure in his skull, aiming right at the heart of the pain there.

"— I'm told you've caused some problems in the past, and I have to say if it's true, I have my own bone to pick with you concerning my new bride. Oh, Jesus -- you're hemorrhaging!" His hand shot behind Miles head, which felt slightly stuck to the old leather. Miles released the pressure in his head, and let it drop forward. The doctor called over his shoulder at the door, "Joseph! Come quick! Bring a towel -- he's bleeding!" He removed his hand, the tips tainted red, and ran to the door.

He was gone, down the hall. Some cursing followed, then another voice, lower, and some arguing. The doctor maintained most specifically: "But why do we have to keep him up here? Do you know there's not even any running water in this house?"

It was cold here, Miles could feel from his stocking feet. The chipped white walls held only small, round windows. A tall brass floor lamp provided the only light in here, besides a single bare bulb out in the hall. Footsteps came up a set up stairs. The waves of darkness began to creep in again as Miles' head hung lower.

STAY ALERT. His head jerked up again. Pain.

Before him two men stood, both concerned, but each about different objects. The young doctor. And the Brahmin. "John," Joseph Barrell began, crossing the room, to a seat by one of the porthole-style windows, "why did you come here?"

The doctor placed a bandage across the back of Miles' head. "Well, good then. It's stopped."

Miles addressed the doctor. "YOU SHOULD LISTEN... If one were to say, 'Let me loose or die', you would take it as a threat when it is just a warning. If one were to simply smile instead, and say nothing, you would think it a sign of mental illness. And if the truth is spoken, someone will be hurt who has suffered enough." Miles attempted to gain strength from a deep breath, but the edge of dizziness stopped it. "A display of power," he said to Barrell, and looked at the doctor. "That is what this is, truth be told, and barely little more."

"It's over, John," the Brahmin sighed as he looked out the window, and patted his knees in confirmation. "But you wanted witnesses, didn't you? A display of power, but with a good chance of getting caught, just like at the courthouse. But somehow you got out of that."

The doctor bowed his head, perhaps out of sadness at Miles' condition, perhaps at Barrell's painfully frank insight.

Miles eyes narrowed in realization. "YOU WANT A CONFESSION." He turned to the doctor, and explained: "A confession is better than evidence itself, remember. It helps when all the pieces don't fit."

"John, we know about your obsession with Meredith. She told me about how you met in that bar over Columbus Day weekend," Barrell sat forward, nodding. "And when she tried to put an end to it a few days later, you snapped, didn't you? You realized you were going to have to see her regularly on a professional basis. So you tried to kill all the people who brought you together -- Lotta, me, even poor John Meares. That, son, is a display of power."

Miles, firmly in the chair, raised his eyebrows and considered, and then stared out at the hall. "You are a very talented manipulator. It is all very feasible, what you say. But there are many ways to interpret events. Yours is motivated by self-interest. Pity. Indeed a waste." He closed his eyes, to gather strength, not to sleep. "I found Fort Washington." In the darkness of his closed eyes, there was silence. Perhaps the sound of a head turning. "I found Florence McCarthy's grave."

Maybe someone's lips mouthed a question.

"I found a deed," he added.

A throat cleared. A breath. The sound over at the window of the Brahmin beginning to stand up, then stopping himself. "What deed?"

Miles opened his eyes. "Clayoquot. I've been there. I just came back."

The Brahmin tried to respond, then broke into a laugh. "No, oh no, John. Oh, is that it? Off to Vancouver Island, hm? All the while under the watchful eyes of the authorities? Yes, I know about your fake illness and your deal with the FBI. Your 'attorney', Bill Connor understands which clients are important and which can be sacrificed for the greater good. Well, I must have made quite an impression on you during our last visit. I didn't think you knew that much about your ancestor, old John Kendrick."

"I didn't. Now I do. I thought it might be you, sir, you who planted the bomb. You, who tried to bribe me the same day you showed me the Columbia medal and told me the tale. You who sent the check not a few days later. You who put immense pressure on the authorities to arrest me, to blame me, when all along I thought it might be you."

"Trying to shift the blame. Denial, John?" The Brahmin countered from his increasingly precarious seat at the window. But he halted, and changed his tone abruptly, "What check?"

The smile almost broke across Miles' face. CONTROL. "The one I cashed just this past week. I used it to tailor this coat and purchase that sword."

The doctor picked up the scabbard resting near the door next to Mile's pair of boots, then promptly put it down. "Meredith told us you must have stolen it from the Kendrick house in Wareham."

"Must I? How must I? The sword came from a collector who found he had a piece of junk sold to him. And this coat," Miles nodded to the broad lapels, "It's my old overcoat – dyed navy blue. I bought the buttons at the Seaport in Aberdeen. The receipt is in the pocket here."

Barrell wanted to stop the doctor, but couldn't think of a convincing reason for him not to. The doctor fished out two pieces of paper, along with a black felt eyepatch which was promptly tossed on the floor. He read the first slip, handed it to the Brahmin, then the next. "Gray's Harbor Historic Seaport?" He shot a look at Barrell, "Joseph, this is dated two weeks ago."

Control carried the Brahmin casually off the window seat, and over to examine the second slip. He, however, did not manage to veil his subsequent puzzlement. The best he could do was: "What is this?"

"REFUTATION. YOU SHOULD HAVE BEEN MORE

CAREFUL." Miles, quickly appealed to the doctor. "Please, if what I'm saying is true, can *he* be right? You are in extreme danger, sir. I know because your name is on a list of victims. A list put on prominent display out in Grays Harbor. Don't you see -- *Gray?* I know this sounds far-fetched, but believe me, I know who you are and I know that the turmoil of this evening will only provoke the person who killed John Meares, Charlotte Bulfinch Coolidge, Simon Woodruffe and Doctor Samuel Roberts --"

Having stopped his mile-a-minute speech, Miles glared at Barrell. "Oh *yeah*, man! Look at him! He's a little worried now, especially when I said those last two names. Samuel Roberts and Simon Woodruffe. You wanna know why? 'Cause they worked for him. Here on the island one summer a dozen years ago. Just like Lotta Coolidge did, but in Boston. He's got this thing about hiring people who were descendants of associates of his ancestor Joseph Barrell, isn't that right? That's why you tried to hire me, just like you did Bernard Magee."

The Brahmin stumbled at recovery. "He -- he's ranting now. Listen --"

"NO. *Listen-to-me.* He's not only immersed himself in the history behind the *Columbia* mission, he's surrounded everyone else in it too. Where the hell did he find you anyway, Lord Pitt? That is who you are -- the Earl of Chatham?"

The doctor nervously played with the remainder of the bandage in his hand. "The -- the title is -- dead, really. But, I could qualify --"

"With enough cash to pay somebody off back home. Sure..." Miles verbally accosted Barrell again, "But it wasn't you who found him, was it? It was probably within the past year, at least. Meredith, your precious student, raised on the myth you sold her, how George Vancouver went out to settle the Nootka Sound Question, sent by the Earl of Chatham, John Pitt, and YOU FOOL! You think he had something to do with Kendrick's death? Your client was right -- *Discovery* was a farce!"

Pitt glanced outside, but Barrell couldn't tear his attention away from the bound man in the chair.

"It was the Padre, you idiot! Joseph Banks sent him to Boston aboard the *Three Brothers* to keep an eye on the Americans. But instead of giving up when Gray brought *Columbia* back owing money, the Yankees didn't stop. Boston sent out *more* ships, not less."

"Banks, not Chatham. You thought the whole British system was monolithic, didn't you? All marching in lock-step? The Whig Party controlled the government then and they were all for free trade, but it was the King and the Tories who stood to lose big if the British East India Company went bust. The Government's approach was to send a warship and a diplomat. The King sent an assassin."

The doctor pulled his attention back to Miles, then to Barrell, who had to ponder this barrage of information. "Why?" Chatham asked. "What is going on? Are you implying Meredith found me intentionally -- just so Joseph here could snuff me out?"

The Brahmin set his hard eyes upon Miles again. The sphinx trick wouldn't work this time. "No," Miles shook his head, "I thought so, especially when he tried to hire me." THE PRIEST addressed Barrell directly: "WHY DID YOU DO THAT? BECAUSE IT HAD WORKED SO WELL BEFORE? DON'T YOU KNOW THE DIFFERENCE BETWEEN RIGHT AND WRONG?" A sigh softened Miles a bit. "I think even he was scared. At first, I thought he might've been scared of himself --"

"Myself!" Barrell was shocked back into animation.

"--Yes! You exhibit obsessive behavior, but mask it well. Same as you thought of me. I thought you fit so well into my mold of crazed murderer. But I took it a bit further, and found you had been out in the Northwest too, looking at *Lady Washington*. Did you know the same time you were out there, Judge Howay's house burned down? I'll bet you knew about Doctor Roberts murder and Simon Woodruffe's death, and suspected... but it would have exposed you. You bastard," Miles was breathing hard, and finally roared: *"I KNOW!"*

The doctor had drifted to the small window and now the sight through it gripped him thoroughly. "Good Lord -- Joseph!"

The Brahmin fought to tear himself away from the accused-turned-prosecutor. When he finally did look out the window, he had barely enough time before the doctor raced out the door. The big man's frame soon followed, but stopped at the door, and turned for one last, somewhat ashamed look, then left.

Alone, in this small attic room the adrenaline wracked Miles' body. The cold was not here, the flush of his body so strong. With a couple great heaves, the chair moved fractions of an inch, but just enough. From here, the sight through the porthole was easy enough to discern.

Stone House, on the opposite hill, was aflame.

CHAPTER FORTY-TWO

Resolution

Friday, November 24, 1995

The lights flicked off soon after. Tied to a chair in the unheated attic of a two hundred year old house on a privately-owned, privately-powered island, watching as the flames from half a mile away consumed a Victorian structure of maybe three-dozen bedrooms seemed to be the most poignant example to date that living was an exercise in powerlessness.

"You're wearing the coat," came a smooth voice from off to his left.

Her. The voice in the darkness was the same he remembered from over a month ago.

"Your coat."

She's come to me. A month ago the voice that had become so soft after the lovemaking, after the wordless passion where he had guided her, and she had responded with greater and greater energy. The voice that said, "I'm sorry" when she finally stopped him, and kissed him and held him, "I'm sorry, just... sorry." He had told her there was no need, and there wasn't. And she climbed atop him and stroked his head, holding it --

He felt fingers touch his skull. *Behind me.*

And the lamp lit, flame set low, was placed on the small table beside him. He felt a cool, wet rag on his skull trying to work away the blood. The fingers caressed their way down around his ears, searching, then back to his ponytail, where the band was removed. Released, his hair was easier to work, the wound easier to clean.

"Yours," her voice repeated.

Hmmm...

"I was listening. You went out to the Coast. For me," her voice said.

Miles spoke not a word, but his breathing ran unevenly as he slowly tried to test the bonds holding him so immobile in this heavy chair.

"You were with me the entire time," she said.

The nylon was unforgiving, the knots pulling against each other so that little, if any, progress was possible without severing an artery.

"With only me. Boston. The Coast. Hawaii," she said.

With me? "You are not Gray," he said at last.

"No," the voice admitted.

"You are not Lady Pitt," he almost proclaimed.

"No."

Miles remembered the photo he had gone back to examine in Barrell's conference room thank to the help of Bernie Magee. The beautiful young woman at the helm of the sailboat. Then he recalled the picture in the school newspaper at Phillips Exeter, with her on the same boat, and proud friends and family around after the trophy for the solo female race. The onlookers in that photo were listed, among others, as Mr. & Mrs. Joseph Barrell, Doctor Samuel Roberts, and dockhand Simon Woodruffe.

And he remembered the letter to Jean-Pierre Hoskins. Her letter. "You are the guiding hand of the *Avenger*," he said, realizing *Avenger* -- the tender to *Lady Washington*.

"Yes."

"Meredith, do you remember your parents dying when you were thirteen?"

Silence. The hands stopped for a moment their caress, then slowly started up again.

"Do you remember the following summer here with your uncle and aunt?"

The hands on his head pulled away.

"Your aunt was ill then, wasn't she?"

The beautiful young woman, lithe and in the prime of her youth, stepped over to the window to watch the lights on the far hill.

"Was it a hysterectomy?"

"*Columbia Rediviva*," her lips, silhouetted against the scene of flames beyond the window spoke, "Columbia Reborn."

"And you took her place."

She reacted as if slapped.

"You were better at it, weren't you? That's it, isn't it?"

Without a hint of emotion, she stood up to leave.

"And the boy."

At the door, through the darkness, the footsteps stopped. A faint sobbing began.

"I saw the photo in your yearbook. You were a chubby girl back then. Nobody would have noticed the first three months. Then, when you came back for Thanksgiving, you lost him... or they took him from you --"

"I got rid of him myself!" she cried from the door. Pain. Anguish.

"And you've had to hold that bitterness inside you. Abandoned by your parents, taken by your uncle, a man you trusted. Forgotten by an aunt who was supposed to protect you. Losing everything before you've even started. And you couldn't say a word. But then one day you saw the image of someone strong, gifted, able to overcome adversity. Someone beset by enemies, and taken down much in the same way as you. Right on that medal. Do you still have it?"

Stepping back into the dim light of the flickering lamp, she held up the copper piece.

"You see the name on the face. It stared at you every day in the law office. Your uncle surrounded you with it."

"... But you changed me."

"Did I?"

"You made me stronger. I was ready to give up, but you invested in and changed me."

"Meredith, that was one night. I didn't even know who you were."

"No, no, you lay me on shore, and instead of using me once and tossing me aside, you held on as long as you could. After they killed you, they took me away and I never saw you again." She knelt down before him, and cradled her head in his lap.

"But here I am."

She looked up, directly back into his eyes. "Yes, John Kendrick."

?

She admitted I am John Kendrick.

YOU ARE.

So who is she?

"I remember the first night you lay within me," she stroked his thighs, around and inside. "I kept you warm, and cradled you, holding you tight. You brought me far from home, far from those who simply wanted to use me. You cared for me and for me alone. You put more into me, and expected nothing in return. You cared for me more than you could have put into me. You realized my inherent value. I sent you that check before we left for London, the back wages you never received from my Owners from our years together."

She rose, placed the coin in his chest pocket, turned, stopped, and removed two small, round burnt orange buttons. Miles recognized them not only as the mates of the one on his dashboard, but also to those adorning the southwest print vest he had worn both on the day of the bombing, and the night he first met her in Chatham. Trophies.

He understood. "You knew who I was."

"From the very first."

"You waited until I left the room to set off the bomb. You never meant to destroy yourself."

"No."

"Because there was still one more brick left. You perceived one last unpunished conspirator. A line that grew wealthy and powerful from the deceit against John Kendrick."

"Yes, yes!" She nearly took flight at his comprehension.

"Lord Pitt, the Earl of Chatham. And you married him. So when he dies, all that ill-gotten inherited British title will pass back to you where it belongs. Then, the books will be in balance."

"You understand" she leaned over to kiss him, and only then did he see she had removed her eyepatch. Nothing but a slight scar and a shut eye indicated the greater physical damage. Her exit into the darkness was slow.

"But if you're wrong?" he asked.

"I'm too tired to care, John," came her answer from the door, followed by the chilling sound, going down the stairs, of a sword sliding out of its scabbard.

Within the gloom of the room, the faint fumes of the oil lamp filling the stale, cold air, Miles understood at last. At the bottom of all those letters to Jean-Pierre Hoskins – two names. Miles had naturally assumed the one on the right to be the signature of the sender. But it only made sense -- *Lady Washington*, besides her master John Kendrick, was herself a Bostoner.

It was amazing a house could take so long to burn. But perhaps the past fifteen minutes of consciousness only seemed like hours. The brilliance of the display lit up the late November sky and the surrounding fields of the island. Perhaps Barrell had already called the state police after that one preemptive bash to Miles' skull, but their nearest barracks was twelve miles away up at the Bourne Bridge. The closest local police, a mile across the strait in Falmouth, wouldn't do for the Brahmin, since his island was a part of the Town of the Gosnold -- jurisdictional problems, if not for them, then for Barrell.

Whatever the case, there were no fire trucks on the island, just as there were no cars. When the lights went out, it meant the Bostoner had gotten to the generator after Stone House, so the water pumps wouldn't be able to supply even the smallest garden hose. Falmouth didn't have anything like a fireboat, and it would take time to ferry over a pumper. By that time, all would be lost.

Next to Miles, the lamp had enough oil for hours, set at this low intensity. Maybe, when everyone else was evacuated from the island, someone might notice the light in the attic of the old mansion. Perhaps the guests and family members, their holiday brought to an abrupt end by the fire and the subsequent loss of utilities, would be too self-absorbed to notice. That is, if the Bostoner succeeded in her errand. *I could be here all winter.*

Thanksgiving, and now the biggest house on the island was occupied. This was a summer retreat, and likely the house afire was not insulated. Nevertheless, the Brahmin had thrown open wide the doors. A post-wedding celebration for Meredith and Lord Pitt, no doubt, to coincide with the most New England of holidays. Barrell's display of power.

HURRY UP OR HE WILL BE DEAD SOON.

I don't care. Miles didn't. Joseph Barrell's health was not of the slightest concern to him. It is not what motivated the man in the chair to bend his hand back as far as the cord allowed, to test the edge of the table next to him.

It wobbled. Nothing like an antique for lack of functionality. The oil in the lamp sloshed about thickly.

WHAT ABOUT PITT? OR MRS. BARRELL? Or anyone else around the island that autumn twelve years ago? In the Bostoner's paranoid mind, Simon Woodruffe had helped run the ferry to bring Doctor Roberts over to care for the young teenage girl who had managed not only to get herself pregnant at school, so her uncle claimed, but to then succeed in upsetting the family's Thanksgiving holiday by inducing an abortion. Her first display of power?

But the Doctor would have known the pregnancy was a little too far along to have been initiated earlier in the semester. He would have had to know it was from that summer, wouldn't he? And wasn't it obvious to the Doctor what was going on? Barrell and his wife hardly spoke, but a great deal of the wealthy man's time was concerned with his niece's condition. And Lotta, his new assistant, had been invited out to the island occasionally for weekends, just as old friend John Meares -- so they must have known what was going on. They *had* to! Didn't they?

NO. JUST AS VANCOUVER HAD NO IDEA WHAT MIGHT HAPPEN TO CAPTAIN KENDRICK IN HAWAII. Just as accidents do happen when a gunner isn't paying attention.

But it fit so well with the tale of injustice her uncle had filled her mind with, of a Captain and his *Lady Washington*, beset by troubles. No, the Bostoner was *not* a reincarnation of Captain John Kendrick, as Miles had spent so much time supposing. The Bostoner was not a person at all, not in the legal sense. No, she was his home and his heart. His Lady. The brigantine *Lady Washington*, herself.

This was not truth. This was not justice. This was a pain and anguish that could never be satisfied.

WHAT IS YOUR DUTY?

I'll do this because I want to. With that, his finger darted at the edge of the table, sending it tipping back, then forward again. The lamp slid off and dashed to the floor, the brittle shards of glass mixing with the oil that spread in a wide, flaming pool under his feet. The warmth from below the chair was instant, followed by a smell of burning wool. The socks barely shielded the intense heat from his feet. That didn't matter too much when the flames leapt up his pant legs.

YOU CAN IGNORE THIS. PAIN IS SIMPLY A LESSON.

I have no time for this lesson. The cord at his feet began to stretch. First slowly, then more so, as the nylon cord quickly set to melting. He lashed out of his legs and they were free. Held up straight before, him, they were slowly but persistently on fire. The image shocked him.

FOCUS. Pulling at the arms rests to which his arms remained tied, the cord budged, but remained fast. The fire had traveled up the cord, and then, far from the main source of fuel, had cooled into a molten mass attached firmly to the leather.

Let go. He flailed in the chair, but both arms remained firmly immobile. The fire crept further and further up his legs, and was becoming unbearable on his feet. The leather was smoldering and the stuffing of the chair was beginning to take light.

He closed his eyes, winced, and clenched his jaw firmly. A growl built up inside of him and exploded as he bolted forward. His feet caught the oil and slid, but he found himself, now hunched over, as the fire more easily crept up his form to the heavy wool coat. A step on a piece of glass caused him to lurch back and the momentum from the heavy chair atop his back sent him stumbling backwards, wrestling to not return to his former position. Two more steps back, the struggle managed to pick up speed.

The sound of the crash was almost unnecessary as he felt himself pulled back and down and out. To his surprise, there had been another window to this room.

Nothing for a second. And almost another more. Then the world exploded.

The chair landed on its back with a horrific crack heard he hoped was not his neck. A few licks of flame poked at the bottom of his trousers as he tried to raise himself up. There was no air in his lungs. It was impossible to inhale, the wind knocked out of him, so he gasped out. The dark sky above him on this side of the hill began to entrance him.

GET UP. He rolled over once, off the wreckage of leather, wood and upholstery. And continued halfway down the hill. The fire out, the cool of the dormant grass soothed the burned skin on his feet and legs. His wrists twinged a little as he lifted himself off the ground, dizzy. Searching about, casting this way and that, he saw the inferno far, so far away this night. *There -- I want to be there.*

GO. Across the field at full run, the heavy coat flapped about him. GET RID OF THIS COAT. YOU CAN MOVE EASIER.

No.

IT'S ONLY IN YOUR WAY.

No, I want it.

YOU CAN GET IT LATER.

No, I want it now.

Quickening his bare-foot sprint, he approached the high stone wall and vaulted over. The edge of the coat caught under his hand as it gripped the stones, and he rolled over onto the soft road on the opposite side. And something else. As he reached to lift himself up out of the rut, he touched the soft texture of cashmere, and a more familiar warm substance spread over it.

The light from the hill cast shadows even here, and darkened the figure in the rut. By the splayed fashion and immense amount of blood he felt on the gravel and grass, Miles knew that the unfortunately-ignorant Earl of Chatham had been split from crown to crotch. *That could have been me.*

IT STILL CAN.

"He didn't deserve this."

GO ON.

Right. Rising, he whipped around, the long hair flying. Anger. He scowled at the darkness, searching. *Where is she?*

In the dark night skies, a thumping began, first faint, then deepening with intensity. *Helicopter. Of course.*

QUICK. BEFORE IT'S TOO LATE.

Dashing up the hill, he brushed past a gaggle of worried family members carrying flashlights. "Hey!" one man called out, and tried to grab Miles' arm. He wrestled free without breaking stride, and continued along the rolling lane towards the burning mansion.

Of the hired help standing well away from the flames, most headed to an adjacent field to guide in the thunderous searchlight descending from the heavens. One employee, bearded and in an old denim coat, held his hand up as he saw a figure approach from down the hill. His attention mostly concentrated on the fire at first, he had to look again at the beast, especially when it whipped him around and held him firmly by the shoulders. *"Where is Barrell?"*

The employee, having never seen this man arrive on the island, tried valiantly to demand, "Who the hell --?"

"TELL ME!" The beast was breathing hard and the employee began to smell the unmistakable stench of burnt hair and flesh, and something more. From the wrists now gripping his lapels hung the melted remains of thick yellow nylon cord.

"Johnny!" came the yell from behind.

The beast whipped around, flung the employee to the ground, and bolted down the path to the water. *I don't have time for this.*

A crowd of men jumped off the helicopter. One, sporting a dark ponytail and black leather jacket, was the first to help the employee up. He was followed by a shorter man with glasses wearing a pea coat, and a middle-aged, gray haired one in a suit and overcoat.

"You okay?" Paulie asked.

"Where'd he go?" Seth demanded.

The employee was dazed, almost as much by the strangers' questions, as by the sudden assault just prior to their arrival. "I dunno. He wanted Mr. Barrell, but --" Then he froze as all eyes followed his to the opposite hill, where the older mansion's top floor showed the first yellow and gold signs of immolation. "Fuck!" and he took off down the path from which the beast had emerged.

It was a flight down the hill to the water. Barely touching the shrubs and grass, it was a battle just to stay vertical. *Water. I must have water.*

She must have water. There was only one place for her to be, to bask in the glory of her next display. Chatham had been left on the road for all coming down from Stone House to find. But they would still have to continue down to the only embarkation spot in this whole island -- the same they arrived at -- the wharf. There they would find an even more gruesome display.

That is why Miles wasn't taking the road. He went straight down. The cliff quickly approaching at the bottom of this hill gave him little choice. The scene had begun.

YOU'RE TOO LATE.

No, I'm not. The coat of the commander of *Washington* flew off his shoulders.

The sword glinted slightly in the first flashlight, but it remained steady. *Lady Washington* – the Bostoner -- despised this woman, Florence. Aunt Florence -- or Florence McCarthy -- which was it? Did it matter? It would be justice to cut off her cold hands and cold, cold heart.

Florence Barrell was speechless with fright, her husband having disappeared after going into the boathouse for a flashlight. What had gotten into this young woman, this niece of hers? She was so intent, so uncaring --

Her thrust was quick, unexpected as it should be. But darkness fell like a ton of bricks.

Wrapping his coat about the middle aged woman as he crashed down the last hillock, the beast shielded most of the blow as he broke the two apart.

Miles whipped himself straight off the ground, his coat off and wrapped about the cowering figure of Florence Barrell. He approached the young woman, wary, stalking. Meredith, in the growing glow of the distant flashlights, beheld the sight of new blood on her blade. She couldn't help but let out a giggle.

Pure animal instinct sent him charging at her, grabbing the blade just before the hilt. She pulled back, but the strength of his rage ripped the weapon from her hands with a savage snarl.

Losing balance, she flipped down on the ground, and as easily back onto her feet again. With another giggle, she disappeared into the boathouse, sliding it quickly aside before Miles barreled into it with all his weight. Nothing. The door -- locked. Nothing. The windows -- none except for the top floor.

"Kendrick!" Seth and Paulie burst through the crowd of stunned family members easing towards Florence Barrell. They were followed closely by a huffing Bill Connor.

"Upstairs!" Miles pointed at the window.

Paulie put a hand on the beast's shoulders. "Calm down. The FBI are right behind us — they brought us along when they heard the fire report."

"No!" Miles yelled. *"No time! She's got him in there!"*

"Kendrick, let the police handle this," Seth was trying to pull Miles back from the structure. "You've done enough."

"Yeah," Bill crowded in closer, "they can negotiate this thing. And if Barrell goes down, so what?"

The beast shot a glare at his attorney. *"There is no time. There will be no negotiation. I don't care about Barrell -- I care about her! It's over if I don't stop her NOW!"*

The Brahmin's large prone frame lay face up as she unbuttoned his shirt. His eyelids fluttered and he began to recognize the almost forgotten sight of her over him, now reaching inside his shirt. The dull thudding in his head wasn't enough to alert him that this time might be different, but the inability to move his arms and legs surely did. His clothes had been nailed to the floor of the sail loft.

She stood framed with her back to the hatch opened to the cove, her breathing unsteady, ranging from controlled to giddy. Strangely, she was placing one small canvas bag after another within his shirt. He tried to speak, to ask her what was happening, to tell her *nothing* could be this bad, but the duct tape held firmly over his mouth. She would have the last word, if she wished.

The stitching had proved faulty on one bag, and it burst open on her pants and chest. Delighting in its contents on her hands and chest, she slowly dripped the contents of black powder and coins about the Brahmin's torso. At last, she bent down, one last time, carefully buttoned each hole in the shirt, zipped up the coat, and placed one last pouch below the man's chin.

It was the cigarette, of all things, that had worried him. She had stopped smoking years ago. But it sat lit nonetheless in its ashtray next to the fuel at his feet. Her steady hand picked it up, drew it to her lips, and held it away as she exhaled and sat down on the floor with the bag within her legs. And she smiled. Teasing.

Tipping the can, she poured a little on the floor in front of her, and lit it with the cigarette. Behold, a small patch of light -- and consumed -- nothing. His heavy, dark eyes watched her actions intently.

There was a thump. The sound of a window being smashed. She

looked up at the air above his head. A single rock met her in the cheek and she veered back. A window sash slid up.

She dropped her cigarette on her pants. The powder ignited. Instinctively, she clasped her legs together, and trapped the fuel can between them. A body rolled in the window, on top of Barrell, and came up onto its knees just in time to watch the first of the gasoline drip out of the can, down onto her chest. Lunging back, Miles threw himself on the floor, only to land face down on the helpless Barrell.

The blast enveloped the sail loft. And then nothing.

Miles slid onto the floor, the fringes of his long hair curled from the heat. He walked to the hatch, eyes down, and remained. Down below, the splintering of wood signaled the entrance of several male voices, as did the many outside along the water. Splashing about the wharf and footsteps up these stairs.

Two companions approached the bard, silent in his audience to the retrieval of the burned, battered woman still gingerly flailing in her charred, water-soaked nudity.

Bill Connor crept in close to Barrell, and whispered in his ear: "I oughta leave you like this. You didn't really think I'd turn my client into the Feds, for you, did you? Hell, they pay better, " and ripped the duct tape off the mouth.

"Shit, Kendrick, thought for a minute we were going to drop you back there," Seth tried to draw attention away from below. "I think you're too top-heavy with all that hair."

"We, uh... we were already camped out at *Nautilus*," Paulie explained, "you know, seemed the best place to look from, and then a call came in from the Coast Guard that Arthur Lewis had been picked up off the Vineyard. He'd gotten drunk and driven his boat up on some rocks... we figured something was goin' on from here... Look -- we all knew you could do it if we just left you alone, and well, you did, right?"

"Hm." Miles hunched down into a squat, and looking about the floor.

"What're you looking for?" Bill asked.

It caught Miles' eye, and he scooped up the prize. Stepping carefully about the Brahmin, he picked his way to the stairs, and slipped a gray stone with a white ring around it back into his pocket. "Luck."

EPILOGUE

Solstice

Thursday, December 21, 1995

Miles examined the barrel of the gun. It defied logic that a projectile small enough to pass through that tiny opening should be able to cause much harm to a human being of any reasonable proportion. It was like being killed by a big peanut.

WHAT IS YOUR DUTY?

"It's over," the bard answered out loud. All debts were paid. All obligations fulfilled. More importantly, irrefutable success and notoriety had been achieved. *I win.*

He was finished. He had learned the rules. He saw how it created such awful suffering – suffering that made him ashamed of whimpering over his own little heartbreaks. It was time to tell Life he simply wasn't going to play anymore.

WHAT ABOUT THOSE WHO COUNT ON YOU?

"Must I continue my life for others? What about me?"

WHAT ABOUT PAIN?

"What *about* pain?"

It would not be in the mouth. Far too homo-erotic, thanks. Too messy, too. He would have an open casket funeral. Much more powerful. *I want them to face me.*

No, it would be in the heart. How poetic! He had considered holding it behind him and firing forward -- shot in the back. *Yes. Good.*

Oh, but what if he missed and someone heard the shot and called the paramedics and, miracle of miracles, his life was saved? Bad publicity. Attempted suicide. A gunshot wasn't like pills. It would be reported big time. He might even get fined for carrying a handgun without a license. What a fantastic fumble -- it would turn him from a hero into a joke.

Holding the gun to his chest, he searched for exactly where his heart was. Up, no, kinda between the lungs and little to the left. The cold of the steel crept through his T-shirt. He leaned back in his chair, balancing the gun with one hand.

It was an automatic. Maybe he might be able to shoot himself twice. Hmmm... Then they might try to pin it on someone else? Oh, eventually they might discover it was suicide, but the media speculation might continue indefinitely, tormenting his tormentors in perpetuity. *Even better.*

YOU SHOULDN'T DO THIS JUST BEFORE CHRISTMAS. AT LEAST WAIT UNTIL AFTER NEW YEARS. He had considered this. What an awful present this would be. On the other hand, was there any *good* time for suicide? He could at least discern the best time.

The family would already be gathered together for the holiday, so no extra expense of traveling to the Cape just for this. And he preferred a funeral in the winter. Spring and summer burials were bizarre, what with everyone wearing black in amidst the sunshine and flowers. Oh, and how devilishly hot! BLEAH! No, now was a terrific time. It would allow people to truly dwell upon it all. Together.

YOU SHOULD DO MORE WITH YOUR TALENTS. MAKE A LASTING CONTRIBUTION.

"I'm so tired..."

This repetitive call to further action thudded painfully upon his head. But it was all so possible now. Keeping the media sharks hungry had made them truly desperate. One interview a couple weeks back provided the cash for his present comfort. Rent was paid a year in advance on *Terminus.* The debts to both commercial and family creditors were history. The rest of the tidy sum was retired with the installation of a wood stove into *Nautilus,* along with the purchase price of the house itself (how could the Marstons refuse their hero-caretaker?).

YOU COULD RESURRECT THIS PLACE YOURSELF. OTHERS WILL RESPECT THAT.

"True, but I don't care about them anymore." In fact, he had already drawn up and executed the documents establishing the Trust. Every asset of his was left to it. His first choice of Trustee was the Professor, but a flash of inspiration had moved him to second choice, should the first-named refuse. Philip Joseph Greenfield would be honored, and, even better, surprised, by the gesture.

Phip.

Miles couldn't help but chuckle at the thought of Phip piloting *Lady Washington* into Boston next summer, then being approached by Seth and Paulie, and informed that he had been named as the administrator of an estate potentially worth millions -- if he acted neither rashly nor timidly. In the mean time, there was at least *Nautilus*. Seth and Paulie were both reserved Life Tenancy within its walls, thus their scarce resources could be channeled toward more important endeavors than simply paying for housing. Besides, this place had a benign effect on all who entered. Should Phip need any more support after the voyage, Miles' two brethren would help. Thus, its many chambers would host the likes of Art, History and Technology. Good. They'd balance each other out.

And what of the woman?

Her -- the Lady.

YOU SHOULD GO VISIT HER IN THE HOSPITAL. ONE LAST TIME. The thought entertained him. He had decided to allow Meredith space until the worst of the skin grafts were over, and she could be permanently transferred to Pocasset. There were other, better-equipped institutions, but she had requested being on the Cape. He hadn't been invited to see her anyway.

But no one can keep me from doing what I want. It would have been in poor taste, though, to go right away. At least the family hadn't been hypocritical. They delivered Barrell his sentence. The news was that the Brahmin had been disowned by the entire family -- wife, children, law partners. They held him responsible for Meredith's injuries. And more.

To his credit, it had all taken effect without any apparent resistance. Joseph Barrell vacating the island, the house in Wellesley, his "retirement" from the law firm, and divorce had been accomplished in the quiet dignity of the condemned.

Where would he go? Miles swung around to the world map on the wall opposite the bed, searching for the possible paths of Joseph Barrell. The Caribbean. Florida. These places sent a chill down his spine. The Brahmin living alone on a houseboat near St. Petersburg -- now *that* was amusing. Mostly because it was absurd but appropriate.

Europe? There at the gaming tables of Monaco, a distinguished middle-aged man with graying temples introduces himself to a Russian beauty, "Barrell. Joseph Barrell." It was so easy to figure out other people's fantasies sometimes. Barrell, the secret agent.

The weight of the gun was starting to dig into Miles' breastbone. He laid it across his stomach, and felt it sinking under his ribs. The map drew his attention back again.

As he leaned ever-so-forward, he felt the gun slip. The phone rang. ANSWER THE PHONE.

The gun!

Left-handed, he caught the pistol before it hit the floor. Good thing it hadn't gone off. A false shot would have brought the police here in a second, thanks to nosy neighbors.

He reached for the phone, then stopped. "Why am I answering this?"

The machine clicked on, played the message and began to record. "Uh, hi, Miles... uh, I'm calling for John Kendrick. This is Philip Greenfield..."

Miles began to laugh. First a chuckle or two to himself, Then he threw back his head in a bellow. "Yes," he said, looking at the machine, "of course it is."

"... I caught you on television when we were in a bar in L.A, and thought, hey, that's great for him -- I wasn't sure how it'd all work out. But I was psyched. Then I realized you mentioned both your roommates who helped you there, but nothing about me..."

That was payback for Seth and Paulie. They got a lot of good exposure. Paulie's head shots of Miles were picked up by the network and he had been asked to do their advance work for big-wig interviews. Meanwhile, the Professor's thumbnail knowledge of the Nootka Sound Incident had been construed to mean he was its leading authority, and so courted by half a dozen universities. The Discovery Channel had called about a consulting position.

"... So how 'bout next time throwing a little limelight my way...?"

THERE WON'T BE A NEXT TIME IF YOU DO THIS. The pistol was heavy in his hand. He laid it down on the old marble coffee table. He closed his eyes from the mental pain, and tried to fight back the smirk. Sure, but Phip was already known to computer geeks everywhere.

"... So, okay, I got the e-mail last night," continued Phip. "See, Roland's interested..."

The man. It was obvious. Only Roland Wolfe had known Phip was in Tofino out of the whole of WolfWorks. He actually assisted the people of

Opitsat in claiming the Columbia Medal from the FBI. Obviously, he wasn't mad at Miles for the theft. Or Phip.

It had to be good, whatever it was. Phip's wealth was mostly stock options. But with Roland's money, anything was possible. Multimedia projects. Travel. Adventure. Everything.

"... He asked me to act as a go-between. I told him about your involvement in the MASE. He sees an inventive, creative guy with the inner drive to get things done..."

I don't work for anyone.

HE JUST WANTS TO TALK.

No. I don't want to talk to him. I don't know him. Anyway, it was too late. Wolfe and all of Life had its chance a long time ago to recognize Miles' talents back when he desperately needed them. But they hadn't seen him, and he sunk to the bottom. Miles was on top now because of what he'd become. And he didn't like it -- not one bit. All the good things people saw about him were simply outgrowths of the bad. Miles had traveled too far from home to return.

It was extremely difficult to allow Phip to hang up the phone. YOU FAILED HIM.

Oh, yeah, like I'm gonna tell him the truth! Hey, Phip, sorry, can't help you there 'cause I'LL BE DEAD!

YOU HAVE AN OBLIGATION.

I've got nothing!

WITH WOLFE'S POWER AND MONEY, YOU COULD DO ANYTHING.

Yes, I could maintain this lofty position. I could crush them and make them pay.

The thought was unappealing. Someone else's money. Someone else's power. Borrowed.

NEVER BORROW SOMEONE ELSE'S POWER FOR THEY WILL EVENTUALLY USE IT AGAINST YOU. That would shut up THE PRIEST.

But I could have it all now!

"It is better to be impetuous than cautious, for fortune is a woman... and it can be seen that she lets herself be overcome by the bold rather than by those who proceed coldly." And a little more Machiavelli quieted *The Rogue.*

The real issue, however, was that he sincerely did not care for revenge anymore. If he had, it would have indicated at least a spark of his humanity remained. In order to think like the Bostoner, he had needed to dredge up all these long-dead feelings. But like a reinflated balloon, they blew up much larger than before. And were far too thin to remain intact for long.

The pistol in his left hand, the cordless phone in his right, Miles held both in front of him. The burns scars still marked his wrists – funny, together with the scar across his throat, he already appeared to bear two marks of suicide.

With his thumb, he flicked off the ringer, and placed the phone on the desk. Slowly, he eased back the chair. He took the pistol in both hands and steadied it against his chest and closed his eyes.

Meredith.

He opened his eyes and looked at the bed. There, in the heat of passion, she had revealed a side to him kept hidden from the rest of the world. The aloof quirkiness she first displayed standing next to him at the local dive was gone. Later, the daunting intellectual front she had assumed came down. But it wasn't the passion that surprised him. No, that level matched his own -- rare indeed. It was her tenderness.

For meeting a woman one evening and spending until the wee hours of the morning plumbing the depths of her psyche, he was totally taken aback by her actions afterwards. He expected to be ignored. He would have been surprised by a little cuddle. But as she crawled on top of his exhausted form, he sensed something different. She reached down, took his head in her hands and stroked in the most absorbing, powerful way imaginable.

She connected with him. Then she connected him to her.

It was the most profound moment he had experienced with anyone. A whisper inside said: *You finally found another like you.*

She was gone now.

So he had found another like him. All that the world had done had brought her to her own destruction. By comparison, his own demise was wholly predictable.

Life had kicked them around and used them up. Instead of crumbling, they had adapted. Those adaptations, however, had horrible side-effects. For her, the suppressed rage was released through delusion. For him, the scars had healed over his nerves until there was no feeling left, and thus pursuit of truth held no pain. Instead of intense pain, he was simply hollow. Success only confirmed this. Life had molded him for this one purpose, to counteract her. And it was over. Now, spurning Wolfe's offer, he knew no one could help him.

The cold, heavy barrel found its now-familiar spot onto the left side of his breastbone. Fully cocked, the gun felt the finger wrap around its trigger.

Very, very far away, the downstairs phone rang.

One last, deep breath.

The phone rang again.

He closed his eyes.

The phone rang.

He exhaled.

His grip tightened on the trigger.

Very, very far away, the phone stopped mid-ring. A soft voice answered, "Hello?"

Miles opened his eyes wide.

His head poked over the corner of the stairs. Shelly called up, smiling. "Miles! Hey sweetie, I'm makin' breakfast! Surprise, huh? Sorry I couldn't get the phone before -- no, don't come down -- take the call. I'll be right up. "

He tried to smile through the shock. "Hey, babe...," he waved the cordless phone, wandering back into the bedroom.

Shelly ran her finger through her hair and caught sight of herself in mirror over the fireplace. Yech! What man would want to wake up to this?

She was worried he might never wake up, at one point. She had spent most of the night, trying to piece together his past few weeks, and finally fell asleep in the chair. When she had woken up, stiff, in the dawn, he hadn't moved an inch. Still peaceful, asleep. So she had decided it might be safe to pull her bags in from the car -- for a little while, at least. See how it goes.

By ten, her hunger overcame her. He was going to have breakfast made for him whether he was awake or not. Walking into the kitchen, she had seen evidence of Miles' handiwork. Not a dish in the sink. Good sign in a man. Wouldn't you know the one time she went to use the bathroom, the phone would ring? She took that as her cue that he was up, and after seeing him on the stairs, had raced back to get the tray of her favorites -- raisin toast, cereal and orange juice. She took special care with the tray as she went up the steep old staircase.

"AAAAAHHH!!!" The eruption from his room froze her on her step. Then the cordless phone exploded on the opposite wall above.

She held tight to the tray and was about to venture up again.

"Mi --?"

It was louder than a pop, but smaller than a blast. Like a car backfiring, except that there was no car parked up in Miles' small corner bedroom. Shelly was at the top of the stairs before she realized she had dropped the tray and stumbled over its contents.

He was slumped in the chair. One hand rested the gun on his thigh. She froze at the door and held her breath. His eyes were open wide. Staring. Glaring.

She couldn't help but follow his gaze up to the wall. A roadmap of the Pacific Northwest. And, quite distinctly, in the center of the coast of Washington, a new, jagged hole about half an inch across.

"Damn it," he finally breathed, and dropped the gun into the drawer, shutting it. As she stepped quietly into the room, he opened his mouth, closed it, and shook his head. "What the *hell* have I done?"

"Miles," Shelly gently approached him, "honey," her hand finally reached his shoulder, "*what* is going on?"

"Hi. I'm sorry. I --" He took a deep breath, stood, and approached the map. The tip of his forefinger circled the bullet hole, tapped on the nearby words "Grays Harbor", and withdrew. "Well, I can't very well go now."

Miles turned a shy, round-eyed face to her, his inhale a little too shaky. The tears would come soon. A brave smile tried an appearance as he took her hand from his shoulder. Then he hugged her. "I'm okay."

In spite of all evidence to the contrary, she believed him, and held him tight. From inside his chest she heard the echo of his words. "My father just passed away."

ACKNOWLEDGEMENTS

Mixing history and psychology, and spinning this tale out of whole cloth was not an easy task, and not one I could have completed without a great deal of invaluable assistance. Therefore, I wish to take this too-brief chance to thank the following for their support, faith and enthusiasm:

Authorities on the early American China trade, Rhys Richards, and the Northwest fur trade, Mary Malloy of Sea Education Association in Woods Hole.

For New England maritime history and marine archaeology, Joshua Smith at the University of Maine.

On either side of the continent, Les Bolton, Director of the Grays Harbor Historic Seaport, and Betty Wright, Curator of the Captain John Kendrick Maritime Museum in Wareham.

Anne Bentley at Massachusetts Historical Society for information on the Columbia Medal. Jan Voogd at the Peabody Essex Museum in Salem for finding just about anything within the Library.

The Maritime Museum of British Columbia and the British Columbia Archives in Victoria, Sturgis Library in Barnstable, the New Westminster Historical Society, the *U.S.S. Constitution* Museum in Boston, and the Bishop Museum and Hawaiian Historical Society in Honolulu.

Jennifer Shibley at the National Mental Health Association, for her knowledge on Borderline Personality Disorder, Dissociative Identity Disorder/Multiple Personality Disorder, Schizophrenia and other disassociative disorders.

Ken Gibson, discoverer of Gray's Fort Defiance, for his knowledge of historical geography in Clayoquot Sound.

Kazuo Sayama for his work on chronicling Captain John Kendrick, first American in Japan.

Katja Lackner, for the cover idea and J. Sanchez for cover photography. Bonnie Foote for the photograph of myself. For those final touches to the cover, Michael Skeggs and Chris LeClaire.

Ben Rollins, chronicler of the Kendrick family genealogy, for web design and hosting. Also, for a host of computer services, printing and layout assistance, John Redfern, Jonathan Redfern and Jake Smith.

For editing and sundry creative guidance, Anne LeClaire, Sally Gunning, Paula Bonnell, Edward O'Toole, Molly Singsen, Dr. Leroy Benoit, Pamela Painter, Risa Decker, Kelly Gunz, Julia Pfrommer, Jeffrey Howell, John Dickson.

For housing and hosting, in Chatham, Benjamin Calloway Jones; in Cambridge, Norman Brisson; in Boston, Andrew MacInnis; in New York, Karol Dixon; in Chicago, Curt and Karen Frost; in the Northwest, Elizabeth Hokanson, Alex Goff, Jennifer Elden, Dawn Merriam, David Gregg, Tamara Klinger and Ondeane-Iona Jurbin; in Paris, Sonia Jeribi and Stephanie Cartaux.

Also, thanks to Joff for help on the Viking stuff.

And most especially, my family, for years of encouragement, and my publisher, Christopher Kelly, for his vision.